WAS THERE A WISDOM TRADITION?

Society of Biblical Literature

Ancient Israel and Its Literature

Thomas C. Römer, General Editor

Editorial Board:
Mark G. Brett
Marc Brettler
Corrine L. Carvalho
Cynthia Edenburg
Konrad Schmid
Gale A. Yee

Number 23

WAS THERE A WISDOM TRADITION?

NEW PROSPECTS IN ISRAELITE WISDOM STUDIES

Edited by
Mark R. Sneed

SBL Press
Atlanta

Copyright © 2015 by SBL Press

All rights reserved. No part of this work may be reproduced or transmitted in any form or by any means, electronic or mechanical, including photocopying and recording, or by means of any information storage or retrieval system, except as may be expressly permitted by the 1976 Copyright Act or in writing from the publisher. Requests for permission should be addressed in writing to the Rights and Permissions Office, SBL Press, 825 Houston Mill Road, Atlanta, GA 30329 USA.

Library of Congress Cataloging-in-Publication Data

Was there a wisdom tradition? : new prospects in Israelite wisdom studies / edited by Mark R. Sneed.
    p. cm. — (Society of biblical literature : ancient Israel and its literature ; Number 23)
Includes index.
Summary: "This collection of essays explores questions that challenge the traditional notion of a wisdom tradition among the Israelite literati, such as: Is the wisdom literature a genre or mode of literature or do we need new terminology? Who were the tradents? Is there such a thing as a "wisdom scribe" and what would that look like? Did the scribes who composed wisdom literature also have a hand in producing the other "traditions," such as the priestly, prophetic, and apocalyptic, as well as other non-sapiential works? Were Israelite sages open to non-sapiential forms of knowledge in their conceptualization of wisdom?"— Provided by publisher.
ISBN 978-1-62837-099-7 (pbk. : alk. paper)— ISBN 978-1-62837-101-7 (ebook) — ISBN 978-1-62837-100-0 (hardcover : alk. paper)
1. Wisdom literature—Criticism, interpretation, etc. I. Sneed, Mark R., editor.
BS1455.W37 2015
223'.06—dc23   2015021474

Printed on acid-free, recycled paper conforming to
ANSI/NISO Z39.48-1992 (R1997) and ISO 9706:1994
standards for paper permanence.

Contents

Abbreviations vii

Introduction
   Mark R. Sneed 1

Part 1: Genre Theory and the Wisdom Tradition

The Modern Scholarly Wisdom Tradition and the Threat of
Pan-Sapientialism: A Case Report
   Will Kynes 11

"Grasping After the Wind": The Elusive Attempt to Define and
Delimit Wisdom
   Mark R. Sneed 39

Three Theses on Wisdom
   Michael V. Fox 69

Wisdom in the Canon: Discerning the Early Intuition
   Douglas Miller 87

Don't Throw the Baby Out with the Bathwater: On the Distinctness
of the Sapiential Understanding of the World
   Annette Schellenberg 115

Deciding the Boundaries of Wisdom: Applying the Concept of
Family Resemblance
   Katharine J. Dell 145

Wisdom, Form and Genre
   Stuart Weeks 161

Part 2: Case Studies

Where Can Wisdom Be Found? New Perspectives on the Wisdom
   Psalms
   Markus Saur 181

Gattung and *Sitz im Leben*: Methodological Vagueness in Defining
   Wisdom Psalms
   Tova Forti 205

How Wisdom Texts Became Part of the Canon of the Hebrew Bible
   Raik Heckl...221

Riddles and Parables, Traditions and Texts: Ezekielian Perspectives
   on Israelite Wisdom Traditions
   Mark W. Hamilton 241

Part 3: Ancient Near Eastern Comparison

The Contribution of Egyptian Wisdom to the Study of the Biblical
   Wisdom Literature
   Nili Shupak...265

Contributors..305
Index of Ancient Works..307
Index of Modern Authors...321

Abbreviations

AAT	Ägypten und Altes Testament
AB	Anchor Bible
ABG	Arbeiten zur Bibel und ihrer Geschichte
ABRL	Anchor Bible Reference Library
AEL	*Ancient Egyptian Literature*. Miriam Lichtheim. 3 vols. Berkeley: University of California Press, 1973–1981.
AIL	Ancient Israel and Its Literature
AnBib	Analecta Biblica
ANE	ancient Near East(ern)
ATANT	Abhandlungen zur Theologie des Alten und Neuen Testaments
ATD	Das Alte Testament Deutsch
ATM	Altes Testament und Moderne
BAe	Bibliotheca Aegyptiaca
BAR	*Biblical Archaeology Review*
BARIS	British Archaeological Reports International Series
BEStud	Brown Egyptological Studies
BETL	Bibliotheca Ephemeridum Theologicarum Lovaniensium
BHT	Beiträge zur historischen Theologie
BibInt	*Biblical Interpretation*
BIFAO	*Bulletin de l'Institut français d'archéologie orientale*
BJS	Brown Judaic Studies
BKAT	Biblischer Kommentar, Altes Testament
BN	*Biblische Notizen*
BO	Bibliotheca Orientalis
BRLJ	Brill Reference Library of Judaism
BSIH	Brill's Studies in Intellectual History
BZABR	Beihefte zur Zeitschrift für Altorientalische und Biblische Rechtsgeschichte

BZAW	Beihefte zur Zeitschrift für die alttestamentliche Wissenschaft
CALS	Cambridge Applied Linguistics Series
CANE	*Civilizations of the Ancient Near East*. Edited by Jack M. Sasson. 2 vols. Peabody, MA: Hendrickson, 1995.
CC	Continental Commentaries
CurBR	*Currents in Biblical Research*
CBQ	*Catholic Biblical Quarterly*
CBQMS	Catholic Biblical Quarterly Monograph Series
CHANE	Culture and History of the Ancient Near East
ConBOT	Coniectanea Biblica: Old Testament Series
CSSH	*Comparative Studies in Society and History: An International Quarterly*
CurBR	*Currents in Biblical Research*
CurBS	*Currents in Research: Biblical Studies*
DSD	*Dead Sea Discoveries*
DtrH	Deuteronomistic Historian/History
ECC	Eerdmans Critical Commentary
ECDSS	Eerdmans Commentaries on the Dead Sea Scrolls
Eg.	Egyptian
EvQ	*Evangelical Quarterly*
EvT	*Evangelische Theologie*
FAT	Forschungen zum Alten Testament
FOTL	Forms of the Old Testament Literature
FRLANT	Forschungen zur Religion und Literatur des Alten und Neuen Testaments
HALOT	*The Hebrew and Aramaic Lexicon of the Old Testament*. Ludwig Koehler, Walter Baumgartner, and Johann J. Stamm. Translated and edited under the supervision of M. E. J. Richardson. 4 vols. Leiden: Brill, 1994–1999.
HAT	Handbuch zum Alten Testament
HB	Hebrew Bible
HBIS	History of Biblical Interpretation Series
HBM	Hebrew Bible Monographs
HDR	Harvard Dissertations in Religion
HKAT	Handkommentar zum Alten Testament
HO	*Hieratic Ostraca*. Jaroslav Černý and Alan H. Gardiner. Oxford: Oxford University Press, 1957.
HPBM	*Hieratic Papyri in the British Museum*

HS	*Hebrew Studies*
HSS	Harvard Semitic Studies
HThKAT	Herders theologischer Kommentar zum Alten Testament
IBT	Interpreting Biblical Texts
ICC	International Critical Commentary
Int	*Interpretation*
IOSOT	International Organization for the Study of the Old Testament
JAOS	*Journal of the American Oriental Society*
JBL	*Journal of Biblical Literature*
JCS	*Journal of Cuneiform Studies*
JEA	*Journal of Egyptian Archaeology*
JEOL	*Jaarbericht van het Vooraziatisch-Egyptisch Geselschap (Genootschap) Ex orient lux*
JNES	*Journal of Near Eastern Studies*
JNSL	*Journal of Northwest Semitic Languages*
JSHRZ	*Jüdische Schriften aus hellenistisch-römischer Zeit*
JSJSup	Supplements to Journal for the Study of Judaism in the Persian, Hellenistic, and Roman Periods
JSOT	*Journal for the Study of the Old Testament*
JSOTSup	Journal for the Study of the Old Testament Supplement Series
JSS	*Journal of Semitic Studies*
KBo	Keilschrifttexte aus Boghazköy
LBA	Late Bronze Age
LHBOTS	Library of Hebrew Bible/Old Testament Studies
LXX	Septuagint
MÄS	Müncher Ägyptologische Studien
MC	Mesopotamian Civilizations
MT	Masoretic Text
NEchtB	Die Neue Echter Bibel
NIB	*The New Interpreter's Bible*. Edited by Leander E. Keck. 12 vols. Nashville: Abingdon, 1994–2004.
NICOT	New International Commentary on the Old Testament
OBO	Orbis Biblicus et Orientalis
OLA	Orientalia Lovaniensia Analecta
OLZ	*Orientalistische Literaturzeitung*
OT	Old Testament
OTL	Old Testament Library

OtSt	Oudtestamentische Studiën
PAe	Probleme der Ägyptologie
PIASH	*Proceedings of the Israel Academy of Sciences and Humanities*
PSB	*Princeton Seminary Bulletin*
RB	*Revue biblique*
SAA	State Archives of Assyria
SAK	*Studien zur Altägyptischen Kultur*
SAOC	Studies in Ancient Oriental Civilizations
SBLDS	Society of Biblical Literature Dissertation Series
SBLMS	Society of Biblical Literature Monograph Series
SBS	Stuttgarter Bibelstudien
SBT	Studies in Biblical Theology
SemeiaSt	Semeia Studies
SESJ	Suomen Eksegeettisen Seuran julkaisuja
SJT	*Scottish Journal of Theology*
SOTSMS	Society for Old Testament Studies Monograph Series
SSEA	Society for the Study of Egyptian Antiquities
StMiss	*Studia Missionalia*
StPohl	Studia Pohl Series Maior
SymS	Society of Biblical Literature Symposium Series
TB	Theologische Bücherei: Neudrucke und Berichte aus dem 20. Jahrhundert
TLZ	*Theologische Literaturzeitung*
TOTC	Tyndale Old Testament Commentaries
TRu	*Theologische Rundschau*
TS	*Theological Studies*
TUAT	*Texte aus der Umwelt des Alten Testaments.* Edited by Otto Kaiser. Gütersloh: Mohn, 1984–.
TynBul	*Tyndale Bulletin*
TZ	*Theologische Zeitschrift*
UTB	Universitäts-Taschenbücher
VT	*Vetus Testamentum*
VTSup	Supplements to Vetus Testamentum
WAW	Writings of the Ancient World
WBC	Word Biblical Commentary
WLAW	Wisdom Literature from the Ancient World
WMANT	Wissenschaftliche Monographien zum Alten und Neuen Testament
WO	*Die Welt des Orients*

WUNT	Wissenschaftliche Untersuchungen zum Neuen Testament
ZA	*Zeitschrift für Assyriologie*
ZABR	*Zeitschrift für altorientalische und biblische Rechtsgeschichte*
ZAH	*Zeitschrift für Althebräistik*
ZÄS	*Zeitschrift für ägyptische Sprache und Altertumskunde*
ZAW	*Zeitschrift für die alttestamentliche Wissenschaft*
ZBK	Zürcher Bibelkommentare

Introduction

Mark R. Sneed

During my days in graduate school, I was taught and read what has been the paradigm position in Hebrew Bible studies concerning the nature of the wisdom corpus. It was described as an alien body in the Hebrew Bible. It never alluded to the pivotal events and persons in Israelite history like the patriarchs or the exodus or the covenants, such as at Sinai. Coupled with this was the view that the priests, prophets, and sages of ancient Israel never seemed to get along and were constantly jockeying for dominance within the political arena. Their respective literatures represent such attempts at persuading others to adopt their perspective. They also were assumed to hold widely differing worldviews and had distinctive theologies and epistemologies. In other words, they saw the world radically differently. The sages were practically empiricists who only considered what could be rationally and empirically verified as legitimate knowledge. Thus, they viewed with suspicion the prophets who received revelations and the priests who divined the future with their Urim and Thummim. They divided the world up into the wise and foolish, the discerning and mocker. The priests were assumed to be obsessed with the purity and cleanness and with ritual matters like sacrifices and circumcision. They saw the world with sacerdotal eyes and divided the world up into the categories of clean and unclean, pure and impure. Both sage and priest were viewed as upper class elites. The prophets were mediators of God's word. They defended the rights of the poor and protested against Israel's many sins, especially unfaithfulness. They challenged the significance the priests gave to the cult and they questioned the piety of the sages. Their world was one of oracles and supernatural revelation. Only they were God's true spokespersons. They emphasized covenant loyalty and social justice. They were viewed as being from the lower classes or at least defenders of those classes. They divided the world up into the righteous and wicked, the faithful and the faithless.

That this approach to the sages, the wisdom literature, and the rest of the intellectual leadership in ancient Israel is still dominant or at least alive and well can be demonstrated by two recent publications. In David Penchansky's recent introduction (2012, 83) to the wisdom literature, he explores ways to explain the gaping silence of the sages regarding the covenant and redemptive events in Israel's history and concludes "that the sages did not regard the Israelite covenants to be important … because they were concerned about other things." Even more recently, John McLaughlin (2014, 281–303) challenges other scholars who have argued that Amos reflects heavy influence from the wisdom tradition. He examines the evidence and concludes that Amos does not display any significant influence from the wisdom circles within ancient Israel (303). He points out that Amos's usage of what appear to be wisdom forms, vocabulary, and ideas is a misnomer because all of these phenomena are employed in distinctly unsapiential ways.

This view was not always the dominant position in biblical studies. At least early German scholarship viewed the sages and their literature as complementary to the other genres and their tradents. For example, Hermann Schultz (1898, 2:83–84) viewed the wisdom literature as philosophical and represented a synthesis of Hebrew thinking for the whole of life. Similarly, Bernhard Duhm (1875, 244–45) believed that this corpus represented a mundane ethic that was lacking in the prophetic material. He also maintained that it was based on Israelite revelatory material.

Hermann Gunkel, with his form-critical approach, marks one of the earliest forms of the current paradigmatic position. As for the *Sitz im Leben* of wisdom literature, Gunkel cites Jer 18:18 (2003, 69–70) and connects the counsel of the sages with old bearded men who sat at the city gates and gave advice to young men. He advocated that the wisdom literature was originally secular in character—rejecting the cult—and that its origins go back to Egypt. He contrasts the sober advice of the sages with the fiery words of the prophets. James Crenshaw (2010, 24–25) is in many ways the direct heir of Gunkel, seeing the wisdom corpus as non-Yawhistic and as representing a worldview distinctive from that of the prophets and priests.

But more recently, there have been attempts to backtrack from Gunkel and this consensus. The essay in this volume by Will Kynes will fill in the details of the inception of this paradigmatic position and the reaction to it. This now leads to the present collection of essays, representing the most recent reassessment of the prevailing consensus. They all in one way or another address this issue: the natue of the wisdom "tradition." Is the wisdom literature rightly a tradition? If so, what kind? Or is it a mode of literature or discourse? Who were the tradents? Can we know with certainty? Does the wisdom literature represent this group's worldview or not? What relationship does the wisdom literature have with the rest of the corpora of the Hebrew Bible? What are the limits or boundaries of the wisdom corpus? How tightly or loosely should they be drawn? These and other questions are the concern of this volume. The contributors fit a spectrum of positions. Some contributors radically question the notion of a wisdom tradition, at least in the sense that this has been understood (Weeks, Sneed, Saur, Heckl, Kynes, Shupak). Others question the paradigm but not in radical ways (Fox and Hamilton). Others occupy more a middle position of sorts, affirming the paradigm but qualifying it in new ways (Dell, Miller, Schellenberg). Forti stands alone as affirming the paradigmatic position without modification.

In "Deciding the Boundaries of Wisdom: Applying the Concept of Family Resemblance," Katharine Dell argues that there is a wisdom tradition, though she uses the term hesitatively. She argues that we should go beyond Gunkel and turns to the notion of family resemblance to define genre, a term from the linguistic philosopher Ludwig Wittgenstein. From this perspective she sees a continuum of relations, with texts being related more closely and more distantly. She follows closely Simon Cheung, who sees three necessary criteria for defining the category of wisdom literature: ruling wisdom thrust, intellectual tone, and didactic intention. She ends up viewing Proverbs and Ecclesiastes as the parents, that is, genuine wisdom literature, and other texts like Job, for example, as more distantly related but not an immediate family member, that is, a cousin.

In "How Wisdom Texts Became Part of the Canon of the Hebrew Bible," Raik Heckl investigates how the books of Job and Proverbs may have entered the emerging canon. He proposes that as the Pentateuch was forming as a semicanonical corpus along with the prophetic books, the books of Job and Proverbs reveal in their frame-narratives a consciousness of this. He argues that their introduction into the larger quasi-canon complements the rest by dealing with the theodicy problem and correcting Deuteronomy (Job) while also providing practical instruction (Proverbs), with both emphasizing that YHWH is a universal deity and not just a god of the Jews with a focus on the individual. Proverbs 8 also connects wisdom with the Torah (Deuteronomy). Thus, even if one could argue that the early wisdom tradition was an elite scribal phenomenon, it becomes democratized by the frame-narratives added to Job and Proverbs. In other words, from a canonical perspective, the form of the wisdom literature within the canon is no longer a separate, idiosyncratic tradition.

In "Where Can Wisdom Be Found? New Perspectives on the Wisdom Psalms," Markus Saur investigates the so-called wisdom psalms and concludes that focusing on whether these psalms should be called such is missing the point. It is their broader implication that is significant. The topics they treat (the deed-consequence nexus, Torah, theodicy) are the very topics that the broader Jewish community was negotiating and not limited to some small group of sages. He points out that the Psalter in many ways has been sapientialized through the inclusion of these psalms, as has the rest of the Hebrew Bible. He concludes that the Psalter represents, *in nuce*, a "little Bible," and that the wisdom psalms within it demonstrate that sapiential concerns were those of the Jewish elite and broader society as whole and not just the parochial concern of the sage.

In contrast to Saur, in "*Gattung* and *Sitz im Leben*: Methodological Problems in Identifying the 'Wisdom Psalm,'" Tova Forti believes such a more narrow focus on wisdom psalms is in fact legitimate and helpful. She critiques the imprecise methodology used by previous scholars in identifying this genre. While admitting the great difficulty of the task, she attempts to provide more robust criteria for determining what psalms should be rightly labeled wisdom psalms. These criteria include thematic, ideational, linguistic, stylistic, lexical, and figurative features. She concludes that the following are legitimate wisdom psalms: 39, 104.

In "Don't Throw the Baby Out with the Bathwater: On the Distinctness of the Sapiential Understanding of the World," Annette Schellenberg assumes the paradigmatic position but tries to soften the boundaries between the various scribal groups that she sees represented by the literature of the Hebrew Bible. For example, though she believes the sages were open to revelation as a source of knowledge, they did not consider it necessary. While she admits that all the Israelites can be viewed as sharing a common worldview, the Hebrew Bible reflects differing theologies and perspectives that confirm that there is indeed a sapiential weltanschauung, though it reflects a dialectical relationship of influence vis-à-vis the other traditions, for example, the priestly and prophetic traditions. She examines biblical, extrabiblical, and ancient Near Eastern literature and argues that the wisdom tradition distinguishes itself in terms of four categories: cosmology, epistemology, ethics/understanding of society, and theology.

In "Wisdom in the Canon: Discerning the Early Intuition," Douglas Miller also maintains the paradigmatic position, but he attempts to reformulate the necessary and sufficient criteria for the parameters of the wisdom tradition in a better way. He first examines seven criteria that previous scholars have proposed as necessary features of wisdom literature and its tradents: form, social location, technical vocabulary, humanistic orientation, didacticism, eudemonism, and weltanschauung. In compliance with recent developments in form criticism and genology, Miller reduces this list heuristically to three criteria: rhetoric (instruction), realized eschatology (focus on present mundane existence), and epistemology (rooted in human experience). He then shows how the other seven categories configure within his triadic grid.

In "Three Theses on Wisdom," drawing on ancient Near Eastern evidence (especially Egyptian), Michael V. Fox challenges much of the consensus position, particularly its postulation of a wisdom school and the view that the sages were an insular professional group within Israel. He argues that (1) there was no wisdom school in ancient Israel (2) the authors of the wisdom literature were not a distinct faction, but (3) there was indeed a generic category of wisdom literature. As for the third item, Fox admits that wisdom literature is a modern scholarly construct and that perhaps another name is necessary. Whatever one calls it, he does believe in a wisdom tradition, which is especially evident in the Egyptian literature, and he defines it as ethical instruction about the successful life and its limitations. And it does this without appealing to revelation or legal material.

In "Wisdom, Form, and Genre," Stuart Weeks takes on the task of critiquing the many form-critical assumptions that come to play in the issue that this volume addresses. He continually points out the many complexities and difficulties of examining genres that is only exacerbated by the baggage of biblical form criticism. Weeks provides many examples of generic complexity throughout his essay, both from classical literature, as well as biblical studies. He basically argues that biblical scholars would be better off moving beyond form criticism—or at least move *less* form-critically—and to embrace the more up-to-date field of genology and to speak in terms of the family resemblance of texts. He attempts to steer wisdom experts away from rigid categorization and the futile attempt to find the closest generic parallel of a biblical wisdom text among ancient Near Eastern literature.

Will Kynes's "The Modern Scholarly Wisdom Tradition and the Threat of Pan-Sapientialism: A Case Report" is the most radical essay in terms of the long-standing paradigmatic consensus on this issue. He essentially deconstructs the notion of a wisdom tradition, even suggesting we abandon the term altogether! Kynes's essay swings between the dangerous poles of, on the one hand, arbitrariness about defining and delimiting what a wisdom tradition means and, on the other hand, what he describes as "pan-sapientialism," which is the tendency to see more and more texts and books from the Hebrew Bible as members of the genre to one degree or another. He begins with a critical survey of the emergence of the notion of a distinctive wisdom tradition among biblical scholars, demonstrating how it is a scholarly construct not necessarily reflecting reality. He then shows the difficulties and arbitrariness in defining wisdom by looking at how both ancient Near Eastern and Qumran scholars have adopted the term to describe various texts; he provides an analogy to pan-sapientialism in "pan-Deuteronomism." In the end, Kynes opts for a robust understanding of intertextuality that would allow scholars to creatively reconfigure, organize, and compare biblical texts—including wisdom ones—in a number of differing ways.

In "Riddles and Parables, Traditions and Texts: Ezekielian Perspectives on Israelite Wisdom Traditions," Mark Hamilton questions the traditional paradigm in terms of the airtight boundaries scholars raise between the various traditions reflected in the Hebrew Bible. He does believe that there were sapiential, priestly, and prophetic traditions but that they interacted in creative ways, not limited to merely textual but also oral phenomena. He first defines what "tradition" should mean as applied to biblical texts, which always involves a social facet. He then investigates Ezekiel as a case study, which demonstrates how a prophetic book has been influenced by what can legitimately be called a priestly and even wisdom tradition, a tradition that was diffused broadly throughout ancient Israelite society. He shows how Ezekiel cites *meshalim* and then comments on them.

In "'Grasping After the Wind': The Elusive Attempt to Define and Delimit Wisdom," I take aim at the view that the wisdom tradition has certain necessary and sufficient conventions, what one could call core elements. I emphasize that this determination is highly subjective and heuristic and is more an intuitive pattern our brains recognize in the literature than an objective taxonomical analysis. I also emphasize that such uncertainty is fine for discussion of genre and emphasize that we will never agree on the boundaries of wisdom entirely. Indeed, one should not pursue such consensus. In the essay I also evaluate wisdom experts around the globe in terms of their consistency with modern generic theory, which includes the notion of generic realism versus nominalism, and the notion of the systemic nature of generic economies. I also compare biblical wisdom experts with ancient Near Eastern scholars. Finally, I offer suggestions for a more healthy approach to the wisdom tradition and its various genres, which includes giving up on the concept of essential features.

In "The Contribution of Egyptian Wisdom to the Study of Biblical Wisdom Literature," Nili Shupak argues that Israelite wisdom, especially Proverbs, has been heavily influenced by the wisdom tradition in Egypt, both in terms of content, perspective, language, and style. She argues that the Egyptian wisdom tradition started out among an aristocratic scribal class and was secular in orientation, not concerned much with the cult, but became more concerned with religion and piety over time, shifting its focus to a more middle-class audience. She distinguishes between didactic and speculative wisdom, the former being more pragmatic and the latter often challenging the status quo, adopting a somewhat prophetic tone—though she rejects such a label for this literature. She demonstrates that one can trace a distinctive and definitive wisdom tradition in Egypt that remained relatively stable for millennia, even though the social class of its tradents and audience changed over time. Shupak essentially argues that Israelite wisdom represents a similar phenomenon but its intended audience was broader and more inclusive than that of Egypt.

Works Consulted

Crenshaw, James L. 2010. *Old Testament Wisdom: An Introduction.* 3rd ed. Louisville: Westminster John Knox.

Duhm, Bernhard. 1875. *Die Theologie der Propheten als Grundlage für die innere Entwicklungsgeschichte der israelitischen Religion.* Bonn: Marcus.

Gunkel, Hermann. 2003. "The Literature of Ancient Israel." Pages 26–83 in *Relating to the Text: Interdisciplinary and Form-Critical Insights on the Bible.* Edited by Timothy J. Sandoval, Carleen Mandolfo, and Martin J. Buss. Translated by Armin Siedlecki. JSOTSup 384. London: T&T Clark.

McLaughlin, John L. 2014. "Is Amos (Still) among the Wise?" *JBL* 133:281–303.

Penchansky, David. 2012. *Understanding Wisdom Literature: Conflict and Dissonance in the Hebrew Text.* Grand Rapids: Eerdmans.

Schultz, Hermann. 1898. *Old Testament Theology: The Religion of Revelation in Its Pre-Christian Stage of Development.* Translated by J. A. Paterson. 2nd ed. 2 vols. Edinburgh: T&T Clark.

Part 1
Genre Theory and the Wisdom Tradition

The Modern Scholarly Wisdom Tradition and the Threat of Pan-Sapientialism: A Case Report

Will Kynes

> Modern historical research itself is not only research, but the handing down of tradition. (Gadamer 2004, 285)

Introduction

Biblical scholarship is currently suffering from a "wisdom"[1] category that is plagued by definitional deficiency, amorphous social location, and hemorrhaging influence, among other maladies.[2] A generation ago, Gerhard von Rad (1993, 7–8) had already raised questions about the genre's survival, asking "whether the attractive codename 'wisdom' is nowadays not more of a hindrance than a help," but prognoses of its imminent demise have recently increased. Weeks (2010, 85) wonders "if, indeed, it is a genre in any meaningful sense." Thanks in large part to its imprecise definition, he also worries that, at least in the discussion of origin and influence, the wisdom category "has become more of a liability than an asset," which these debates "would do well to retire" (141). Similarly, Matthew Goff (2010, 325) has observed that

> The prospects of wisdom as a viable category of genre can seem rather bleak. One might suppose that in the next generation of scholarship the term "wisdom" might seem like a rather antiquated scholarly term, such

---

1. The quotation marks encompassing the category's title reflect the fact that it is a scholarly convention. For ease of reading, I will henceforth dispense with them. "Wisdom" is used here interchangeably with the fuller title, "wisdom literature."

2. For a recent incisive discussion of the current difficulties in the study of wisdom, see Weeks 2010 and the summary in Kynes forthcoming.

as the amphictyony, the putative tribal federation of ancient Israel, or the Elohist source.

Indeed, the session at the SBL Annual Meeting in 2012 that discussed whether a wisdom tradition ever existed, inspired by Mark Sneed's article, "Is the 'Wisdom Tradition' a Tradition?" (2011), suggests that the category, if not on life support, is certainly in critical condition.

Goff (2010, 334–35), like von Rad (1993, 7) and Weeks (2010, 144), however, thinks the wisdom category is worth preserving despite its significant difficulties as long as scholars are willing to acknowledge that it is a subjective, modern projection onto the texts, which could be mistaken (see, similarly, Fox 2012, 232). A brief overview of the past century of wisdom study will suggest, however, that this modern scholarly tradition may, in fact, be the source of wisdom's definitional problems. As a result, the survival of the category will require significant changes in lifestyle. I will suggest the discussion of biblical wisdom exercise more hermeneutical restraint, cut back on its exclusive claims to define the texts it includes and their historical origins, and add more intertextual connections to its interpretive diet. Otherwise, the category risks succumbing to meaninglessness, either as an unexamined scholarly consensus or as an all-encompassing and indistinct umbrella term, thereby, indeed, acting as more of a hindrance than a help. The treatment of this ailment must, however, be determined by a diagnosis of its underlying causes, and this begins with the patient's history.

Case Presentation

According to common accounts, wisdom developed as a distinct subject with a corresponding corpus in the Hebrew Bible soon after the turn of the twentieth century.[3] Though closer study of the history of wisdom

---

3. E.g., Ludger Schwienhorst-Schönberger (2013, 119), who does not identify a specific originating work. James Crenshaw (1976, 3) suggests Johannes Meinhold, in his *Die Weisheit Israels in Spruch, Sage und Dichtung* (1908), was the first to recognize the separate existence of wisdom. Crenshaw is apparently following Walter Baumgartner (1933, 261). R. N. Whybray (1995, 1) is the only modern scholar I have encountered who posits a date before the twentieth century, pointing to S. R. Driver's *An Introduction to the Literature of the Old Testament* (1891, 369) as an early indication of the category.

interpretation reveals this date to be at least half a century too late,[4] the discovery of a definite literary relationship between Prov 22:17–24:22 and the Egyptian Instruction of Amenemope in 1924 did indeed ignite new scholarly interest in the subject (Erman 1924a, 1924b; cf. Scott 1970, 23–24; Crenshaw 1976, 5–6). By the outbreak of World War II, a deluge of research addressed many of the questions that continue to shape the study of wisdom, such as the extent of parallels from the ancient Near East, the structure of wisdom thought, and the identification and social setting of wisdom forms (Crenshaw 1976, 6).[5]

Despite the initial interest in wisdom, its contribution to biblical scholarship more broadly remained unclear. After World War II, this new darling of biblical study fell into disfavor. The enthusiasm for finding connections between biblical wisdom texts and those from the ancient Near East became a liability when a new scholarly movement brought the theological significance of Israelite history and Hebrew thought to the fore. Crenshaw (1976, 1–2) offers G. Ernest Wright (1952) and Horst D. Preuss (1970) as representative bookends for this trend. Both considered wisdom's affinity with foreign wisdom an indication of a worldview they did not hesitate to call pagan. Wisdom began to be considered a *Fremdkörper* ("foreign body") in the Hebrew Bible (Gese 1958, 2) and treated as a virtual "vermiform appendix" to Old Testament theology (Scott 1970, 39). In fact, in the first volume of von Rad's *Old Testament Theology* (2001, 355), wisdom is a *literal* appendix, tacked on at the end as "Israel's answer" to the Lord. During this period the common and continuing tendency to define wisdom negatively, by what it lacks, is pronounced. The absence of revelatory content, Israel's covenant with Yahweh, the law revealed at Sinai, and Yahweh's intervention in history on behalf of his chosen people all contribute to the definition and consequent marginalization of wisdom. Characterized as secular, empirical, humanistic, international, and universal, it found only a secondary place in relation to the sacred traditions

---

4. Already in 1851, Johann Bruch had published *Weisheits-Lehre der Hebräer*, which focused on the wisdom corpus still widely accepted today and was influential in the discussion of wisdom in the latter half of the nineteenth century. For the development of the wisdom category in the nineteenth century, see Kynes forthcoming.

5. For further bibliography from this period, see Baumgartner 1933, 259–61; Scott 1970, 23 n. 3. Many of these issues had already been raised in the previous century (see Smend 1995, 267; Dell 2013; Kynes forthcoming), however the attention wisdom received during this period did expose them to a broader audience.

and specific Yahwistic beliefs that loomed large in the theological thought of this period, suffering "the fate of one who is insufficiently Hebraic at a time when a premium is placed on Hebrew thought" (Crenshaw 1976, 2; see also Murphy 1969, 290).

Over the course of the 1960s, however, the emphasis on Israelite history that had sidelined wisdom eventually fell into disfavor itself. Perhaps due to a new appreciation for wisdom's "universalism" (Crenshaw 1976, 3; see also 1998, 1), its relationship to the rest of the canon swung to the opposite pole as studies on purported wisdom influence proliferated. According to these studies, wisdom played a formative role in books across the canon.[6] Wisdom, once disregarded, now gained new prominence, inspiring Roland Murphy (1969, 290) to ask, "Where has Old Testament wisdom failed to appear?"

The arguments for wisdom influence were based on affinities in vocabulary, subject matter, and worldview (Crenshaw 1976, 9). The same types of arguments continued to be made with ancient Near Eastern texts (though with greater caution), so in this period the number of texts connected to the wisdom movement was expanding in both directions at once, across the canon as well as the ancient Near East, with the biblical wisdom texts testifying to ancient Near Eastern influence on Israelite wisdom, and other biblical texts from across the canon revealing wisdom's influence in Israel. Thus, though this development was an about-face in regard to the relationship between wisdom and the rest of the canon, it continued to see wisdom as something distinctive in Israel, defined to a large degree by its contact and similarity with other texts from the ancient Near East. This attempt at the reintegration of wisdom with the rest of the canon did not make wisdom more Israelite, but Israel more sapiential, as the emphasis on wisdom's *influence* suggests.[7]

---

6. The texts that have been claimed to demonstrate wisdom influence include the Primeval History (Gen 1–11), the Joseph narrative (Gen 37–50), Exodus, Deuteronomy, the Succession Narrative (2 Sam 11–20; 1 Kgs 1–2), Esther, the historical books as a whole, Isaiah, Jeremiah, Ezekiel, Daniel, Amos, Jonah, and Habakkuk (see Crenshaw 1969; 1976, 9–13; Morgan 1981; Weeks 2010, 135).

7. Von Rad could therefore both place wisdom in a poorly integrated appendix to his Old Testament theology and argue that in postexilic Israel "the entire theological thinking of late Judaism came more or less under the sway of wisdom: at any rate it found in the general concept a unity and an all-embracing binding factor such as Israel had not possessed until then" (2001, 1:441).

However, each connection with another text diluted that very distinctiveness of wisdom which influence studies had depended on to be both convincing and significant (Weeks 2010, 140).[8] The texts and associated features that defined wisdom expanded as the popularity of these studies initiated a chain reaction, in which arguments for one purported wisdom-influenced text invited the association of yet another with wisdom. Thus, Hans Walter Wolff's (1964) conclusion that Amos's intellectual home was the wisdom of tribal society built on Johannes Fichtner's (1949) earlier argument that the prophet Isaiah was a product of a wisdom school (see Scott 1970, 36–37). Similarly, R. N. Whybray's (1968) argument for wisdom influence in the Succession Narrative (2 Sam 9–20; 1 Kgs 1–2) and Shemaryahu Talmon's (1963) reading of Esther as wisdom both grew out of von Rad's (1953) earlier suggestion that the Joseph narrative (Gen 37, 39–50) is an example of the didactic literary novel as a form of wisdom literature (see Crenshaw 1969, 129; Sheppard 1980, 8–9). Fueled by the tendency "to describe as 'wisdom thinking' not just concepts which are found in every wisdom text, but concepts which are found in any wisdom text" (Weeks 2010, 107–8), from its place as an appendix, wisdom was spreading like an infection throughout the Hebrew Bible.

James Crenshaw (1969) recognized the threat of this enthusiasm for wisdom influence and attempted to provide a methodological antibiotic to limit the infection. His basic argument, as becomes clear in a later article (1976, 9–13), is that these purported wisdom-influenced texts were either not distinctive enough from the rest of the canon or not united enough with wisdom to justify the sapiential association. For example, Crenshaw argues that von Rad's suggestion that the Joseph narrative is designed to demonstrate courtly wisdom fails because, on the one hand, the anthropological concern he claims connects the story with wisdom is found in texts across the canon, and, on the other hand, numerous nonwisdom themes appear, such as appeals to special revelation and theophanic visions, sacrifice, and *Heilsgeschichte* (1969, 135–37). Crenshaw's approach assumes, however, that wisdom is composed of a discrete group of texts that can be distinguished formally and thematically from the rest of the canon. His attempts to justify this assumption reveal the weakness of this limit to wisdom.

---

8. See Crenshaw's counterarguments below, which consistently aim to demonstrate that these influence studies do not reflect a sufficiently distinct view of wisdom.

Crenshaw claims that one of the "distinct disadvantages" of these influence studies is that "they cannot escape circular reasoning" due to the fact that "the wisdom corpus alone (itself the result of a subjective decision on the part of each interpreter) defines what is in the last resort 'wisdom'" (1976, 9). Using Whybray's (1968) work as an example, he explains, "If, then, the succession narrative is by definition wisdom, a study of thematic considerations in wisdom literature and in the 'historical' account turns up nothing that contradicts the hypothesis and proves nothing unassumed from the outset" (Crenshaw 1976, 9). When it comes to his own study of wisdom based on the limited grouping of Proverbs, Job, Ecclesiastes, Ben Sira, Wisdom of Solomon, and a few psalms, Crenshaw admits the "subjective nature" of his "assumption" (1976, 5).[9] Nevertheless, he claims elsewhere, "However much the five books ... differ from one another, they retain a mysterious ingredient that links them together in a special way" (1998, 9).

Crenshaw's restricted wisdom corpus is itself essentially just a series of studies in wisdom influence that have been generally accepted, so it shares this liability to the charge of circularity. His attack on the expansion of wisdom reveals the weakness of the category's current limits and causes the grouping either to disintegrate or to expand indefinitely as each added text contributes further aspects to what defines it. Though he never acknowledges this dilemma, he does fear that influence studies will eviscerate wisdom of meaning by constantly extending its definition (1976, 13). These studies challenge wisdom study more fundamentally, however, by exposing its circularity. In his effort to curb them, Crenshaw resorts to circular reasoning himself, arguing that "wisdom influence can only be proved by a stylistic or ideological peculiarity found primarily in wisdom literature" (1969, 132), in spite of the fact that the content of wisdom literature was exactly what was up for debate.[10] His work likewise "proves nothing unassumed from the outset." Thus, his oft-cited definition of wisdom literature merely lists the features of texts in his wisdom corpus:

---

9. Crenshaw would later (2000) question the existence of wisdom psalms altogether.

10. Dell (1991, 62 n. 23) recognizes this circularity in Crenshaw's approach to limiting wisdom. Sheppard (1983, 479) notes a similar circular reliance on the traditional grouping of wisdom books to evaluate arguments for wisdom influence in his review of Morgan's work (1981), which takes a similar approach.

Formally, wisdom consists of proverbial sentence, or instruction, debate, intellectual reflection; thematically, wisdom comprises self-evident intuitions about mastering life for human betterment, gropings after life's secrets with regard to innocent suffering, grappling with finitude, and quest for truth concealed in the created order and manifested in a feminine persona. When a marriage between form and content exists, there is wisdom literature. (Crenshaw 1998, 11)

Thirty-three years after his initial arguments against wisdom influence, with the debate continuing, Crenshaw admits that "conclusive criteria" for distinguishing which texts derive from a "sapiential milieu" are still lacking (1993, 176). The "mysterious ingredient" that links them together is evidently still the subjective presuppositions of modern interpreters. Thus the problem, the traditional wisdom corpus, with the difficulties it poses to definition, becomes the solution to the problem of wisdom's spread across the canon.

For a generation, Crenshaw's retrenchment of wisdom in the traditional scholarly wisdom corpus has dominated wisdom scholarship. However, recently, in the midst of a "great bloom" of wisdom research (Witte 2012, 1159),[11] Crenshaw's paradigm has begun to lose its hold on the field. Increasingly, it is cited in order to be criticized as new approaches to wisdom are offered. Crenshaw's definition is said to be "only really a way of encapsulating the problem of definition, rather than of solving it" (Weeks 2010, 142–43). In light of evidence from Qumran, it is charged with illegitimately tying sapiential instruction to "a particular kind of content or a single worldview" (Collins 1997, 278; see also 266). Due to the diverse worldviews represented in Qumran wisdom texts, its marriage between form and content "ends in divorce" (Goff 2010, 325; see also 318, citing Collins 1997, 280). Its "list-of-features approach" to genre, which depends on "binary logic" and cannot account for "the diversity inherent in the wisdom tradition," should be replaced with a prototype-theory approach that allows for "fuzzy" generic borders (Wright 2010, 292, 314; see also 290). The previous generation's infection of influence has developed a

---

11. The attraction of the international character of wisdom remains in scholarship, though Witte adds further reasons for its recent popularity, such as its reflections on the limits of human knowledge and freedom, the relationship of the individual and community, conceptions of life and ethics, and representations of God in the world (Witte 2012, 1160).

resistance to Crenshaw's antibiotic, and, as will become apparent, it has returned stronger.

Discussion and Diagnosis

Sneed provides the most extensive recent attack against the traditional approach to wisdom that Crenshaw represents. His article is exemplary in the way it raises important questions to which it offers provocative answers that have ignited a healthy dicussion among scholars interested in wisdom. It provides, therefore, an opportunity to diagnose the current stage of the scholarly wisdom tradition's progression. Sneed (2011, 53–54) takes issue with the common presentation of the wisdom tradition, which he associates with Crenshaw and summarizes as "the view that Hebrew Wisdom Literature represents a worldview, tradition, and movement distinct from those of the priests and prophets and that it provides an alternative to Yahwism, that it is anti-revelatory." In order to argue instead that wisdom complemented other biblical literature, Sneed appeals to two recent developments in scholarship since those influence arguments of a previous generation: the first involves a new understanding of the nature of genres and the second reenvisions the scribal setting in which biblical texts were produced and preserved.

First, according to Sneed, this new understanding of the nature of literary genre asserts its independence from worldviews, which are too large for a genre to convey, from setting (contra Gunkel), since genres may be used in more than one setting, and even ontological existence (52, 54–57). In contrast with generic realism, which considers genres to be stable, static, ontological categories, and thus focuses on determining their specific features and which texts are in and out, Sneed, following Kenton Sparks (2005, 6–7), advocates a generic nominalism that recognizes that genres are taxonomic inventions with loose, constantly shifting boundaries (66–67). However, Sneed goes on to argue that wisdom should not even be considered a genre at all, but a mode, which is a broader, more abstract category (e.g., *comic* play or *heroic* epic, or, in the Bible, *legal* material or *historical* books). The abstraction of modes, which in the case of wisdom literature "represents, in many ways, an arbitrary collection of only loosely connected works," actually in itself suggests that speaking of corresponding settings or "worlds" and, presumably, worldviews is inappropriate for wisdom (57).

Sneed follows the exemplary definitions he provides from Derek Kidner, John Goldingay, and Richard Clifford in the widespread practice of defining Hebrew wisdom negatively, claiming much of its distinctiveness can be explained by recognizing that "it is not historical; it is not apocalyptic (except for hybrid examples in early Judaism); it is not prophetic, and so on" (68). However, he argues, wisdom is not opposed to these other features of Israelite thought. Instead, as one of several "complementary" modes in the Hebrew Bible (54), its focus simply lies elsewhere. Thus, with its primary purpose the enculturation of elite youth, the wisdom mode is defined by two broad characteristics: didacticism and moralizing, which, though evident in other modes, are "more overt and distilled" in wisdom (68–69).

Second, wisdom's educational function supports Sneed's main opposition to a separate wisdom tradition. Wisdom's complementary relationship to the rest of the Hebrew Bible is grounded, he argues, in the texts' common scribal origins, in which "scribal scholars," such as the wise in Proverbs 22:17; 24:23, were responsible, not only for producing the wisdom literature, but also for "the preservation, composition, utilization, and instruction of the other literary genres of our Hebrew Bible" (62–64).[12] This scribal role should be "given more weight" in the biblical authors' worldview than other roles they may have simultaneously held, such as Ezra's role as priest. Though the Israelite scribal scholars were not "one homogeneous whole," Sneed claims, "their worldview was largely the same, especially in light of their common academic heritage and common goals in teaching." The wisdom literature, then, particularly Proverbs, was central in the academic development of scribes, serving as a primer (cf. Carr 2005), but, since the other genres and traditions were also taught and studied in this setting, the entire Bible similarly contributed to scribal training (66, 71). Thus, in effect, Sneed does away with a purported distinctive wisdom tradition by arguing the whole Hebrew Bible came from the same tradition, and that this tradition was actually shaped by wisdom, with "these same Israelite wisdom writers or scribal scholars" producing and preserving all the biblical texts (62–63).

---

12. For a similar attribution of nonwisdom texts, and even the entire Bible, to scribes, Sneed refers to J. L. McKenzie 1967, 4–9; Weinfeld 1967, 249–62; Sparks 2005, 56; Clifford 1997, 1, 7; van der Toorn 2007a, 75–108, 143–72. He also refers to Carr's view that the wisdom literature was employed in the initial training of all biblical authors (see Carr 2011, 410). Sneed's citations of each of these scholars, with the exception of van der Toorn, explicitly connect this scribal setting to wisdom.

Ludger Schwienhorst-Schönberger (2013, 127–28) provides a potential diagnosis to explain the pan-sapiential propensity in Sneed's work when he identifies two opposing tendencies in wisdom scholarship: one, exemplified by von Rad, aims toward integrating the wisdom literature with the rest of the canon and makes it the center (*Mitte*) of Old Testament theology,[13] and the other, exemplified by Preuss, emphasizes wisdom's distinctiveness in a way that makes it theologically problematic and pushes it toward the edge (*Rand*). As the brief survey above suggests, the last century of wisdom scholarship could be interpreted as a pendulum swinging between these two extremes, constantly overcorrecting and thereby missing the golden mean between them. Thus, even in his attempt to limit early wisdom influence studies, Crenshaw (1969, 142 n. 54) acknowledged that they offered a "reminder that we have compartmentalized Israelite society far too rigidly." Sneed's work could then be understood as a swing back toward an integrated view of wisdom after Crenshaw's efforts to restrict its spread.

However, Sneed's methods for reaching his conclusion suggest more is at stake than how to properly balance the medications to manage the tensive relationship between wisdom and the rest of the canon. Sneed's attempt to distinguish the wisdom mode from other modes of biblical literature indicates he does not intend to advocate pan-sapientialism. This makes the pan-sapiential tendency of his argument all the more revealing of the current state of scholarly affairs. While employing his loose approach to genre, he never clearly explains how he reaches the conclusions about what wisdom is and is not concerned with. His reticence to list a number of wisdom texts from which he distills these essential traits is understandable given his opposition to a taxonomically focused generic realism. However, in its place, he offers only the admittedly "arbitrary"

---

13. Murphy (1967, 407 n. 2) suggests von Rad's attractive presentation of wisdom in his *Old Testament Theology* was a possible impetus for the popularity of wisdom influence studies (similarly, Scott 1970, 21). The fact that Murphy also criticizes von Rad for relegating wisdom to a "peripheral or secondary" position as Israel's response to God demonstrates the conflicted nature of the interpretation of wisdom and von Rad's particularly complex involvement in its development in the twentieth century. Murphy's observation that the entire Hebrew Bible might legitimately be considered "Israel's answer" to Yahweh (1969, 290) may be the key to reconciling these apparently contradictory effects of von Rad's work: the characterization of wisdom as response rather than revelation, which marginalized it when Hebrew thought was valued, enabled its popularization when universal ideas became more popular.

and "loosely connected" mode of wisdom literature, and a nominalist view of genre, which understands genre as "an unstable entity, constantly changing and dynamic," so that one could, for example, include Daniel, the Song of Songs, and wisdom psalms, or exclude Job (66–67). When Sneed combines his nominalist view of the wisdom genre, or mode, with a scribal setting shared with the entire Hebrew Bible, he takes these recent developments in the discussion of wisdom to an untenable extreme. If the worldview of those who composed and preserved the biblical texts militates against a distinctive wisdom worldview because the same scribal scholars, which Sneed and the scholars he cites associate with wisdom, composed and preserved them all, wisdom and nonwisdom alike, then wouldn't their worldview ultimately define the entire Bible? Sneed's approach to genre enables *anything* to be considered wisdom, while the shared scribal setting enables *everything* to be considered wisdom, and if wisdom can mean anything and everything, then it means nothing.

Though Sneed's combination of the redefinition of genre with a widespread scribal setting makes clear the pan-sapiential potential of these two responses to the traditional approach to delimiting wisdom, scholars have already recognized the lack of control suggested by each approach individually and attempted to provide some methodological limits to the sapiential expansion they facilitate. The failure of the proposed solutions to maintain the wisdom category while limiting its spread, apart from appealing circularly to the scholarly consensus, suggests the problem with Sneed's argument does not stem ultimately from his methods or their combination, but from the wisdom category itself.

First, in regard to genre, Benjamin Wright provides a more methodologically developed generic nominalist approach to the wisdom genre in his study of wisdom at Qumran by incorporating a prototype theory of genre. Wright (2010, 291, 297) acknowledges the lack of consensus on what constitutes wisdom as a literary genre and the fact that its existence could be questioned altogether. However, because scholars "almost universally agree" on a group of wisdom books, he believes it legitimate to discuss wisdom as a genre. He believes prototype theory, which does not require the identification of clearly defined classificatory criteria, may enable the category's continued use (297–98). Taking this approach, he begins with the prototypical exemplars of the genre by "general consensus" (Proverbs, Qoheleth, Job, Ben Sira, and Wisdom of Solomon) and distills four properties that serve as a template for judging other potential members: (1) pedagogical form and intent; (2) concern for acquiring wisdom through study and learning; (3) engagement with earlier sapiential tradition; and (4) interest in practical ethics (298–99; see further 294–95). Though other texts may share several of these traits, what is important for a prototype approach is the structural relations between them (301). This approach, then, provides two primary advantages over the more traditional taxonomic list-of-features approach: it removes the need to worry about whether borderline cases belong in the genre or not, and it enables the borders between genres to be blurred and overlap (302–3).

Despite its methodological clarity, Wright's article is a clear example of the *ex post facto* justification of wisdom that characterizes the current discussion. Beginning with the scholarly consensus on the contents of the genre, he looks for a means of explaining it, finding one in prototype genre theory. What the field lacks is an analysis that reaches back *before* the wisdom category became a fact to the origins of this grouping that scholars must go to such lengths to justify. The basis for the categorization of this "universally" agreed upon group of wisdom texts remains "a legitimate question" (Collins 2010, 429).

Second, in regard to scribal setting, Katharine Dell (2000, 350) observes that in the earlier discussion of wisdom influence the question of whether these affinities with wisdom resulted from an early formative influence on the authors' thought or from later literary editing was never answered (cf. 352–53). Though few did so explicitly, the earlier influence arguments in the 1960s and 1970s tended to explain the affinities between those texts and wisdom with the first explanation (as the term influence suggests).[14] This view has recently been given a new historical explanation in David Carr's arguments that wisdom was at the heart of the enculturation of Hebrew scribes (Carr 2005, 2011). The latter view of later sapiential editing built on a notion that wisdom came to dominate the theology of late Judaism, which is already evident in von Rad's *Old Testament Theology* (see n. 7 above). Gerald Sheppard (1980, 13) proposed a means through which this thinking seeped back into earlier texts by taking the use of wisdom as a "hermeneutical construct," already recognized in Sir 24 by von Rad (1993, 245), and arguing that it was applied in the editing of texts across the Hebrew Bible. Similar arguments expanding on his thesis soon followed (e.g., Wilson 1992; Van Leeuwen 1993). By attributing the entire

---

14. This despite the fact that the wisdom books are predominantly dated later than the texts wisdom is said to have influenced (see Weeks 2010, 136).

canon to "scribal scholars," Sneed combines the school setting with that of scribal editing and conflates wisdom as an early formative influence with the later sapiential editing of texts of other genres.[15] In so doing, he demonstrates the diachronic pincer movement by which wisdom has invaded the broader canon.

Dell's response to such influence arguments is again indicative of the current state of wisdom scholarship. Though the influence of wisdom on biblical material beyond the "so-called wisdom books" was "significant," she argues, "if we want a stable definition of what wisdom literature proper actually includes, we need to restrict it to that material containing in large measure the forms, content, and context of wisdom and this brings us back to the mainline wisdom books" (2000, 353). She continues,

> It is interesting that the tradition has preserved wisdom as a separate entity with its own forms, content, and theology and it may well have belonged to a distinctive context in the social world of the Israelites. This suggests that consideration of its literature should focus on the major biblical wisdom books plus a few wisdom psalms, and that the issues of wisdom influence elsewhere in the Old Testament, and its context of origin and development, should have these books as their point of reference.

Her supposition that the tradition has preserved wisdom as a separate entity, especially if that entity is associated with the "mainline wisdom books," is based on modern views of the definition of wisdom literature that only gained prominence in the mid-nineteenth century; it is a *scholarly* tradition. This, in the end, is the final recourse she (and the field more broadly) has available to limit wisdom's spread so that it can have a stable definition.

The diverse contents of the wisdom corpus have consistently given attempts to define its distinctive features a certain instability, characterized by vague, abstract, and potentially all-encompassing definitions (see Weeks 2010, 108), such as a "shared approach to reality" (Murphy 1978, 48–49), which is broad enough to make all literature wisdom literature (Whybray 1982, 186). Crenshaw considered his work a dam to hold back

---

15. Note his consistent linkage of "composition and/or preservation" in his description of these scribal scholars' role in the shaping of the canon (Sneed 2011, 54; see also 63, 71).

the spread of wisdom throughout the Hebrew Bible. Wisdom, held in its own distinctive reservoir by Crenshaw's appeal to the consensus, has, now that that dam has started to crumble, begun to rush across the canon again. If Crenshaw's definition of wisdom circularly both starts and ends with the scholarly tradition, this more recent approach's start in a traditional consensus, the justification for which scholars are increasingly recognizing to be problematic, leaves it without a way to end apart from an appeal back to that same consensus. Sneed's work is a prime example of how a broad discomfort with the marginalization of wisdom from the rest of the Hebrew Bible and its theology has led, not so much to a theologization of wisdom in scholarship akin to the one once proposed to have existed within the Israelite wisdom movement itself,[16] as to a sapientialization of the theology of the Hebrew Bible.[17] Thus, Sneed can cite approvingly Clifford's view: "Rather than wisdom books influencing other biblical books, however, it is more likely that wisdom thinking was in the main stream of biblical literary production from whence its style and ideas radiated throughout biblical writings" (Clifford 2006, 1; cf. Sneed 2011, 64). The wisdom worldview is seen as "an important part of the background for most of the literature in the Old Testament" (Høgenhaven 1987, 99–100). So, Carr (2011, 407) argues, "'In the beginning' was the writing-supported teaching of 'the wise.'" Or, as Dell (2000, 370) writes, "The richness and diversity of wisdom, and the extent of its influence, lead one to suspect that wisdom's proper place is at the heart of the Israelite experience of God." The appendix has become the heart. From there, it threatens to infect the entire canonical corpus.

ANALOGOUS CASES

Wisdom at Qumran

Recent research on the Dead Sea Scrolls provides a helpful parallel to the attempts to bring the pan-sapiential epidemic in the Hebrew Bible under

---

16. E.g., McKane 1970. For criticism of this view, see, e.g., Crenshaw 1998, 76–82; Dell 2000, 357–58.

17. See the subtitle of Sheppard's influential book *Wisdom as a Hermeneutical Construct: A Study of the Sapientializing of the Old Testament*. For recent discussion of sapiential influence on texts across the Hebrew Bible, see Saur 2011, 447–48; Witte 2012, 1173–74.

control, which is related by both analogy and extension to that phenomenon.[18] Qumran scholars had an advantage over Hebrew Bible scholars, however; they were able to approach their texts as a blank slate without preestablished consensuses on which books were wisdom and which were not (Newsom 2010, 276–77), however, this tabula rasa was quickly piled up with scholarly assumptions and is no longer available (Collins 2010, 425). This has fostered widespread debate, though a generally agreed-upon group of primary Qumran wisdom texts has emerged.[19] In this discussion, however, a number of the same problematic tendencies have arisen as in the pan-sapiential epidemic in the study of the Hebrew Bible.

Goff's approach to defining wisdom at Qumran, though it stands somewhere between a chastened list-of-features approach and a family resemblance approach, is nearly indistinguishable from Wright's prototype-theory approach to the question (see pp. 21–22 above). Both start with the general scholarly consensus on wisdom texts in the Hebrew Bible (Goff 2010, 319, 331; Wright 2010, 298) and draw in Qumran texts that interact with this tradition to greater or lesser degrees, integrating other features, such as Torah or apocalyptic interests. For both this follows a chain-reaction process similar to that in wisdom influence studies. Texts are associated with wisdom because of a particular affinity with a single wisdom text, such as 4QInstruction with Ben Sira, or even a section within it, such as 4QWiles of the Wicked Woman with Prov 7 (Wright 2010, 304–6). This has the effect of expanding the definition of wisdom (see Collins 2010, 424), so that, according to Goff, Ben Sira links Proverbs to the Torah, which then allows the Qumran texts 4Q185 and 4Q525, which share this trait, to be connected to wisdom, while 4QInstruction takes Proverbs in a different direction, toward apocalypticism,[20] enabling the book of Mysteries and the Treatise of the Two Spirits to be considered wisdom texts, as well (Goff 2010, 330, 322). As a result, Goff concludes, "one can consider a Qumran composition a wisdom text, even if it has little in common with

---

18. For a survey of the extensive relevant literature, see Goff 2009.
19. 4QInstruction (1Q26, 4Q415–418, 423) (also known as *musar le-mebin*), the book of Mysteries (1Q27, 4Q299–301), 4QWiles of the Wicked Woman (4Q184), 4QSapiential Work (4Q185), 4QWords of the Maśkil (4Q298), 4QWays of Righteousness (4Q420–421), 4QInstruction-like Composition B (4Q424) and 4QBeatitudes (4Q525). See Goff 2010, 316–17.
20. Wright argues, however, that 4QInstruction was primarily associated with wisdom through its similarity to Ben Sira, not Proverbs.

biblical wisdom or includes much that is alien to older sapiential texts" (2010, 321).[21] To hold these disparate texts together, both scholars end up with short lists of rather vague and abstract common wisdom traits.[22] Whether the various developments in the genre are seen as texts at the boundaries of multiple genres, as Wright would put it, or as "several types of sapiential discourse," which may stem from different traditions, as Goff says, the genre has spread so far in both their treatments that, as Goff declares, "Engagement of a given wisdom composition with other sapiential texts must be established, rather than assumed on the basis of the genre label" (2010, 334). This being the case, however, the value of the genre label is drastically reduced, since it can provide little interpretive guidance. As Goff puts it, once the Qumran texts are considered, "wisdom as a literary category, which was somewhat loose to start with, is now even looser" (2010, 335).

The progression from scholarly consensus to vague definition to chain-reaction extension and consequent dilution of the genre's interpretive significance common to these two studies is shared by attempts to define wisdom in the Hebrew Bible. The attempt to begin with the general consensus of wisdom from Hebrew Bible scholarship and provide definitions of wisdom at Qumran that give the genre a definition distinct enough to provide interpretive guidance and prevent potential pan-sapiential expansion fails, in my opinion, not because of their erudite efforts, but because of the unwieldy wisdom category handed down to them in the scholarly tradition. In order to encapsulate the diverse wisdom texts in the Hebrew Bible, this classification is already so vague and abstract that any attempt to categorize other texts on this basis "threatens to become an all-encompassing category" (Tanzer 2005, 42, quoting Collins 1994, 2).

---

21. By tracing the affiliations between texts, Goff's analysis resembles a family resemblance approach. For an explicit family resemblance approach to defining wisdom, see Fox 2000, 17. John Swales (1990, 51) has observed that "a family resemblance theory can make anything resemble anything," and the chain reactions in Goff's article seem to support this judgment.

22. Goff suggests two defining features of wisdom that encapsulate the diversity of wisdom texts both in the Hebrew Bible and at Qumran, which he acknowledges are "somewhat ambiguous": (1) a noetic purpose, which, in addition to instructing, fosters a desire to search for understanding; and (2) significant participation in a sapiential discourse by engaging with traditional Israelite wisdom as exemplified by Proverbs (2010, 327–28, 330). For Wright's list, see pp. 21–22 above.

Wisdom in the Ancient Near East

The situation in Qumran scholarship in the past half-century of scholarship is similar to the one scholars faced with ancient Near Eastern texts in the half-century before that: scholars had the opportunity to evaluate texts that had appeared unencumbered by a tradition of generic classification. Here also, however, scholars studying both ancient Egyptian (Williams 1981, 1; Lichtheim 1996, 261) and ancient Mesopotamian texts (Lambert 1960, 1; Beaulieu 2007, 3) defined ancient Near Eastern wisdom literature based on the scholarly consensus on the biblical wisdom corpus.[23] Texts that resembled Proverbs and others that resembled Ecclesiastes or Job were grouped together in a common category of ancient Near Eastern wisdom literature.

Just as the texts from early Judaism do, these additional texts stretch the concept of wisdom in various ways, as they incorporate aspects foreign to the traditional understanding of biblical wisdom. For example, John Gray repeatedly notes that the Babylonian texts that have the most affinities with Job also share them with psalmic laments. He claims that both the Babylonian texts and Job reflect the conventional language of that common literary type, which was used in fast-liturgies in Mesopotamia and Israel and concludes, "All those texts indicate how intimately wisdom in the ancient Near East was connected with religion" (Gray 1970, 268; cf. 255, 256, 263). Similarly, Paul-Alain Beaulieu (2007, 8–11) discusses how the Mesopotamian reflections on pious suffering were set in the context of exorcism, which indicates the "fully integrated nature of wisdom, religion, ritual, and divination" in Mesopotamian texts. In fact, he observes, exorcism, divination, and rites of intercession were all characterized as *nēmequ* ("wisdom") or associated with Ea, the god of wisdom, so attempting to define wisdom based on the Mesopotamian understanding would lead to an extensive corpus quite unlike the traditional characterization of biblical wisdom literature (12).

It is little surprise, then, that in ancient Near Eastern scholarship, as in the study of the Dead Sea Scrolls, wisdom literature has continued to expand, now including texts as diverse as the Epic of Gilgamesh[24] and the

---

23. Beaulieu observes, "In ancient Mesopotamia, there was no such concept or category as wisdom literature" (2007, 3).

24. Van der Toorn 2007b, 21; cf. Beaulieu (2007, 7), who claims the work's sapiential themes "cannot easily be separated from the larger context of religion and ritual."

preceptive hymns, Hymn to Ninurta and The Shamash Hymn.[25] Once again, using the biblical wisdom corpus as an unexamined starting point leads to the expansion of the genre and dilution of its hermeneutical significance, and therefore the potential distortion of the interpretation of its contents.

Pan-Deuteronomism

The difficulties in defining wisdom at Qumran and in the ancient Near East, which can, in both cases, be traced back to the consensus regarding the content of biblical wisdom, indicate that this scholarly tradition is the source of the pan-sapiential infection. However, a further analogous case demonstrates that methodological factors have contributed to its spread. The struggle to quarantine a category that threatens to spread across the canon is not a unique phenomenon within biblical studies. In 1999 a collection of essays undertook to evaluate a growing "pan-Deuteronomism" before "the fever" reached "epidemic proportions" (Schearing 1999, 13). Continuing the analogy, Crenshaw (1999, 146, 145), in his contribution to the volume, notes the "astonishing" likeness this pan-Deuteronomistic tendency in scholarship bears to "a pan-sapientialism [that] infected much research relating to the Hebrew Bible" thirty years before. He charges both with circular reasoning and a lack of widely agreed upon controlling criteria, though he identifies five criteria commonly employed by both: (1) phraseological similarities; (2) thematic considerations; (3) social location; (4) creative adaptation; and (5) oppositional ideology (146).[26]

As the methodological reflections by Richard Coggins, Norbert Lohfink, and Robert Wilson included in the volume indicate, pan-Deuteronomism shares a number of other similarities with recent wisdom scholarship beyond their common recourse to circular reasoning, lack of adequate controls, and use of similar criteria.

(1) Associated "movement": Just as "speculation" and "misunderstanding" characterize discussion of the wisdom "movement" in ancient

---

Van der Toorn also includes Etana, the Series of the Fox, Sidu, and the Series of the Poplar among the ancient Near Eastern wisdom texts (2007b, 22).

25. See Lambert 1960, 118–38, and discussion in Scott 1970, 32.

26. Similarly, Wilson (1999, 78) observes that "although a growing number of scholars agree that much of the Hebrew Bible is Deuteronomistic, they do not agree on what makes it Deuteronomistic."

Israel (Weeks 2010, 133), so evidence is also lacking for the purported tradents of Deuteronomism and the "movement" or "tradition" to which they belonged (Coggins 1999, 26–27; cf. Lohfink 1999). Coggins even entertains the idea that the "Deuteronomists" were not a group at all, but that instead the similar rhetoric that enables scholars to infer their existence is no more than "just a kind of language" used for particular types of religious prose (32).

(2) Terminology: Confusion results from the use of wisdom (often used interchangeably with scribal and sapiential) to refer to a concept, a genre, and a movement, with illegitimate transfers from one category occasionally made to another, so that "scribal circles become 'wisdom circles' and schools become 'wisdom schools' almost by default, and therefore anything scribal or educational becomes 'wisdom' as well" (Weeks 2010, 141; cf. Crenshaw 1969, 130). Deuteronomism is similarly plagued by terminological confusion. Deuteronomic and Deuteronomistic are often used in an overlapping fashion, muddling together the name for a book, a literary process, and an ideological movement. Using the terms this way "is to invite a breakdown in understanding" (Coggins 1999, 34–35).

(3) Chain-reaction expansion: Just as a chain-reaction process has enabled the expansion of wisdom across the canon (see p. 15 above), Lohfink (1999, 39) explains how through a similar process the starting point for determining what is Deuteronomistic has expanded from simply the book of Deuteronomy (or even just the law in Deuteronomy 12–26), to the commonly accepted canon of Deuteronomistic texts (Deuteronomy, the Former Prophets, and parts of Jeremiah), to texts that share features with that broader canon, even if they lack direct connections with Deuteronomy. For both phenomena, this extension has reached a point where every part of the canon, and nearly every book, has been associated with each (Coggins 1999, 22–23; Wilson 1999, 68, see n. 6 above).

(4) Recourse to scholarly consensus: A recourse to the scholarly consensus emerged above as a repeated response to the threat of pansapientialism. Lohfink takes a similar approach to attempt to limit "pan-Deuteronomistic chain reactions." He suggests reserving the word "Deuteronomistic" only for describing textual affiliation, so that only books "within the *basic Deuteronomistic canon already known*" may be designated "Deuteronomistic," and beyond that, it could serve only as an adjective for specific phenomena such as "Deuteronomistic formulation" (1999, 39, emphasis added). The semantic distinction Lohfink attempts to make

is analogous to the one in wisdom study between wisdom literature and literature that demonstrates wisdom influence (see p. 16 above).

Along with their methodological similarities, it appears the two scholarly phenomena may now face the same drastic alternatives: either a nearly all-encompassing embrace or abandonment. The wisdom category now seems poised between capacious proposals like Sneed's and the potential demise entertained by von Rad, Goff, and Weeks. Pan-Deuteronomism may force a similar choice. Thus, on the one hand, Wilson (1999, 82) argues that the extensive literary activity attributed to the Deuteronomists may make it necessary "to explore the possibility that Deuteronomism was a wide-ranging movement that was much more diverse than scholars commonly think and that was active over a very long period of time." However, on the other hand, he continues, "Recent research may in fact have demonstrated, unwittingly, that the concept of Deuteronomism has become so amorphous that it no longer has any analytical precision and so ought to be abandoned." He concludes, "Current trends in Deuteronomistic research may thus force scholars to take seriously the possibility that if everybody is the Deuteronomist, then there may be no Deuteronomist at all."

PROPOSED TREATMENT

This comparison with Deuteronomism appears to suggest two potential courses of treatment for biblical scholarship's sapiential appendicitis: amputating the infected category or letting the contagion spread throughout Hebrew Bible interpretation; the significant difficulties of defining the wisdom genre given the diversity of its contents have left previous mediating approaches untenably unstable. However, the resemblance between the two scholarly phenomena also suggests another treatment option may be available: the interpretation of connections between the texts associated with each movement and other biblical texts as the result of scribal familiarity and intertextual citation or allusion rather than of a unified, distinct school, movement, or tradition in Israelite culture. Lohfink, for example, claims the use of Deuteronomistic content or language in later works may be better explained simply as the result of the widespread familiarity with the Deuteronomistic writings gained in an educational context. Similar to the way Chronicles takes up passages from the Deuteronomistic History yet is not considered Deuteronomistic as a result (S. L. McKenzie 1999, 269), other writers could refer their readers to Deuteronomy or other Deuteronomistic texts through allusions and citations, perhaps even in their redaction of earlier books, without being involved in a Deuteronomistic movement (Lohfink 1999, 65; see further S. L. McKenzie 1999, 264).[27]

Wisdom may require a more radical application of this treatment. Due to the intractable difficulty of determining the genre's limits, a much more limited understanding of the genre is called for. I would prescribe that the so-called wisdom genre no longer be considered the exclusive caterogization for the books it purportedly contains nor the grounds on which to draw conclusions about movements to which their authors belonged, but simply one of many ways to draw intertextual connections among them and other texts in the Hebrew Bible. I would agree with Weeks, who is willing to use the title wisdom literature for Proverbs, Ecclesiastes, and Job "so long as this is taken simply as a description of subject-matter, and not of form or origin" (1999, 27). But I would add the further caveat that this subject not be taken as the only, or even necessarily the main, topic with which the three books are concerned. When compared with one another, the three books demonstrate certain similarities that illuminate their interpretation, but comparing the books with other texts would bring other aspects to light. For example, before the wisdom category was developed, W. M. L. de Wette (1807) grouped Job, Ecclesiastes, and the lament psalms together in a study of the prominence of *Unglück* or "misfortune" in Israelite religion (Kynes forthcoming). More recently, Claus Westermann has argued that the disproportionate use of the word רשע ("wicked") in Proverbs, Job, and the Psalms (particularly individual laments) compared to the rest of the Hebrew Bible, indicates "a relationship of these three complexes to one another" (Westermann 1995, 81).[28] Both these comparisons shed new light on the books, but they certainly do not justify positing misfortune literature or wicked literature as categories of biblical books with shared distinctive worldviews and traditions. And yet similar thematic and lexical connections are the basis for the wisdom literature category. Jonathan Culler (1975, 147) explains, "A work

---

27. Lohfink offers the intentional citation of Jeremiah in Zech 1:1–6, the pluses in the MT of Jeremiah, and imitations of the Deuteronomistic prose of Jeremiah in Dan 9 and Baruch as examples.

28. For more examples of the interpretive value of tracing connections between wisdom books and texts across the canon and beyond, see Dell and Kynes 2013 and 2014.

can only be read in connection with or against other texts, which provide a grid through which it is read and structured by establishing expectations which enable one to pick out salient features and give them a structure." The wisdom category is only one of the many structures through which the so-called wisdom texts can and should be interpreted.

Wisdom, like any genre, is indeed a scholarly construct, the formalization of intertextual comparisons made by a group of readers (see Newsom 2010, 273). Attempts to identify links with wisdom in other texts in the Hebrew Bible (i.e., wisdom influence), at Qumran, or in the ancient Near East are simply extensions of the same process that originally brought Proverbs, Ecclesiastes, and Job together. Some of these similarities may be the results of later authors intentionally referencing earlier texts (diachronic intertextuality) and others may be the products of readerly comparison (synchronic intertextuality) (see Kynes 2013, 202). As long as the possibilities of other connections are acknowledged, the discussion of such similarities is unproblematic. However, the reification of these intertextual connections through their connection to a particular ancient tradition or movement complete with its own social setting and group of authors and tradents sets unwarranted boundaries on the interpretation of the so-called wisdom books (see Nickelsburg 2005, 36; Weeks 2013, 19, 24). Sneed, then, provides half of the solution to the problem of wisdom's marginalization produced by the modern scholarly wisdom tradition in his appeals to a nominal view of genre like the one I have just described. But his argument, which attempts to connect his wisdom mode with a setting in scribal education, and then expands this setting to the entire Hebrew Bible, brings the entire canon within those boundaries instead of breaking them down. Yes, genres are social phenomena, but the wisdom genre as it is currently understood is a modern construct, so attempts to interpret its social dimensions must start with the last century and half of biblical scholarship before they address a purported setting in ancient Israel (see Kynes forthcoming).[29]

---

29. For the widespread tendency of critics to read earlier texts through the genre categories of their own time as if those genres were static and universally applicable, see Fowler 1982, 51.

Conclusion

Attempts to define wisdom literature, whether at Qumran, in ancient Near Eastern texts, or in the Hebrew Bible itself, resort eventually to the scholarly consensus concerning which biblical texts make up the category's core. With the other arguments resting upon it, this factor carries all the weight in the current debates about wisdom, and yet little research has been put into how this consensus developed, leaving it a "gray area" in biblical scholarship (Dell 2013, 605–6 n. 2). If an understanding of wisdom based on the scholarly consensus either turns circularly back on itself or expands indefinitely, then perhaps that consensus is itself the problem. Instead of starting and ending at this point or starting here and never ending, I propose evaluating how this modern tradition started and interrogating its driving presuppositions to determine how they may be affecting the current discussion of the ancient wisdom tradition. In the meantime a more consciously intertextual approach to the so-called wisdom texts would foster a more healthy relationship between the texts associated with the category and the rest of the biblical corpus.[30]

Works Consulted

Baumgartner, Walter. 1933. "Die israelitische Weisheitsliteratur." *TRu* 5:259–88.

Beaulieu, Paul-Alain. 2007. "The Social and Intellectual Setting of Babylonian Wisdom Literature." Pages 3–19 in *Wisdom Literature in Mesopotamia and Israel*. Edited by Richard J. Clifford. SymS 36. Atlanta: Society of Biblical Literature.

Bruch, J. F. 1851. *Weisheits-Lehre der Hebräer: Ein Beitrag zur Geschichte der Philosophie*. Strassburg: Treuttel & Würtz.

Carr, David M. 2005. *Writing on the Tablet of the Heart: Origins of Scripture and Literature*. Oxford: Oxford University Press.

———. 2011. *The Formation of the Hebrew Bible: A New Reconstruction*. Oxford: Oxford University Press.

Clifford, Richard. 1997. "Introduction to the Wisdom Literature." *NIB* 5:1–16.

---

30. I would like to thank James R. Edwards and J. Matthew Kynes, MD, for providing helpful feedback on an earlier version of this essay. I am also grateful to Mark Sneed for his insightful editorial suggestions.

Coggins, Richard. 1999. "What Does 'Deuteronomistic' Mean?" Pages 22–35 in Schearing and McKenzie 1999.

Collins, John J. 1994. "Response to George Nickelsburg." Paper presented at the Annual Meeting of the Society of Biblical Literature. Chicago.

———. 1997. "Wisdom Reconsidered, in Light of the Dead Sea Scrolls." *DSD* 4:265–81.

———. 2010. "Epilogue: Genre Analysis and the Dead Sea Scrolls." *DSD* 17:418–30.

Crenshaw, James L. 1969. "Method in Determining Wisdom Influence upon 'Historical' Literature." *JBL* 88:129–42.

———. 1976. "Prolegomenon." Pages 1–60 in *Studies in Ancient Israelite Wisdom*. Edited by James L. Crenshaw. Library of Biblical Studies. New York: Ktav.

———. 1993. "Wisdom Literature: Retrospect and Prospect." Pages 161–78 in *Of Prophets' Visions and the Wisdom of Sages*. Edited by Heather A. McKay and D. J. A. Clines. JSOTSup 162. Sheffield: Sheffield Academic.

———. 1998. *Old Testament Wisdom: An Introduction*. 2nd ed. Louisville: Westminster John Knox.

———. 1999. "The Deuteronomists and the Writings." Pages 145–58 in Schearing and McKenzie 1999.

———. 2000. "Wisdom Psalms?" *CurBS* 8:9–17.

Culler, Jonathan D. 1975. *Structuralist Poetics: Structuralism, Linguistics and the Study of Literature*. London: Routledge & Kegan Paul.

Dell, Katharine J. 1991. *The Book of Job as Sceptical Literature*. BZAW 197. Berlin: de Gruyter.

———. 2000. "Wisdom in Israel." Pages 348–75 in *Text in Context: Essays by Members of the Society for Old Testament Study*. Edited by A. D. H. Mayes. Oxford: Oxford University Press.

———. 2013. "Studies of the Didactical Books of the Hebrew Bible/Old Testament." Pages 603–24 in vol. 3.1 of *Hebrew Bible, Old Testament: The History of Its Interpretation*. Edited by Magne Sæbø. Göttingen: Vandenhoeck & Ruprecht.

Dell, Katharine, and Will Kynes, eds. 2013. *Reading Job Intertextually*. LHBOTS 574. New York: Bloomsbury T&T Clark.

———. 2014. *Reading Ecclesiastes Intertextually*. LHBOTS 587. New York: Bloomsbury T&T Clark.

Driver, S. R. 1891. *An Introduction to the Literature of the Old Testament*. New York: Scribner's Sons.

Erman, A. 1924a. "Das Weisheitsbuch des Amen-em-ope." *OLZ* 27:241–52.

———. 1924b. "Eine ägyptische Quelle der 'Sprüche Salomos.'" *Sitzungsberichte der Preussischen Akademie der Wissenschaften, philologisch-historische Klasse* 15:86–92.

Fichtner, Johannes. 1949. "Jesaja unter den Weisen." *TLZ* 74:75–80.

Fox, Michael V. 2000. *Proverbs 1–9*. AB 18A. New York: Doubleday.

———. 2012. "Joseph and Wisdom." Pages 231–62 in *The Book of Genesis: Composition, Reception, and Interpretation*. Edited by Craig A. Evans, Joel N. Lohr, and David L. Petersen. Leiden: Brill.

Fowler, Alastair. 1982. *Kinds of Literature: An Introduction to the Theory of Genres and Modes*. Oxford: Clarendon.

Gadamer, Hans-Georg. 2004. *Truth and Method*. Translated by Joel Weinsheimer and Donald G. Marshall. London: Continuum.

Gese, Hartmut. 1958. *Lehre und Wirklichkeit in der alten Weisheit: Studien zu den Sprüchen Salomos und zu dem Buche Hiob*. Tübingen: Mohr.

Goff, Matthew. 2009. "Recent Trends in the Study of Early Jewish Wisdom Literature: The Contribution of 4QInstruction and Other Qumran Texts." *CBR* 7:376–416.

———. 2010. "Qumran Wisdom Literature and the Problem of Genre." *DSD* 17:315–35.

Gray, John. 1970. "The Book of Job in the Context of Near Eastern Literature." *ZAW* 82:251–69.

Høgenhaven, Jesper. 1987. *Problems and Prospects of Old Testament Theology*. Sheffield: JSOT Press.

Kynes, Will. 2013. "Intertextuality: Method and Theory in Job and Psalm 119." Pages 201–13 in *Biblical Interpretation and Method: Essays in Honour of Professor John Barton*. Edited by Katherine J. Dell and Paul M. Joyce. Oxford: Oxford University Press.

———. Forthcoming. "The Nineteenth-Century Beginnings of 'Wisdom Literature,' and Its Twenty-First Century End?" In *Perspectives on Israelite Wisdom: Proceedings of the Oxford Old Testament Seminar*. Edited by John Jarick. LHBOTS. New York: Bloomsbury T&T Clark.

Lambert, W. G. 1960. *Babylonian Wisdom Literature*. Oxford: Clarendon.

Lichtheim, Miriam. 1996. "Didactic Literature." Pages 243–62 in *Ancient Egyptian Literature: History and Forms*. Edited by Antonio Loprieno. PAe 10. Leiden: Brill.

Lohfink, Norbert F. 1999. "Was There a Deuteronomistic Movement?" Pages 36–66 in Schearing and McKenzie 1999.

McKane, William. 1970. *Proverbs: A New Approach*. OTL. London: SCM.

McKenzie, John L. 1967. "Reflections on Wisdom." *JBL* 86:1–9.

McKenzie, Steven L. 1999. "Postscript: The Laws of Physics and Pan-Deuteronomism." Pages 262–71 in Schearing and McKenzie 1999.

Meinhold, Johannes. 1908. *Die Weisheit Israels in Spruch, Sage und Dichtung*. Leipzig: Quelle & Meyer.

Morgan, Donn F. 1981. *Wisdom in the Old Testament Traditions*. Atlanta: John Knox.

Murphy, Roland E. 1967. "Assumptions and Problems in Old Testament Wisdom Research." *CBQ* 29:101–112 (407–18).

———. 1969. "The Interpretation of Old Testament Wisdom Literature." *Int* 23:289–301.

———. 1978. "Wisdom–Theses and Hypothesis." Pages 35–42 in *Israelite Wisdom: Theological and Literary Essays in Honor of Samuel Terrien*. Edited by John G. Gammie, Walter A. Brueggemann, W. Lee Humphreys, and James M. Ward. Missoula, MT: Scholars Press.

Newsom, Carol A. 2010. "Pairing Research Questions and Theories of Genre: A Case Study of the Hodayot." *DSD* 17:270–88.

Nickelsburg, George W. E. 2005. "Wisdom and Apocalypticism in Early Judaism: Some Points for Discussion." Pages 17–37 in *Conflicted Boundaries in Wisdom and Apocalypticism*. Edited by Lawrence M. Wills and Benjamin G. Wright. SymS 35. Atlanta: Society of Biblical Literature.

Preuss, Horst Dietrich. 1970. "Erwägungen zum theologischen Ort alttestamentlicher Weisheitsliteratur." *EvT* 30:393–417.

Rad, Gerhard von. 1953. *Das erste Buch Mose : Genesis Kapitel 25,19-50,26*. ATD 4. Göttingen : Vandenhoeck & Ruprecht.

———. 1993. *Wisdom in Israel*. Translated by James D. Martin. Harrisburg, PA: Trinity Press International.

———. 2001. *Old Testament Theology*. OTL. Louisville: Westminster John Knox.

Saur, Markus. 2011. "Die literarische Funktion und die theologische Intention der Weisheitsreden des Sprüchebuches." *VT* 61:447–60.

Schearing, Linda S. 1999. "Introduction." Pages 13–19 in Schearing and McKenzie 1999.

Schearing, Linda S., and Steven L. McKenzie, eds. 1999. *Those Elusive Deuteronomists: The Phenomenon of Pan-Deuteronomism*. JSOTSup 268. Sheffield: Sheffield Academic Press.

Schwienhorst-Schönberger, Ludger. 2013. "Alttestamentliche Weisheit im Diskurs." *ZAW* 125:118–42.

Scott, R. B. Y. 1970. "The Study of Wisdom Literature." *Int* 24:20–45.
Sheppard, Gerald T. 1980. *Wisdom as a Hermeneutical Construct: A Study in the Sapientializing of the Old Testament.* BZAW 151. Berlin: de Gruyter.
———. 1983. Review of Donn F. Morgan, *Wisdom in the Old Testament Traditions. JBL* 102:479–80.
Smend, Rudolf. 1995. "The Interpretation of Wisdom in Nineteenth-Century Scholarship." Pages 257–68 in *Wisdom in Ancient Israel.* Edited by John Day, Robert P. Gordon, and H. G. M. Williamson. Cambridge: Cambridge University Press.
Sneed, Mark. 2011. "Is the 'Wisdom Tradition' a Tradition?" *CBQ* 73:50–71.
Sparks, Kenton L. 2005. *Ancient Texts for the Study of the Hebrew Bible: A Guide to the Background Literature.* Peabody, MA: Hendrickson.
Swales, John M. 1990. *Genre Analysis: English in Academic and Research Settings.* CALS. Cambridge: Cambridge University Press.
Talmon, Shemaryahu. 1963. "'Wisdom' in the Book of Esther." *VT* 13:419–55.
Tanzer, Sarah J. 2005. "Response to George Nickelsburg, 'Wisdom and Apocalypticism in Early Judaism.'" Pages 39–49 in *Conflicted Boundaries in Wisdom and Apocalypticism.* Edited by Lawrence Wills and Benjamin G. Wright. SymS 35. Atlanta: Society of Biblical Literature.
Toorn, Karel van der. 2007a. *Scribal Culture and the Making of the Hebrew Bible.* Cambridge: Harvard University Press.
———. 2007b. "Why Wisdom Became a Secret: On Wisdom as a Written Genre." Pages 21–29 in *Wisdom Literature in Mesopotamia and Israel.* SymS 36. Edited by Richard J. Clifford. Atlanta: Society of Biblical Literature.
Van Leeuwen, Raymond C. 1993. "Scribal Wisdom and Theodicy in the Book of the Twelve." Pages 31–49 in *In Search of Wisdom: Essays in Memory of John G. Gammie.* Edited by Leo G. Perdue, Bernard Brandon Scott, and William Johnston Wiseman. Louisville: Westminster John Knox.
Weeks, Stuart. 1999. "Wisdom in the Old Testament." Pages 19–30 in *Where Shall Wisdom Be Found? Wisdom in the Bible, the Church and the Contemporary World.* Edited by Stephen C. Barton. Edinburgh: T&T Clark.
———. 2010. *An Introduction to the Study of Wisdom Literature.* New York: T&T Clark.

———. 2013. "The Limits of Form Criticism in the Study of Literature, with Reflections on Psalm 34." Pages 15–25 in *Biblical Interpretation and Method: Essays in Honour of John Barton*. Edited by Katharine J. Dell and Paul M. Joyce. Oxford: Oxford University Press.

Weinfeld, Moshe. 1967. "Deuteronomy: The Present State of Inquiry." *JBL* 86:249–62.

Westermann, Claus. 1995. *Roots of Wisdom: The Oldest Proverbs of Israel and Other Peoples*. Edinburgh: T&T Clark.

Wette, W. M. L. de. 1807. "Beytrag zur Charakteristik des Hebraismus." Pages 241–312 in vol. 3.2 of *Studien*. Edited by Carl Daub and Friedrich Creuzer. Heidelberg: Mohr.

Whybray, R. N. 1968. *The Succession Narrative: A Study of II Samuel 9–20; I Kings 1 and 2*. London: SCM.

———. 1982. "Prophecy and Wisdom." Pages 181–99 in *Israel's Prophetic Heritage: Essays in Honour of Peter R. Ackroyd*. Edited by Richard Coggins, Anthony Phillips, and Michael Knibb. Cambridge: Cambridge University Press.

———. 1995. *The Book of Proverbs: A Survey of Modern Study*. HBIS 1. Leiden: Brill.

Williams, Ronald J. 1981. "The Sages of Ancient Egypt in the Light of Recent Scholarship." *JAOS* 101:1–19.

Wilson, Gerald H. 1992. "The Shape of the Book of Psalms." *Int* 46:129–42.

Wilson, Robert P. 1999. "Who Was the Deuteronomist? (Who Was Not the Deuteronomist?): Reflections on Pan-Deuternomism." Pages 67–82 in Schearing and McKenzie 1999.

Witte, Markus. 2012. "'Weisheit' in der alttestamentlichen Wissenschaft: Ausgewählte literatur- und theologiegeschichtliche Fragestellungen und Entwicklungen." *TLZ* 137:1159–76.

Wolff, Hans Walter. 1964. *Amos' Geistige Heimat*. WMANT 18. Neukirchen-Vluyn: Neukirchener Verlag.

Wright, Benjamin G. III. 2010. "Joining the Club: A Suggestion about Genre in Early Jewish Texts." *DSD* 17:289–314.

Wright, G. Ernest. 1952. *God Who Acts: Biblical Theology as Recital*. London: SCM.

"Grasping After the Wind": The Elusive Attempt to Define and Delimit Wisdom

Mark R. Sneed

"I know it when I see it" was United States Supreme Court Justice Stewart Potter's famous threshold test for defining pornography (*Jacobellis v. Ohio* [1964]). No specific criteria could be mustered except the vague notion that pornography had to have some sort of social or artistic value to distinguish it from obscenity. Yet no one would deny that pornography as a genre exists.

Genres exist, but the important question is, Where do they exist? The reality is that genres do not exist in texts themselves but only in the minds of authors and readers. Genres are essentially agreed upon patterns and conventions with built-in assumptions that enable communication to take place. No one communicates without them; no one can escape their use. Our socialization by parents and school is the main way genres are learned. They become so ingrained in us that we are largely unconscious of them. While genres usually enable communication, they can sometimes be used creatively by communicators to produce an estrangement effect. Mixing genres does this. For instance, comedy-horror combines the conventional expectations of both genres to produce novel effects neither genre alone could create. A communicator can thus cunningly manipulate an audience by subverting generic expectations.

But if socialization is an important component for identifying genres, this means ancient literature presents serious difficulties for moderns in discerning the pact ancient authors and readers made between themselves that enabled them to communicate with each other. It means we can never definitively discern or map out the generic world ancient authors and readers understood unconsciously. We can only discern ancient generic patterns indirectly. This means that our task, then, is largely heuristic and highly subjective.

Old and New Ways

Generic Realism versus Generic Nominalism

In modern genre theory, two general approaches prevail: generic realism and nominalism, with the former increasingly eclipsed by the latter. Kenton Sparks has perhaps done the most to make this distinction for the study of biblical genres. About the former, he states, "Generic realism posits that texts are uniquely and intrinsically related to the generic categories in which we place them" (Sparks 2005, 6). It views genres ontologically: they actually exist in texts. Genres are viewed as static, and the business of genre analysis is primarily about taxonomy, much like an entomologist who views her main task as identifying the genus and species of particular insects.[1] With this perspective, the boundaries between genres are clearly defined, and any fuzziness must be dispelled.

Generic nominalism, however, Sparks notes, assumes that "there is a flexible and partially arbitrary character to all classifications ... generic categories are essentially taxonomic inventions" (2005, 6). This perspective views genres as dynamic and constantly changing and generic boundaries as largely permeable and shifting. To best identify what camp a particular scholar occupies, one must pay close attention to how rigidly or loosely generic boundaries are defined. A good way to clarify the distinction between the two camps is to think back to the cave allegory that Plato uses to describe the difference between the eternal Forms and their mere reflection or instantiation in the world. The slaves who mistake the shadows for reality would be generic realists, while those who could recognize the shadows as shadows would be generic nominalists.

The Systemic Nature of Genres or Modes of Literature

In a 2011 article I pointed out a faulty assumption that wisdom experts often make with regard to genres (Sneed 2011, 55). They assume falsely that a genre can encapsulate a worldview. Modern genre experts speak of genres creating worlds, not worldviews.[2] This is an important distinction and reveals the nature of genres. Genres are inherently systemic. One

---

1. For criticism of the taxonomic approach to genres, see Fowler 1982, 37–53; Frow 2006, 51–55; Dowd 2006, 11–27; Collins 2006, 55–68.

2. See Frow 2005, 75–77, 85–87. Bakhtin scholars refer to literary genres convey-

genre exists at the expense of another. What makes a particular genre a genre is that it is not another genre; it does not share its conventions. Thus, genres occupy certain niches within the larger economy of genres, and this cluster of genres treats all the various facets of life. Genres fulfill all kinds of social functions within a culture. One could say that all the combined genres of a culture would adequately reflect that culture's worldview, but no modern genre critic would ever say that a single genre is capable of doing that.

Yet that is what biblical wisdom experts often assume. They maintain that the wisdom literature or tradition reflects the worldview of a particular group, the sages. However, this is impossible. Worldview is an anthropological and comparative religion term that signifies the way a culture makes sense of its world. The facets of worldview usually include the following: doctrinal, mythical, ethical, ritual, experiential, and social (Smart 1983, 7–8).[3] The wisdom literature primarily focuses on the ethical dimension. It does not explore the mythical, which is about the etiological stories that explain why things are the way they are to a people. Rather, it assumes it. The closest the wisdom tradition comes to this is Woman Wisdom in Prov 8, though most anthropologists would see this story as too abstract to count within this category. The wisdom corpus also rarely invokes the ritual dimension. It alludes to the other elements only marginally. Thus, the wisdom tradition, in terms of the complete Israelite worldview, represents only the legs of a statue, without the trunk or arms or head. The wisdom tradition only explores a certain niche of the total Israelite worldview. The reality is that all the Israelites held the same worldview, though there were certainly differences in theology, politics, and the assessment of the status quo (social class perspectives).

This fits its character as a genre or, better, mode of literature,[4] as systemic.[5] Part of what makes the wisdom tradition the wisdom tradition is

---

ing worldviews, but even they admit that these are not complete (Newsom 2007, 30; Mitchell 2007, 34).

3. Susan Niditch applied Smart's schema of worldview components to ancient Israelite culture (1997).

4. For the argument that the wisdom literature should be described as a mode of literature and not a tradition proper, see Sneed 2011, 50–71. Mode refers to a higher level of generic abstraction. Usually, modes are indicated by an adjective, such as *comic* play, or *heroic* epic, or *didactic* literature.

5. See Buss: "*The Hebrew Bible is largely arranged according to what appear to be*

that it neither focuses on history as do the historical texts, nor on legal affairs as does the priestly tradition, nor on divining the future as does the prophetic literature. The wisdom tradition, from a genre theory perspective, is simply one among many genres or modes of literature that make up the totality of genres within the Israelite literary system. And, again, it cannot be viewed as representing the complete worldview of a group of sages. Genres or modes of literature are not created to serve that purpose.

Evaluating Wisdom Expertise from a Modern Genre Critical Perspective

In the following, I will evaluate representative wisdom experts in terms of two matters: (1) whether they reflect generic realism or nominalism; (2) whether they are sensitive to the systemic nature of genres (and modes) and the worlds they produce.

American Wisdom Experts

James Crenshaw

James Crenshaw easily fits into the generic realist camp. He views generic boundaries rather rigidly and as impermeable. He has carefully discerned what he considers the core of the wisdom tradition and what books constitute its corpus: Proverbs, Job, Ecclesiastes, Sirach, and Wisdom of Solomon (2010, 5). Crenshaw becomes rather vitriolic when countering scholars who want to be flexible with these boundaries and extend them to other corpora. For example, the exchange between him and Kenneth Kuntz about the prospect of wisdom psalms is quite animated (Crenshaw 2003, 155–58; Kuntz 2003, 145–54).

By bracketing off the wisdom corpus and then circularly distilling its essence, Crenshaw defines wisdom as "the reasoned search for specific ways to ensure personal well-being in everyday life, to make sense of extreme adversity and vexing anomalies, and to transmit this hard-earned knowledge so that successive generations will embody it" (2010, 4). He discerns certain specific conventions and themes and concludes: "When

---

culturally significant genres, which each represent a dimension of life and which engage metaphorically in a dialogue with each other" (2007, 13, emphasis original).

a marriage between form and content exists, there is Wisdom Literature. Lacking such oneness, a given text participates in biblical wisdom to a great or lesser extent" (2010, 12). Crenshaw views the wisdom tradition as an alternative to Yahwism and as essentially nonrevelatory (2010, 243–47). It is obvious that any revelatory elements (e.g., the vision of Eliphaz in Job 4:12–21) are viewed as anomalies that have crept into the tradition over time (2010, 211–14). Wisdom's embrace of Torah as exemplified by Sirach is also seen by Crenshaw as a new development, though several scholars (e.g., Schipper 2013, 55–80) have noted that the usage of the word *torah* in Prov 1–9 is dependent on Deuteronomy (e.g., Prov 6:20–35 parallels Deut 6).

When Sparks criticizes generic realism among wisdom experts about the nature of wisdom, he probably has Crenshaw especially in mind:

> Although Old Testament scholars generally agree that there are several books in the Hebrew Bible that fall into the category called "wisdom literature." … there is an ongoing discussion about what wisdom literature is and about what texts fit, or do not fit, into this category. Although some of this discussion has been healthy and valuable, much of the debate has been fueled by the subtle assumption that wisdom literature is a thing that already exists, that the task of scholarship is merely to correctly identify it by isolating its salient features from the wisdom texts. Generic nominalism helps to diffuse these needless debates by averring that there may be many legitimate ways to define wisdom literature. As a result, our intellectual energies can be productively focused on more important matters. (2005, 6–7)

A key part of this debate has been what to make of the lack of references in the earliest wisdom literature to the Israelite covenants, the patriarchs, the Sinaitic law, the Exodus, or any salvation-historical events. Crenshaw sees great significance in their absence: it means the sages were not Yahwistic. Crenshaw's mistaken assumption that the wisdom literature represents a complete worldview leads him to make such a radical assertion.

Michael V. Fox

Michael Fox can be classified as a generic realist, but he is certainly a more sophisticated example of this approach. He does not go as far as Crenshaw does in viewing the wisdom tradition as non-Yahwistic. But he still seems to assume that the wisdom literature is a thing that already exists in the texts, and that our goal in terms of genre is to extract its salient features. He also views wisdom's epistemology as clearly distinct from that of the other types of literature in the Hebrew Bible in that it is nonrevelatory. But is this phenomenon a generic convention or the epistemological perspective of the sages? The latter, which I think Fox actually assumes, would constitute a move in line with assuming that the wisdom literature represents a distinctive worldview. This is because epistemology is a significant component of a person's worldview. To not accept revelatory experiences as the basis for ethical instruction for individuals (wisdom literature à la Fox) would certainly pit the sages over against both priests and prophets.

In his commentary on Proverbs, Fox defines wisdom as "the capacity of the human mind to determine the right course of behavior and to apply this knowledge in achieving a successful life" (2009, 921). The reason Fox includes the phrase "human mind" is because he assumes, as do most wisdom experts, that "wisdom is not communicated by divine revelation" (2009, 921). Fox insists that when it comes to individual ethical behavior, the sages were nonrevelatory. They felt no compulsion to draw on divine revelation for composing their sapiential instructions and aphorisms. In the series of essays on the sages' view of ethics, revelation, and epistemology, Fox spends a great deal of energy and space toward expunging any residue of revelatory elements in the wisdom tradition, and this is the place where Fox reveals a faulty view of equating a generic convention with a worldview (2007b, 75–88; 2007a, 669–84; 2009, 934–76; 2000, 347–59). In other words, if the seemingly nonrevelatory epistemology of the sages is a generic convention—which I maintain it is—then it is incorrect to infer that the sages' epistemology is limited to or constrained by this convention per se.

Fox indeed assumes, as many other Old Testament scholars do, that there is a distinctive wisdom tradition that has its own particular epistemology. He even finds that the authors of the Hebrew Bible appear to have been conscious of such distinctiveness. We will look at just two of the many examples Fox gives that supposedly demonstrate this. He succinctly states what he perceives is the primary ethical axiom of the book of Proverbs: "that *the exercise of the human mind is the necessary and sufficient condition of right and successful behavior in all reaches of life: practical, ethical, and religious*" (2009, 934, emphasis original). He notes that certain other biblical authors perceived this distinctive epistemology and responded to it by downplaying such claims.

Fox admits that Deuteronomy has been heavily influenced by the wisdom tradition. But he believes Deuteronomy constantly subordinates wisdom to the Law. For example, Fox quotes Deut 4:6: "You shall observe [these laws] diligently, for this will be your wisdom and understanding in the eyes of the nations who, when they hear all these statutes, will say, 'Surely this great nation is a wise and discerning people!'" He then notes, "This verse shows that the Deuteronomist was aware of a way of thinking that knew about foreign wisdom and sought to emulate it—which is exactly what Proverbs does, as is most evident in Prov 22:17–24:22" (2009, 953). Here Fox is alluding to the probability that Proverbs reflects a reliance on The Instruction of Amenemope.

This seems a real stretch. How do we go from a verse in Deuteronomy about a wise nation to the book of Proverbs, let alone a section of Proverbs supposedly dependent on an Egyptian instruction? Ockham's razor is best employed here. Deuteronomy is not alluding to any wisdom tradition but rather to wisdom as a general skill and disposition that was highly esteemed in the ancient Near East. Of course, Deuteronomy does subordinate wisdom to the Torah here, but not the wisdom tradition per se; Fox is often guilty of this kind of equivocation.

A second example is Fox's discussion of Agur's oracle (Prov 30:1–9). He notes that while this passage is now joined to Proverbs, it is really a reaction to it. He states, "In his [Agur's] view, God himself now must do what the sages (of Prov 1–9, at least) considered to be fully in the power of human wisdom: to harden a man against temptation" (2009, 957). Fox then argues that Agur has replaced wisdom with the fear of God. Fox concludes, "The editor who added Agur's poem sought to rectify the lack of concern for divine revelation in the book of Proverbs that had reached him" (2009, 957).[6]

It is quite evident that Fox does not feel that this oracle belongs in Proverbs or really constitutes a wisdom genre. Revelatory items, for Fox and Crenshaw both, are anomalies in the wisdom tradition, not constituent parts. In connection with this, Fox works hard in his discussion of Woman Wisdom in Proverbs to prevent her from holding any revelatory features at all, in spite of the fact that she is the firstborn of creation and God's darling (Prov 8) (2000, 271–95, 331–45)! Fox argues that the word

---

6. See Bernd Schipper, who also finds Agur's view of wisdom as largely antithetical to the rest of Proverbs (2013, 69–76).

'*amon* should be translated "growing up" and not "artisan" in 8:30, as is sometimes suggested (2000, 285–89), though 3:19 states that the Lord created the world by wisdom. Richard Clifford's translation may be preferable. Clifford vocalizes the word as '*oman*, an Akkadian loanword from *ummanu*, meaning "scribe, sage; heavenly sage," which had fallen out of usage by the time of the LXX and other versions (1999, 100–101). Clifford notes that an *ummanu* was "a divine or semi-divine bringer of culture and skill to the human race" (1999, 101). This, of course, alludes to the Mesopotamian antediluvian semidivine sages who passed on their wisdom to humans through Zisudra or Utnapishtim (the Babylonian Noah), after the flood, in the form of the buried tablets that contained the Instruction of Shurupak. In other words, Woman Wisdom here is the Hebrew Prometheus! Though she might not be involved in any acts of creation, she stands alongside God ready to transmit wisdom to the crown of his creation: humanity.

Beyond this, Woman Wisdom certainly displays revelatory features. In chapter 8 she speaks with a prophetic voice and is as inspired as any prophet, if not more so. There is no doubt that she is divine and that she speaks with divine authority. Her status as firstborn of creation lends her supreme honor and credibility. So, whatever claims of inspiration and authority Woman Wisdom holds, so do the wisdom of the father who appeals to the youth in chapters 1–9 and the wise men who composed the aphorisms and instructions in the latter collections. Kovacs's description is accurate:

> What is the wise man's warrant? The prophet has *koh 'amar yhvh*; the priest has torah, tradition, and rite. ... '*etsah* does not mean simply giving advice which can then be accepted or rejected according to the whims of the hearer. When given as counsel, it is the divine word no less than torah or oracle. Not surprisingly, then, "mashal" can mean "oracle" as well as "proverb." The word of Ahithophel amounted to a divine oracle (2 Sam 16:23). In the admonitions of the wise, the motivating clause is no more essential to the saying's authority than are such clauses for torah and oracle. In this sense, wisdom is authoritative *dabhar*, the word of Yahweh. (1974, 184–85)

A notion of divine inspiration for the sages needs further attention by wisdom experts. Even if the instructions and aphorisms of the wise are based primarily on experience, this still does not exclude the notion of inspiration. Prophets, the gurus of inspiration, also drew on life experiences for their arguments and appeals. Not every word of a prophet was considered verbatim citation of God. In fact, little of the prophetic material fits that description.

Raymond Van Leeuwen

Raymond Van Leeuwen is sensitive to the systemic nature of genres. He addresses the silence in the wisdom literature concerning major theological ideas and significant events:

> This silence does not imply that the various authors of the book had no interest in matters of redemptive history or in other biblical books … Like most books, Proverbs does not reveal the full range of its authors' concerns. … Such silences in wisdom writings are a function of their genre and purpose, and too much should not be concluded concerning the isolation of the sages from Israel's historical traditions. (1994–2004, 5:21)

Van Leeuwen is correct on both counts. First, the wisdom corpus does not reflect all of the concerns of its authors. This is another way of saying that a mode like the wisdom literature does not represent a worldview. Genres convey conventional worlds, nothing more (Frow 2006, 75–77, 85–87). A genre is not comprehensive enough to reflect a complete worldview, and from the broader ancient Near Eastern perspective, the scribes who composed and studied wisdom literature composed and read various other genres, all of which occupied important niches in their training and education. Most of these genres are parallel with those of the Hebrew Bible. More particular, it is interesting that the scribes of ancient Emar, in Northern Syria, during the LBA, were often simultaneously diviners or medical experts and studied omens and medico-magical incantations, as well as wisdom literature (Cohen 2009, 2, 4, 47 54, 121–46, 194–238). Also, interestingly, Egyptian scribes who composed wisdom literature were often simultaneously lector priests (Instruction of Amenemope, Complaints of Khakheperre-sonb, and Instruction of Ankhsheshonq). The clear-cut distinctions biblical scholars make between prophets, priests, and sages, and their respective literatures does not fit the broader ancient Near Eastern pattern.

Second, Van Leeuwen is correct that the wisdom corpus as a mode of literature is focused on its own purposes and not those of the other modes. In other words, what makes the wisdom literature wisdom literature is its differences from the prophetic literature, the Torah, and the apocalyptic and historical literature. What makes wisdom wisdom is not just what it teaches, but what it does not teach.

Richard Clifford

Similarly, Richard Clifford, referring to the wisdom literature, notes, "Missing from them are politics, economics, and history as well as national and international affairs, for these are not (for the most part) subject to *personal* decision and reflection. Wisdom literature is personal and familial" (1998, 19, emphasis original). He also argues that the supposed wisdom influence in nonsapiential modes of literature in the Hebrew Bible can be explained as due to the common education of scribes, who all studied wisdom literature (Clifford 1997, 1, 7).

If one considers the other ancient Near Eastern wisdom traditions, as a whole, there is a similar pattern. There are few allusions to core theological tenets or historical events of the respective cultures. For example, the Instruction of Ptahhotep makes few allusions to the main tenets of Egyptian theology. It occasionally refers to the gods but only generally. It alludes occasionally to the concept of Maat, but this notion is highly relevant for a discussion of ethical behavior, which is the focus of the work. Also, the maxims in the Mesopotamian Instructions of Shuruppak make even less reference to respective core beliefs or historical figures/events. Again, all of this suggests that this feature is in the nature of wisdom literature, which focuses on the mundane and ethics, and not on historical or international events or core mythological stories.

British Wisdom Experts

Katharine Dell

While Katharine Dell is more a realist than a nominalist; her approach to the wisdom literature is more sophisticated than most and she seems able to be more flexible about categorization.[7] Her exclusion of Job (and almost Ecclesiastes) from the category of wisdom literature is innovative and fascinating, even if few scholars have followed her lead (1991, 147). Her work

---

7. Her dissertation on the generic categorization of the book of Job is an outstanding work, though she relies too much on older form-critical assumptions. She does not incorporate enough *literary* genre theory in her analysis (Dell 1991).

on the wisdom psalms demonstrates how permeable the boundaries are between the wisdom corpus and the other corpora of the Hebrew Bible (e.g., 2004, 445–58).

Derek Kidner and Stuart Weeks

Early on Derek Kidner was a pioneer of the notion of the systemic nature of the biblical genres. He assumed that the book of Proverbs as wisdom literature addresses the particular domain of values and ethics: "There are details of character small enough to escape the mesh of the law and the broadsides of the prophets, and yet decisive in personal dealings. Proverbs moves in this realm, asking what a person is like to live with, or to employ; how he manages his affairs, his time and himself" (1964, 13). More recently, Stuart Weeks's introduction to the wisdom literature is certainly in line with generic nominalism and the systemic nature of genres, though he never utilizes genre theory per se (2010, 1–7, 107–44).

Continental Wisdom Experts

Karel van der Toorn

The Dutch Karel van der Toorn is more sensitive to the systemic nature of the biblical genres, but he does not go far enough. He maintains that the Hebrew Bible was originally written by scribes and for scribes, but not as part of a curriculum (2007, 2, 247). He also speaks of differing types of scribes like royal, Temple, and Levitical scribes (2007, 82–96). But when he examines the book of Deuteronomy, he sees four types of scribes behind it: legal scholar (covenant), educated cleric (history), priest (Torah), and teacher (wisdom), each type with its own distinctive worldview or perspective (2007, 150–66). So we have one step forward, and then back.

Ludger Schwienhorst-Schönberger and Markus Saur

Though two recent German-language articles do not appeal to current genre theory per se, they embrace its spirit and suggest promising venues for interpreting the wisdom corpus. Ludger Schwienhorst-Schönberger surveys older and more recent scholarship on the place of wisdom literature in the canon. He finds a return to an earlier form of interpretation that does not rigidly separate the wisdom corpus from the other corpora (2013, 118–42). He shows how scholarship on the wisdom literature has shifted from form-critical and history of religion concerns to intertextual, canonical approaches. He ends by noting that although historical-critical concerns are legitimate, the fact that wisdom literature was preserved within the context of the canon cannot be ignored.

Schwienhorst-Schönberger cites Markus Saur as an example of a younger scholar who has contributed to the new approach he documents (2013, 126–27). In a recent article, Saur argues that the wisdom corpus should be viewed as functioning as the first inner-biblical, theological hermeneutic of the canon (2011, 236–49). He describes it as a hermeneutical discourse that not only revaluates other nonsapiential books, but contains its own inner-wisdom dialogue where different theologies compete with one another. The importance of the recent essays by Schwienhorst-Schönberger and Saur is that they represent a Continental trajectory that meshes well with scholars in the United Kingdom, who are transforming the way we view the wisdom corpus.

Israeli Wisdom Experts

Tova Forti

Two Israelis help to show that this issue is also continuing to be debated there. Tova Forti, although a literary critic, is not sensitive to the systemic nature of genres; she upholds the consensus view that the wisdom tradition is a distinct tradition with its own particular theological perspective and worldview. In her book on animal imagery in Proverbs, she speaks of the teacher's distinctive perspective in comparison with the other modes of literature in the Hebrew Bible. The following quotes will sound familiar:

> His main concern is not the national history of Israel or the people's fidelity to its covenant with the Lord. Instead the teacher addresses individuals, urging them to internalize behavioral values to promote integration into the social order. ... The teacher's dicta do not claim to have the same authority as The Commandments and the Law of God. Although his precepts are referred to as *miṣwâ* 'injunction/teaching' (x 8) and, implicitly, as *leqaḥ* 'internalized teaching' (i 5; x 8), they are counsels (*ṣēṣṣâ*) rather than categorical injunctions. (2008, 9–10)

She also refers to the teacher's perspective as anthropocentric, reflected in his appeals made through reasoning, common sense, and deliberation (2008, 10). She maintains that the animal imagery in Proverbs "reinforces the wise man's empirical observations and worldview, which give meaning and direction to the daily conduct of human beings" (2008, 10).

Nili Shupak

But another Israeli, Nili Shupak, goes the opposite direction and views the Hebrew wisdom literature as one among many modes of literature the Israelite scribes composed and studied. In an article on the *Sitz im Leben* of the book of Proverbs, she shows evidence via common vocabulary and conceptuality that the Israelite scribes who composed Proverbs were heavily influenced by the Egyptian scribal institution, including its school system (1987, 98–119). She concludes that scribal schools existed in ancient Israel, modeled on the Egyptian system, where wisdom texts were one among many genres studied, and that this explains why "wisdom" elements can be found outside the wisdom corpus in the Hebrew Bible (1987, 118). She further elaborates:

> There is nothing surprising in the existence of a vocabulary common to both Hebrew and Egyptian Wisdom writings and compositions in other genres. All of these works were the creations of a single type of author—namely the scribe. And scribes received their education at schools, where they sometimes also taught, and were in this capacity responsible for committing Wisdom compositions to writing; these, in turn, served as learning texts in the very same schools.
>
> The assumption of an influence of the Wisdom tradition upon literary works that are unrelated to Wisdom cycle in the Bible appears therefore to be quite legitimate, and there would seem to be no reason to reject such a view, as a number of scholars in the field have attempted to do. (1987, 119; cf. Carr 2004)

Ancient Near Eastern Scholars

In the following we will now turn to representation of Assyriologists and Egyptologists who have focused on the wisdom literature to see how well they fare regarding conformity to modern genre-critical standards.

William Lambert

The Assyriologist W. G. Lambert admits adopting the term wisdom literature from biblical studies for his study of Babylonian didactic literature (1996, 1). He points out that the term is technically a misnomer because the texts he considers wisdom literature rarely focus on it or the concept, and when they do, it is largely without the moral connotation typical of biblical wisdom (cf. Edzard 1928, 45; Röllig 1928, 59). However, he feels the term is useful, and so he applies it to several Babylonian works. He generally describes these texts as reflecting primitive forms of what we would call philosophy. Many other Assyriologists seem to concur with Lambert and utilize the term and identity a particular corpus with it, though rarely do the lists of works completely agree. But there has been no consternation about this lack of consensus, unlike in biblical studies.

Giorgio Buccellati

The exception is the Assyriologist Giorgio Buccellati, who argues that there is no Mesopotamian wisdom corpus per se, because wisdom themes are too diffused throughout a variety of Mesopotamian genres. Rather, he sees only a cultural phenomenon called wisdom, which is to be separated from literature (1981, 35–47). This resembles R. N. Whybray (1974), who argued that the wisdom literature was not a literary but intellectual tradition that is diffused throughout the Hebrew Bible. Both approaches suffer from inadequate grounding in current generic theorization. And Buccellati incorrectly assumes that form and content are both necessary components of a genre and that all typical generic conventions must be present in particular examples.

Miriam Lichtheim

As far as Egypt is concerned, Miriam Lichtheim takes a reactionary position relative to the term "wisdom literature." She prefers to use the term "didactic literature" for the Egyptian version of wisdom literature because she notes, similarly to Lambert, that these texts rarely make the word "wisdom" or the concept a focal concern (1997, 1–8; 1996, 243–62). Again, Lichtheim erroneously assumes that the concept of wisdom and its terminology are the only criteria for identifying a genre. Among Egyptologists, again, different corpora of wisdom literature have been delineated, with none exactly the same. For example, The Admonitions of Ipuwer is sometimes categorized as prophetic literature (Shupak 1990, 81). But neither concerted effort to create a rigid canonical list, nor any protracted debate about what belongs or not, has occurred.[8]

Kenneth Kitchen

To the contrary of Lichtheim, Egyptologist Kenneth Kitchen (1977, 69–114) has no problem with applying the term wisdom to literature of the ancient Near East. He mentions the resistance to this nomenclature, "The epithet 'Wisdom' is sometimes criticized because it is periodically abused in practice; however, *any* classification would be subject to this 'occupational hazard', and the epithet 'Wisdom' does distinguish a well-accepted group of writings in each case" (1979, 236, emphasis original). He divides this group of texts up into practical everyday wisdom and reflective wisdom or social literature, which he regards as prephilosophical (1979, 236–37). Examples of the former would be the older instructional literature like the Instruction of Ptahhotep. The latter category would include, for example, from the Middle Kingdom, The Eloquent Peasant, The Dispute Between a Man and his Ba, and the Admonitions of Ipuwer (1979, 237–38). Kitchen also emphasizes the creativity and flexibility of ancient Near Eastern writers in modifying sapiential genres (1979, 243; cf. idem 1998, 363), so Kitchen easily falls within the category of generic nominalist.

The "Argument from Silence"

The wisdom experts who fail to comprehend the systemic nature of genres are often guilty of employing the *argumentum ex silento* or argument from silence to explain why the wisdom literature lacks certain major theological tenets and allusion to significant redemptive events. The assumption is that if the biblical wisdom literature does not include these, then the authors must not have viewed them as significant, and, consequently, the

---

8. See the discussion by Nili Shupak concerning the differing generic categorizations of Egyptian works such as The Admonition of Ipuwer, The Tale of the Eloquent Peasant, The Dispute between a Man and his Ba, The Prophecies of Neferit, and The Complaints of Khakheperre-sonb and her classifications of them all as wisdom literature (1990, 81–102).

sages stand out as a minority subculture in ancient Israel. However, philosophers and rhetoricians point out that the argument from silence is an inherently weak form of argument. In fact, it is usually treated as a fallacy (Duncan 2012, 83). This is because "the assumption that considering apparent lack of evidence as evidence of actual lack of evidence is to go too far, which in turn raises the question of how any lack of evidence can ever be established as meaningful" (Duncan 2012, 84). In other words, the absence of evidence is not evidence of absence! The argument from silence is technically a variation of *argumentum ad ignorantiam* or appeal to ignorance, such as someone arguing that there must be ghosts because no one has ever proven that they do not exist (Copi 1982, 101).

However, Mike Duncan (2012, 83–97) does not throw the argument completely out. While acknowledging it as a very weak form of argument, he maintains it can be useful as a stepping stone to further research and for counter arguments that eventually arise (2012, 88). Conveniently, Duncan alludes to an example from biblical studies. The argument is made that because Paul does not allude much to Jesus's precrucifixion life found in the Gospels, then that means he was largely ignorant of it (2012, 89–93). This has produced counterarguments to explain the absence: Paul viewed his own revelation as more authentic than the experiences of the twelve apostles, so he avoids alluding to this information; Paul assumed his audience would have already known this information, so he does not mention it; Paul saw the Gospel material as authentic but not agreeable with his teaching and emphases.

In the vein of Duncan's comments, there have been several counterarguments to the view that the wisdom literature must represent an idiosyncratic tradition within the canon of the Hebrew Bible because of the absence of significant theological tenets of other types of literature. For example, David Carr has argued that the book of Proverbs does not reflect what are considered the core Yahwistic elements because these tenets had not yet become dominant among the Israelites (Carr 2011, 407).

This leads to another counterargument that helps explain the lack of distinctively Israelite tenets within the wisdom corpus: its rhetoric. Since wisdom literature seeks to counsel moral guidelines for daily life, these instructions must assume the ideology of universalism (Eagleton, 1991, 56–58). In other words, the truths and knowledge about living wisely promoted in the wisdom literature cannot be parochial, for sectarian "truth" is no truth at all. The instructions that wisdom literature promulgates must be true for any individual, not just a particular ethnicity or nationality. For example, the wisdom writers prohibit the well-to-do from taking advantage of the poor:

> Oppressing the poor to increase himself,
> Giving to the rich,
> Only results in loss! (Prov 22:16)[9]

The author of this maxim would not have thought that it would only apply to Israelites. Like Immanuel Kant and his Categorical Imperative, he would have viewed his aphorism as being valid only if it applied to everyone, no matter what ethnicity or nationality. Concern for the poor is also a frequent motif in the other non-Israelite corpora of wisdom literature. For example, in the Instruction of Ptahhotep there is counsel against attacking a poor man when in a dispute with him: "Wretched is he who injures a poor man" (*AEL* 1:64). There is no indication that the author believed that this applied exclusively to the Egyptians. The non-Israelite sapiential authors have adopted the same universalistic ideology as the Israelite wisdom writers.

This rhetorical strategy becomes especially visible when non-Israelites are deliberately invoked in the biblical wisdom literature. The inclusion of the advice of king Lemuel's mother (Prov 31), Agur, and the characterization of the Edomite Job and his three (four) friends are good examples of this strategy. The inclusion of foreigners in these texts serves to legitimate the truth of texts whose veracity one might suspect as parochial. Outside the wisdom corpus, it is found in the story of the Queen of Sheba, who acknowledges Solomon's great wisdom (1 Kgs 10).

Even when particularism starts becoming a part of the wisdom "tradition," it always begins with a universalistic perspective. For example, when Ben Sira praises Wisdom in Sir 24, he describes her as wandering the whole earth looking for a resting place. But then after she had traveled the compass of the earth, the Lord finally commanded her to light in Jacob and in Jerusalem. Without the universalistic scope at the beginning, Wisdom would not have been legitimate and resting in Judah would have meant little. In the Wisdom of Solomon, similarly, when the description of Wisdom's creation is recounted in chapter 7, it is couched in universalistic terms, and the many dimensions of her knowledge reflect the typical subjects in a Greek school. But then in chapter 8, she

---

9. Unless otherwise indicated, all translations of Hebrew are mine.

is depicted metaphorically as becoming Solomon's bride. Likewise, in chapter 10, Wisdom is depicted as guiding Adam and early men before Israelite history begins.

Another counterargument to the notion that Israelite wisdom is unconcerned about dominant theological tenets is that much of the terminology in the wisdom literature makes little sense without the rest of the canon. Words like wisdom and righteousness remain largely abstract concepts without the plethora of narratives in the Hebrew Bible that provide concrete examples of what these virtues mean. For example, Abigail demonstrates what Israelite wisdom means when she uses her wits to save her family from slaughter by David, whom her husband Nabal, nicknamed fool, had insulted (1 Sam 25). She is described as *ṭovah śekel*—literally "good of insight" (25:3), and David pronounces her wise because of her deeds: "Blessed be your good sense (*ṭaṭam*)" (25:33). Wisdom becomes defined as intelligence but also respect and self-sacrifice for the good of the family. Nabal, to the contrary, demonstrates what folly looks like: greed and disrespect. It is highly doubtful that the sages of ancient Israel would have considered such stories as *unnecessary* for developing the skill of moral discernment!

The Sages and the Nonsapiential

While it is true that sapiential literature cannot be viewed as primarily revelatory in nature, this does not exclude its categorization as inspired literature, as we argued earlier. Wisdom experts often repress the not infrequent inclusion of revelatory materials in the wisdom corpus: the *massa'* (oracles) of Lemuel and Agur in Proverbs, the revelatory dreams of Job (7:13–14), Eliphaz (Job 4:13–21), and Elihu (Job 33:15–16), and the divine speeches (Job 38–41), not to mention Ben Sira and his embrace of the Torah. These revelatory elements signify that revelation was a significant though not dominant component of the total pool of sapiential resources drawn upon for wisdom compositions. It is true that the sages did not define their role primarily as revelatory conduits of God's verbatim words and will, as did the prophets. But the degree of difference between sage and prophet is just that: one of degree, not category. Prophets primarily drew on revelatory resources, though not exclusively, and sages primarily drew on sapiential resources, but, also, not exclusively. Significantly, this does not mean the sages' epistemology for wise behavior is limited to the nonrevelatory or that they denied prophetic claims of access to the divine will.

The sages were interested in all forms of knowledge, whether revelatory or not. They were perennially curious about all mysteries of the cosmos and sought to penetrate them as far as they could.

This typical sapiential, cosmopolitan curiosity is demonstrated by Ben Sira, a scribe and sage, who is fascinated with both prophecy and the Torah (Sir 38:34–39:3). His interest in these nonsapiential concerns is not as some latecomer as is often claimed. Baruch, a sixth century royal scribe and official, was also apparently very interested in his mentor's prophecies, unless one wants to argue that he was mercenary! Further, in Jer 8:8, wise scribes, perhaps Levitical priests, claimed to have the Torah = Deuteronomy (Bright 1965, 63–64) and, no doubt, taught it. Jeremiah does not question the authority of the Torah. What he disagrees with is these scribes' claim that the Torah was *necessary* and *sufficient* for determining God's will. If Jeremiah and Baruch are to be trusted, we have direct evidence of wise scribes, who relished things nonsapiential and who loved prophecy and Torah. This fascination and interest in things nonsapiential by the sapiential is, thus, no late development! Ben Sira represents a continued trajectory that goes back to preexilic days.

With respect to Jeremiah, Edward Greenstein persuasively argues that the author of Job is heavily dependent on Jeremiah. The author of Job often takes material from Jeremiah and hyperbolizes it, like the curse of Jeremiah's birthday (Jer 20:14–18), which the Joban author (Job 3) expands to include even the curse of the day of his conception (2004, 102–3). Greenstein also convincingly argues that the character Job actually confesses receiving divine revelation in Job 4, with Eliphaz deriding it in chapters 5 and 15 (2004, 105–7). If this is so, it shows that revelation is far from being foreign or anomalous to the book of Job, even when not considering the divine speeches (Job 38:1–42:6) and the frame narratives (Job 1–2; 42:7–17), where God's speech is recorded.

Suggestions for a More Healthy Approach

How should we define wisdom literature and identify its scope and limits, from a modern, critical generic perspective? First of all, we should abandon the notion of required conventions and even the notion of a core (Fowler 1982, 39; contra Brown 2011). The one constant of genres is that they are continually changing and shifting; they are inherently unstable. The wisdom literature of the Dead Sea Scrolls shares the form and some of the vocabulary but the content is quite different from the standard wisdom corpus of the Hebrew Bible (Kampen 2011, 5–15 and Goff 2013, 12–23). It is quite apocalyptic and could be called sectarian wisdom.[10] It even broadens the intended audience to include women (4Q415 2 ii; Goff 2013, 32)! But would all these differences justify denying its categorization as wisdom literature? Dead Sea Scroll experts have found such terminology and classification helpful. The shift in the wisdom tradition evident in this literature has forced John Collins (1997, 281) to simply refer to it as "instructional literature," which means he defines the corpus by its function, one of many ways to do it, according to current genre theory—but not the only one!

Various conventions have been posited by wisdom experts as essential, but all of them are problematic. Some have suggested a focus on the concept of wisdom and, relatedly, the high frequency of sapiential vocabulary, as what should determine the limits of the wisdom corpus (e.g., Whybray 1974; Lichtheim 1997, 1–8).[11] Obviously this is a reasonable suggestion. Unfortunately, it cannot be the sole deciding factor. By this criterion, many wisdom psalms would be excluded, including Ps 1, which neither uses distinctively wisdom terms, nor focuses on the concept of wisdom itself. Yet almost all scholars agree that the notion of wisdom psalms is legitimate, except for Crenshaw (2003, 155–58), of course.

Others have noted that this corpus focuses on the individual instead of the nation (e.g., Goldingay 1979, 194). Several aphorisms express national concerns: for example, Prov 11:14; 14:34; 24:24. Many maxims express neither individual nor national concerns but rather describe life or reality in general, such as several of the numerical proverbs (Prov 30). These proverbs simply describe phenomena to ponder, connoting the notion of profundity.

A proverb is often defined as "the wisdom of many and the wit of one," and the various genres within the wisdom literature certainly involve high artistry and clever subtly. Could this be the determining criterion? Robert Alter, in fact, in his book *The Art of Biblical Poetry*, entitles his chapter on Proverbs "The Poetry of Wit" (1985, 163). While wit and subtlety are certainly features of proverbs, many pedantic proverbs that repetitively

---

10. On the confluence of apocalypticism and wisdom in Judaism, see Collins 1993, 165–85.

11. See Crenshaw's criticism of word tabulation for determining wisdom texts (1969, 132–33).

instruct on retribution exist (e.g., 12:5; 15:1; 24:3), as even Alter is forced to admit (1985, 163–64).

Another way to distinguish wisdom literature is to emphasize its distinctive, original audience: young elite males (Prov 1:4 and many references to "my son"). But even here exceptions exist. The reference in the prologue to the older wise (1:5) and several proverbs that counsel advice about raising children (e.g., 22:6) indicate that youths are not exclusively the intended audience. And 4QInstruction addresses poor agrarian males and sometimes women (e.g., 4Q415 2 ii; Goff 2013, 23–27, 31–41, 207)!

Another potential center that might hold the wisdom corpus together is wonder, as William Brown advocated in a 2011 SBL presentation (Brown 2011). However, the notion that Qoheleth expresses wonderment about the cosmos is one about which most wisdom experts would not concur.

As has been demonstrated, no matter what definition one constructs or what criteria one posits or what center one proposes, it will not be *necessary* and *sufficient* for delimiting what should and should not be included within the wisdom category, nor will it be comprehensive enough for the inclusion of all the elements present. The reality is that no core exists and that what counts as wisdom literature can depend on a number of factors, with none by itself being entirely sufficient.

Second, rather than demanding essential features and conventions, one should speak of family resemblances and be more flexible and creative with various possible ways of drawing up collections, corpora, and subdivisions (Fowler 1982, 41). Proverbs, Job, Ecclesiastes, the wisdom psalms, Sirach, and the Wisdom of Solomon surely belong to the same family. Some might expand it to include writings from the Dead Sea Scrolls, as we have seen, or Daniel, perhaps denoting it as mantic wisdom but wisdom nonetheless, or perhaps Jonah—classifying it as a didactic tale (Strauß 2004, 393–95). The latter possibility would help resolve the perennial problem of prophetic experts trying to make sense of such an unusual prophetic book. Within the wisdom corpus itself, experts already distinguish between optimistic (Proverbs, Sirach, Wisdom of Solomon) and pessimistic wisdom (Job and Ecclesiastes), which includes other ancient Near Eastern examples. This would base genre definition on mood, which is very common (Fowler 1982, 67). In genre theory, there are no hard and fast rules, and these kinds of generic nuances can be quite helpful for interpretation.

Third, we should not restrict ourselves to investigating how the wisdom writers imitated generic conventions; we should explore how they subverted them or created new ones (Fowler 1982, 28–29; Frow 2006, 23–25)! For example, C. L. Seow has shown how Qoheleth undermines the conventional royal autobiography in chapters 1–2 (1995, 275–87). Instead of bragging about all his royal accomplishments and assets, Qoheleth as king declares them all vanity! Also, Dell's dissertation is an excellent example of this move. She demonstrates how the author of Job constantly parodies established genres (see especially 1991, 125–27). This possibility resonates with Derrida's notion of law versus counterlaw in generic formation, that is, how genres exist in a perpetual dialectic between rules and their subversion.[12] If a person wants to do something new generically, then it cannot be entirely new or else it would not be understood. One can never transcend generic conventions completely, though the always partially successful attempt makes for interesting effect!

Why Have Wisdom Experts Propagated the Notion of an Insular Wisdom Tradition?

Why have wisdom experts rigidly separated the wisdom corpus off from the rest of the corpora? Of course, much blame could be leveled at outmoded generic theorization. But apparently it runs deeper than this. Egyptologists and Assyriologists in general do not appear to have followed the same path and artificially separated their respective wisdom corpora from the other literary corpora and concomitantly pitted priest against scribe against diviner and magician, with each profession representing distinctive worldviews. Source and form criticism were two important catalysts for orienting biblical scholars in a rather idiosyncratic direction. Both types of criticism were analytic in nature and served to predispose biblical scholars to focus on differences and tensions in Scripture rather than on how it cohered.[13] These methodological predispositions, coupled with many of Gunkel's erroneous form-critical assumptions, served to predispose biblical scholars to turn priest against prophet and each against sage,

---

12. Derrida 1980, 55–81; he uses the example of *La Folie du jour* by Maurice Blanchot to show this dialectic (66–81). Blanchot calls this piece an "account" but breaks all the rules that accounts should follow!

13. For a comparison of the source and form-critical approaches with the contextual approach of an Assyriologist, see Hallo 2010, 677–97.

as well as each other, and one type of literature against or in competition with another.[14]

This is not to imply that there are no distinctive theologies in the Hebrew Bible, but theological differences do not usually divide along modal (e.g., wisdom literature versus prophetic literature) or professional lines (e.g., priest versus prophet) alone. For example, Patricia Dutcher-Walls has argued persuasively that the Deuteronomistic movement was not instigated by one particular group, such as the formerly northern Levitical priests or royal scribes or the king, but rather by a political faction of scribes, courtiers, prophets, priests, peasants, and the king (1991, 77–94). It is also significant that the Deuteronomistic "tradition" is found in numerous genres and in distinctive modes of literature and not just one (e.g., parts of Jeremiah, Hosea, and some of the psalms [e.g., Ps 78])!

Also, biblical scholars seem to have adopted the Greek notion of competing philosophical schools with their differing epistemologies and theoretical perspectives and applied this to the Hebrew Bible (Michael V. Fox, pers. comm.). Thus, a purported polemic between the priests, prophets, and sages is assumed, comparable to that between, say, the school of Aristotle and the sophists over rhetoric, or the Epicureans and Stoics over the summum bonum, and, closer to home, between the Pharisees, Sadducees, Essenes, and Zealots. With this perspective, the priests are viewed as very sacerdotal and hold a priestly worldview and have a epistemology where only knowledge that can be elicited from Urim and Thummim or the Torah can count as legitimate for discerning God's will. The prophets naturally consider oracular revelation as the only valid medium of reliable knowledge for humans, and thus, the prophetic worldview differs from that of the priests, who are more like diviners and fixated on cultic matters. The prophets focused more on social justice. The sages, contrarily, limited reliable and truthful knowledge to what can be discerned by nonrevelatory means through human rationality alone. The sages were early rationalists, though not true empiricists. Scholars, like Michael Fishbane, speculate that there were even separate scribal schools for prophets, priests, and sages, which specialized in their own respective genres and modes of literature and traditions (1988, 78–79). But where is the evidence for this?

The almost unconscious drive to discern an ever more fractured and dissentious Scripture no doubt ultimately derives from the Enlightenment

---

14. See Sparks's critique of Gunkel and form criticism (2005, 5–21).

need to curtail the authority of the Bible. A Bible divided against itself cannot legitimately serve as a hegemonic source of authority to be welded by those in power against the powerless. However, we should ask ourselves whether we have not gone too far as biblical scholars in this endeavor and are perceiving divisions and distinctions that are really not there? It is appropriate to be critical, but have we taken our analysis to an extreme?

Assyriologists and Egyptologists do not start from the same source- and form-critical assumptions as biblical studies. In many ways, these experts have tried to put distance between themselves and biblical studies. Consequently, they do not appear to perceive the degree of diversity and distinctiveness of worldview in the respective corpora they study that biblical scholars see in the Hebrew Bible. They certainly do not see distinctions aligning chiefly along modal and generic lines as biblical scholars have. One also rarely sees the ancient Near Eastern scholar pitting priest against sage and both against prophet or each other, the way biblical scholars have done. Distinctions and differences are perceived, but not to the degree of biblical studies and not along modal and/or generic and professional lines.

Conclusion

While all the books scholars usually designate as wisdom literature share a family resemblance, striking differences exist among them. Job is the odd book in. No essential features exist except perhaps a focus on the concept of wisdom or a high frequency of sapiential vocabulary. But these are highly diffuse criteria, and they exclude subgenres like the wisdom psalms. More than one way is possible to identify a wisdom corpus, where, for example, Daniel, Jonah, and certain Dead Sea Scroll texts might be included, while others, like Job, could be excluded (à la Dell 1991). Each wisdom book might be included in another modal category that includes nonsapiential books. Qoheleth, Lamentations, certain psalms, and Job might be included in a corpus of pessimistic or lament literature. We should also devote attention to how the wisdom writers subverted the rules of generic conventions and not just how they abided by them.

What criteria do we use to identify wisdom literature in the Hebrew Bible and the ancient Near East? As much as we might hate to admit it, basically you know it when you see it! That should not perplex us. The conventions of this literature exist, but only as our minds detect the patterns. We cannot enter into the minds of the ancient authors and clearly and definitively detect these conventions. We might grasp the general features, but never the details. This means the boundaries can never be hard and fast and that there may be more than one way to configure them. We might even come up with a novel pattern the ancients missed. The Israelite and ancient Near Eastern modes of literature have never been static, never homogenous, their borders never tightly drawn. They have always been evolving, ever changing. Again, that is how modes and genres do their business—and that is okay!

Works Consulted

Alter, Robert. 1985. *The Art of Biblical Poetry.* New York: Basic Books.
Boer, Roland, ed. 2007. *Bakhtin and Genre Theory in Biblical Studies.* SemeiaSt 63. Atlanta: Society of Biblical Literature.
Bright, John. 1965. *Jeremiah.* AB 21. Garden City, NY: Doubleday.
Brown, William P. 2011. "Wisdom's Wonder: A New Heuristic Framework for the Sapiential Literature of the Hebrew Bible." Paper presented at the Annual Meeting of the Society of Biblical Literature, San Francisco, CA, November 21.
Buccellati, Giorgio. 1981. "Wisdom and Not: The Case of Mesopotamia." *JAOS* 101:35–47.
Buss, Martin J. 2007. "Dialogue in and among Genres." Pages 9–18 in Boer 2007.
Carr, David M. 2004. "Wisdom and Apocalypticism: Different Types of Educational/Enculterational Literature." Paper presented at the Annual Meeting of the Society of Biblical Literature, San Antonio, TX, November 21.
———. 2011. *The Formation of the Hebrew Bible: A New Reconstruction.* Oxford: Oxford University Press.
Clifford, Richard J. 1997. "Introduction to the Wisdom Literature." *NIB* 5:1–16.
———. 1998. *The Wisdom Literature.* IBT. Nashville: Abingdon.
———. 1999. *Proverbs: A Commentary.* OTL. Louisville: Westminster John Knox.
Cohen, Yoram. 2009. *The Scribes and Scholars of the City of Emar in the Late Bronze Age.* HSS 59. Winona Lake, IN: Eisenbrauns.
Collins, Jeff. 2006. "The Genericity of Montage: Derrida and Genre Theory." Pages 55–68 in *Genre Matters: Essays in Theory and Criticism.* Ed. Garin Dowd, Lesley Stevenson, and Jeremy Strong. Bristol, UK: Intellect.

Collins, John J. 1993. "Wisdom, Apocalypticism, and Generic Compatibility." Pages 165–85 in *In Search of Wisdom: Essays in Memory of John G. Gammie*. Edited by Leo G. Perdue, Bernard Brandon Scott, and William Johnston Wisemen. Louisville: Westminster John Knox.

———. 1997. "Wisdom Reconsidered, in Light of the Scrolls." *DSD* 4:265–81.

Copi, Irving M. 1982. *Introduction to Logic*. 6th edition. New York: Macmillan.

Crenshaw James L. 1969. "Method in Determining Wisdom Influence upon 'Historical' Literature." *JBL* 88:129–42.

———. 2003. "Gold Dust or Nuggets? A Brief Response to J. Kenneth Kuntz." *CBR* 1:155–58.

———. 2010. *Old Testament Wisdom: An Introduction*. 3rd ed. Louisville: Westminster John Knox.

Dell, Katharine. 1991. *The Book of Job as Sceptical Literature*. BZAW 197. Berlin: de Gruyter.

———. 2004. "'I Will Solve My Riddle to the Music of the Lyre' (Psalm XLIX 4[5]): A Cultic Setting for Wisdom Psalms?" *VT* 54:445–58.

Derrida, Jacques. 1980. "The Law of Genre." *Critical Inquiry* 7:55–81.

Dowd, Garin. 2006. "Introduction: Genre Matters in Theory and Criticism." Pages 11–27 in *Genre Matters: Essays in Theory and Criticism*. Edited by Garin Dowd, Lesley Stevenson, and Jeremy Strong. Bristol, UK: Intellect.

Duncan, Mike. 2012. "The Curious Silence of the Dog and Paul of Tarsus: Revisiting the Argument from Silence." *Informal Logic* 32:83–97.

Dutcher-Walls, Patricia. 1991. "The Social Location of the Deuteronomists: A Sociological Study of Factional Politics in Late Pre-exilic Judah." *JSOT* 52:77–94.

Eagleton, Terry. 1991. *Ideology: An Introduction*. London: Verso.

Edzard, Dietz Otto. 1928. "Literatur." Pages 45–46 in vol. 7.1-2 of *Reallexikon der Assyriologie*. Edited by Erich Ebeling et al. Berlin: de Gruyter.

Fishbane, Michael. 1988. *Biblical Interpretation in Ancient Israel*. Rev. ed. Oxford: Clarendon.

Forti, Tova. 2008. *Animal Imagery in the Book of Proverbs*. VTSup 118. Leiden: Brill.

Fowler, Alastair. 1982. *Kinds of Literature: An Introduction to the Theory of Genres and Modes*. Cambridge: Harvard University Press.

Fox, Michael V. 2000. *Proverbs 1–9: A New Translation with Introduction and Commentary*. AB 18A. New York: Doubleday.

———. 2007a. "The Epistemology of the Book of Proverbs." *JBL* 126:669–84.
———. 2007b. "Ethics and Wisdom in the Book of Proverbs." *HS* 48:75–88.
———. 2009. *Proverbs 10–31: A New Translation with Introduction and Commentary.* AB 18B. New Haven: Yale University Press.
Frow, John. 2006. *Genre.* The New Critical Idiom. London: Routledge.
Goff, Matthew J. 2013. *4QInstruction.* WLAW 2. Atlanta: Society of Biblical Literature.
Goldingay, John. 1979. "The 'Salvation History' Perspective and the 'Wisdom' Perspective within the Context of Biblical Theology." *EvQ* 51: 194–207.
Greenstein, Edward L. 2004. "Jeremiah as an Inspiration to the Poet of Job." Pages 98–110 in *Prophecy in the Ancient Near East: Essays in Honor of Herbert B. Huffmon.* Edited by John Kaltner and Louis Stulman. JSOTSup 378. London: T&T Clark.
Hallo, William W. 2010. *The World's Oldest Literature: Studies in Sumerian Belles-Lettres.* CHANE 35. Leiden: Brill.
Kampen, John. 2011. *Wisdom Literature.* ECDSS. Grand Rapids: Eerdmans.
Kinder, Derek. 1964. *Proverbs.* TOTC. Downer's Grove, IL: InterVarsity Press.
Kitchen, Kenneth A. 1977. "Proverbs and Wisdom Books of the Ancient Near East: The Factual History of a Literary Form." *TynBul* 28:69–114.
———. 1979. "The Basic Literary Forms and Formulations of Ancient Instructional Writings in Egypt and Western Asia." Pages 235–82 in *Studien zu altägyptischen Lebenslehren.* Edited by Erik Hornung and Othmar Keel. OBO 28. Freiburg: Universitätsverlag; Göttingen: Vandenhoeck & Ruprecht.
———. 1998. "Biblical Instructional Wisdom: The Decisive Voice of the Ancient Near East." Pages 346–63 in *Boundaries of the Ancient Near East: A Tribute to Cyrus H. Gordon.* Edited by Meir Lubetski, Claire Gottlieb, and Sharon R. Keller. JSOTSup 273. Sheffield: Sheffield Academic.
Kunzt, J. Kenneth. 2003. "Reclaiming Biblical Wisdom Psalms: A Response to Crenshaw." *CBR* 1:145–54.
Lambert, W. G. 1996. *Babylonian Wisdom Literature.* Oxford: Oxford University Press, 1960. Repr., Winona Lake, IN: Eisenbrauns.
Lichtheim, Miriam. 1975. *Ancient Egyptian Literature: The Old and New Kingdoms.* Vol. 1. Berkeley: University of California Press.

———. 1996. "Didactic Literature." Pages 243–62 in *Ancient Egyptian Literature: History and Forms*. Edited by Antonio Loprieno. PAe 10. Leiden: Brill.

———. 1997. *Moral Values in Ancient Egypt*. OBO 155. Freiburg: Universitätsverlag; Göttingen: Vandenhoeck & Ruprecht.

Mitchell, Christine. 2007. "Power, *Eros*, and Biblical Genres." Pages 31–42 in Boer 2007.

Newsom, Carol A. 2007. "Spying Out the Land: A Report from Genology." Pages 19–30 in Boer 2007.

Niditch, Susan. 1997. *Ancient Israelite Religion*. New York: Oxford University Press.

Röllig, Wolfgang. 1928. "Literatur." Pages 59–61 in vol. 7.1–2 of *Reallexikon der Assyriologie*. Edited by Erich Ebeling et al. Berlin: de Gruyter.

Saur, Markus. 2011. "*Sapientia discursive*: Die alttestamentliche Weisheitsliteratur als theologischer Diskurs." *ZAW* 123:236–49.

Schipper, Bernd U. 2013. "When Wisdom Is Not Enough! The Discourse on Wisdom and Torah and the Composition of the Book of Proverbs." Pages 55–79 in *Wisdom and Torah: The Reception of 'Torah' in the Wisdom Literature of the Second Temple Period*. Edited by Bernd U. Schipper and D. Andrew Teeter. JSJSup 163. Leiden: Brill.

Schwienhorst-Schönberger, Ludger. 2013. "Alttestamentliche Weisheit im Diskurs." *ZAW* 125:118–42.

Seow, C. L. 1995. "Qohelet's Autobiography." Pages 275–87 in *Fortunate the Eyes That See: Essays in Honor of David Noel Freedman*. Edited by Astrid B. Beck, Andrew H. Bartelt, Paul R Raabe, Chris A. Franke, and John F. Craghan. Grand Rapids: Eerdmans.

Shupak Nili. 1987. "The 'Sitz im Leben' of the Book of Proverbs in the Light of a Comparison of Biblical and Egyptian Wisdom Literature." *RB* 94: 98–119.

———. 1990. "Egyptian 'Prophetic' Writings and Biblical Wisdom Literature." *BN* 54:81–102.

Smart, Ninian. 1983. *Worldviews: Crosscultural Explorations of Human Beliefs*. New York: Scribner's Sons.

Sneed, Mark. 2011. "Is the 'Wisdom Tradition' a Tradition?" *CBQ* 73:50–71.

Sparks, Kenton L. 2005. *Ancient Texts for the Study of the Hebrew Bible: A Guide to the Background Literature*. Peabody, MA: Hendrickson.

Strauß, Hans. 2004. "Weisheitliche Lehrerzählungen im und um das Alte Testament." *ZAW* 116:379–95.

Toorn, Karel van der. 2007. *Scribal Culture and the Making of the Hebrew Bible.* Cambridge: Harvard University Press.
Van Leeuwen, Raymond. 1994–2004. "The Book of Proverbs: Introduction, Commentary, and Reflections." *NIB* 5:19–264.
Weeks, Stuart. 2010. *An Introduction to the Study of Wisdom Literature.* T&T Clark Approaches to Biblical Studies. London: T&T Clark.
Whybray, R. N. 1974. *The Intellectual Tradition in the Old Testament.* BZAW 135. Berlin: de Gruyter.

Three Theses on Wisdom

Michael V. Fox

Bible scholars, acting on the form-critical axiom that every *Gattung* has its *Sitz im Leben*—a situation in the life of a society in which literature of a certain sort was produced and used—have constructed a wisdom school to serve that end. In my view, (1) there was no wisdom school; and (2) the authors of wisdom literature were not a distinct faction; but (3) there was a wisdom literature.[1]

There Was No Wisdom School

"School" can mean an institution dedicated to teaching or a school of thought, like the Greek philosophical schools (which were likely the model for the invention of the concept of "wisdom school"). There was no wisdom school in the ancient Near East in either sense.[2] The following arguments support the basic thesis argued by Sneed (2011) in this regard.

There were scribal schools in Egypt and Mesopotamia, and we know a fair amount about their curricula. Wisdom literature (a term I will use in the traditional loose but functional way until I define it more closely below) was certainly taught there, but so were a great variety of other texts. The existence of schools in Israel cannot be proved but seems likely.[3] A

---

1. In this essay I enter into discussion in particular with two innovative articles: Mark Sneed (2011) and Will Kynes (forthcoming). I thank Dr. Kynes for making his essay available to me before publication. I take issue with some of his ideas because of their significance to the field. I should note that I did not have access to the articles in the present anthology, but I understand Sneed's and Kynes's continuing work to be consistent with the above-mentioned essays.

2. I argued this earlier in Fox (1996).

3. See the survey by H.W. Fischer-Elfert (2001, 438–42). Brunner's study of Egyptian education (1957) is still valuable. We know something of the curricula of the

school need be no more than a room in which a group of boys were taught to read and introduced to the more technical aspects of their future professions, especially in connection with the temples and law courts. It is likely that there were schools attached to the temple and possibly the court, as in Egypt and Mesopotamia, for the Jerusalem temple followed foreign models in many regards. The Second Temple in Jerusalem had a library. Such libraries would form a locus for advanced learning, like the House of Life in Egyptian temples. In the following discussion, I will use Egyptian wisdom as my primary non-Israelite example, because it has preserved the greatest number of wisdom instructions and provides information about their authors.

Schools are not a necessary or sufficient condition for the composition and transmission of wisdom literature. There is no evidence that wisdom books were written *for* the schools, to serve as school texts.[4] The Egyptian wisdom instructions do not present themselves as originating in the schools or any other specific social locus. Some of their authors are called scribes, but any literate man could have that title as a professional designation. (Egyptian *sš* literally means "writer"—as does Hebrew *sôpēr* and English "scribe.") The wisdom books are ascribed to men from a variety of professions and classes, ranging from king and vizier to ordinary scribes of different ranks. Some ascriptions may be fictitious, but some certainly are not, for their authors are described in terms too specific to be typological, and their status, while respectable, does not have the luster possessed by typological sages, which comes from their antiquity or royalty status.

The Authors of Wisdom Were Not a Distinct Faction

The old assumption that there was a class of professional wise men called חכמים who constituted an ideological-political faction was effectively

---

Twelfth Dynasty from the masses of ostraca found throughout Egypt, especially in Deir el-Medineh. (Papyrus was used by the more advanced pupils.) Wisdom texts, especially the Wisdom of Amenemhet, are well represented. According to Fischer-Elfert (ibid.), the core of instruction was a set of three texts taught in sequence: The Instruction of Chety, the Instruction of a Man for His Son, and the Loyalist Instruction. These are all distinctively didactic wisdom and are titled instruction.

4. For a fuller discussion of this issue, see Fox (1996). I argue that the school was not the *Sitz im Leben* of didactic wisdom literature. The social location of some of the collections of the book of Proverbs was the royal court, in the broad sense of the royal service. Other books and individual sayings had other social locations.

undermined by N. Whybray in 1975. He examined every occurrence of
חכם and showed that none had a specialized sense. To be sure, it is possible that there was such a faction even if wise men does not have that precise denotation in the Bible, but this is not the picture we get from the sources. We may add that there is no evidence of a faction of wisdom-authors in Mesopotamia or Egypt either. The following sections survey wisdom book ascriptions that are probably actual, not pseudonymous.

Egypt

The ostensive, and often actual, authors are men from various walks of life who are speaking to their sons. In the Middle Kingdom, the putative authors are kings and viziers. In the New Kingdom they are scribes of a lower order, respectable but not illustrious. (For bibliography, see the end of this essay.) Most of these persons are not lofty in rank or antiquity and unlikely to attract pseudepigraphic ascriptions. The following ascriptions are credible:

1. *Duachety* (or *Chety*): No professional designations are given to the author of this very popular instruction (of which some 250 whole or partial copies remain). He instructs his son while sailing with him to his future school.
2. *Amenemope*: Overseer of the fields, overseer of grains, and so on. (Amenemope lists his various offices, which involve overseeing taxation, demarcations of fields, etc.). His wife's titles, too, are listed, as are his son's religious functions. The book is spoken to Amenemope's actual son, Ho-em-maakher. The instruction is relevant to an indefinitely broad reading audience, but it is directed in the first instance to Amenemope's son, who would be expected to inherit his father's positions, for nepotism was the standard practice in Egyptian scribal offices. This means that Amenemope's admonitions about honest marking and measuring of the fields, correct allocation of temple rations, and generosity in assessments from a poor man (§§5, 6, 13, 17) are spoken with an actual person, his own son, in mind.
3. *Anii*: Scribe of the palace of Queen Nefertari. This is not a particularly illustrious position. No further information is given.
4. *Amennakhte* son of Ipuy: He was "scribe of the tomb," "scribe of the vizier," "royal scribe," "scribe of the Residence," "scribe in the

House of Life," and held some other functions as well. The House of Life was a scribal center in the temple that included a library and a school, and the "Scribe of the Tomb" apparently had supervisory responsibilities in education. But Amennakhte does not call himself a schoolteacher, and he does not cast this book as a school instruction. His case shows that a scribe could serve the needs of a school even while filling a variety of other offices.

5. *Hori*: a scribe of the tomb, probably working under the supervision of Amennakhte. He was also called "Designer" and "Chief of Designers in the Place of Truth."

Even the ascriptions that were or might be fictional show what an Egyptian reader could be expected to envision as the setting of wisdom instruction. Three works are ascribed to viziers. Ptahhotep was a vizier in the Old Kingdom, but the language of his book belongs to the Middle Kingdom. The father (whose name is lost) who speaks to Kagemeni was a vizier in the Old Kingdom, and Kagemeni was to become one as well; Ankhsheshonqy was a vizier wrongly deposed as the victim of slander. This event is a topos found in a number of books, including Ahiqar, and was probably fictional.[5]

Even a pseudepigraphic book can be historically credible. Amenhemhet I, a king, was not the author of the instruction he gives, because he apparently speaks from the realm of the dead, having been assassinated in a palace coup. We happen to know the actual author of this book. In the New Kingdom Pap. Chester Beatty IV (6.13–14; Lichtheim 1973–1981, 2:177), it is said of the eminent scribe named Chety (= Duachety) that it was he "who wrote a book as an instruction for king Sehetipre' [= Amenemhet] when he had gone to rest, etc." This Chety was probably the author of his own wisdom book, mentioned above (as Duachety). This is a case where a work can be pseudepigraphic and yet be rooted in the historical situation it describes. The instruction to Merikare was by a king, obviously not the real author because he too is speaking from the realm of the dead. We cannot know if Prince Hardjedef was the actual author of his teaching.

Nothing suggests that the authors of wisdom instructions wrote exclusively in that genre. The composition In Praise of Ancient Scribes[6]

---

5. On the topos of "disgrace and rehabilitation of the vizier," see Fox 2012, 258–60.
6. Or The Immortality of Writers: P. Chester Beatty IV, verso 2.5–3.11; Brunner 1988, 218–30; Lichtheim 1973–1981, 2:175–78.

mentions six ancient authors. Of them, two, possibly three, wrote known wisdom compositions. These six sages, it is said, "Foretold the future. What came from their mouth occurred; it is found as (their) pronouncement. It is written in their books" (see Lichtheim 1973–1981, 2:177). The sages are praised for their prophecies, for that too is wisdom. Of the books mentioned and extant, Chety and Ptahhotep do not foretell the future, but Neferti does (*ex eventu*). It is significant that the sages all are grouped together. There is no hint of a sages-versus-prophets division.

We know something about the range of one scribe's compositions. Amennakhte composed numerous administrative and judicial documents (Bickel & Mathieu 1993, 37–38). Five of Amennakhte's credited literary works are extant: an Educational Instruction (partially preserved in five copies), a poem of nostalgia for Thebes, a satirical poem, two hymns to Ramses IV, and another hymn to a god (Bickel and Mathieu 1993, 38; translations ibid. 35–48). Of course, Amennakhte may have had underlings doing the actual composition or editing, but he is credited with the work and at least directed their creation. Strikingly, some extant administrative documents seem to have been inscribed by Amennakhte himself (ibid., 38).

Mesopotamia and Syria

Of the named authors of Mesopotamian and Syrian wisdom, Shupe'awilum and Ahiqar could have been actual authors, but this cannot be determined. Shuruppak is obviously pseudepigraphic since he lived before the flood. In all cases the instructions are spoken by a father to his son (or adopted son), not to pupils in a school.

Israel

Most of Israelite wisdom is anonymous. Most of the book of Proverbs is ascribed, pseudonymously, to the archetypal sage Solomon (1:1; 10:1; 25:1), but some parts are associated with anonymous sages (22:17 [emended[7]]; 24:23). Proverbs 30:1–9 is the teaching of one Agur, apparently a non-Israelite king (possibly spoken to his son, named Ithiel) while 31:1–9 is the teaching of a woman, the mother of an otherwise unknown

---

7. Read דברי חכמים at the beginning of Prov 22:17, based on G's λόγοις σοφῶν.

king Lemuel (31:1). The historicity of these persons cannot be determined. The lectures in Proverbs 1–9 are spoken by a father to his son or sons. This is a literary fiction based on ancient practice (see further Fox 2003, 155–60). Qoheleth is not a historical character but only takes on the guise of royalty for two chapters.

We know only one author of Israelite wisdom by name: Ben Sira. Ben Sira was a scribe who served in several capacities, mainly as agent to the wealthy (to whose ranks he does not belong). There is a hint of the father-to-son setting in Ben Sira, for he speaks to "my son" (e.g., 3:8; 3:12, 17 [2x], 18; 4:20) and "my sons" (41:14) and calls himself "father" (3:1a). Since the book was translated to Greek by his grandson, it may have actually been transmitted in the family. It is possible that Ben Sira offered instruction, but the invitation to his "house of instruction" in 51:23, commonly taken to refer to a school, metaphorically alludes to his *book*, for he goes on to offer his wisdom "without money" (51:25). Ben Sira is much like the Egyptian sages of the ethical instructions: learned in the writings, experienced in political and economic offices, educating his son or sons with a view to future generations.

There is no reason to suppose that the authors of Israelite wisdom belonged to a certain school and subscribed to a distinctive ideology. To be sure, we do not know for a fact that "the same authors who composed the wisdom literature are also responsible for the composition and/or preservation of the other types of literature" (Sneed 2011, 73), but they could well have been. This is not to say that there are no stylistic and theological differences between wisdom books and most other biblical genres. Before Ben Sira, Israelite wisdom says nothing about the national history and little about the cult, but this does not show an ideological rift. Wisdom is simply not about those topics.[8] The purpose of didactic wisdom is to shape the personal character of young men, while other wisdom books probe broad human issues of justice and life's meaning. The distinctive styles and ideas of Israelite wisdom literature are features of the genre's goals, not of the authors' mentality.

---

8. Perdue (1977, *passim*) shows that that the authors of wisdom were by no means hostile to the cult or even indifferent to it.

There Was a Wisdom Literature but Perhaps It Needs a New Name

Studies by W. Kynes (forthcoming) and M. Sneed (2011) have challenged the validity of the traditional scholarly ideas of wisdom literature. Sneed (2011, 57) thinks that there was a genre adequately called wisdom literature (although he prefers to call it a "mode" [2011, 57]), but he fundamentally rethinks the social location and function of this category. Kynes rejects the term wisdom literature and denies that there was such a genre. He makes a fresh contribution to the history of scholarship in his survey of the origin and early uses of the concept of wisdom literature and his exploration of the concept's ideological setting. He shows that the term was poorly defined from the start and was used in multifarious ways. Consequently he advocates that this term be avoided as a scholarly artifact and repudiates the assumption that there ever was such a genre.

In my view, these observations do not justify abandoning the concept of wisdom literature or the recognition of wisdom literature as a genre. If it is a scholarly artifact, the same may be said of most of our literary and linguistic categories and concepts, such as detective story or phoneme. From Kynes's survey, it is clear that modern scholars have shared an approximate idea of a type (which is to say, *Gattung* or genre) of literature reasonably called wisdom literature and have communicated satisfactorily using this term. To be sure, the category is often stretched too far, sometimes even being made to include Psalms and Song of Songs. (The latter can be included in wisdom only by construing that book allegorically.) Nevertheless, there is still a core group of works that all recognized, and extraneous texts placed in the category were little more than a distraction.

Wisdom literature is a heuristic genre, which is valid insofar as it helps bring together texts that can be fruitfully compared, both for similarities and differences. The fact that, as Kynes shows, scholars of wisdom have drawn on intellectual and religious ideas of their contemporaries does not invalidate the terminology they used or even the concepts that infused their thought. It only shows that they were not intellectually inert. (Is feminist Bible scholarship crippled by being influenced by feminist intellectual and ideological goals?[9]) In any case, a scholar today can borrow a theory from nineteenth-century scholars and philosophers while setting aside

---

9. The answer is yes, but only when the ideology predetermines the conclusion.

extraneous assumptions those scholars held. Consider that modern biology is fundamentally Darwinian even while rejecting Darwin's assumptions about the inheritance of acquired characteristics.

W. G. Lambert (1960) is often cited for doubting the validity of the concept of wisdom literature. Though he named his anthology "Babylonian Wisdom Literature," he felt uneasy with the term. In an often-quoted declaration he warns: "Wisdom is strictly a misnomer as applied to Babylonian literature, because, unlike biblical ḥokmah, the Babylonian terms for wisdom rarely have moral content" (1960, 1).[10] Still, Lambert says, "'wisdom' has been used for a group of texts which correspond in subject-matter with the Hebrew wisdom books, and may be retained as a convenient short description" (1960, 1). (This seems to me like a good reason to use the term, and it grants that there is such a "group.") In spite of his hesitations, Lambert is clear enough about the boundaries of the genre. While including a broad array of texts in his anthology, he omits some texts because "they are clearly distinguished from the more openly rational attitude displayed in our texts" (1960, 1). In the end, Lambert says, he "has included all those works which obviously belong, but in the matter of border-line cases he has been compelled to use his own judgment" (1960, 2). (Which is of course what a scholar should do.) For all his compunctions, Lambert has a notion of a wisdom genre, with a group of works "that obviously belong" and a number of texts on the margin.

Though the criteria of Lambert's editorial choices are never explained, the title he gave his book has functional clarity. When I ordered his book, I knew I was going to get at least Shuruppak, Babylonian Counsels of Wisdom and Ludlul Bēl Nēmeqi, but probably not Gilgamesh. Whenever I look at an introduction to wisdom literature, I can expect reference to certain members of the group. If marginal items are included as well, that does not cause harm, unless one were to naively transfer features of a marginal work to another work under study—or, for that matter from one core work to another. We must be sensitive to differences whether or not we class works together. Indeed, the best way to detect differences is to compare one work with another one that is similar enough to make the differences significant.

---

10. In fact, חכמה also has no inherent moral valence outside wisdom literature. Wisdom literature alone claims that there is no wisdom that is not in accord with ethical and religious principles; see Fox (2000, 32–34; idem, 2009, 934–40).

Sneed distinguishes two theories about genres: realism and nominalism. In Sneed's view (following Sparks [2005, 6–7]), genre realism assumes that "wisdom literature is a thing that already exists, that the task of scholarship is merely to correctly identify it by isolating its salient features from the wisdom texts" (66). It further assumes that genres are "rigidly defined, with clear boundaries between them" and are "stable and static" (66). But this description is something of a caricature of both scholars. H. Gunkel and J. L. Crenshaw, whom Sparks and Sneed identify as genre realists, do assert the social-historical reality of genres but do not insist on their immutability or strict discreteness. Gunkel was certainly aware of—and intrigued by—genre fluctuation, growth, and mixing.[11] Crenshaw lists a series of formal and thematic features that together characterize wisdom literature and aptly observes: "When a marriage between form and content exists there is wisdom literature. Lacking such oneness, a given text participates in biblical wisdom to a greater or lesser extent" (1998, 11). For both scholars, the fuzziness inevitable in all (reasonable) typologies does not contradict the ontological reality of the genres.[12] Genre nominalism, in contrast, holds that "there is a flexible and partially arbitrary character to all classifications … generic categories are essentially taxonomic inventions" (Sneed, 66, quoting Sparks, 6).

---

11. In his *The Stories of Genesis* (1994), Gunkel gives only the loosest typology of the stories (9–26), with much overlapping. There are "etiological stories" and "ethnological stories," but the latter are certainly etiological, for "they are written for a purpose, or to explain something" (18). There are "etymological legends" and "ceremonial legends," but the latter can hold etymologies (as in the explanation of Pesaḥ; Exod 12:27). Gunkel was very aware of "mingling of motifs" (24–25), though he is vague on what it is that is being "mingled." Indeed, "There are almost always a number of different motifs united in the stories and mingled together in a variety of ways" (24). In fact, what interests Gunkel is the development of the literary (and religious) features of Genesis, and he sets up categories as a means of describing these features. His work is characterized by enthusiasm for the ancient literature and its social rootedness, not by dry generic typologies; nor is Crenshaw's.

12. Both scholars show some inconsistency. Gunkel repeatedly asserts that every genre has a specific social location (later labeled *Sitz im Leben*), but he does not assume that every development in form creates a new genre that reflects a different social setting. Crenshaw, in spite of his important recognition that texts can participate in the wisdom genre to varying degrees (quoted above), sometimes guards the borders strictly, as when he definitively excludes wisdom Psalms from participation (2000). Since I regard genres as fuzzy sets in which degrees of membership are possible (see n. 13), I would say rather that certain psalms belong to wisdom literature *to a fair degree.*

In my view, some genres are real, some nominal. The former have a reality independent of scholarly definitions. The reality in question is that of social constructs. Science fiction really exists—as a construct, of course. It has its own magazines, its own publishers, and its readers who expect to find certain kinds of stories in its publications. Of course one can argue about whether this or that book belongs to the genre (*1984*?), but all would agree that a given book can participate in more than one genre. A book can be both science fiction and, say, a mystery story. Nominal genres are created for various purposes by scholars. "Skeptical wisdom," for example, exists only insofar as scholars assign different works to this category and others find it useful. (Otherwise it would be a dead end.)

Molly Zahn provides a valuable survey of genre theory, with a selective bibliography of the field. Her most important point is that genres are not exclusive categories. They are flexible and change in their composition and details over time, like a flock of birds. Hence, "we can speak of texts 'participating' in genres: dipping into them, employing their elements in modified fashion, combining them. In this model, texts can participate in multiple genres simultaneously" (2012, 277). Zahn draws on cognitive psychology to observe that in practice people do not form categories by making checklists, "but rather by comparison to some object that is taken as prototypical" (278). This, I believe, is applicable to both real and nominal genres. For wisdom literature, the prototypical member has undoubtedly been Proverbs, with other texts admitted to the category insofar as they resemble this book.

I suggest that we can best describe literary genres as *fuzzy sets*. An element in a fuzzy set can have *degrees* of membership, and not only a binary yes/no qualification.[13] Certainly Proverbs and Amenemope have a high degree of belonging. Psalm 119 may belong to wisdom literature, but to a lesser degree than Proverbs.

Wisdom literature is undoubtedly a loosely defined category, but refinements are possible. If we give up on "wisdom," we'll need a substitute

---

13. Fuzziness is "the vagueness concerning the description of the semantic meaning of the events, phenomena or statements themselves" (Zimmermann 1985, 3). The Wikipedia article http://en.wikipedia.org/wiki/Fuzzy_sets offers a clear elementary explanation of fuzzy set theory with reference to works in various areas. Pattern recognition is one area in which fuzzy set theory is applied. Someone who controls the necessary mathematics, which I do not, might be able to provide a mathematical model of literary genres.

term, because we're going to want to talk about works like Amenemope, Ahiqar, Proverbs, Ben Sira, Qoheleth, and others, without repeating the whole list every time. (Putting "wisdom literature" in scare quotes does not solve the problem. Nor does calling it "so-called," as Kynes sometimes does).

For the core group of wisdom literature, that is to say, the works included explicitly or implicitly by all who have used this concept, the more precise term didactic wisdom literature has served well enough for some time and has engendered little confusion. It is clear that Amenemope and Proverbs belong here while Job does not. One justification for the term is that Proverbs, Qoheleth, and Ben Sira are explicitly concerned with wisdom and use words for wisdom and the wise with great frequency. But this terminology is less prominent in the Egyptian and Babylonian counterparts. It is, however, reasonable to extend a term most relevant to Israel to other literary cultures, but maybe a new term is in order.

All the Egyptian texts that offer boys counsel in leading a wise, virtuous, and productive life are called (insofar as their beginnings are intact) *sb'ywt* "instructions" (singular *sb'yt*). (Egyptologists too usually speak of the genre in this way.) This is not an exclusive designator, because the term is also used of other types of instructions, such as a king's directives, a god's teaching to believers, encyclopedic lists, last testaments, and rules of letter writing (see Shupak 1993, 76). Still, the label is adequate, for two reasons. First, a reader who sees *sb'yt* soon recognizes what sort of teachings the book offers. Second, in most instructions, the title *sb'yt* does not stand alone. Often a prologue immediately defines the book's contents with greater precision. Amenemope describes his teachings as "The beginning of the teaching for life, the instruction for well-being, all the rules for relations with elders, ... to guide one in the way of life" (1.2–3, 7).[14] Similar prologues are found in other instructions. But an even more precise designation is available.

Several New Kingdom instructions are designated *sb'ywt mtrwt* "educational instructions." *Sb'yt mtrt* is the title of the instructions of Hori, Amennakhte, the fragmentary Instructions in Negative Form,[15] and Anii. Anii also uses the term in his epilogue, where his son says "A youth cannot fulfill [lit. 'do'] the *sb'yt mtrt*" (22.17). This is in contrast to what he believes

---

14. Similarly in Proverbs, the loose designation *mišley-* in 1:1 is defined in the next five verses.

15. Ostraca of the British Museum 5631 verso; see Brunner 1957, 215–17.

a youth *can* do, namely, "recite the sayings from a scroll" (22.15–16). A *mtrt* is thus a teaching that demands more than mechanical recitation.

Sb'yt and *mtrt* are synonyms, but *sb'yt mtrt* is not a pleonasm. *Mtr* is an alternate writing of *mty*, which means "straight(ness)," "rectitude," hence "good character."[16] There are different ideas about the exact meaning of *mtr*. According to Quack (1994, 83) *sb'yt* is more theoretical and *mtrt* more practical. Shupak says that *mtr* is instruction in which relations between teacher and pupil are on a personal level (1993, 36). Other senses of *mtr/mty* are chastisement and testimony. Looking at the root meaning of *mtr* and its various connotations, it is clear that it refers to education in the virtues of good character, in other words, ethics. We can call the genre in question "ethical instruction." Given the intertwining of practical good sense and religious virtues in these texts,[17] this term than can be unpacked as "instructions in leading an ethical and successful life."

Israelite wisdom books do not have ethical instruction in their titles, but the concept does exist. Proverbs' promise to teach "wisdom and discipline" and "the discipline of insight, righteousness, justice, and rectitude" (Prov 1:2, 6) could be restated as ethical instruction. Ben Sira's encapsulation of his book as "the instruction of insight and skilled [?] proverbs" (Sir 50:27) places it squarely in the tradition of the ethical instruction. The book of Qoheleth belongs here, because it sets out to discover and teach "what is good for a man to do under the heavens during the few days of his life" (Qoh 2:3b), and the epilogue describes Qoheleth as a teacher of knowledge "to the people" (12:9). (The address to "my son" in 12:12 is a reminiscence of the ancient practice of speaking ethical instructions to one's son.) The fact that this title is not used in every text that belongs in the group does not disqualify it as a genre label. Most detective stories do not call themselves by that term but manage to find their way to the same shelf in the bookstore.

A text can belong to this genre without having *only* ethical instructions in it. Amenemhet relates a historical event—his own assassination (M 1.6–3.5)—and Merikare's father speaks of his own accomplishments, reports on a rebellion, and even confesses a failing (P 68–74; 94–100). These matters are relevant to the immediate audiences of the instructions, namely, the sons who are receiving the instruction, and for these royal listeners

---

16. For the various writings, see Faulkner 1962, 120–21. *Mtrt* is a noun and feminine adjective from *mtr*.

17. Discussed in Fox 2009, 934–39.

the instructions have ethical weight. Qoheleth relates his own (fictitious) autobiography in the course of pronouncing ethical instructions. His autobiography is at the fore in Qoh 1:12–2:26, but the entire book until 12:8 relates his experiences. Ben Sira's is the first (known) ethical instruction in Israel to dwell at length on Israel's history (in his praise of the fathers, Sir 44:1–50:24) and to speak of Israel's Torah as wisdom (Sir 24:1–29). This passage sets Israel's Torah at the pinnacle of wisdom. Hymns and prayers are very rare in wisdom literature, but the praise of the Creator in Merikare (P 130–138) is hymnic, and Ben Sira includes several hymns (Sir 1:1–10; 18:1–7; 39:12–35; 42:15–43:33; 50:22–24; 51:12) and two prayers of petition (22:27–23:6 and 36:1–22). All these works are pushing the boundaries of the genre and enriching it in doing so, but they remain ethical instructions. (Amenemhet, Merikare, and Qoheleth are *also* testaments. Works need not be confined to a single genre.)

To Sneed's question, "Is the 'Wisdom Tradition' a Tradition?" the answer (if we confine wisdom to ethical instructions) is certainly yes. Egyptian ethical instructions formed a self-aware tradition, one in which later works drew on earlier ones and adapted their counsels to new settings. Egyptian wisdom books frequently cite and adapt earlier wisdom texts. Extensive evidence for this can be found in Egyptological research, notably Brunner's study of quotations from wisdom instructions (1979, 105–71) and Schipper's 2005 examination of the way that Proverbs draws on Amenemope and Amenemope draws on his own predecessors. Ancient recognition of the genre is demonstrated by the way an extract from Amenemope was adopted smoothly into Hebrew wisdom and then taken into Proverbs. A Hebrew editor considered the Amenemope to be compatible with the book he was writing and could use it as a direct source both for its language and its ideas. Ahiqar was the source of several sayings in Proverbs.[18] Ben Sira drew upon much of the biblical canon, but he mainly cited Proverbs and modeled most of his teachings on Proverbs' style and forms.

Ethical instruction was a real genre. It had the reality of a social construct, one native to a culture and in some way recognized in it. It is my claim that the ancient Egyptians recognized the ethical instruction as a distinct genre, and called it *sb'yt* or, more narrowly, *sb'yt mtrt*. And, in

---

18. I review the literature on Proverbs' use of Amenemope and Ahiqar in Fox 1996 and add some supportive considerations in Fox 2009, 753–69.

view of the strong affiliations between the Egyptian instructions and didactic works in Israel and Mesopotamia, the concept can be extended to the latter as well.

Wisdom literature, in distinction, is a heuristic genre, a construct of modern scholarship. So are a great many other important categories—prose, and morphology, and parallelism, for example. Such constructs are valid to the extent that they are useful in describing the interconnections among ancient texts. Scholars who see deep affinities between, say, Proverbs and the book of Job (or some voices within it) or some psalms can reasonably class these works as wisdom literature.[19] (The affinities can take the form of direct disagreements.)

One problem with the notion of wisdom literature is that it has too often been spread too wide. Some scholars include fables or contest literature and popular sayings in it and then find the category to be too loose to be useful (thus in Lambert's anthology). But this is just a reason to be more restrained in including works too distant from the rest of the family genre and to justify inclusions by showing their utility.

Here is how I define wisdom literature, that is to say, how I delineate a set of texts whose similarities make them a useful grouping for literary and ideological comparisons. A wisdom book purports to discover and teach insights about the ethical and successful life (including the limitations on attaining it). It meditates on and teaches about such matters as the moral relation between deed and consequence and the efficacy of moral rules. It thinks about the powers and validity of wisdom itself. And all this without appealing to revelation or laws.[20]

---

19. D. Carr has studied education in the Near East in depth (2005, 17–173). He says that "'wisdom' or 'gnomic' instructions often played roles particularly in the early stages of a broader curriculum of literature used for teaching" (132). He feels that the concept of "wisdom literature" (always in quotation marks) "can be misleading insofar as it suggests that didactic tales and sage instructions were separated from other forms of literature by their educational usage" (ibid.). He does not explain how the term "gnomic" avoids this difficulty. A better solution is just to avoid the mistaken assumptions. In any case, few people would suppose that Job and Ecclesiastes were part of elementary education.

20. The book of Job culminates in a divine revelation, but the book itself is not supposed to be revealed. Yahweh's words in the theophany are revealed to Job (and perhaps to his friends), but they are scripted into a drama in which Yahweh is one of the personae. The same is true of the divine message at the end of Ludlul Bēl Nēmeqi. Some behaviors can be proscribed by both wisdom and *law*, but the motivations and

It is not the label wisdom that makes it valuable to think about Job in terms of Proverbs, or about Proverbs in terms of certain psalms, but rather the affinity among these works in ideas (including repudiated ideas), form, and style (in the friends' frequent proverb-style couplets) that makes defining them as a set useful. A wisdom book—Job, say—can be placed in other sets as well—of individual laments, for example—and read with profit in that context. It is not the case (as Kynes worries) that classifying Job as wisdom literature leads to ignoring its intertextual connections with Psalms. That has not happened. If people have misused the concept of wisdom literature, the problem is with the misuse, not the concept.

Works Consulted

Ancient Works Mentioned

The following listing is meant to provide quick access to a translation of the texts mentioned. Bibliography for the sources can be found in the anthologies cited and in Fox 2009, 1119–20. Citations are according to their numeration in the major manuscript of the work (usually column/line). In the case of Amenemope, chapter numbers are also given, marked by §.

Egypt (in approximate chronological order)

Kagemeni (i.e., *to* Kagemeni): Lichtheim 1973–1981, 1:59–61; Brunner 1988, 133–36.
Ptahhotep: Lichtheim 1973–1981, 1:61–80; Brunner 1988, 104–32. (A Middle Kingdom dating is possible.)
Merikare (i.e., *to* Merikare): Lichtheim 1973–1981, 1:97–109; Brunner 1988, 196–217.
Amenemhet I: Lichtheim 1973–1981, 1:135–139; Brunner 1988, 169–77.
Loyalist Teaching (mainly from the stele of Sehetibre; on the sources see Brunner 1988, 178–79): Lichtheim 1973–1981, 1:125–29 (partial); Brunner 1988, 178–84.

---

consequences are quite different. The consequences of violation of wisdom admonitions are not executed by humans as *penalties* but come about by natural causation or (which is ultimately the same thing) are imposed by God.

Duachety (or Chety): Lichtheim 1973–1981, 1:184–92; Brunner 1988, 155–68.
A Man to His Son: Brunner 1988, 185–93.
Anii: Lichtheim 1973–1981, 2:135–46; Brunner 1988, 196–217.
Amenemope: Lichtheim 1973–1981, 2:146–63; Brunner 1988, 234–56; Laisney (2007).
Amennakhte: Bickel and Mathieu 1993, 33–35; Brunner 1988, 231–33.
Hori: Bickel and Mathieu 1993, 49–50.
Pap. Chester Beatty IV (a miscellany of wisdom texts): Gardiner 1935, 37–44; Brunner 1988, 218–30.
Ankhsheshonqy: Lichtheim 1973–1981, 3:159–84; Brunner 1988, 257–91.

Mesopotamia and Syria

Shuruppak: Alster 1974, 33–51.
Shupe'awilum: Foster 1993, 1:332–35; Hurowitz 2007.
Counsels of Wisdom: Foster 1993, 1:328–31.
Ludlul Bēl Nēmeqi: Foster 1993, 1:308–25
Ahiqar: Porten and Yardeni 1993, 3:24–53.

Modern Scholarship

Alster, Bendt. 1974. *The Instructions of Suruppak: A Sumerian Proverb Collection*. Mesopotamia 2. Copenhagen: Akademisk.
Bickel, Susanne, and Bernard Mathieu. 1993. "L'écrivain Amennakht et son enseignement." *BIFAO* 93:31–51.
Brunner, Helmut. 1957. *Altägyptische Erziehung*. Wiesbaden: Harrassowitz.
———. 1979. "Zitate aus Lebenslehren." Pages 105–71 in *Studien zu altägyptischen Lebenslehren*. Edited by Erik Hornung and Othmar Keel. OBO 28. Freiburg: Universitätsverlag; Göttingen: Vandenhoeck & Ruprecht.
———. 1988. *Altägyptische Weisheit*. Zürich: Artemis.
Carr, David. 2005. *Writing on the Tablet of the Heart: Origins of Scripture and Literature*. New York: Oxford University Press.
Černý, Jaroslav, and Alan H. Gardiner. 1957. *Hieratic Ostraca*. Oxford: Oxford University Press.
Crenshaw, James L. 1998. *Old Testament Wisdom: An Introduction*. Louisville: Westminster John Knox.

———. 2000. "Wisdom Psalms?" *CurBR* 8: 9–17.
Faulkner, Raymond. 1962. *A Concise Dictionary of Middle Egyptian*. Oxford: Griffith Institute.
Fischer-Elfert, H.W. 2001. "Education." Pages 438–42 in vol. 1 of *The Oxford Encyclopedia of Ancient Egypt*. Edited by Donald B. Redford. 3 vols. Oxford: Oxford University Press.
Foster, Benjamin R. 1993. *Before the Muses*. Bethesda, MD: CDL.
Fox, Michael V. 1996. "The Social Location of the Book of Proverbs." Pages 227–39 in *Texts, Temples, and Traditions*. Edited by M. V. Fox, V. A. Hurowitz, A. Hurvitz, M. L. Klein, B. J. Schwartz, and N. Shupak. Winona Lake, IN: Eisenbrauns.
———. 2000. *Proverbs 1–9*. AB 18A. New York: Doubleday.
———. 2003. "Wisdom and the Self-Presentation of Wisdom Literature." Pages 153–72 in *Reading from Right to Left: Essays on the Hebrew Bible in Honour of David J. A. Clines*. Edited by J. Cheryl Exum and H. G. M. Williamson. JSOTSup 373. Sheffield: Sheffield Academic.
———. 2009. *Proverbs 10–31*. AB 18B. New Haven: Yale University Press.
———. 2012. "Joseph and Wisdom." Pages 231–62 in *The Book of Genesis: Composition, Reception, and Interpretation*. Edited by Craig A. Evans, Joel N. Lohr, and David L. Petersen. VTSup 152. Leiden: Brill.
Gardiner, Alan H. 1935. *Hieratic Papyri in the British Museum: Third Series; Chester Beatty Gift*, pls. 37–44. London: British Museum.
Gunkel, Hermann. 1994. *The Stories of Genesis*. Edited by William R. Scott. Translated by John J. Scullion. Berkeley: BIBAL.
Hurowitz, Victor A. 2007. "The Wisdom of Šūpê-amēlī—A Deathbed Debate Between Father and Son." Pages 37–51 in *Wisdom Literature in Mesopotamia and Israel*. Edited by Richard J. Clifford. SymS 36. Atlanta: Society of Biblical Literature.
Kynes, Will. Forthcoming. "The Nineteenth-Century Beginnings of 'Wisdom Literature,' and Its Twenty-First Century End?" In *Angles on Israelite Wisdom: Proceedings of the Oxford Old Testament Seminar*. Edited by John Jarick. LHBOTS. New York: T&T Clark.
Laisney, Vincent P. M. 2007. *L'enseignement d'Aménémopé*. Rome: Pontifical Biblical Institute.
Lambert, W. G. 1960. *Babylonian Wisdom Literature*. Oxford: Clarendon.
Lichtheim, Miriam. 1973–1981. *Ancient Egyptian Literature*. 3 vols. Berkeley: University of California Press.

Perdue, Leo. *Wisdom and Cult: A Critical Analysis of the Views of Cult in the Wisdom Literatures of Israel and the Ancient Near East.* SBLDS 30. Missoula, MT: Scholars Press, 1977.

Porten, Bezalel, and Ada Yardeni. 1993. *Textbook of Aramaic Documents from Ancient Egypt, 3: Literature, Accounts, Lists.* Jerusalem: Hebrew University.

Quack, Joachim F. 1994. *Die Lehren des Ani: Ein neuägyptischer Weisheitstext in seinem kulturellen Umfeld.* OBO 141. Freiburg: Universitätsverlag; Göttingen: Vandenhoeck & Ruprecht.

Schechter, Solomon, and C. Taylor. 1899. *The Wisdom of Ben Sira: Portions of the Book of Ecclesiasticus from Hebrew Manuscripts in the Cairo Genizah Collection.* Cambridge: Cambridge University Press.

Schipper, Bernd U. 2005. "Die Lehre des Amenemope und Prov 22,17–24,22: Eine Neubestimmung des literarischen Verhältnisses." *ZAW* 117:53–72, 232–48.

Shupak, Nili. 1993. *Where Can Wisdom Be Found? The Sage's Language in the Bible and in Ancient Egyptian Literature.* OBO 130. Freiburg: Universitätsverlag; Göttingen: Vandenhoeck & Ruprecht.

Sneed, Mark. 2011. "Is the 'Wisdom Tradition' a Tradition?" *CBQ* 73:50–71.

Sparks, Kenton L. 2005. *Ancient Texts for the Study of the Hebrew Bible: A Guide to the Background Literature.* Peabody, MA: Hendrickson Publishers.

Whybray, R. N. 1974. *The Intellectual Tradition in the Old Testament.* BZAW 135. Berlin: de Gruyter.

Zahn, Molly. 2012. "Genre and Rewritten Scripture: A Reassessment." *JBL* 131: 271–88.

Zimmermann, H. J. 1985. *Fuzzy Set Theory and Its Applications.* Boston: Kluwer-Nijhoff.

Wisdom in the Canon:
Discerning the Early Intuition

Douglas B. Miller

Biblical scholars of the past century have been asking a form of the question (to borrow from Stanley Fish), "Is there a wisdom text in this Bible?" We thought so, then became less sure.[1] Yet the term *wisdom* persists: there is something attractive about identifying Job, Proverbs, and Ecclesiastes in the Hebrew Bible/Old Testament (often also the apocryphal Ben Sira and Wisdom of Solomon) as distinctive within the canon and similar to each other.

The goals of this essay are modest: to discern the initial intuition that led to the identification of wisdom literature in the Hebrew Bible/Old Testament, and to evaluate its potential for addressing some scholarly puzzles.[2] Thus, it is primarily an argument about scholars and their perceptions. Rather than counting publications and making a statistical case, I reflect on the proposals of representative scholars. The history of the identification of wisdom as a literary category has been recounted in some detail. I begin with an overview that includes highlights of that history,

---

1. Norman Gottwald's reference to "the way in which Israelite sages made use of a genre that had reached definitive form long before Israel had become a nation" is typical of earlier expressions of confidence (Gottwald, 1959, 463–64). In his later introduction to the Hebrew Bible, however, he declared the characterization of wisdom to be "increasingly complicated and vexed." He complained that if one would posit that wisdom is nonrevelatory, with a humanistic orientation and a didactic drive, "it is easy to see 'wisdom' almost everywhere in the Hebrew Bible where there is no direct speech of God" (Gottwald 1985, 564, 567).

2. James Crenshaw, in reference to the five wisdom texts cited above, puts it this way: "However much these literary productions differ from one another, they retain a mysterious ingredient that links them together in a special way" (Crenshaw 1981, 17, and also in the second and third editions [1998, 2010] of his wisdom introduction).

then summarize some developments within the practice of form criticism and recent insights in genre theory. From this background I isolate three characteristics identified by scholars and argue that these together constitute the original intuition by which wisdom literature was identified. In the process, I hope to show that this intuition was justified due to the significance of the three attributes, and because this thesis explains why other commonly recognized characteristics of wisdom literature are less central. I conclude with some reflections on the relevance of this determination.

PROPOSING WISDOM LITERATURE'S ATTRIBUTES

The exploration of wisdom as a distinct literary category in the Bible is primarily a twentieth-century phenomenon that continues to the present.[3] For our discussion, it will be helpful to organize the proposals according to the four components of Berlo's (linear) communication theory: source, message, channel, and receiver. The source is the *wisdom enterprise*, composed of putative sages, schools, traditions, and authors. The message is *wisdom* (including proposals concerning a distinctive theology and/or worldview), and the channel is the macro-genre *wisdom literature* (with its forms, i.e., genres and subgenres).[4] The receiver, addressed only implicitly in this essay, would include *readers* (and/or hearers) actual, intended, and implied.[5] This essay addresses primarily the channel in Berlo's model.

Interestingly, the identification of wisdom literature in the Hebrew Bible was initially broader than Job, Proverbs, and Ecclesiastes; then it narrowed in focus to those three books; and now, for many, it has expanded beyond them again. That oscillation largely reflects the uncertainty of wisdom's definition. Gerhard von Rad, in his *Old Testament Theology* (1962), considered wisdom to be "practical knowledge of the laws of life and of the world, based on experience," an enterprise that eventually focused on

---

3. Crenshaw identifies the initiation of scholarly wisdom study with Hans Meinhold, *Die Weisheit Israels in Spruch, Sage und Dichtung*, 1908 (Crenshaw 1976, 3). Even so, Smend provides an interesting overview of nineteenth-century developments in the study of the wisdom books through a focus on Proverbs (Smend 1995).

4. With John Collins, I understand the quest for distinguishing wisdom literature as part of the search for "macro-genres"—he cites prophecy as another—that hold together a "cluster of related forms" (Collins 1997, 266).

5. Cf. Crenshaw's statement that "wisdom is an attitude, a body of literature, and a living tradition" (Crenshaw 1976, 4).

the task of education; he continues, in his later *Wisdom in Israel*, to examine how "experiential knowledge" (*Erfahrungswissen*) was expressed in Israel's "didactic" (*didaktisch*) literature.⁶ Others interested in the wisdom enterprise noted the purpose of wisdom in specific life contexts. So James Crenshaw distinguished nature, juridical and practical, and theological wisdom, each of which seeks mastery of understanding in its own arena (Crenshaw 1969, 130, 132; see also Wolff 1973, 118–20).

The study of wisdom literature was early entwined with the Hebrew term *ḥokmâ* (usually translated as "wisdom") and eventually other terms found within the wisdom corpus. The word *ḥokmâ* refers to skill for a specific task, such as sewing (Exod 28:3) and working with bronze (1 Kgs 7:14). The adjectival form of the word is used to describe a variety of skilled professionals, such as magicians, boatmen, and mourners (Exod 7:11; Ezek 27:8; Jer 9:16 [Eng. 9:17]). The second major meaning of *ḥokmâ* indicates the ability more generally to assess complex situations, determine the issues involved, and then make the best possible decisions.⁷ This more general sense is where the Bible's wisdom writings focus. Such a skill, for this too can be acquired, involves gaining information to some extent, but even more it means being the kind of person who can live well in a world of complex challenges. Particularly in the book of Proverbs, wisdom is associated with a variety of life habits—often called virtues—that contribute to the prospect of a successful life.

The pursuit of clarity in the definition of wisdom literature and the effort to find appropriate methods for its discernment led to a variety of proposals that I have organized into seven categories. Form is one prominent determinant of this literature.⁸ The one-line (two stich) verse was proposed as basic to wisdom, a form that expanded later to more complex poetry (cf., e.g., the shorter forms in Prov 10–20 with the longer ones in 1–9). Simple evolutionary theories in regard to form have been roundly critiqued, however. Yet sympathy remains for associating

---

6. Von Rad 1962 (German, 1957), 418, 431–32. In *Weisheit in Israel* (German, 1970), he questioned whether the designation wisdom was more of a hindrance than a help; see von Rad 1972, 1–14.

7. While possibly ethically neutral elsewhere, in Proverbs the term denotes a moral virtue (e.g., Prov 1:2–7; cf. Deut 4:6); see Fox 1999, 72.

8. Collins proposes three ways of approaching wisdom's distinctiveness: literary form, worldview, or function and setting (Collins 1997, 265).

wisdom with specific literary types, such as wisdom sayings, fables, disputation, and parables.[9]

A second area of identity is social location. Hermann Gunkel's assumption that each piece of literature belonged to only one genre, and that each of the latter was nestled in a unique *Sitz im Leben* was influential in this effort.[10] Some, as mentioned above, have proposed several loci of wisdom; further examples include court, clan, and family. Buss has correctly argued that though particular literary forms have a specific target audience and setting, these should not be artificially connected with an institution.[11] One dimension of the social location issue is the proposition that wisdom experts, or sages, existed in leadership roles within ancient Israelite society, and that they taught with a certain status or authority. This supposition is largely based on evidence of similar roles in Egypt and Mesopotamia. Within Israelite literature we find only hints, such as the reference or allusion to scribes in 2 Sam 25:30 and Prov 25:1, and the mention of "the wise" in Isa 19:12; 29:14; Jer 8:8; 9:22–23 [Eng. 9:23–24]; 18:18, and elsewhere (Whybray 1990).[12] Regardless of whether such a class or profession can be demonstrated in Israel, it would be incorrect to limit the promotion of wisdom, however defined, to such a group.[13] This is partly because no direct evidence of authorship is available for these writings, but also because any literate person should in principle be capable of producing any type of literature.

A third strategy identifies a list of technical vocabulary or themes that are central to the wisdom enterprise. Those works considered paradigmatic

---

9. See, e.g., the taxonomies of Roland Murphy and John Gammie (Murphy 1981b; Gammie 1990).

10. See the overview in Buss (1999, 244–54), and the discussion of generic realism and generic nominalism in Sparks (2005, 6–7). Gunkel advocated that mood, form, and *Sitz im Leben* were the criteria for identifying the genre of a text.

11. See the historical presentation of this issue in Buss (1999, 357–406). As Raymond Van Leeuwen states, "Matters of religion are *human* functions, and while certain institutions may specialize in those functions, prayer, adoration, celebration, sacrifice, piety, and religious instruction are not per se institutional functions" (Van Leeuwen 2003, 82, emphasis original).

12. Other important texts include Prov 1:6; 22:17; 24:23; Job 15:18; Eccl 12:11. For a discussion of this question, see esp. Whybray (1974, ch. 2).

13. The possibility of a supportive role played by wisdom tradents within Israel's royal establishment, along with its connection to epistemology, has been explored by Walter Brueggemann (e.g., Brueggemann, 1978).

of wisdom, such as the biblical books of Proverbs and Job, were examined for typical vocabulary. Various words for wisdom (e.g., the root *ḥkm* as discussed above) and related concepts were identified, in addition to terms such as fool/foolish(ness), discipline, plan, path, favor, and phrases like the fear of Yahweh. Whybray, in his critique of this approach used to identify wisdom influence elsewhere, notes that two criteria are essential: the proposed vocabulary must be characteristic of Job, Proverbs, and Ecclesiastes, and it must reflect the topics that are distinctive to those books, that is, problems faced by human society and human individuals. More specifically, he identifies human conduct, the consequences of such conduct, and the search for knowledge and prosperity. Recognizing that the choice of such a list will always involve subjective factors, he notes several challenges to the effort, such as the fact that even in regard to distinctive topics, terminology is certain to be used that also is used frequently in nonwisdom texts. He identifies nine terms in addition to *ḥkm* that may be genuinely distinctive of the wisdom tradition (Whybray 1974, ch. 4). Characteristic themes include the two ways and the so-called doctrine of retribution (the righteous are blessed, the wicked are judged).[14]

A fourth perspective sometimes goes by the label humanism.[15] The fundamental purpose of wisdom has been called a quest for self-understanding with attention given to the way wisdom writings begin with the human condition, its perceptions, questions, and needs. This approach recognizes that wisdom writings tend to focus on the individual more than the group, and the family more than the entire culture, though exceptions to the latter include references to the king and to other leaders (e.g., Prov 8:15–16; 14:35; Eccl 4:9–16; 8:1–9). Wisdom writings are also discerned to be more international in their approach (low reference to Israel as a distinctive people) and secular (low reference to God and to religious matters).[16] The most obvious exceptions to these criteria are Ben Sira and

---

14. Oliver Rankin (*Israel's Wisdom Literature*, 1936) listed God as creator, divine and human responsibility, divine providence, reward and punishment, and belief in a future life (cited by Rowley 1951, 211–12).

15. So Driver (1897, 393); Oliver Rankin (*Israel's Wisdom Literature*, 1936, 3), cited in Davidson (1964, 154).

16. As found in Rowley's summary (Rowley 1951, 211). Murphy calls the "most striking" characteristic of wisdom literature the "absence of what one normally considers Israelite and Jewish" (Murphy 1990, 1). This aspect is also identified in nineteenth-century scholarship (Smend 1995, 263–64, 266).

the Wisdom of Solomon. Some propose that these noncanonical books—with their celebration of Israel's Torah, salvation history, and heroes—reflect a merging of two spheres later in Israel's history, that this constitutes an injection of *Heilsgeschichte* (the record of dramatic divine intervention) into the more secular wisdom enterprise. However, regarding that supposed secularity, we find worship allusions in all three canonical books, along with numerous references to the deity: Job (well over 200 times), Proverbs (over 100 times), Ecclesiastes (*'ĕlōhîm* 40 times), for an average of four references per chapter in each book. Some have claimed that the presentation of God is less personal in Job, Proverbs, and Ecclesiastes than elsewhere in the Hebrew Bible, yet most admit that the theophany of Job is a major exception. Further, the use of *Yahweh*, Israel's personal name for the deity, is prominent in Proverbs and in the framing story of the book of Job.

A fifth approach has focused on wisdom as didactic, a major motivation in the texts to teach about life. Wisdom wishes to pass along matters of importance to those in one's community and in particular to the next generation. Inspired by the reformer Martin Luther, Hans Walter Wolff titles a section of the Hebrew canon "The Books of Teaching," which were "intended to cast light on the present life." These include Job, Proverbs, and Ecclesiastes, along with Psalms and didactic stories (Wolff 1973, 101–37). Zimmerli also refers to wisdom writings as "instructing" the student and others (Zimmerli 1978, 157; also Davidson 1964, 143–44). In Scott's succinct description of those who speak for wisdom in Israel, he emphasizes that "their method is counsel and instruction, and, at a later stage, persuasion and debate" (Scott 1971, 5).[17]

Approach six embraces both major meanings of *ḥokmâ* cited above and emphasizes that wisdom was concerned with practical daily success, the ordering of one's life, and the manipulation of creation for success and prosperity. Zimmerli, in his outline of Old Testament theology, titles his discussion of wisdom "Mastery of Everyday Life and Its Concrete Secrets" (Zimmerli 1978, 155). Crenshaw's list of wisdom attributes, all of which he significantly qualifies, includes eudaemonism: a commitment to happiness and personal well-being (Crenshaw 1985, 369). Wisdom literature

---

17. Scott's summary also includes a focus on the individual, setting aside concern for institutional religion and Israel's sense of special relationship with Yahweh, a concern for the everyday world, and an authority that arises from "the moral experience and trained intelligence of genuinely religious men" (1971, 4–5).

makes the most of life in this world, both by avoiding problems and by maximizing life's potential.

A seventh approach contends that a distinctive version of Israel's worldview underlies the wisdom writings. Smend summarizes that, for an extended period, nineteenth-century scholars identified wisdom with philosophy (Smend 1995, 265–66). In particular, a focus on creation (even a creation soteriology) was often cited as characteristic of true wisdom and sometimes also an empiricist methodology (von Rad 1972, 314; Murphy 1979). Certainly empirical tendencies can be recognized, particularly in Ecclesiastes (e.g., 4:1–8, 13–16). But in fact, both in Israel's writings and among its neighbors the proposed wisdom texts were thoroughly (poly) theistic and allowed for revelatory experiences beyond those typically attributed to the five senses. Even Qoheleth draws upon theological tradition to state the things that he knows about God (e.g., Eccl 2:24–26; 3:10–15, 17; 4:16–5:6 [Eng. 5:1–7]; 7:29; 8:12–13, 16–17). Another element often highlighted is the deed-consequence relationship (typically connected with the so-called doctrine of retribution or the search for order), promoted by Proverbs but challenged by Job and Ecclesiastes.[18] Proposed wisdom worldviews involve a vision of a distant, fearful, and powerful Creator who oversees and directs human lives according to a mysterious plan.

This brief review illustrates attempts to identify wisdom literature as that which exists in certain forms, involves certain vocabulary or themes, manifests in certain social contexts, is humanistic, is concerned with teaching, seeks practical success, and/or reflects a distinctive philosophical or worldview orientation. Each of these categories seems inadequate in itself to embody the distinction that is wisdom, and yet each represents an important aspect of wisdom's characterization. The fifth, sixth, and seventh items will be discussed further below.

Developments in Form Criticism and Genology

Studies in theory and method may help evaluate the efforts given to understand wisdom literature. Marvin A. Sweeney and Ehud Ben Zvi, in

---

18. Wisdom's search for order was emphasized by von Rad (1972, 308) and others (see discussion in Kaiser 1975, 367–68). Crenshaw traces the journey of Murphy who began with a conviction that order was central to wisdom and later abandoned it (Crenshaw 1987). Crenshaw disagrees with Murphy's eventual conviction that the sages embraced Yahwism and therefore were committed to divine freedom.

the introduction to the essay collection they edited on future directions in form criticism, summarize how a shift has taken place from a more diachronic approach (with focus on *Sitz im Leben*) to a more synchronic approach (with more concern for *Sitz in der Literatur*). This shift has been complemented by increased attention to rhetorical criticism and canonical intertextuality, among others. Though still considered important, the difficult-to-recover social location of forms or of a given text has given way to more concern for the interrelation of a text and forms with other texts (Sweeney and Ben Zvi 2003, 1–11).

Carol Newsom's helpful review of developments within genology, the theory of genres, provides a way to understand the impasse in wisdom studies as well as perhaps a way forward (Newsom 2007). She points out that "genre recognition involves some sort of mental grouping of texts on the basis of perceived similarity" (Newsom 2007, 22) and yet, as Alastair Fowler notes, "genres at all levels are positively resistant to definition" (Fowler 1982, 40). Like the study of the apocalypse that Newsom uses as an example, wisdom research has pursued an intuition that a particular genre exists, and similarly, has identified characteristic traits of various sample texts (see Sparks 2005, 9). She reviews Wittgenstein's proposal that we typically group texts according to family resemblances. Yet this has complications. For example, if we consider three texts classified together by this principle—text 1 with traits a, b, and c, text 2 with b, c, and d, and text 3 with d, e, and f—all three texts would have elements in common. Yet texts 1 and 3, with no such similarities, would be classified in the same family.

The intertextual approaches of Jonathan Culler and Alastair Fowler seek to overcome this limitation by focusing upon the way texts are distinguished through their relationship with other texts (Culler 1975; Fowler 1982). In their view, genres are fluid and dynamic, sometimes playfully subverted; all texts are influenced by encounters with other texts, producing multiple generic variations in response to what has come before (Fowler 1982, 41–43).[19]

Building on that understanding, those who advocate cognitive theories of categories as applied to literature emphasize that prototypical

---

19. Though taking a more diachronic approach, Fowler is concerned to avoid direct identification between the tracking of genre family resemblances and source criticism. As distinctive examples of the former, he cites such phenomena as polygenesis and remote influences.

examples are central to genre recognition.[20] A good example, provided by Newsom, is the New Testament book of Revelation as a prototype for the apocalypse. "As applied to genre categories, prototype theory requires an identification of exemplars that are prototypical and an analysis of the privileged properties that establish the sense of typicality" (Newsom 2007, 24). Some properties are considered central while others are considered peripheral. A recognition of genre takes place within a gestalt structure of textual elements.[21]

Job, Proverbs, and Ecclesiastes are the acknowledged "prototypes" for wisdom literature. Yet how could such diverse writings be considered part of the same macro-genre?[22] I propose to identify three characteristics that operated as central and essential markers of wisdom within the biblical canon, a gestalt structure of elements. The relationship of these three provides an inner coherence for wisdom literature; the remaining four elements (from the list of seven above) are peripheral and inconsistently present.

Discerning the Initial *Discrimen*

It is not too difficult to craft a narrative of theological favor and disfavor within the community of texts we call the Hebrew Bible or Old Testament. Whatever the process of their initial incorporation, once the canon was recognized, the individual members were celebrated for representing the "age-long dialogue between Yahweh, Israel's covenant God, and this people which he had chosen to hear his call, obey his commandments, and serve his purposes on earth" (Scott 1971, 2). The books we now identify as wisdom were immensely popular in Europe's medieval period (Murphy

---

20. Similarly, Fowler speaks of paradigmatic authors (Fowler 1982, 57).

21. Notice how, when it comes to a canon and other such formations of text communities, the usual distinction between synchronic and diachronic becomes suspended. The canon forms its own artificial synchronism by which the texts relate to each other suspended in time. A text (arguably) from the far reaches of Israel's past becomes associated with those from a much more recent era, and readers distinguish these two in relation to each other (as well as in relation to all the others).

22. Crenshaw, in reference to the mysterious ingredient that links these books together, adds, "This bond is so powerful that it prompts interpreters to use these works as a norm" (Crenshaw 1981, 17). I am postponing a discussion of Ben Sira and the Wisdom of Solomon because they were never acknowledged as part of the Hebrew Bible canon.

1990, ix). Subsequently, the effort to achieve a biblical theology (traced by many to Johann Gabler in 1787 but preceded by many other efforts) began respectfully enough for the wisdom writings. As long as biblical texts were used primarily to support the tenets of the historic creeds or dogmatics (during much of seventeenth- and eighteenth-century Europe), or when the theology of the Bible was simply discussed in canonical order, they were welcome on the playground.[23] Eventually the biblical theology venture, and especially the Old Testament effort, moved away from dogmatics and gave greater opportunity to the texts to speak for themselves. In the process, the wisdom writings became devalued. Sometimes they were considered late in the historical development of Israel's religion—as if the glow of God's great activity with Israel was fading and being replaced by the pagan thinking of unwelcome neighbors. More thematically oriented works, such as the magisterial accomplishments of Walther Eichrodt and Gerhard von Rad in the mid-twentieth century, placed prominent emphasis, respectively, on God's covenant with Israel and on the testimony of God's faithfulness in salvation history. In both cases, Proverbs, Job, and Ecclesiastes were further marginalized. Fortunately, out of such exclusion came efforts to discern commonalities among these wisdom books.

Initially, these books tended to be identified by characteristics they lacked: no mention of Israel's covenant, no emphasis on special revelation, no emphasis on the mighty acts of Israel's God, the creation of the world but not the creation of Israel as a people, and so on. And yet intuitively, scholars recognized that these works belonged to each other—not just for what they lacked, but for what was similar among them. I propose that the scholarly intuition that distinguished the Bible's wisdom books from others in the canon involved the confluence of three attributes: (1) persuasion in their rhetoric (i.e., instruction), (2) realized eschatology (the goal of making the most of present existence), and (3) an epistemology rooted in human experience.[24] For each in turn, I will substantiate

---

23. For an example of the former, though beginning to break the bonds of dogmatic theology, see notably Cocceius (1648). For an example of the latter, see Oehler (1883), who devotes only thirty pages of a nearly six-hundred-page tome to wisdom, yet with admiration for its role in Israel's writings.

24. See also Crenshaw's discussion of defining wisdom. His first point connects biblical wisdom to those elsewhere in the ancient Near East because they too are instructions; his third point evaluates wisdom as a worldview that begins by asking "what is good for men and women," and in addition "it believes that all essential

the scholarly attention given, then show their legitimacy as indicators of wisdom literature.

Persuasive Rhetoric

Wisdom is didactic literature. We begin with the last of von Rad's defining attributes for wisdom texts. What is didactic (instructional) about certain writings, and how can this characteristic be discerned? If we consider literature to be the combined corpus of rhetorical and poetical writings, the Bible contains both, but more of the former than the latter.[25] In classical terms, rhetorical speech, including written works, are "those instances of formal, premeditated, sustained monologue in which a person seeks to exert an effect on an audience" (Corbett 1990, 3). These effects are of three types, the first two being forensic (a focus on the past in which someone defends or condemns someone's actions) and epideictic (a focus more on the present concerned to reinforce values already believed). The third type is deliberative, with a focus on the future. The latter writings "seek to persuade someone to do something or to accept [the writer's] point of view" (Corbett 1990, 28–29).

The Old Testament illustrates mostly the second and third types.[26] Some writings are more epideictic: they reinforce and inspire persons to stay the course. Examples include the narratives of Israel's history, which demonstrate positive choices to emulate and negative ones to avoid. The Psalms, as well as worship pieces scattered throughout the canon, also fill such a role. The same rhetoric is notable among the legal-like material in

---

answers can be learned in experience" (Crenshaw 1981, 17–18). In contrast, Katharine Dell contends "that a study of form, content and context is a valid method, and that only when we have these three aspects in large measure can a book be strictly defined as 'wisdom literature'" (Dell 2000, 5).

25. Of the four primary elements of written communication (source, message, channel, receiver), poetic works emphasize the message itself and rhetorical works emphasize the receiver. That is, rhetorical works attempt to accomplish goals apart from the work itself, while poetic works have a goal not apart from the works. I draw here upon Boucher who concludes, "The biblical writings are essentially rhetorical; that is true of the Bible as a whole, of most of the books within the Bible, and of most of the smaller units within the books" (1977, 16).

26. Forensic literature is most obvious in the criticisms made by prophets such as Amos, but may also be discerned in the DtrH narrator's assessment of monarchs and others.

Exodus, Leviticus, Numbers, and Deuteronomy. Deliberative rhetoric is found among the energizing prophets, such as Amos and exilic Isaiah and Ezekiel, as they seek to motivate faithfulness in the midst of Israel's various challenging circumstances. We find a similar function in the hortatory sections of Ezra and Nehemiah, as well as in many of the lament psalms.

In most cases, the process of education involves epideictic rhetoric.[27] It seeks to reinforce adherence to values already believed by the audience or the community of which the audience is a part. Such a purpose is stated overtly in Prov 1:2–6. This instruction encourages alignment with understandings that will change the way one acts and/or thinks moving forward. It encourages the listener/student to adopt virtues of humility, diligence, respect for God, fidelity in relationships, self-mastery, a devaluing of wealth compared to other values that are more important, and many more. Cultivation of virtues, through study, reflection, and mentoring, requires repeated decisions until life habits are formed (Brown 1996, ch. 1).

Wisdom writings employ a variety of techniques to encourage just such choices. Most often action is commended for being advantageous, for example, Wisdom promises wealth to those who love her (Prov 8:21). Occasionally a choice is commended for being good, that is, aligning with Yahweh's values or character. Wisdom declares that her nature is to hate evil and pride (Prov 8:13). Sometimes the status of the teacher is emphasized, as when the title of mother and father are invoked in Proverbs 1:8. Similarly, the status of Qoheleth as a sage is cited in the epilogue of Ecclesiastes (12:9–11). Job and his story are commended to the reader by establishing that Job was "blameless and upright, one who feared God and turned away from evil" (Job 1:1 NRSV).

Where the determination of the type of rhetoric becomes more slippery is when an educator sharply challenges the values of the audience.[28] Qoheleth urges his audience to change their thinking and practice in a variety of ways, for example, in chapter 4. The dialogue at the center of the book of Job may be an example of how all three types of rhetoric intersect and overlap: the intent to defend or condemn past actions, to commend

---

27. See the discussion in Perelman and Olbrechts-Tyteca (1969, 47–54). Thus Scott makes the case that Psalm 1 is wisdom because it is didactic; its purpose is "to commend and justify the choice of a devout life rather than a wicked or worldly one" (Scott 1971, 193).

28. On the conception of epideictic rhetoric and its role in motivating change, see Sheard, who speaks of epideictic's "deliberative functions" (1996, 784–87).

good and disparage wrong values, and to motivate a radical change with future implications. For our purposes, the terms instruction and didactic will embrace both values-affirming and change-oriented rhetoric.

In sum, Job, Proverbs, and Ecclesiastes are didactic: "information is being passed on by someone in authority, and someone is being instructed about human conduct or about life in general" (Murphy 1981b, 7).[29] Further, they have a common instructive emphasis: in the form we now find them, all three seek to reinforce the fear of God, an understanding that engages all of one's life and efforts (Job 1:1, 8–9; 28:28; Prov 1:7; 9:10; Eccl 5:1, 6 [Eng. 5:2, 7]). In what sense, however, does such a determination distinguish these writings from others in the Hebrew canon?

One could argue that in some sense the entire Hebrew canon is didactic. The texts have been gathered to instruct present and future generations on the history, character, and values of the community's relationship with God. But much of this is literature put to secondary use. The purpose of worship material is to help lead people in worship. It can be instructive, and we have reason to believe that the book of Psalms has been edited to heighten that potential. But the essential purpose of Psalms is to aid the practical worship life of the community.[30]

Similarly with law. A community's legal material is not literature by the definition given above, but in the Pentateuch it has become part of a literary work (premeditated, sustained monologue). This is most obvious in Deuteronomy where codes are now part of Moses's last testament to the people. Such casuistic-type legal material presents community-administered consequences for certain actions or lack of action. But in the Pentateuch, this material has been put to secondary use: a record of the history and values of the community. Thus it is instructional, a form of epideictic rhetoric, and as such has affinities to wisdom. This secondary use of prescriptions in the Torah overlaps with the appeals of the sages to seek out one's best advantage in daily life; the law and wisdom genres began to influence each other (Blenkinsopp 1995, esp. chs. 5 and 6).[31] Likewise, stories told to celebrate the cleverness of an underdog or to illustrate God's

---

29. Collins asserts that the "coherence of wisdom literature ... lies in its use as instructional material rather than in literary form, strictly defined" or by worldview, as he demonstrates through various wisdom writings from Qumran (Collins 1997, 281).

30. Whether we find wisdom psalms among this collection is a separate question.

31. Note his treatment of Pss 1, 19, and others that celebrate the value of Torah for successful living.

providential care for the ancestors, put to secondary use in the sacred canon, became instructional in a broad sense.

In each of these cases—worship, law, narrative—generic forms began to influence each other. The content of psalms became a source for reflection; legal material began to instruct beyond the implication of community-imposed consequences; folklore and other narrative assumed parabolic roles.[32] Certainly stories may be used tropically to carry a message indirectly. So, in the case of Joseph, we may recognize a message not simply about God's providential care for a family who tote a bouquet of promises that will play themselves out over many generations. Rather, we suspect that behavior is described in detail to serve as a model for making choices in the midst of strained and threatening circumstances.[33] Thus, regarding wisdom writings, von Rad and others were correct to discern the didactic concern as an essential part of their identity. Yet the wisdom designation becomes of little value if every text put to secondary instructive use is for that reason considered wisdom literature.

Realized Eschatology

Wisdom literature concerns practical knowledge of the laws of life and the world. The term eschatology refers to the study of last things, the ultimate goal toward which all things are traveling, the outcome often proposed to be achieved by a future cataclysm. For present purposes, however, I intend not to use eschatology so narrowly. Rather I use it to designate the divine direction or plan that is promoted by a given outlook or orientation to reality. In the sense that I will use, every canonical piece

---

32. See, e.g., Landes 1978. As Boucher insists, the terms *māšāl* and *parabolē*, essentially identical as they are used in the biblical texts, were "in flux and undefined in both the Semitic and classical traditions. All that can be said is that the words … were used by the ancients to refer to any unusual or striking speech. Their meanings were no more precise than this" (Boucher 1977, 13). Thus, in such literary investigations we need our own terms, and carefully defined, to speak clearly. Landes discusses five different forms identified as *māšāl* in the Hebrew Bible and concludes that all have a didactic function (Landes, 139–46).

33. Boucher helpfully describes direct and indirect forms of communication and locates the terms *allegory* and *parable* within the variety of tropical modes available to a writer (Boucher 1977, 18–25). Von Rad demonstrates numerous ways in which Joseph models the virtues of Proverbs as well as articulating the theology of that book (von Rad 1966). See also Wills (1990).

of didactic literature has an eschatology, that is, a vision for life's ultimate goal. This may be hopeful or it may be more pessimistic, but it radically shapes the educational enterprise.[34]

For many, the eschatology of Israel is located primarily in the imaginative proclamations of its prophets and the visions of its apocalyptic seers. For example, Zephaniah (1:14–18) and Amos (5:18–20) announce the anticipated "day of Yahweh," and the book of Daniel contains apocalyptic visions (Dan 7–12). Yet the broader conception of eschatology developed by C. H. Dodd in his assessment of the Gospels' presentation of Jesus's kingdom teachings may have value for the Hebrew Bible as well. Dodd argued convincingly that there is in New Testament understanding both a present inbreaking of the kingdom and an ultimate fulfillment yet to come. In his view, and also that of Joachim Jeremias, Jesus announced the act of God that burst onto the historical scene yet left a tension reflected in two of Jesus's phrases: "Thy kingdom come" and "The kingdom of God has come upon you" (Dodd 1961, 167).[35] Such a realized eschatology has certain affinities to texts within Israel's canon—not the fulfillment of the future foreseen by prophets, but a parallel understanding that God blesses in the ongoing present.

A tension between present and future may be found, for example, in the book of Psalms. Thanksgiving psalms celebrate God's work in the past, while psalms of lament long for a future healing of harms. But the praise hymns envision a present blessed reality in which God's wishes for the creation are now taking place. Hymns of praise celebrate the God who blesses and gives life, much as we find in the narrative accounts of Gen 1–3 (see, e.g., Pss 82:8; 68:20–35; 76:12; 97:1–6; 104:31–35; 108; 144).

Israel's covenants similarly present a hopeful vision for the ongoing life of the people with their God. The call of God to Abraham anticipated blessing to the whole world (Gen 12:1–3). The law that accompanied the covenant through Moses presented a hopeful vision of vibrant life in the present with provision for failures that could occur. The new covenant (Jer 31:33; Ezek 36:26–28; 37:13–14; Joel 2:28–29) offered even more hope. We

---

34. In fact, it could be argued that all forms of literature present or imply a story (past) and cast or imply a vision (future), however near or far that future may be conceived. See the discussion of this issue, from Plato to John Dewey, in Groome 1980, 7–10.

35. According to Jeremias, Dodd agreed with his own formulation: "eschatology that is in the process of realization" (Jeremias 1972, 230).

should also note the psalms that celebrate Torah instruction (e.g., Pss 1, 19, 119) as a reflection of divine goodness and standards that promote hope in the midst of shortcomings.

This small sample reminds us that there is a diversity of eschatological vision (in the broad sense) among Israel's canonical writings. Some obviously emphasize a future salvation, while others display an expectation of God's present blessings.

The vision of the wisdom writings is addressed more to the present reality within this canonical continuum.[36] Granted, wisdom also refers to ending points. Proverbs speaks of final accountability when it warns of the end of the wicked or the outcome of certain actions (e.g., Prov 2:22; 5:11; 6:12–15; 14:12; 16:18, 25; 18:12; 20:21; 24:20) and promises eternal and future blessing for the righteous (e.g., 10:25, 30; 13:21; 16:20; 19:20; 24:14; note the contrasts in 10:7–9, 16–17; 23:17–18). But Proverbs most of all invites disciples to a life of ongoing training in blessedness in the midst of challenges (2:20–21; 3:35; 4:18; 12:18; 13:14–17; 15:24). In particular, Lady Wisdom embodies this vision (e.g., ch. 8).

The speculative wisdom voices of Job and Ecclesiastes question loudly whether the hopefulness embodied in standard wisdom rings true. Yet what I am calling the realized eschatology of wisdom literature holds even for these books, for they engage the tension inherent in the issue.

The book of Job symbolizes the unjust suffering of one righteous person and alludes to that of others; however, though he considers Sheol his ultimate resting place (e.g., 7:9; cf. 3:11–19), Job's cries also include hope for positive developments in this world (19:25–27; 23:10), culminating in the appearance and engagement of the deity (38:1–42:6). In a marvelous display of community deliberation that fails to resolve the mystery of life's incongruities, the book manifests a hopeful vision in motion: an abused righteous man who retains his integrity is reinstated, strained and battered relationships are restored, and the deity's oversight brings good out of bad.[37]

As for Ecclesiastes, we must first recognize that some read the book as an extremely pessimistic treatise while others discern more hopeful notes

---

36. "The worldview usually ascribed to wisdom has a markedly this-worldly character. It might be described as a kind of natural theology, that is by no means secular" (Collins 1997, 267).

37. This, of course, is not an attempt to summarize the message of the book, as Newsom warns against (2003, 259–64).

among the hard tunes the author plays on his instrument. For our present discussion, given these different approaches, we ask what vision the book communicates for the present or future. I propose that several characteristics of Ecclesiastes transcend the polarized interpretations of the book as a whole. The first of these is Qoheleth's assessment of the wisdom enterprise, which is positive though highly qualified. Notably Qoheleth adopts the methods and agenda found in Job and Proverbs, such as the exploration of human experience (Eccl 1:13; 2:1; 4:1), deliberation upon it (1:14-15; 2:2; 4:2-3), and pronouncement of practical conclusions for the benefit of the reader/student (2:24; 3:12-13; 4:9-12).[38] Further, he never advises to embrace folly or wickedness but advocates for wisdom and righteousness (consider 5:1-7; 7:11-12, 15-18; 9:13-18). Second, he demonstrates determined confidence that God is just and deserving of fear, and that ultimately it will be well for the righteous (3:16-17; 8:12-13; 11:9). Finally, we find the assessment of the epilogist (either a disciple or a self-commendation) that Qoheleth is a sage whose words are carefully chosen and worthy of embracing (12:9-11). As for a vision of the end, what Qoheleth presents appears bleak: darkness, death, the breath of life returns to God who gave it. But for matters of the present, his major focus, we find an outlook a bit more cheering. Life contains at least pockets of pleasure that should be enjoyed, though in themselves they will not satisfy (e.g., 2:24-26, preceded by 2:1-23). His encouragement that life in community (4:9-12) can overcome competitive, individualistic, and workaholic patterns (4:4-8) contrasts with his discussion of oppression and political futility in that same context (4:1-3, 13-16). He also holds insistently to a confidence that God will justly judge those who deserve it (8:12-13).

In sum, the canonical wisdom writings focus upon and advocate for a successful life in the present.

Experiential Epistemology

Finally, wisdom literature is based on experience. This kind of writing motivates its students to be and to act for the present good by an appeal to the broad range of human experience: what the wise have observed and passed along, but also what the pupil can discern by looking to his neigh-

---

38. Some interpreters, of course, insist that the book is primarily a venting of Qoheleth's frustrations. Yet even such readers recognize that the sage, as mentioned above, advocates for certain choices, however tinged with cynicism they find them to be.

bor's fields and to the ants at his feet. Other canonical examples of such appeals to human experience, sometimes attributed to wisdom influence, may be better accounted for as part of the diversity of ways the divine was understood to communicate with human beings.

I believe that Roland Murphy was correct that wisdom writings reflect "an approach to reality that was shared by all Israelites in varying degrees" (Murphy 1978, 39).[39] Thus, a distinction between what is sometimes called general revelation on the one hand and special revelation on the other is a matter of a continuum in Israel's literature.[40] As Murphy proposed, there is a shared view in Israel that God sometimes works through the regular and predictable, and sometimes through the unusual and unexpected.[41] Nor is there any particular tension that God does either one or the other in greater abundance. Reading through the accounts of God's amazing encounters with Abraham, Sarah, Isaac, Jacob, Joseph, Moses, the prophets, and others, one easily spots the tremendous periods of silence from God that sometimes, as with the promise of Isaac's birth, become an important part of the plot. One might even consider that the modus of general revelation is a way of maintaining communion with the will and ways of God in between those special times of communication that Moses, Abraham, and others could never predict.

Examples on the more experiential end of the epistemological range within the canon include the implication of providence in Mordecai's suggestion to Esther that she attained a royal position "for just such a time as this" (Esth 4:14 NRSV); the predicament of the daughters of Zelophahad that led to a reformulation of divinely approved law (Num 27:1–11); divine direction traced through the Joseph novella (Gen 37–50); and the books of Ezra and Nehemiah. Little or nothing of direct divine encounter or communication is found in these accounts, and yet there are indications that God is providentially involved.

---

39. James Barr previously argued for revelatory "axes" in addition to holy history that he believed were "equally pervasive and important" within the canon of Scripture (1963, 10).

40. Epistemological contrasts have been noted, esp. between sages and prophets. Prophets may need to challenge the inherent social conservatism of some versions of wisdom, but this does not mean that the modes of discerning God's direction are inherently at odds. See Brueggemann 1978 and Scott 1971, 101–35.

41. Also see his argument in Murphy 1981a.

What we find in biblical wisdom writings avoids complete empiricism on one extreme, and on the other does not require (yet allows for) special revelatory events.[42] The latter is especially notable with the appearance and speeches of God to Job for which he longed and cried (Job 38–41), but also more subtly in the assertions of Qoheleth that certain things about God can indeed be known (Eccl 1:13; 3:10–11, 14–15, 17–18; 5:1–7; 6:1–2; 7:13–14; 8:17; 9:1; 11:5, 9; 12:7). As in the book of Proverbs, Qoheleth draws upon traditions about God that cannot be accounted for through everyday observation.

In fact, Fox argues convincingly that the sages only occasionally reference their experience to justify the content of their teaching. He says Qoheleth differs by attempting to be thoroughly empirical, though he is not consistent (Fox 1999, 80–82). It is more accurate to say that Qoheleth gives the appearance of an experience-based epistemology and rhetoric. He does this by citing the experiments he has conducted and the things he has seen (e.g., Eccl 1:12–2:11; 4:1–3) while relying much more on ethos, his credibility, to be convincing (Miller 2000). Yet neither do Job nor Proverbs, on the whole, appeal to divine encounter to justify their insights.

In sum, it is correct to conclude that in the range between personal and empirical data as the basis for conclusions, on the one hand, and special divine encounters and communication on the other, the wisdom writings emphasize the former over the latter.

---

42. Some scholars, such as William McKane and Diethelm Michel (cited in Fox 1999), have proposed that old wisdom is empirical and lacking in ethical elements, so that what we find in the Bible reflects a mixture of the old with the more pietistic (McKane 1965, 16–17; Fox 1999, 80–82). In a related issue, McKane, Scott, and, more recently, Penchansky claim that some of the material in Proverbs assumes human effort to achieve wisdom and other sections understand wisdom to be God's gift (McKane 1970, e.g., 302–6; 420–21; Penchansky 2012, 22–25; Scott 1965, 15–17). We should consider that there could be such differences, especially between traditional proverbial wisdom and the forms produced in a more culturally developed context. It is important to recognize, however, that wisdom-like writings elsewhere in the ancient Near East likewise reflect an openness to divine interruption and to knowledge obtained not strictly through ordinary experience with the five senses. Only rarely, however, do we find explicit claims to a divine source in such wisdom. On the other hand, a lack of reference to the divine does not necessarily imply a nontheological understanding of wisdom. In Prov 2:1–8, for example, both aspects of this paradoxical, or perhaps synergistic, understanding are manifest together in the same wisdom poem (to paraphrase): "if you make wisdom high priority and seek it with all your being, you will find it … because YHWH gives wisdom" (see Murphy 1990, 114–15).

Relation to Other Proposed Characteristics

Our focus has been limited to literature within the Hebrew canon. I have proposed a three-part gestalt—instructional rhetoric, realized eschatology, experiential epistemology—from which we can now consider whether the other four characteristics of this literature we noted at the outset are central or peripheral.

Specific Forms

The diversity of forms among Job, Proverbs, and Ecclesiastes means that form is not a central determinant of Hebrew Bible wisdom. A few of the forms proposed in Murphy's study are found among two or more of these three books, for example, admonition, anecdote, appeal to ancient tradition, better saying, description of experience, disputation, example story, instruction, numerical saying, paraenesis, proverb, reflection, and wisdom poem. But not all apply to all three, some to only one, and the literary concept of each is different: Job is primarily a disputation, Proverbs instruction, and Ecclesiastes a complex interplay and parody of forms such as fictional royal autobiography, instruction, and reflection. Elsewhere in the canon, disputation by prophets, instruction by priests, and anecdotes by those who govern are not strong indicators of wisdom literature. Outside of the canon, each of the three books has its analogs. Yet in other ancient Near Eastern instructional material as well as in later Israelite examples, the disjunction between form and content is continually manifest.[43]

Specific Themes and Vocabulary

Neither themes nor vocabulary can be considered central to the determination of canonical wisdom literature. Some topics are certainly shared among the three books, for example, wisdom, passing generations, labor, judgment, blessing. Creation has been proposed as a theme that unites Job, Proverbs, and Ecclesiastes, yet not every reference to creation in the canon has wisdom associations (cf. Gen 1–3; Pss 8; 104; and Isa 40–55 with such texts as Prov 8; Job 38–41; and Eccl 12:1–7). Themes in common

---

43. Collins demonstrates through the Qumran material that "the forms of sapiential instruction are not necessarily tied to a particular kind of content or a single worldview" (Collins 1997, 278).

that arise from a similar eschatology and epistemology, not to mention a larger shared worldview, are to be expected. Whybray has shown the limited usefulness of overlaps in vocabulary. His caution concerning the difficulties of avoiding circular arguments applies to themes as well as to terms (Whybray 1974, 155–56). Outside the canon, instructional literature has shown both similarity to and diversity from the canonical books.

A Particular Social Context

This issue can be approached from two directions. One argues historically concerning the situation and people involved in the wisdom enterprise and/or the receivers of the literature. Most of the arguments in regard to social context have been of this type and have been based upon speculated similarities to what is known in other ancient Near Eastern cultures, for example, sages, schools. A second approach employs only the literature itself in regard to implied authors or implied audience. Staying within the scope of the present study, and taking up the latter, we could note arguments that the implied audience for the three canonical books has similarities, for example, middle classes, literate, male. Because of their pervasiveness, however, these specific aspects are not helpful for distinguishing genre. Certainly the confluence of the three gestalt attributes suggests the *plausibility* of a particular social role: a teacher who draws upon the insights obtained from everyday experience (and from others who have done the same) and who offers shrewd practical advice. Outside the canon, arguments of the second type have been aided by the prologue to Ben Sira and such references as to a "house of instruction" as in Sir 51:23. In sum, very little concerning social context in Job, Proverbs, and Ecclesiastes, if anything, will lead us to conclusions that distinguish this literature from others in the canon.

Humanism

Israelite wisdom literature's eschatology and epistemology suggest it has a close connection to human experience, goals, and longings. That is one sense of the term *humanism*, and all apply to Job, Proverbs, and Ecclesiastes. In addition, we could add their international character, if by that we mean a downplaying of Israelite distinctives, such as the call of Yahweh, the history of God's acts on their behalf, lack of concern for the land of promise, and even religious practice in general. Yet claiming these elements amounts to an argument from silence. Further, each of the three books has a definite Israelite connection: Job's use of the name Yahweh; the same for Proverbs; and Ecclesiastes's statements regarding David, Jerusalem, the "house of God" (Eccl 4:17 [Eng.. 5:1]), plus its allusions to Solomon. All refer to religious practice in some ways, and notably Job contains several references to divine communication in addition to its theophany (Job 4:12–21; 33:14–18; 36:2–4; 38–42). Thus, a determination that the three books are humanistic is not very helpful for distinguishing them from other canonical literature. Other texts are also very concerned with this-worldly prosperity (Deuteronomy, Ezra, Nehemiah), and others mention little or nothing about the God of Israel or even the divine realm (Ruth, Esther, Song of Songs). So on the one hand, we can say that this element does fit nicely with our prototypical wisdom texts in the canon, but on the other that this is of little consequence and better set aside. The same applies to literature outside the canon. All ancient Near Eastern instructional texts reflect a religious worldview, and later Israelite texts make their theological perspective even more prominent and yet also more diverse.[44]

Conclusion: Relevance

I have argued that among the seven major categories of characteristics used to define Israel's canonical wisdom literature, three are significant as a gestalt by which to appreciate this macro-genre. Job, Proverbs, and Ecclesiastes should be understood as the prototypes. They are instructional, primarily epideictic rhetoric (they reinforce values but also challenge toward new understandings). They display an eschatology with more emphasis on the present realization of God's blessings than a future catastrophic inbreaking. And their epistemology is broadly based on the potential for insight through creation, not in the sense of being opposed to special revelatory events, but with primary attention to ongoing divine communication through life experiences.

---

44. Collins notes the apocalyptic judgment scenario in the Wisdom of Solomon and the diversity of worldviews that are found among the didactic literature of Qumran: "The new evidence from Qumran shows that wisdom, even Hebrew wisdom, cannot be identified with a single worldview" (Collins 1997, 279–81). He cites texts with futurist eschatology, an appeal to special revelation, and instruction in sectarian matters. See also Kampen (2011).

Thus I submit that the three-part gestalt proposed here for wisdom accurately discerns the intuition of the scholars who first identified wisdom as a distinct genre. This is not my own very nonwisdom-like claim to clairvoyance, only a decision about what works. This gestalt works because each element rings true to Job, Proverbs, and Ecclesiastes in relation to other canonical texts, as explained above. Further, it aligns with what the scholars were proposing for wisdom definitions while accounting for the optional nature of four characteristics that are commonly associated with such writings. This proposal is not an attempt to define the heart of wisdom literature for all places and times. Rather it shows how a particular collection of texts relates to each other.

The present discussion has focused almost exclusively on the question of wisdom literature and its character. We alluded in the previous section to elements necessary for establishing the wisdom enterprise, that is, whatever individuals or groups and settings were responsible for producing the literature that later was brought into the canon. As for wisdom itself, the message of the literature, we can say that what we find in the canon is material of a practical and mainly present-world focus (reflects a realized eschatology), derived primarily from ordinary human experience (experiential epistemology), and drawn as well from the insights of living traditions (an implication of the instructional rhetoric).

Very briefly, let us consider the significance of these determinations for other ongoing questions. One debate has centered around so-called wisdom influence: some propose that biblical texts that have affinities with Job, Proverbs, and Ecclesiastes were edited by sages, in other words, wisdom tradents. The approach to genology described above explains why biblical texts that have become instructional secondarily are not, merely because they are now used instructionally, properly called wisdom.[45] Neither does this rule out the possibility of such editing, however.

Scholars have also debated whether wisdom literature as identified in this essay reflects a distinctive worldview as part of its message. We saw that in each of the three significant aspects—rhetoric, eschatology, and epistemology—wisdom fits within the range evident in other canonical writings. From this review it seems that the canonical wisdom writings reflect a distinctive configuration within Israel's worldview. Such diver-

---

45. Note esp. Crenshaw's critique of von Rad's thesis that "the Joseph narrative is a didactic wisdom-story" (von Rad 1966, 300; Crenshaw 1969).

sity has long been recognized within the Hebrew Bible (see, e.g., Goldingay 1987).

As for comparative literary analysis with extracanonical ancient Near Eastern texts, the proposed gestalt does nothing to dampen the possibility of influence, as has been proposed. The concept of prototypes explains how scholarly associations could happen with extracanonical ancient Near Eastern texts having attributes similar to those in the Hebrew Bible. At the same time we can see the impossibility of establishing a concept of a wisdom macro-genre that transcends time and culture.

I conclude by mentioning two areas for which I find this determination particularly valuable. The first is the recognition of a distinctive Israelite wisdom voice or perspective in the canon, arising alongside prophecy, priestly concerns, political leadership, and perhaps more, that overlap and complement each other in regard to values, theology, and ethics. The second is a literary basis from which to seek further historical evidence of the wisdom enterprise as it functioned in Israelite society, however diverse that enterprise may have been. May both of these contribute to the engagement of wisdom by contemporary communities of faith.

Works Consulted

Barr, James. 1963. "Revelation through History in the Old Testament and in Modern Theology." *PSB* 56:4–14.

Blenkinsopp, Joseph. 1995. *Wisdom and Law in the Old Testament: The Ordering of Life in Israel and Early Judaism*. Rev. ed. Oxford Bible Series. Oxford: Oxford University Press.

Boucher, Madeleine. 1977. *The Mysterious Parable*. CBQMS 6. Washington, DC: Catholic Biblical Association of America.

Brown, William P. 1996. *Character in Crisis: A Fresh Approach to the Wisdom Literature of the Old Testament*. Grand Rapids: Eerdmans.

Brueggemann, Walter. 1978. "The Epistemological Crisis of Israel's Two Histories (Jer 9:22–23)." Pages 85–105 in Gammie 1978.

Buss, Martin J. 1999. *Biblical Form Criticism in Its Context*. JSOTSup 274. Sheffield: Sheffield Academic.

Cocceius, Johannes. 1648. *Summa Doctrina de Foedere et Testamento Dei*. Elseviriorum: Lugduni Batavorum.

Collins, John J. 1997. "Wisdom Reconsidered, in Light of the Scrolls." *DSD* 4:265–81.

Corbett, Edward P. J. 1990. *Classical Rhetoric for the Modern Student*. 3rd ed. New York: Oxford University Press.

Crenshaw, James L. 1969. "Method in Determining Wisdom Influence Upon 'Historical' Literature." *JBL* 88:129–42.

———. 1976. "Studies in Ancient Israelite Wisdom: Prolegomenon." Pages 1–45 in *Studies in Ancient Israelite Wisdom*. Edited by James L. Crenshaw. New York: KTAV.

———. 1981. *Old Testament Wisdom: An Introduction*. Atlanta: John Knox.

———. 1985. "The Wisdom Literature." Pages 369–407 in *The Hebrew Bible and Its Modern Interpreters*. Edited by Douglas A. Knight and Gene M. Tucker. Chico, CA: Scholars Press.

———. 1987. "Murphy's Axiom: Every Gnomic Saying Needs a Balancing Corrective." Pages 1–17 in *The Listening Heart*. Edited by Kenneth G. Hoglund, E. F. Huwiler, J. T. Glass, and R. W. Lee. JSOTSup 58. Sheffield: JSOT Press.

Culler, Jonathan. 1975. *Structuralist Poetics: Structuralism, Linguistics, and the Study of Literature*. Ithaca, NY: Cornell University Press.

Davidson, Robert. 1964. *The Old Testament*. Philadelphia: Lippincott.

Dell, Katharine. 2000. *"Get Wisdom, Get Insight": An Introduction to Israel's Wisdom Literature*. Macon, GA: Smyth & Helwys.

Dodd, C. H. 1961. *The Parables of the Kingdom*. Rev. ed. New York: Scribners.

Driver, S. R. 1897. *An Introduction to the Literature of the Old Testament*. Repr. Meridian Library. New York: Meridian, 1957.

Fowler, Alastair. 1982. *Kinds of Literature: An Introduction to the Theory of Genres and Modes*. Cambridge: Harvard University Press.

Fox, Michael V. 1999. *A Time to Tear Down and a Time to Build Up: A Rereading of Ecclesiastes*. Grand Rapids: Eerdmans.

Gammie, John G. 1990. "Paraenetic Literature: Toward the Morphology of a Secondary Genre." *Semeia* 50:41–77.

Gammie, John G., Walter Brueggemann, W. Lee Humphreys, and James M. Ward, eds. 1978. *Israelite Wisdom: Theological and Literary Essays in Honor of Samuel Terrien*. Missoula, MT: Scholars Press

Goldingay, John. 1987. *Theological Diversity and the Authority of the Old Testament*. Grand Rapids: Eerdmans.

Gottwald, Norman K. 1959. *A Light to the Nations: An Introduction to the Old Testament*. New York: Harper.

———. 1985. *The Hebrew Bible: A Socio-literary Introduction*. Philadelphia: Fortress.

Groome, Thomas H. 1980. *Christian Religious Education: Sharing Our Story and Vision*. San Francisco: Harper & Row.

Jeremias, Joachim. 1972. *The Parables of Jesus*. 2nd rev. ed. New York: Scribners.

Kaiser, Otto. 1975. *Introduction to the Old Testament: A Presentation of Its Results and Problems*. Translated by John Sturdy. Minneapolis: Augsburg.

Kampen, John. 2011. *Wisdom Literature*. ECDSS. Grand Rapids: Eerdmans.

Landes, George M. 1978. "Jonah: A *Māšāl*?" Pages 137–58 in Gammie 1978.

McKane, William. 1965. *Prophets and Wise Men*. London: SCM.

———. 1970. *Proverbs, a New Approach*. OTL. Philadelphia: Westminster.

Miller, Douglas B. 2000. "What the Preacher Forgot: The Rhetoric of Ecclesiastes." *CBQ* 62: 215–35.

Murphy, Roland E. 1978. "Wisdom—Theses and Hypotheses." Pages 35–42 in Gammie 1978.

———. 1979. "Wisdom and Salvation." Pages 177–83 in *Sin, Salvation, and the Spirit*. Edited by Daniel Durken. Collegeville, MN: Liturgical Press.

———. 1981a. "Israel's Wisdom: A Biblical Model of Salvation." *StMiss* 30:1–43.

———. 1981b. *Wisdom Literature: Job, Proverbs, Ruth, Canticles, Ecclesiastes, and Esther*. FOTL 13. Grand Rapids: Eerdmans.

———. 1990. *The Tree of Life: An Exploration of Biblical Wisdom Literature*. ABRL. New York: Doubleday.

Newsom, Carol A. 2003. *The Book of Job: A Contest of Moral Imaginations*. New York: Oxford University Press.

———. 2007. "Spying Out the Land: A Report from Genology." Pages 19–30 in *Bakhtin and Genre Theory in Biblical Studies*. Edited by Roland Boer. SemeiaSt 63. Atlanta: Society of Biblical Literature.

Oehler, Gustav Friedrich. 1883. *Theology of the Old Testament*. 2 vols. Edited by George E. Day. New York: Funk & Wagnalls.

Penchansky, David. 2012. *Understanding Wisdom Literature: Conflict and Dissonance in the Hebrew Text*. Grand Rapids: Eerdmans.

Perelman, Chaim, and Lucie Olbrechts-Tyteca. 1969. *The New Rhetoric: A Treatise on Argumentation*. Translated by John Wilkinson and Purcell Weaver. Notre Dame: University of Notre Dame Press.

Rad, Gerhard von. 1962. *Old Testament Theology*. Translated by D. M. G. Stalker. Vol. 1. New York: Harper & Row.

———. 1966. "The Joseph Narrative and Ancient Wisdom." Pages 292–300 in *The Problem of the Hexateuch and Other Essays*. Translated by E. W. Treman Dicken. London: SCM.

———. 1972. *Wisdom in Israel*. Translated by James D. Martin. Nashville: Abingdon.

Rowley, H. H., ed. 1951. *The Old Testament and Modern Study: A Generation of Discovery and Research*. Oxford: Clarendon.

Scott, R. B. Y. 1965. *Proverbs, Ecclesiastes*. AB 18. New York: Doubleday.

———. 1971. *The Way of Wisdom in the Old Testament*. New York: Macmillan.

Sheard, Cynthia Miecznikowski. 1996. "The Public Value of Epideictic Rhetoric." *College English* 58: 765–94.

Smend, Rudolf. 1995. "The Interpretation of Wisdom in Nineteenth-Century Scholarship." Pages 257–68 in *Wisdom in Ancient Israel: Essays in Honour of J. A. Emerton*. Edited by John Day, Robert P. Gordon, and H. G. M. Williamson. Cambridge: Cambridge University Press.

Sparks, Kenton L. 2005. *Ancient Texts for the Study of the Hebrew Bible: A Guide to the Background Literature*. Peabody, MA: Hendrickson.

Sweeney, Marvin A., and Ehud Ben Zvi, eds. 2003. *The Changing Face of Form Criticism for the Twenty-First Century*. Grand Rapids: Eerdmans.

Van Leeuwen, Raymond C. 2003. "Form Criticism, Wisdom, and Psalms 111–112." Pages 65–84 in Sweeney and Ben Zvi 2003.

Whybray, R. N. 1974. *The Intellectual Tradition in the Old Testament*. BZAW 135. Berlin: de Gruyter.

———. 1990. "The Sage in the Israelite Royal Court." Pages 133–39 in *The Sage in Israel and the Ancient Near East*. Edited by John G. Gammie and Leo G. Perdue. Winona Lake, IN: Eisenbrauns.

Wills, Lawrence M. 1990. *The Jew in the Court of the Foreign King: Ancient Jewish Court Legends*. HDR 26. Minneapolis: Fortress.

Wolff, Hans Walter. 1973. *The Old Testament. A Guide to Its Writings*. Philadelphia: Fortress.

Zimmerli, Walther. 1978. *Old Testament Theology in Outline*. Translated by David E. Green. Atlanta: John Knox.

Don't Throw the Baby Out with the Bathwater: On the Distinctness of the Sapiential Understanding of the World*

Annette Schellenberg

Differences between the wisdom books of the Old Testament (Job, Proverbs, Ecclesiastes, Sirach, Wisdom of Solomon) and similarities between the wisdom and nonwisdom books make it difficult to define "wisdom." Despite these and other problems, however, the traditional consensus holds that there is a wisdom tradition, which is distinguished by a specific worldview, held by a specific group of sages, who produced the wisdom books (e.g., Crenshaw 2010, esp. 11, 24–25, 27; Grabbe 1995, 171; Steck 1982, 303–315).[1] Recently, however, this consensus was questioned (again), most pointedly by Mark Sneed and Stuart Weeks (Sneed 2011; Weeks 1999; 2005; 2010, 6–7, 107–144). They point out several problems with the traditional view and argue that the "current consensus ... is incredibly simplistic and rigidly stereotypical" (Sneed 2011, 54). Their arguments differ in detail, but both make the point that it is only the genre and subject matter of the wisdom books (and wisdom psalms) that set them apart from other

---

* I thank Bob Coote and Thomas Krüger, who gave me valuable feedback to earlier drafts of this essay, and Mark Sneed, who invited me to contribute to this volume. The task was more challenging than I anticipated—an indication of the importance of this volume and the question concerning the character of the wisdom tradition.

1. The consensus was always quite variable, and it was questioned early on by Whybray (1974), who argued that the wise did not constitute a professional class, that the wisdom books were not linked to an institution, that the authors of these books "constituted a separate 'tradition' only in the sense that they concerned themselves more than the majority of their contemporaries in an intellectual way with the problems of human life" (70), and that this intellectual tradition can be found in many other texts of the Old Testament as well.

biblical books. As much as they acknowledge that there are wisdom books, they deny that these texts reflect a unique worldview that is different from the worldview reflected in other books of the Old Testament.[2] Thus, they conclude that the "wisdom tradition" is "not a tradition or movement" but only a "mode of literature" (Sneed 2011, 71) or even "a phantasm in Old Testament scholarship" (Weeks 1999, 30).

In my view, Sneed and Weeks start with legitimate questions and are right to debunk some of the common views about wisdom as too simplistic. However, by concluding that there was no wisdom tradition, they throw the baby out with the bathwater. In the following I will counter their conclusion by concentrating on the question of worldview.[3] Though this word might be too grandiose, in my view the fact remains that, despite their differences, the five wisdom books share some basic premises in their understanding of the world that are different from the premises reflected in other books of the Old Testament. After some preliminary remarks (1), in the following I will describe these premises of the sapiential understanding of the world, addressing cosmology (2), epistemology (3), ethics and understanding of society (4), and theology (5).

---

2. For a skeptical assessment of a distinct sapiential understanding of the world, see also Murphy (1981), who maintains that "the sapiential understanding of reality was shared by all Israelites" (3); Collins (1993), who focuses on the newness of the apocalyptic "view of the world that is sharply at variance not only with the biblical wisdom books, but with the Hebrew Bible as a whole" (170); Collins (1997b), who states that the different wisdom texts (from the Old Testament and beyond) reflect a "variability of sapiential worldviews" (279); and Dell (2006, 125–200), who (with good reasons, see §1 below with n. 14) questions whether "the idea of a completely separate worldview" is realistic (15) and argues against too sharp a separation of wisdom from the rest of the Old Testament.

3. Reflecting on the character of wisdom tradition, it is helpful to remember that one can address the issue from three different angles: genre (literary forms and respective topics and focuses), worldview (basic assumptions about the world), and setting in life (function of the texts; social location of the people embodying and handing down the tradition). These three aspects are interrelated and all three are constitutive of the character of the wisdom tradition (like other traditions). However, they are not always or necessarily congruent with each other; in such cases it is one's preconceptions that determine where to see the center of the wisdom tradition and where to allow departures from the norm. On this problem, see Collins (1997b), with observations on the wisdom texts from Qumran, which combine "wisdom forms with an apocalyptic worldview" (277). On the problem of the term worldview, see §1 below with n. 10.

1. Preliminary Remarks

Both Sneed and Weeks integrate more general considerations about the scribal milieu in ancient Israel into their argumentation and point out that there is no evidence that the wisdom books were composed and transmitted by a distinct group of scribes (Weeks 2010, 127–44; Sneed 2011, 61–64). Whereas Weeks leaves open whether he would say the same for all the other books of the Old Testament as well, Sneed explicitly argues that "these same Israelite wisdom writers or scribal scholars, in addition to producing the wisdom literature, were involved in the preservation, composition, utilization, and instruction of the other literary genres of the Hebrew Bible" (Sneed 2011, 62–63) and holds that the "biblical materials' common scribal matrix and the exposure of scribes to a multitude of genres and traditions … discredit the notion of distinctive worldviews in the Hebrew Bible" (Sneed 2011, 64). In my view, this position as stated mixes correct observations with invalid conclusions.

It is correct that most if not all books of the Old Testament were produced by professional scribes (Carr 2005; Schmid 2011; van der Toorn 2007), people who underwent thorough training that turned them into scribal experts with profound knowledge of older writings and traditions and the skills to interpret them and compose new writings in continuation of the tradition. In addition to comparative evidence from the ancient Near East, this is indicated by the biblical books themselves, which are highly literary, show clear traces of a long formation history, and contain many passages that reflect knowledge of older traditions and writings. Though many of the Old Testament books had oral origins in different settings of life, at some point in history they all came into the hands of professional scribes, who studied the respective texts and traditions in light of other such texts and traditions, composed/edited the writings, and handed them down to the next generation. Unfortunately, our knowledge of these processes and the scribal guild in ancient Israel is extremely limited. The Old Testament mentions scribes in different contexts—royal administration (e.g., 1 Kgs 4:3), temple/priesthood (e.g., Ezra 7:11), military (e.g., 2 Kgs 25:19), schools (see Sir 51:23), and private employment (e.g., Jer 36:32)—but it is unlikely that all these scribes were scholars who composed books. Thus, we can only speculate how many groups of scholar-scribes existed in given periods,[4]

---

4. With terms such as *Deuteronomists* and *Priestly school, theocratic* and *eschato-*

how numerous they were,[5] with which institutions they were connected,[6] whether all scribes received the same kind of training, what exactly they did besides composing the books that became canonical, how dependent they were on their employers,[7] whether some of them were independent,[8] and how these groups developed over the course of time.

The evidence in the Old Testament clearly shows that there were major theological/ideological disagreements, and at least some of them have to do with different groups (e.g., Jer 8:8–9). On the other hand, it is also clear that we cannot posit too many scribal groups for ancient Israel, as sociologically such an assumption is very unlikely. Furthermore, as many controversies are reflected in one and the same book (e.g., Ezek 34:11–16, 23; Amos 9:8), there are additional practical considerations that caution against interpreting every difference as an indication of different scribal groups. Moreover, ancient Near Eastern archives/libraries and the scrolls from Qumran show that it was common for one and the same group to study diverse writings. Along with the problems of discerning who the wise are (Weeks 1994, 74–91; Whybray 1974, 15–54), it thus seems premature to assume that the wisdom books must have been written by a distinct scribal group of sages. Though this is a possibility, we simply do not know enough about the scribal milieu in ancient Israel to be sure about it.

---

logical streams of thought (Plöger), or *Zadokite Judaism, Sapiential Judaism*, and *Enochic Judaism* (Boccaccini), scholars normally imply that there were different scribal groups. Others, however, stress that for postexilic Judah we must assume just *one* scribal group (e.g., Ben Zvi 2003, 293–95; similarly Sneed 2011, 54, 60–64; VanderKam 2007, 18–20). See also nn. 6 and 7.

5. Most scholars agree that the scribes constituted "a very small intellectual elite in society" (Ben Zvi 2003, 293). However, it remains open what "very small" means.

6. For the postexilic period, many scholars point to the temple as the place where the Old Testament books originated (e.g., van der Toorn 2007, esp. 86–89). Others have considered the royal court/administration (e.g., Schniedewind 2004) or the educational system (e.g., Carr 2005). Some scholars argue that these options do not contradict each other, either pointing out the connections between them (e.g., van der Toorn 2007, 85, 88) or assuming that the Old Testament books were produced in different institutional settings (e.g., Perdue 2007, 327–29).

7. The prophetic books, especially, contain such heavy criticism of the political and religious leaders that one wonders whether some of them might have originated outside of an institutional setting (Schellenberg 2010, 295–302 with n. 66).

8. Ben Sira describes the scribe as one "who has little business" and "the opportunity of leisure" (Sir 38:24).

However, that we cannot trace every difference between and within Old Testament books to distinct groups of scribes does not mean that these differences are irrelevant. The question of the *scribal* milieu in which ancient texts were produced is only one facet of the question of the *social* milieu of the people who shared the views reflected in these texts. Though it is possible that scribes upheld different positions just for the fun of it, passages in which proponents of different positions are criticized (e.g., Jer 8:8–9) and others in which hierarchies are established (e.g., Num 12:6–8; Deut 18:15, 18; 34:10) show that such differences often were not just a game. Rather, they have to do with differences in ideology/theology, often related to different group's relative power. Whether one explains the differences as reflecting different scribal groups or high heterogeneity within one group, it is clear that these ideologies/theologies were not developed in isolation but in intensive disputes. The wisdom books reflect such disputes (e.g., Schmid 2008; Schipper 2012; Krüger 1997b), as do most of the other books. In later times the writings of the Old Testament show an increased tendency of the scribes to find compromises between different positions and to reconcile differences (e.g., Deut 4:6; Lev 26:3, 9, 14–15, 44[9]). This has to do with the emergence of the canon, which in a way binds all the different books and ideologies/theologies together. However, it is part of the beauty of this canon that it is extremely diverse and leaves texts with different ideologies/theologies to stand side by side.

In the following I will focus on this aspect of ideology/theology, that is, basic premises that guide how one understands the world. As just outlined, the difficulty of pinpointing different scribal groups is not an argument against diversity in the ideologies/theologies expressed in the books produced by these scribes. What is disputed in the case of the wisdom books is whether their distinctness lies only in the form (genre) and the topics and focuses connected with it or whether it goes deeper and has to do with a specific understanding of the world, which is shared by some people but not by others. Whereas Sneed and Weeks argue for the first explanation for the distinctness of the wisdom books, in the following I will argue for the second, which is the traditional view. What I intend to describe is often described as the sapiential worldview. However, it might be better to avoid this term, not only because it has philosophical connotations[10] but also

---

9. Nihan (2009) argues that Lev 26 provides a reinterpretation of the Deuteronomic understanding of covenant in light of the Priestly understanding of covenant.

10. The term worldview (*Weltanschauung*) is used differently by different people.

because it is very "high up" and one can legitimately argue that everyone in ancient Israel (and the ancient Near East in general) shared the same worldview.[11] Nonetheless, not everyone thought the same way. In addition to differences on the individual level, there were also differences between groups caused by different ideologies/theologies, that is, sets of premises that influenced how the world was perceived and interpreted.[12] How comprehensive such sets of premises were and whether/how they were connected to a controlling body differed from group to group. In the case of the wisdom tradition, the set of premises (outlined below) is quite encompassing—hence the temptation to call it a worldview. The question of the social location of the wise is hard to answer and lies beyond the scope of this article. Here one would have to make further distinctions, as wisdom is not only an ancient Israelite phenomenon but is attested throughout the ancient Near East. Furthermore, there were major historical developments, as attested already in the Old Testament wisdom books and even more so in the later apocryphal Jewish wisdom writings.

In the following I will concentrate on the five wisdom books of the Old Testament[13] and only occasionally refer to ancient Near Eastern wisdom writings and noncanonical Jewish wisdom texts. In many instances they

---

According to a well-known definition by Leo Apostel and Jan van der Veken, a worldview gives answers to seven questions: (1) What is? (Ontology); (2) Where does it all come from? (Explanation); (3) Where are we going? (Prediction); (4) What is good and what is evil? (Axiology); (5) How should we act? (Praxeology); (6) What is true and what is false? (Epistemology); (7) Where do we start in order to answer those questions? (Vidal 2008, 4–5).

11. See Krüger (2006, 239–40), who distinguishes three levels of abstraction: (1) "sehr allgemeine Konzepte des Denkens, die weitgehend im gesamten Alten Testament und seinem kulturellen Umfeld vorausgesetzt werden"; (2) "'Vorstellungen,' 'Denkmodelle' oder 'Theologien'"; (3) "sehr konkrete Konzepte von alltäglichen Gegenständen, Sachverhalten und Handlungsabläufen." Obviously, one cannot sharply distinguish between these three levels; nonetheless the distinction is helpful. On the ambiguity of whether the sapiential premises constitute a "worldview," see n. 39.

12. Interestingly, in his important article "Strömungen theologischer Tradition im Alten Israel," Steck (1982) does not use the term worldview (*Weltanschauung*), even though he makes a strong case for different streams of traditions (among them the wisdom tradition), carried by different circles of tradents. Instead, in addition to "Traditionsströmung" Steck uses terms like "Vorstellung," "Denkbewegungen," "Position," "Denkansatz," and "eigengeprägte, konturierte Konzeption von Erfahrungsbewältigung" (e.g., 299, 300, 302, 301, 316).

13. The focus on the Old Testament wisdom *books*, which leaves out the wisdom

confirm the picture, in others they add to the variety within the sapiential tradition. This variety is a consequence of different cultural contexts and of historical developments. Particularly noteworthy is the influence of apocalypticism on the later wisdom tradition. Even within the five Old Testament books there is considerable variety and much overlap with other books. Nonetheless, the traditional notion of a specific sapiential view of the world is not wrong. Indeed, the five Old Testament wisdom books are connected with each other (and other wisdom texts) by family resemblance—not only with regard to genre (form and respective topics) but also with regard to underlying premises.[14]

As I am defending the traditional consensus, in the following I will obviously repeat many arguments that are well known. However, I still hope to contribute to the understanding of the sapiential view of the world by modifying some of the common notions about its premises— for example, that the sapiential view is distinguished from other views by the notion of world order, creation theology, and empiricism—which are indeed too simplistic and stereotypical, as Weeks, especially, has pointed out (Weeks 2010, 107–26).

2. COSMOLOGY

As is well known, both the topic of creation and the idea of a nexus of deed and consequence are important in all the wisdom books. Though these

---

psalms, is motivated by practical considerations; obviously there are several psalms that are as sapiential as the wisdom books.

14. See Collins 1997a: "In the Hebrew Bible, wisdom is characterized by a particular view of the world or theological perspective. That perspective, however, changes over time, and there is vast difference between Qoheleth's view of the world and that of the Wisdom of Solomon. Wisdom, in short, is a tradition, held together by certain family resemblances rather than by a constant essence" (1). This lack of a "constant essence" in the sapiential understanding of the world makes defining this understanding difficult, as there are members (texts) for whom it is not clear whether they still belong to the family—the decision depends on the focus and is a matter of definition. Nonetheless, the lack of a "constant essence" is not an argument against a sapiential understanding of the world—as long as one does not assume that such an understanding must be unchangeable and totally different from all other understandings. The latter seems to be assumed in some formulations of Weeks (Weeks 1999, 30: "wholly separate school of thought"; Weeks 2005, 299: "wholly or largely distinct from other Jewish thought").

books approach the two topics quite differently (Weeks 2010, 111–13), they still reflect a common view, namely the assumption that the cosmos is stable, that there is an order inherent in the world that will not change. Though this notion is expressed explicitly only a few times (see most clearly Eccl 1:3–11), it is reflected implicitly in numerous statements from all five wisdom books. In detail, each of them expresses the notion of a stable order of the world differently, and on some important points they disagree. Nonetheless, in one way or another, the notion that the world will remain the same forever is fundamental in all five of them. It is important to note that the difference from other books of the Old Testament is *not* the notion of world order. This notion is important throughout the entire ancient Near East (Schmid 1966; 1968). However, as the following examples show, in different ideologies/theologies this order is seen in effect in different places, and in some there is still room for fundamental changes. Such changes are not expected in wisdom literature.

No doubt, the wisdom books are not the only books in the Old Testament that reflect the belief that the world will more or less remain the same forever. Another important exponent of this view is the Priestly text. In addition to Gen 1, where the stability of the cosmos is explained in detail, P includes other passages, such as 9:8–17 (which states that there will never again be a flood) and Gen 17 (which describes God's everlasting covenant), that make clear that God orders the world in a way that guarantees that it remains the same forever. Similarly, some passages in the Prophets (see, e.g., Isa 54:9–10; Jer 31:35–37; 33:20, 25–26) refer to cosmic stability to convey that God's special relationship with Israel will endure forever. Many other books do not address the question of the order of the world at all. In some cases, this might be an indication that the scribes behind them could not imagine that the world would not be stable. Conversely, many books of the Old Testament contain statements about radical changes in the future. That such changes can also concern the cosmos is most clearly expressed in Isa 65:17; 66:22 (God creates a new heaven and a new earth) and Jer 4:23–26 (the order of creation reverts back to chaos). No doubt, these two passages stand out within the prophetic corpus. As a general tendency, however, major changes are expected in most prophetic books, and there are several other passages that indicate that these changes also concern the order of the world (e.g., Isa 40:4; Joel 2:10; Amos 8:8–9; Hag 2:6, 21–22). This is most clearly the case in the protoapocalyptic texts (e.g., Isa 24:1–6; Ezek 38:19–20; Zech 14:6–8), which predict an end time in which the world will be fundamentally shaken. Based on the assessment that the current world is bad beyond repair, later apocalyptic texts often describe its destruction (e.g., 1 En. 1:7) or the total collapse of its order (e.g., 4 Ezra 5:1–13).[15] In all these examples, the stable or unstable state of the world is addressed in connection with statements about the stable or unstable state of YHWH's relationship with Israel. Apparently, for many these two belong together. Thus, one wonders whether or not all statements that describe YHWH's special relationship with Israel as conditional are a faint reflection of the understanding that the order of the world is *not* a matter of course. At least, it is noteworthy that Deuteronomy, which is the parade example of such a conditional theology, contains a whole chapter of curses, of which many have to do with reversal of order (e.g., Deut 28:23–24, 30, 43).[16] Another interesting text is Ps 72, as it points to an important nuance relating to the notion of order. As is typical of royal ideology, Ps 72 presents the king as the one who (together with God) guarantees order, including the order of nature and society. The text does not say that the king is also responsible for the order of the cosmos, but this cosmic order is mentioned indirectly—tellingly, in all three cases in formulations that equate the duration of the king's reign with the duration of the cosmos (see 72:5, 7, 17). As much as these formulations aim at emphasizing how stable and everlasting the king's reign is, they implicitly also show that according to royal ideology the stability of the cosmos is *not* a given but, rather, has to

---

15. On a different level, the notion of order is strongly confirmed in apocalypticism as well, as indicated not only by cosmological passages but also in the prediction of the destruction of the wicked and the salvation of the righteous. This idea of an eschatological judgment is also expressed in Wisdom of Solomon (see Wis 1–5) and in the eschatological wisdom texts from Qumran. Obviously, here wisdom is influenced by apocalypticism. What distinguishes the apocalyptic view from the wisdom view at this point is not the assessment of the goodness/wickedness of people and their afterlife but rather the assessment of the goodness/wickedness of the (current) world and the stability of its order. Whereas the Qumran texts are more influenced by the apocalyptic view in this regard, Wisdom of Solomon clearly confirms this goodness/stability (see below).

16. Obviously, on another level the curses and blessings of Deuteronomy are an apt expression of order, namely in that they confirm the rule of a nexus of deed and consequence. Unlike in the wisdom texts, here, however, the nexus of deed and consequence concerns not only individuals but the entire people, so that the consequences are an expression of whether Israel remains in the realm of order or falls into the realm of chaos (see Deut 30:15–20 with the alternatives of life and death).

be upheld.[17] Finally, through the figure of Job the book of Job seriously questions whether the order of the world is as it ought to be (see below). Though at the end the book affirms the notion of order, it nonetheless shows that not everyone in ancient Israel took it for granted.

Against the background of these diverse Old Testament texts that in one or another way reflect awareness that the order of the world might be shaken, it is noteworthy how strongly all five wisdom books affirm that the order of the world is stable. In the older parts of Proverbs (Prov 10–29), this is indicated indirectly, namely through the many proverbs that express that there is a nexus of deed and consequence. Though many of them merely express logical connections (e.g., Prov 11:15; 13:20) or point to the community as the entity that connects deed to consequence (e.g., Prov 11:26; 14:35), many others either point to God (e.g., Prov 16:7; 24:12) or imply some kind of automatism (e.g., Prov 11:3; 13:21; 22:8). While the question thus remains open as to how the nexus of deed and consequence works, it is firmly asserted that such a nexus exists. The myriad examples pertaining to diverse aspects of human life imply that it is a reflection of an order that permeates the entire world.[18]

Similarly, Prov 1–9, Sirach, and Wisdom of Solomon strongly affirm the theory of a nexus of deed and consequence. In these younger wisdom texts, however, the notion of order is also explained more explicitly, pointing to God as creator.[19] In all three of these texts, the linking of order and creation happens through inclusion of divine wisdom: with different emphases, they express that wisdom, often described as a woman, existed from the very beginning and was present when God created the world (see Prov 3:19–20; 8:22–31; Sir 1:1, 4, 9; 24:1–9; Wis 8:1, 4; 9:9; see also Job 28:25–27). Thus, they imply or express that wisdom permeates the entire world (see also Wis 7:21–8:1). This saturation of the entire world with wisdom is not only an apt expression or explanation of the world's order

---

17. This notion is more clearly expressed in Egyptian texts, with the opposition of *maʿat* and *isft* (Assmann 2006, 213–22).

18. For Egypt, see Assmann (2005, 94): "Was den Tun-Ergehen-Zusammenhang garantiert, ist weniger eine 'logische natürliche Folge', als vielmehr eine Ordnung der Dinge, die vom Schöpfergott eingerichtet und vom Menschen in seinem Tun verwirklicht wird, das Prinzip Maat ('Wahrheit, Gerechtigkeit, Ordnung')."

19. Prov 10–29 also contains statements about God the creator (e.g., Prov 14:31; 16:4) but they do not, or only very implicitly, pertain to the notion of order in the world.

but also the reason why, according to these same three texts, humans have the chance to understand this order (see §3 below). Sirach contains several more passages that emphasize the order of the world as God's work. Noteworthy in particular are Sir 33:7–15, where Ben Sira explains the distinction between righteous and sinful people as the work of God's wisdom, and Sir 42:15–43:33, where he praises the wonders of creation, highlighting both the power of God and the stability of God's work.[20] Under the influence of Stoic philosophy with its idea of tension and relaxation, the author of Wisdom of Solomon approaches the question of stability of the world from a new angle. He mentions changes of the elements (see Wis 19:18) and even describes the event at the Red Sea as a new creation (see Wis 19:6). However, Wis 7:17–20 and 19:18 in particular leave no doubt that he considers these exceptions and is very clear that overall the stability of the cosmos remains (Collins 2005b, 153–57).

It certainly is no coincidence that the stability of the cosmos is affirmed most explicitly in Job and Ecclesiastes, the two wisdom books that deal with the problem that the theory of a nexus of deed and consequence often is contradicted by experience. To some extent, the character of Job still holds on to this nexus, in the sense that he shares the notion that humans *should* be treated according to their deeds. However, as he is exposed to suffering that cannot be reconciled with the theory, he questions God, going so far as to make the accusation that God is "wicked" (רָשָׁע), a deity who does not commit to any order but randomly attacks the innocent (see Job 9:23–24). Though Job refers to God as the one who created the structure of the world and put the chaotic elements in their place (see Job 9:8; 26:7–10, 12–13), he does so to point out not the order of the world but God's power. In his view, God does not use this power only to establish order but also to tear it down (e.g., Job 9:5–7; 12:14–19; 26:11). In this, Job not only questions the theory of a nexus of deed and consequence, but also God's righteousness and the stability of the order of the world. In the last two points, however, the book overall does not confirm the position of the character Job. Rather, in Job 38–41 the scribes behind the book give YHWH a voice and through his speeches strongly affirm that there is an order to the world, which is established and upheld by God, its creator.

---

20. Sirach contains one passage that mentions earthshaking events (Sir 16:18–19). However, the relevant words probably refer to a theophany. And, more importantly, they are disqualified as the "thoughts of one devoid of understanding" (Sir 16:23) who foolishly thinks that God does not pay attention to him.

Along the same lines, they conclude the book with narrating how God restored Job's fortune (Job 42:10–17). Similarly, the book of Ecclesiastes affirms the stability of the cosmos (see esp. Eccl 1:3–11) and that there is an order (see esp. Eccl 3:1–8), even though humans are not capable of fully understanding it (see §3 below). Probably in rejection of apocalyptic ideas (Krüger 1997a), Ecclesiastes explicitly stresses that the world with its order—that is, God's creation—will remain the same forever and that on the large scale there will be nothing new (see Eccl 1:4, 9–10; 3:14–15).

3. Epistemology

Another realm where one can observe a major difference between the wisdom books and other books of the Old Testament is epistemology. The difference is not the one of empiricism versus revelation, as is often proposed. Revelation is one of the sources of cognition that some of the wisdom books consider reliable. However, as much as the five wisdom books disagree regarding both sources and limits of human cognition (Schellenberg 2002, 204–40), they all agree that there is no need for a human mediator who conveys knowledge that he gained through special revelation to others. In this respect, the wisdom books obviously stand in sharp contrast to many other books from the Old Testament, particularly Exodus–Deuteronomy and the Latter Prophets, which present large parts of their content as the words of the Lord revealed to special persons (Moses, the prophets), who then conveyed them to the people.[21] As foreshadowed already in Ezek 40–48, Zech 1–6, and Dan 7–12, in later times a similar model becomes important in apocalypticism. Various texts present themselves as written records of insights into divine mysteries that famous visionaries such as Enoch or Baruch received through revelations.[22] Often, they include additional angelic mediators who explain the significance of the visions to the visionaries.

---

21. No doubt, these same books also include passages that do not mention a mediator but stress that knowledge/wisdom is accessible to all (e.g., Deut 30:11–14; Jer 31:33–34). They are reflections of the scribes' disputes on the epistemological question.

22. Often, these revelations and visionaries are described in sapiential terms (Collins 1990; Lange 2008). Obviously, here (mantic) wisdom and apocalypticism influence each other. On the eschatological wisdom texts from Qumran, see below with n. 24.

In contrast to these epistemological models that highlight human (and angelic) mediators, the wisdom books are characterized by an epistemology of immediacy. In the process of gaining knowledge, other humans are only important in their capacity as teachers or as famous sages of the past who composed wisdom books (Solomon). In their cognitive capacities, however, these teachers and sages are not presented as special. Rather, most wisdom books emphasize that all humans have the same capacity to gain insight. Those that do make distinctions always consider an entire group to be privileged, namely the "righteous/wise" as opposed to the "wicked/foolish."

In line with their educational goal, many wisdom books admonish their addressees to listen to the teachings of their fathers and to seek wisdom (e.g., Prov 1:8; Sir 6:18, 32–37; Wis 6:12–16). In this, they imply that anyone has the capacity to gain wisdom if he only tries hard enough. Sirach 17:6-7 explains this general cognitive ability of humans with reference to God's creation of humans. Others are more pessimistic in this regard. Triggered by experiences that contradict the traditional view of a nexus of deed and consequence (see §2 above), the books of Job and Ecclesiastes and some other passages stress the inaccessibility of wisdom and the inability of humans to understand the order of the world (e.g., Job 11:7–9; 28; 38:4–5; Prov 20:24; Eccl 3:11, 22; 7:14; 11:5–6). However, here as well this judgment concerns *all* human beings alike. The addressees are admonished to accept this general limitation. Several passages are formulated in a way that might reflect controversies with others who claim to know ways to gain special insights (see Job 15:7–8; Prov 30:3–4; Eccl 6:11–12; 8:16–17; 10:14; Sir 3:21–24; 34:5–7).

Only a few passages in the wisdom books are not formulated on the assumption that all humans have the same cognitive capacities. All the examples have to do with tracing wisdom and insight directly back to God, mainly to praise God (e.g., Job 32:8; Sir 39:6; Wis 8:21) or to remind people that ultimately God decides the destiny of humans (e.g., Eccl 2:26; see also Sir 33:7–15). Several of these passages still point to humans as the ones who with their behavior decide whether God gives them wisdom/insight (e.g., Prov 2:6 after 2:1, 5; Sir 1:10, 26; 15:1, 7–8; 43:33; Wis 1:4; 2:21–22). None of them aims at singling out a prophetic mediator.[23]

---

23. Only Wis 7:7, 15–21 shows some tendencies toward the idea of a special revelation to a special person (Solomon). However, the same passage also contains

As stated at the beginning of this section, the difference between the wisdom books and other books of the Old Testament is not between empiricism and revelation: Though all wisdom books consider experience crucial—either in the form of personal experience or in the form of tradition as condensed experience—most of them also are at ease with the concept of direct revelation. Many formulations indicate that for the scribes behind these books revelation is nothing but a way that God grants someone wisdom/insight (e.g., Job 32:8, 18; Sir 39:6; Wis 7:7, 15). Thus, those who receive such revelations are also not described as being special visionaries. In the wisdom books, Job stands out as a recipient of direct revelation (Job 38–41). The content of the revelation he receives, however, is nothing more than natural theology, and God does not appoint him to convey his words to others. Even more telling are the descriptions of divine revelations in Prov 1–9 (see Prov 1:20–33; 8:1–36; 9:1–6). These are portrayed as highly public events, with Woman Wisdom crying out in the streets. Everyone has the chance to receive wisdom, notwithstanding that this wisdom is revealed through a divine figure.

Only Sirach and Wisdom of Solomon contain some statements that point to a more exclusive understanding of revelation. In Wisdom of Solomon one finds the phrase "mysteries of God" (μυστήρια θεοῦ; Wis 2:22). It is noteworthy that this recalls the phrase רז נהיה ("mystery to come"), which is prominent in the eschatological wisdom texts from Qumran (see esp. 4QInstruction, Book of Mysteries) (Collins 2005a; Goff 2007, 9–103). In both cases the mystery has to do with eschatological judgment, which brings eternal life to the righteous and destruction to the wicked. Whereas the texts from Qumran imply that only the מבינים ("understanding ones"), the elect group of addressees, have the chance to learn about and contemplate the "mystery to come,"[24] Wis 2:21–24 states that anyone could know/understand the mystery if only their wickedness did not blind them. Thus, even though the terminology and content is reminiscent of apocalyptic revelations, the author still argues on the basis of an epistemology of immediacy. And this same epistemology is also reflected in other verses,

---

statements that make clear that Solomon was a mostly ordinary person and is just an example of a wise person (see Wis 7:1–6, 14).

24. As this group seems rather big (Goff 2007, 47–65), in itself this focus on the righteous ones is still in some sense in line with the epistemology of other wisdom texts. However, 4QInstructions also mentions a "vision of Hagu" and with that introduces a visionary, as typical of apocalyptic epistemology.

most clearly in Wis 1:1; 6:1-2, 9, 21, where the author addresses the "rulers of the earth," and in Wis 12:27; 13:8-9, where he argues that even non-Israelites had the chance to recognize God, and that it is their own fault that they failed to do so.

Ben Sira is less clear on this subject. Though in Sir 16:15-16 he makes the same argument as the author of Wisdom of Solomon (the Egyptians could have recognized God), at other points he recalls the special revelations to Moses and the prophets (see Sir 45:5; 48:3, 7, 22, 24-25; 49:8), and in Sir 24 he identifies (divine) Wisdom with the Torah (see 24:23) and describes how Wisdom settled in Jerusalem. These texts clearly present wisdom not only as revealed but also as revealed to the Israelites only (see §5 below). However, Ben Sira's main interest lies in praising and promoting wisdom and not the Torah as such (note the lack of references to specific laws and formulations, as in Sir 19:20). Through closely associating wisdom with Torah—see also verses that highlight the Torah as a source of wisdom (e.g., Sir 15:1; 24:25-29) and verses in which the two terms are put in parallel (e.g., Sir 17:11)—he renders wisdom (teaching) as a form of Torah (teaching), and thus emphasizes its importance.[25] Wisdom itself, for him, goes beyond the Torah. Thus, in Sir 38:34-39:8, his description of how the scribe acquires wisdom (see also Sir 39:24), he first points to the Torah but then also mentions studying other traditions, traveling to foreign countries, and being filled with wisdom by God directly (see also 6:34-37; 44:1-15). That overall, despite his equation of wisdom with the Torah, Ben Sira also adheres to an epistemology of immediacy is most clearly confirmed in what he says—and does not say—about Moses. Obviously, he is familiar with the tradition that the Torah was revealed through Moses, and he also refers to it in the paragraph on Moses, in his praise of the ancestors (see Sir 44:5; further 46:1). However, in Sir 24:23 he reduces Moses's role to "commanding" (ἐντέλλομαι) the law to the Israelites, and in Sir 17:11-14 he alludes to the revelation at Mount Sinai without mentioning Moses at all. Rather, here he describes a very public revelation, in which everyone "saw" and "heard" God—tellingly leaving open whether "they" are all humans or the Israelites only (see §5 below).

The examples from Wisdom of Solomon and Sirach show that the difference between the epistemologies of the wisdom books and those of the books of the Pentateuch and the Prophets cannot be explained with

---

25. See also Sir 24:33, where Ben Sira equates his wisdom (teaching) with prophecy.

the content of these books alone (thus Weeks 2010, 115): though the contents of these books do differ, there is also a considerable amount of overlap, as the wisdom books are not only concerned with daily life affairs, nor are the books of the Pentateuch and the Prophets only concerned with affairs relating to the relationship between YHWH and Israel. Likewise, the difference in their epistemologies cannot be explained in reference to epistemology only: The scribes behind Exodus–Deuteronomy and the Prophets must have been well aware that many of the words in these books were added by them. Though we do not know whether they understood themselves as some kind of (literary) prophets and their additions as some kind of revelations, it must at least have been clear to them that these revelations were not mediated through Moses and the (oral) prophets. Thus, it seems fair to conclude that they utilized the concept of revelation as a means to strengthen the authority of their books (van der Toorn 2007, 205–32). The scribes behind the wisdom books employed similar strategies, namely their version of the concept of revelation (see above), the attribution of some of their texts to Solomon, and the equation of wisdom with the Torah. The striking difference is that they did not point to human mediators of divine revelation. As in other respects these scribes prove to be quite elitist (see §4 below), this absence of mediators can hardly be a reflection of an egalitarian understanding of humans. Rather, it might be a consequence of the scribes' reflections on the cosmic significance of wisdom. Alternatively, it may reflect their investment in education, which accords not only with upholding tradition and reflection but also with the view that wisdom is not just revealed to special individuals but can be acquired by anyone who works hard enough.

4. Ethics and Understanding of Society

The wisdom books' ethics and understanding of society is another area where one can observe major differences from other Old Testament books. An important point here is that the focus of the wisdom books is on the individual, whereas in many other biblical books it is on Israel and, thus, the community. To a large extent this difference has to do with the different contents of these books—after all, the wisdom books are not concerned with Israel but with the question of how individuals can lead a successful life. However, as this question could be answered in many different ways, the uniformity of the answers given in the wisdom books is striking.

In one way or another, they all reflect the conviction that it is important to please God and that the best way to do so is to lead a decent life, guided by integrity, diligence, and moderation. Since humans live in community, frequently the wisdom books address interactions with others. And especially in these instances where the broader community is in view, it is striking how much the focus remains on the individual. Besides passages that praise friendship and solidarity as beneficial for the individual (e.g., Prov 17:17; Eccl 4:7–12; Sir 6:5–17) and others that point to society as a place where the deeds of individuals have consequences (e.g., Job 19:13–19; Prov 3:3–4; Eccl 8:10; Sir 10:6–7), this is most obvious in passages that deal with the weak in society. Such passages occur in most of the wisdom books (Ecclesiastes is an exception to a degree, but see below) and in some of them quite frequently. However, their primary concern clearly is not the health of society and the well-being of its weakest members. Rather, being generous to those in need is addressed because it is considered an integral aspect of a lifestyle that distinguishes a wise/righteous person from a foolish/godless one. As with all the other admonitions in the wisdom books, the major concern is the question of how one can please God (e.g., Job 31:16–17, 19–21; Prov 28:27; Sir 3:30–4:10; Wis 2:10–12).

In this respect, the wisdom books stand in contrast to other books in the Old Testament, in which the health of society and the well-being of the weak are a real concern—first and foremost several of the prophetic books and the Pentateuch (Schellenberg 2012). Though in all of these books the question of what behavior pleases God is important as well, they reflect higher awareness of structural problems causing poverty and powerlessness (e.g., Isa 5:8; 10:1–2; Amos 5:11–12; 8:4–5; Mic 2:1–2), do not shy away from pointing out the members of the upper class as those who exploit the weak (e.g., Isa 1:23; Jer 22:11–17; Ezek 22:6–12; Amos 6:1–6; Mic 3:1–3), expand the circle of those who must be treated with mercy and evoke a sense of solidarity (e.g., Exod 22:20–21; Deut 16:11–12), and contain at least some ideas about how the system could or should be changed—be it through a direct divine intervention (e.g., Isa 1:25–27; Ezek 34:20–22; Mal 3:5), a messianic figure (e.g., Isa 11:4–5; 61:1–3; Jer 23:5), or laws, which not only transform helping the weak from an act of mercy to a legal obligation (e.g., Exod 22:20–26; Deut 24:6, 10–15, 17–22) but in some cases also stipulate real social reforms to the benefit of the powerless (see esp. Exod 21:2–11; Lev 25; Deut 15:1–18).

Without a doubt, many statements on how one should deal with the weak sound similar, regardless of whether they are part of a wisdom book, a prophetic book, or the Pentateuch.[26] Nonetheless, in view of passages like the ones mentioned above, one can hardly overlook that the wisdom books are less socially conscious than other books of the Bible. This becomes even more obvious when one notes how directly the wisdom books link wealth with righteousness—the lack of social consciousness inherent in this link is evident when poverty is explained as one's own fault (thus frequently in Proverbs, e.g., Prov 10:4; 13:18; 21:17; see also Job 25:29; Eccl 4:5; Sir 18:33)—and how derogatorily some passages speak of slaves (e.g., Prov 29:19, 21; Eccl 2:7; Sir 33:25–32) and others in need (e.g., Prov 6:1–3; Sir 29:4–6). Clearly, the wisdom books reflect the view of people who are not interested in changing the system.[27] To an extent, this disinterest is an extension of the assumption that the cosmos is stable and that the order of the world will remain the same forever (see §2 above). According to this belief, the stability of social hierarchies is an apt reflection of cosmological stability, and major changes would be out of place. This is not the only factor at play, however. A look at the laws of the Pentateuch shows that the aim of transforming society into a more just place resonates with the notion of a stable cosmos. In the case of the scribes behind the wisdom books, their disinterest in such changes is also a reflection of their own social location. Though in antiquity the scribal profession made all scribes part of the elite, the wisdom books stand out not only in that they reflect this upper-class background more clearly than other books[28] but also in that they contain passages that show how frightening the prospect of societal changes was in the minds of the people behind them (see esp. Prov 19:10 and 30:21–23; further Job 3:19; 12:17–21; Eccl 10:7; Wis 18:11). The more critical wisdom books Job and Ecclesiastes might be reflections of changes that lowered the status of those by and for whom these books were written (Sneed 2012, 125–154; van der Toorn 2004, 128–129). Tell-

---

26. Compare, e.g., Job 31:19 with Exod 22:25; Isa 58:7; Ezek 18:7 (clothing); or Prov 22:22–23 with Exod 23:6; Amos 5:12 (fairness at court).

27. This is also true for the Egyptian instructions, even though here one finds at least one more radical idea of how to deal with the problem of poverty: in ch. 13 of the Instruction of Amenemope, the addressee is admonished to forgive a poor man two-thirds of the debts. Within the Old Testament, Sirach stands out through some kind of social-criticism (Collins 1997a, 29–30). However, this goes hand in hand with admonitions such as how to behave at banquets.

28. See especially admonitions that are addressed to rulers (e.g., Prov 31:1–9; Wis 1:1; see also Sir 10:1–5) or to those in high positions (e.g., Prov 25:6–7; Eccl 8:2–4; Sir 31:12–32:13).

ingly, however, not even they contain reflections on the necessity of societal changes. Rather, the character Job maintains that he should be treated with the respect that is owed to a patron like him (see Job 29–31), and God does not contradict him but rather, at the end, takes his side against the friends and restores him to his former position (Job 42:7–16). And even Ecclesiastes, who is aware of the suffering of others and realizes that there are injustices that come with the system, only observes this and does not admonish his addressees to work toward change (see Eccl 3:16; 4:1; 5:7).

5. Theology

The biblical wisdom books are also distinguished from other Old Testament books in the area of theology in the narrow sense of the word, that is, in the understanding of God and how God is present in the world. In one way or another, they all depict God as the creator of the world and thus, (1) highlight God's universal power, without entering the debates about polytheism and monotheism,[29] (2) show no interest in God's/YHWH's special relationship with Israel but rather, (3) focus on God's relationship with individuals, thereby (4) highlighting the aspect of justice, that is, fair retribution, which (5) is assumed to be experienced naturally. Though none of these aspects is unique to wisdom literature, in combination they reflect a distinct theology.

In itself, the notion of creation does not set the wisdom books apart from the rest of the Old Testament. In one way or another this notion is widespread throughout the ancient Near East. However, in the wisdom books the belief that God is the creator has much more weight than in other texts, and it influences most other aspects of the understanding of God. Probably, the monotheistic tendency (Weeks 2010, 117–19) even in wisdom texts that originated in premonotheistic times (in addition to the oldest ones from the Old Testament, this includes those from the ancient Near East) has to do with this influence as well. Most importantly, the wisdom texts reflect an understanding of God as the creator that is closely connected with the notion of order (see §2 above). Based on the assumption that God is the one who established the order of the world, they reflect

---

29. Wisdom of Solomon 13 is the only Old Testament wisdom text that reflects these controversies. Even more surprising than the lack of references to other gods and idols is the way some wisdom books talk about Woman Wisdom (see §3 above), namely, without any indication that there might be questions about her divine status.

on God's maintenance of it. By pointing out God's justice in blessing the righteous and cursing the wicked (Proverbs, Sirach, Wisdom of Solomon), God's (apparent) injustice in attacking the righteous (Job), or God's unpredictability in acting in ways that cannot be understood by humans (Ecclesiastes, Job), they all describe God as rather impersonal but at the same time heavily involved in individuals' lives. The God of the wisdom books pays close attention to humans' doings (e.g., Prov 15:3; Sir 17:15, 19–20; Wis 1:8) and interferes with their lives, either in keeping with expectations (e.g., Prov 15:29; Sir 2:8; Wis 1:9) or against them (e.g., Job 19:4–11; Eccl 9:1–3).

Though normally not expressed to this degree, most other Old Testament books reflect the understanding that God/YHWH pays attention to humans' deeds, assesses their righteousness, and influences their well-being (see esp. Deuteronomy and the Prophets). At the same time, many of these books depict YHWH as a more personal deity, frequently referring to his emotions (e.g., Exod 20:5; Isa 54:6–8)[30] and mentioning divine actions that are not reactions to human actions (e.g., Gen 12:1; Deut 7:6–8). Furthermore, only a few of these books/texts depict God as interested in the individual (in particular the psalms of the individual); the majority, however, focus on how YHWH interacts with Israel. In themselves, neither of these differences is fundamental: in the case of the depiction of God we are dealing with questions of degree, and focusing on individuals and the entire people are not mutually exclusive. However, in most books the focus on Israel and the emphasis on YHWH's emotions and unexpected actions are connected with further theological assumptions, which are not in line with the understanding of God reflected in the wisdom books.

Most importantly, in one way or another all Old Testament books that focus on Israel share the conviction that Israel is special because YHWH has established a special relationship with it (election, covenant, etc.). Though this assumption may well be connected with the notion that YHWH is the creator of the entire world (see Gen 1 as the beginning of P; the praise of YHWH as creator in Deutero-Isaiah), it outshines it as the relationship with Israel is presented as more personal than this general creator-creature relationship. As in one way or the other this special

---

30. The wisdom books mention some emotions of God as well. In the book of Job, the wrath of God is important as this is the way Job experiences God (e.g., Job 14:13; 16:9). In Sirach and Wisdom of Solomon, God's "mercy" is mentioned frequently (e.g., Sir 16:11–12, 16; 18:11–14; Wis 3:9; 11:23).

relationship between God/YHWH and Israel is highly important in most other books of the Old Testament, it is striking that it is not mentioned in Proverbs, Job, and Ecclesiastes and is only partially integrated in Sirach and Wisdom of Solomon (see below). Whereas for the oldest wisdom texts one can speculate on the extent to which the salvation history traditions were already developed and known at that time,[31] for the later ones it is clear that the scribes behind them must have known them.[32] So how is one to understand the wisdom books' silence on this subject? It cannot be explained on the basis of the focus on the individual—after all, as an individual one is still part of one's people and interacts with the same God who also interacts with the people as a whole. Although in theory this second point could be an option, none of the Old Testament texts point in this direction. Further, the wisdom texts, while they prefer generic terms such as "El" or "Elohim," sometimes also use the proper name "YHWH" and thus clarify that the God they are talking about is none other than the God of Israel. Neither can the wisdom books' silence on God's relationship with Israel be explained with universalistic thinking in the sense of an inclusive theology that decidedly holds that foreigners are as worthy as Israelites. Though the wisdom books do imply that they talk about humanity in general and mention some non-Israelites in prominent roles (see Job 1:1; 2:11; 32:2; Prov 30:1; 31:1; also Wis 1:1, etc.), the idea of equality is never expressed explicitly and there are statements (like Sir 8:18; 11:34) that contradict it.[33] Rather, the casual way foreigners are mentioned (see also Sir 10:22) indicates that the question of equality/difference between Israelites and others is not theologically important in the wisdom books. Israel's salvation history is not mentioned because the scribes behind the wisdom books did not consider it relevant, either for understanding God or for knowing how an individual Israelite should behave.

Interestingly, this impression is even confirmed in Wisdom of Solomon, though about half of this book deals with Israel's salvation history

---

31. See Carr 2011, 403–7, who uses the silence about these traditions in Proverbs as an argument for dating the whole book early.

32. In addition to the explicit references in Sirach and Wisdom of Solomon, this is clear because Proverbs, Job, and Ecclesiastes reflect knowledge of Old Testament books (or earlier forms of them) in which these traditions are prominent.

33. That wisdom is an international phenomenon would only be relevant for the question of whether the wisdom texts reflect a universalistic perspective if there was an international wisdom movement in the sense of an organization. This is most unlikely.

(see Wis 10–19). The formulations indicate that this history is retold not for its own sake but rather as an illustration. In addition to the use of general terms (righteous, ungodly, foolish, etc.) to describe the Israelites and their enemies, this lack of emphasis is most evident in those passages that draw lessons from the Israel's salvation history (see Wis 11:21–12:2; 12:11–18). They describe God's actions without alluding to a special relationship with Israel, instead stressing that God is the creator of the entire world and cares for all. Accordingly, Wisdom of Solomon is addressed to the "the rulers of the earth" (see §3 above). Only in Sirach does the notion of a special relationship of YHWH with Israel have more importance. To an extent, this has to do with Ben Sira's professional pride as a scribe who is well acquainted with all the traditions of his people (see Sir 38:34; 39:1–8). For him, the ancestors and the ancient traditions are important as a source of wisdom (see Sir 44:1–15). He especially highlights the Torah as a source of wisdom. Primarily, this is a strategy to demonstrate the relevance of wisdom (see §3 above). Nonetheless, in connection with this strategy, Ben Sira does sometimes highlight the special relationship of God with Israel. This is most clearly the case in Sir 24:8–12, where he describes how God advised Wisdom to settle in Jerusalem. Here, the notion of an exclusive relationship between God and Israel influences how Ben Sira describes wisdom. However, in Sir 17:11–12 the influence is the other way around. There, the argument that God is the creator of all humanity and has equipped everyone with intellectual abilities influences how Ben Sira describes the revelation at Mount Sinai and the covenant—namely, in a paragraph where it remains open whether he still speaks about all humans (see Sir 17:1) or about the Israelites only, as in the continuation (see Sir 17:17). Ultimately, YHWH's special relationship with Israel is not that important in Sirach either.

Furthermore, connected with the notion of a special relationship of YHWH with Israel, several Old Testament books describe extraordinary actions of God, for example, miracles like the one at the Red Sea, revelations like the one at Mount Sinai, or transformations like the one described in Ezek 36:26. Admittedly, here we have to be careful as the ancients did not distinguish between natural and supernatural as we do, so the notion that God influences the well-being of an individual is only slightly different from the notion that God influences the well-being of a people (compare, for example, Prov 21:31 and Isa 45:17), and descriptions of supernatural actions of God in the past can also be explained by faithfulness to the tradition (as in the case of Sirach and Wisdom of Solomon) and do not necessarily reflect the theology of the scribes who composed/edited these books. Nonetheless, it remains noteworthy that, for the most part, the wisdom books describe God as being experienced naturally (that is, through factors like longevity, health, wealth, offspring, etc.) and, unlike many other books from the Old Testament, contain very few statements about happenings that we today would describe as supernatural.[34]

That the wisdom books exhibit an understanding of God that is distinct from the understanding exhibited in other Old Testament books, finally, is also reflected in what they say about questions of piety and worship. No doubt, in this area there is considerable variety throughout the Old Testament and many of these understandings can be explained with the specific contents of the respective books. Nonetheless, with their emphasis on the fear of YHWH/God[35] and their disregard of cultic issues (purity, sacrifices, festivals, etc.),[36] the wisdom books stand out so clearly that it seems likely that the difference has something to do with different theologies. Indeed, the emphasis on the fear of YHWH/God fits in very

---

34. In addition to the few descriptions of direct divine revelations (see §3 above), most of them are found in the passages in Sirach and Wisdom of Solomon that deal with Israel's salvation history. Sirach 36 is another exception, but many consider this chapter a late insertion (Collins 1997a, 109–11).

35. The wisdom books reflect some variety in their understanding of the fear of YHWH or fearing God; however, with the exception of Wisdom of Solomon, the notion is important in all of them. Normally it is closely connected with wisdom (here, Ecclesiastes is the exception), and in all cases it describes the right attitude of humans vis-à-vis God. Other Old Testament books mention the fear of YHWH, fearing God, and the like as well. Normally the notion does not have the same importance as it has in the wisdom books, though. Striking in particular is that within the prophetic books the notion of the fear of God is important only in Isaiah, even though several others share the wisdom books' reserved attitude toward the cult.

36. It is striking both how seldom the wisdom books address issues related to the cult and how many of the few allusions reflect a distancing (e.g., Prov 15:8; 21:3; Eccl 4:17; 5:1; Sir 7:9; 35:15). Certainly, there are also some positive statements about sacrifices and the like (e.g., Job 1:5; 42:8; Eccl 9:2; Sir 7:30; 35:6–13; 38:11). Ben Sira, especially, has a positive attitude toward the cult, as reflected in the length of the passage on Aaron (see Sir 45:6–22), the inclusion of Aaron's grandson Phineas among the ancestors to be praised (see Sir 45:23–26), and the culmination of this entire section with a long passage on the high priest Simon (see Sir 50:1–21). At the same time, however, Ben Sira stresses that observing cultic laws is less important than following ethical norms and leading a life in righteousness (see Sir 34:21–24, 30–31; 35:1–5). On this point he is agreement with many of the prophets.

well with the wisdom books' understanding of God and their focus on God's power. Likewise, the disregard of cultic issues might be explained by the connection of cult and national concerns/salvation history,[37] or with the role that religious specialists (priests) play in it as mediators between ordinary humans and God,[38] or with the tension between the concept of atonement and the focus on justice/righteousness.

Conclusion

When at the end of his introduction to the wisdom literature Weeks concludes that "at the level of ideas, it is difficult to find anything in the wisdom literature as a whole which is not found elsewhere as well" (Weeks 2010, 142), he is right. However, in my view, he downplays the fact that the wisdom books share many ideas that are distinct from the ideas reflected in other books—if not all of these ideas, then still many. And these distinctive ideas are not just random, but are connected with each other. For example, the assumption that the order of the world will not change is related to the conservative view of society; and the epistemology of the wisdom books is congruent with their focus on creation/the order inherent in the world (empiricism) and their disregard of Israel's salvation history (no mediators; the difference between Israelites and non-Israelites irrelevant). At this point it becomes difficult to argue that all these differences from the other books are just a consequence of the wisdom books' genres and their particular focuses. Rather, the evidence indicates that the wisdom books share a distinct set of theological/ideological premises, which are all interrelated and influence the wisdom books' understanding in areas as diverse as cosmology, epistemology, ethics, and theology. Thus, it seems appropriate to speak about a sapiential understanding of the world (if not worldview).[39]

---

37. It is at least striking that Sirach, where the special relationship of YHWH with Israel has at least some importance, is the wisdom book that speaks most positively about the cult and priests (see n. 36).

38. Interesting in this regard is the book of Job: it mentions sacrifices but neither priests nor the temple (see Job 1:5; 42:8).

39. See again the worldview questions mentioned in n. 10. The sapiential understanding of the world as outlined above includes answers to most, but not all, of these questions. The decision of whether this qualifies as worldview depends on how many different worldviews one wants to distinguish. In a fundamental way, the sapiential understanding is not different from all other ancient Near Eastern understandings of the world, as all of them share the basic conviction that the world and everything in it

In my view, the pendulum has swung from one extreme to the other, and it is time to let it rest in the middle. The wisdom tradition was neither a *Fremdkörper* in ancient Israel (Gese 1958, 2; Preuß 1970, 414), nor was it no tradition at all but only "a mode of literature" (Sneed 2011, 71). The family resemblance among the wisdom books speaks against letting go of the notion of a sapiential understanding of the world, as clear as it is that this understanding was neither set in stone once and forever nor distinct from other understandings on each and every issue. The problem of pinpointing the people who shared and promoted this sapiential understanding of the world makes it hard to determine how widespread it was. However, the inclusion of three wisdom books in the Hebrew canon and five in the Greek, the existence of wisdom psalms in the Psalter, the wisdom influence in other books, and the efforts to prove sapiential compatibility with the Torah (see Deut 4:5–8; 30:11–14) indicate that it had influential proponents.

Works Consulted

Assmann, Jan. 2005. *Theologie und Weisheit im alten Ägypten*. Munich: Fink.

———. 2006. *Ma'at: Gerechtigkeit und Unsterblichkeit im Alten Ägypten*. 2nd ed. Munich: Beck.

Ben Zvi, Ehud. 2003. "The Prophetic Book: A Key Form of Prophetic Literature." Pages 276–97 in *The Changing Face of Form Criticism for the Twenty-First Century*. Edited by Marvin A. Sweeny and Ehud Ben Zvi. Grand Rapids: Eerdmans.

Carr, David M. 2005. *Writing on the Tablet of the Heart: Origins of Scripture and Literature*. Oxford: Oxford University Press.

———. 2011. *The Formation of the Hebrew Bible: A New Reconstruction*. Oxford: Oxford University Press.

Collins, John J. 1990. "The Sage in the Apocalyptic and Pseudepigraphic Literature." Pages 343–54 in *The Sage in Israel and the Ancient Near East*. Edited by John G. Gammie and Leo G. Perdue. Winona Lake, IN: Eisenbrauns.

---

is created and influenced by God/divine powers. With regard to details, however, there are many differences.

———. 1993. "Wisdom, Apocalypticism, and Generic Compatibility." Pages 165–85 in *In Search of Wisdom: Essays in Memory of John G. Gammie*. Edited by Leo G. Perdue, Bernard Brandon Scott, and William Johnston Wiseman. Louisville: Westminster John Knox.

———. 1997a. *Jewish Wisdom in the Hellenistic Age*. OTL. Louisville: Westminster John Knox.

———. 1997b. "Wisdom Reconsidered, in Light of the Scrolls." *DSD* 4:265–81.

———. 2005a. "The Mysteries of God: Creation and Eschatology in 4QInstruction and the *Wisdom of Solomon*." Pages 159–80 in *Jewish Cult and Hellenistic Culture: Essays on the Jewish Encounter with Hellenism and Roman Rule*. JSJSup 100. Leiden: Brill.

———. 2005b. "The Reinterpretation of Apocalyptic Traditions in the Wisdom of Solomon." Pages 143–58 in *Jewish Cult and Hellenistic Culture: Essays on the Jewish Encounter with Hellenism and Roman Rule*. JSJSup 100. Leiden: Brill.

Crenshaw, James L. 2010. *Old Testament Wisdom: An Introduction*. 3rd ed. Louisville: Westminster John Knox Press.

Dell, Katharine J. 2006. *The Book of Proverbs in Social and Theological Context*. Cambridge: Cambridge University Press.

Gese, Hartmut. 1958. *Lehre und Wirklichkeit in der alten Weisheit: Studien zu den Sprüchen Salomos und zu dem Buche Hiob*. Tübingen: Mohr.

Goff, Matthew J. 2007. *Discerning Wisdom: The Sapiential Literature of the Dead Sea Scrolls*. VTSup 116. Leiden: Brill.

Grabbe, Lester L. 1995. *Priests, Prophets, Diviners, Sages: A Socio-Historical Study of Religious Specialists in Ancient Israel*. Valley Forge, PA: Trinity Press International.

Krüger, Thomas. 1997a. "Dekonstruktion und Rekonstruktion prophetischer Eschatologie im Qohelet-Buch." Pages 151–72 in *Kritische Weisheit: Studien zur weisheitlichen Traditionskritik im Alten Testament*. Zurich: Pano.

———. 1997b. "Die Rezeption der Tora im Buch Kohelet." Pages 173–93 in *Kritische Weisheit: Studien zur weisheitlichen Traditionskritik im Alten Testament*. Zurich: Pano.

———. 2006. "Überlegungen zur Bedeutung der Traditionsgeschichte für das Verständnis alttestamentlicher Texte und zur Weiterentwicklung der traditionsgeschichtlichen Methode." Pages 233–45 in *Lesarten der Bibel: Untersuchungen zu einer Theorie der Exegese des Alten Tes-

taments. Edited by Helmut Utschneider and Erhard Blum. Stuttgart: Kohlhammer.

Lange, Armin. 2008. "Sages and Scribes in Qumran Literature." Pages 271–93 in *Scribes, Sages, and Seers: The Sage in the Eastern Mediterranean World*. Edited by Leo G. Perdue. FRLANT 219. Göttingen: Vandenhoeck & Ruprecht.

Murphy, Roland E. 1981. *Wisdom Literature: Job, Proverbs, Ruth, Canticles, Ecclesiastes and Esther*. FOTL 13. Grand Rapids: Eerdmans.

Nihan, Christophe. 2009. "The Priestly Covenant, Its Reinterpretation, and the Composition of 'P.'" Pages 87–134 in *The Strata of the Priestly Writings: Contemporary Debate and Future Directions*. Edited by Sarah Shectman and Joel S. Baden. ATANT 95. Zurich: TVZ.

Perdue, Leo G. 2007. *Wisdom Literature: A Theological History*. Louisville: Westminster John Knox.

Preuß, Hans Dietrich. 1970. "Erwägungen zum theologischen Ort der alttestamentlichen Weisheitsliteratur." *EvT* 30:393–417.

Schellenberg, Annette. 2002. *Erkenntnis als Problem: Qohelet und die alttestamentliche Diskussion um das menschliche Erkennen*. OBO 188. Fribourg: Universitätsverlag; Göttingen: Vandenhoeck & Ruprecht.

———. 2010. "A 'Lying Pen of the Scribes' (Jer 8:8)? Orality and Writing in the Formation of Prophetic Books." Pages 285–309 in *The Interface of Orality and Writing: Speaking, Seeing, Writing in the Shaping of New Genres*. Edited by Annette Weissenrieder and Robert B. Coote. WUNT 1/260. Tübingen: Mohr Siebeck.

———. 2012. "Hilfe für Witwen und Waisen: Ein gemein-altorientalisches Motiv in wechselnden alttestamentlichen Diskussionszusammenhängen." *ZAW* 124:180–200.

Schipper, Bernd U. 2012. *Hermeneutik der Tora: Studien zur Traditionsgeschichte von Prov 2 und zur Komposition von Prov 1–9*. BZAW 432. Berlin: de Gruyter.

Schmid, Hans Heinrich. 1966. *Wesen und Geschichte der Weisheit: Eine Untersuchung zur altorientalischen und israelitischen Weisheitsliteratur*. BZAW 101. Berlin: Töpelmann.

———. 1968. *Gerechtigkeit als Weltordnung: Hintergrund und Geschichte des alttestamentlichen Gerechtigkeitsbegriffes*. BHT 40. Tübingen: Mohr Siebeck.

Schmid, Konrad. 2008. "The Authors of Job and Their Historical and Social Setting." Pages 145–53 in *Scribes, Sages, and Seers: The Sage in the Eastern Mediterranean World*. FRLANT 219. Edited by Leo G. Perdue. Göttingen: Vandenhoeck & Ruprecht.

———. 2011. "Schriftgelehrte Arbeit an der Schrift: Historische Überlegungen zum Vorgang innerbiblischer Exegese." Pages 35–60 in *Schriftgelehrte Traditionsliteratur: Fallstudien zur innerbiblischen Schriftauslegung im Alten Testament*. FAT 77. Tübingen: Mohr Siebeck.

Schniedewind, William M. 2004. *How the Bible Became a Book: The Textualization of Ancient Israel*. Cambridge: Cambridge University Press.

Sneed, Mark R. 2011. "Is the 'Wisdom Tradition' a Tradition?" *CBQ* 73:50–71.

———. 2012. *The Politics of Pessimism in Ecclesiastes: A Social-Science Perspective*. AIL 12. Atlanta: Society of Biblical Literature.

Steck, Odil Hannes. 1982 [1978]. "Strömungen theologischer Tradition im Alten Testament." Pages 291–317 in *Wahrnehmungen Gottes im Alten Testament: Gesammelte Studien*. TB 70. Munich: Kaiser.

Toorn, Karel van der. 2004. "Revelation as a Scholarly Construct in Israel and Mesopotamia." Pages 125–38 in *Theologie in Israel und in den Nachbarkulturen: Beiträge des Symposiums "Das Alte Testament und die Kultur der Moderne" anlässlich des 100. Geburtstags Gerhard von Rads (1901–1971), Heidelberg, 18.–21. Oktober 2001*. Edited by Manfred Oeming, Konrad Schmid, and Andreas Schüle. ATM 9. Münster: LIT.

———. 2007. *Scribal Culture and the Making of the Hebrew Bible*. Cambridge: Harvard University Press.

VanderKam, James C. 2007. "Mapping Second Temple Judaism." Pages 1–20 in *The Early Enoch Literature*. Edited by Gabriele Boccaccini and John J. Collins. JSJSup 121. Leiden: Brill.

Vidal, Clément. 2008. "What Is a Worldview?" Published in Dutch as "Wat is een wereldbeeld?" Pages 71–85 in *Nieuwheid denken: De wetenschappen en het creatieve aspect van de werkelijkheid*. Edited by Hubert van Belle and Jan van der Veken. Leuven: Acco. English version at http://cogprints.org/6094/.

Weeks, Stuart. 1994. *Early Israelite Wisdom*. Oxford: Oxford University Press.

———. 1999. "Wisdom in the Old Testament." Pages 19–30 in *Where Shall Wisdom Be Found? Wisdom in the Bible, the Church and the Contemporary World*. Edited by Stephen C. Barton. Edinburgh: T&T Clark.

———. 2005. "Wisdom Psalms." Pages 292–307 in *Temple and Worship in Biblical Israel*. Edited by John Day. LHBOTS 422. London: T&T Clark.

———. 2010. *An Introduction to the Study of Wisdom Literature*. London: T&T Clark.
Whybray, R. N. 1974. *The Intellectual Tradition in the Old Testament*. BZAW 135. Berlin: de Gruyter.

Deciding the Boundaries of "Wisdom": Applying the Concept of Family Resemblance

Katharine J. Dell

The Proverb and the Book of Proverbs

At the heart of wisdom is the proverb.[1] Someone, somewhere first coined a proverb. The aim was to make a comparison of human behavior with a well-known image and to contrast the positive effect of one type of behavior with its negative opposite. The mainspring of it was personal experience, the point of saying it was to tell of that experience to another so that they would learn it too. The style had to be pithy, short, memorable, even clever, to show off a great wit and intellect, but it also had to be true, or at least relatively so. Relatively because its second line could be replaced with an alternative depending on who was being addressed or whether a variation in topic was desired. It had to draw images from the world that both coiner and recipient shared and yet avoid the mundane or the obvious despite its everyday appearance. It needed to provide alternative paths for the good and bad adherent–an ethical choice was at stake. It was about right and wrong even if it was sometimes embellished with clever imagery or even talk of God or king. It might have been written by a father to his son or a mother to her child, or a teacher to their pupil, or even a king to his subjects, not that those roles are not overlapping and complementary to some extent. In Israel, it might have been coined by a great king called Solomon, or by one of his courtiers, or by the Queen of Sheba, his old sparring partner (1 Kgs 10), but the original speaker, and indeed the original proverb, has been lost in the mists of time–what is now in front of me,

---

1. So Sneed (2011, 65) writes, "The proverb or sentence is the most fundamental, and thus, the primary genre of the wisdom literature" and cites Sumerian parallels.

a reader far removed from that original coining, is just the proverb, and many more like it, indeed a whole book of Proverbs.

In 2000 I wrote that the book of Proverbs is "a book universally acknowledged as the supreme example of traditional Israelite wisdom" and of the proverb, "the proverb is the basic form of all wisdom and in that sense is at the heart of the enterprise." (Dell, 2000, 5). I stand by those statements. Although there may be older proverbs and collections from the ancient Near East,[2] the proverb is the mainspring of the biblical wisdom enterprise. The proverb is both an oral and a literary phenomenon[3] and hence one is immediately drawn into questions of oral (and written) context as well as literary genre. The question of who coined and used each proverb is just as relevant as who collected them and who produced the finished literary product. While the whole procedure of speaking of a wisdom genre is to take a literary approach and to perceive wisdom as a literary tradition,[4] it did not always have this character. I would suggest that there are oral precedents that need to be taken into account which lead us back to questions of context, itself an essential part of the genre definition. What Sneed (2011) critiques Gunkel (1926), the father of form criticism, for doing is for assuming that a genre leads to a group, that a literary tradition leads to those who produced it, and to the question of who they were. Sneed argues that we have been too prescriptive about the so-called sages or scribes who produced the literature, seeing a genre as narrowly tied to a context, to the degree that we have been unable to see beyond this linkage to a broader picture. I will return to this point.

Classifying Wisdom

The recognition of the primary place of Proverbs and within it the proverb helps us in any classification of wisdom. We may choose to count the occurrences of חכמה/חכם, like Whybray (1974), to ascertain this classification. We may wish to note the elements of Proverbs that go beyond

---

2. E.g., Sumerian collections of proverbs coming from the late second millennium BCE; see Alster (1997).

3. Contra Sneed (2011, 66). I do not agree that proverbs "are literary products meant to be read and studied, not used orally," I believe they function on both levels. Sneed overprioritizes the literary context in my view.

4. Sneed (2011, 50) opens his article with this point: "Few commentators have any problem referring to the Hebrew wisdom literature as a distinctive literary tradition."

simply the proverb and which provide us with the context for reading them—so Prov 1–9 with its longer instructions[5] and poems (1:20–33, 3:13–18; 8) that reveal the uniting figure of Wisdom (חכמה) who embodies the didactic, intellectual and ethical core of the wisdom quest. Miscellaneous proverbs and poetry cohere under the umbrella of Wisdom, at once a female character and an abstract idea. These roads lead us back to Proverbs, the head of the family of wisdom books. It is where to go from here that becomes more challenging.

Van Leeuwen (2005, 638) writes "Proverbs is the foundational wisdom book of the Bible, teaching the ABCs of wisdom and introducing more complex issues that are further elaborated in Ecclesiastes, Job and the wisdom teaching of the New Testament." It is here, at the point of going beyond Proverbs, that disagreement begins among scholars over what exactly to include in the wisdom category and what the criteria for inclusion should be.[6] Once we have more than one book we have a category, or we can speak of influence or even common purpose. Scholars of the past used different labels—writings, poetry, philosophy. The question is raised: How should we carve up the canon?

That Job and Ecclesiastes should also form this biblical core of wisdom books and that the category should be further defined by the apocryphal books of Ben Sira and the Wisdom of Solomon is usually taken for granted,[7] but the material is actually very diverse in nature and genre. There seems to be a common concern with wisdom issues among these books, (books that we have, in circular fashion, labeled wisdom on the basis of such issues) and some have more commonalities than others, but is this enough? It all depends on one's criteria. Then the question arises, should the net be widened to other parts of the Old Testament, to narratives such as the Joseph narrative (von Rad 1966) and the Succession Narrative (Whybray 1968) or to a slippery selection of psalms that appear to

---

5. There is some debate among scholars as to whether these sections of Proverbs 1–9 should be called instructions, following Egyptian precursors. Whybray (1974) argues for ten short instructions in Prov 1–9. Fox (2000), while maintaining similar boundaries, prefers to call them "interludes." Weeks (2007) argues that since Egyptian instructions were much longer, the word is a misnomer for these short pieces.

6. This is to pick up on an older debate. For a summary see Dell 2005, ch. 1.

7. This is taken for granted in all introductions to the wisdom literature, e.g., Crenshaw 2010; Weeks 2010.

be wisdom in character,[8] to Song of Songs[9] and beyond. There are then the parallels from the ancient Near Eastern world, themselves not classified as wisdom,[10] but recognizably part of the same didactic and ethical quest.[11] The criteria for inclusion can be kept narrow[12] or they can become very broad (Morgan 1981).

Genre Criteria

A highly successful set of criteria—not of what was wisdom, but in reference to wider literary convention—was established by Gunkel (1926) in his form-critical method. He stressed form, content, and context as the three main elements that established a *Gattung* or genre. His aim was to discover the historical evolution of different genres, and so the contextual aspect was always primary. This idea of genre classification has held the field for a long time, although I would argue that its application has become more literary over time. It was on a narrow form-critical literary definition that I argued (Dell 1991) that Job is not strictly wisdom[13] in genre because on the level of small forms there are many taken from other walks of life, the lament and the law court in particular (and often parodied, e,g., Job 7:7–8/Ps 8:4).

Weeks questions whether wisdom is a separate category at all[14] and argues that the heavily intertwined nature of the genres within its books

---

8. First noted by J. F. Bruch (1851), who noticed "gnomischen Psalmen." A precursor to Gunkel's classification of wisdom psalms, O. Zöckler (1867) anticipated him with three categories for didactic psalms, those of content, form, and didactic tendency.

9. Which most scholars do not see as wisdom in genre, but which Roland E. Murphy (2002) includes in his introduction to the wisdom literature.

10. W. G. Lambert (1960) famously made the point that Babylonian wisdom literature (the title of one of his books) was only so named because of the scholarly grouping of Israelite wisdom literature.

11. See Weeks (2010) who begins his introduction with the ancient Near Eastern material seeing these as forming criteria for selecting Israelite texts of a similar character.

12. Crenshaw has always maintained that a narrow definition is best. In the third edition of *Old Testament Wisdom* (2010), he does not want to attribute any wisdom psalms to the sages (in a change from his earlier view), showing how the classification is, for him, linked to context, i.e., wise authors/sages.

13. I am avoiding terms such as *wisdom literature* in order to keep the wisdom classification simple, but the discussion could, of course, be more nuanced.

14. Weeks (2010, 142) certainly sees "wisdom literature" as "our category, not one bequeathed to us by the biblical writers themselves."

make distinguishing them a circular enterprise. He writes, "This works both ways: if the sentence literature in Proverbs can pose sometimes as instruction, so too can the instructions sometimes borrow the style of sentence literature" (2010, 24). While I acknowledge the closely integrated nature of these smaller genres, I still would argue that there is another layer of genre above the individual ones that make up the larger category of "wisdom." Sneed (2011, 57) also argues that genre classification has to be at the smaller level and that "Hebrew wisdom literature should be described as a mode of literature and not strictly a genre." Mode of literature is a broader category, but surely genre categorization can operate on a number of different levels so that small sections and whole works or groups of works can be described using this terminology. I maintain that Proverbs with its emphasis on wisdom/Wisdom has established a wisdom genre thematically and that common forms such as the proverbs and a context in teaching (and let us not forget the context aspect of genre) support the idea that there is a recognizable genre of wisdom here. The question is one of degree—how much wisdom does a book need to be classified as such?[15] Should one remain conservative or become liberal on this issue?

Sneed argues that it was Gunkel's association of the genre with a specific group of sages or scribes that led scholarship down the rather false path of assuming a tradition in a specific, narrow context. I would contest, with Sneed against Gunkel, that, despite uncertainties about the context, all genres must have contexts, probably more than one as time goes by. Sneed also makes the point that given that the scribes were the elite and educated of society, they probably composed the whole of scripture, and so to confine them to a small part of the canon is mistaken. However, in my view, there is a distinction to be made between the sages who may have taught and disseminated proverbs and instructions, and the scribes who were their successors in forming the literary canon that we have today. Another important distinction needs to be made between the oral transmission and early written stages of the material, and the later bringing together of entire sections and books. It may be true that context has tended to drive the discussion too much—and I would agree with Sneed that a more literary starting point is what is needed in such questions of

---

15. Weeks cites my own decision not to classify Job as wisdom in a narrow sense of smaller genres as evidence that the genre system does not work, but, in fact, I believe this decision upholds the point that genres work on different levels and refer to different amounts and groupings of material.

genre definition; that is largely the route I am taking here. Context cannot be limited and fixed—although each proverb or any other genre has its original somewhere. Context is an ever-changing aspect of genre, as form and content find new addressees—and so it needs careful definition.

Widening the net of possible wisdom contenders highlights the criteria problem. Should we include narrative texts about Solomon which would link the narrative about him in Kings with his attributed books? That would then be an argument for the inclusion of the love song of the Song of Songs too—it contains five references to the great king (Dell 2010). Should we see political intrigue and human self-sufficiency in the Succession Narrative as sufficient to call this wisdom (Whybray 1968)? If wisdom was the preserve of kings and courtiers, then such a narrative would not be out of place, nor that about Joseph, the ideal wise man (von Rad 1966), nor Daniel, the wise interpreter of dreams (see Goldingay 1989). Two questions arise: How do we define wisdom in terms of its influence and, once we have attempted to do so, how do we classify any text showing significant influence from the wisdom genre? For example, using traditional form-critical categories, wisdom psalms[16] could be said to be both wisdom and psalms; their form may be quite different from wisdom books (except for the lament sections of Job) and their context is likely to be cultic rather than didactic, not that these two are necessarily mutually exclusive.[17] Furthermore some psalms show considerable wisdom elements, for example, Pss 37 and 49, while others are on the edge of such a classification.[18] How then do we evaluate significant wisdom influence?

An Alternative to Form Criticism?

In an attempt to solve this problem Simon Cheung (forthcoming) suggests some new criteria that take us away from form criticism. Building on the

---

16. There are almost as many scholarly suggestions as to which psalms are wisdom psalms are as there are scholars. See the chart in Cheung forthcoming, 200–201.

17. See Dell (2003), where I argued against Mowinckel and others that the wisdom psalms could well come from a cultic context.

18. Cheung (2015) distinguishes helpfully between different levels of wisdom influence on psalms in his use of examples both from generally agreed upon wisdom psalms such as 37 and 49 and of more disputed wisdom psalms such as 128, 32, 39, and 19.

findings of speech-act theory he suggests that three new elements should define any wisdom (or didactic) psalm. First, there needs to be a "ruling wisdom thrust," that is, an overall dominance of wisdom concerns in the piece. Second, there needs to be an "intellectual tone." This involves stylistic devices weaved together in an intellectual way by the use of reason and is an acknowledgement that, as with the proverbs themselves, wisdom is an art of cleverness. Third, there should be a "didactic speech intention," that is, the teaching role, whether formal or informal, is another key raison d'être for the wisdom genre, as most fully explicated in Proverbs (Cheung forthcoming, 36–37). This is an attempt to uncover the essential elements of wisdom without being tied to the form, content, and context structure of form criticism, although there are undoubtably similarities between these three alternative sets of classifications and form criticism.

So, the "ruling wisdom thrust" acknowledges that the content of wisdom must be there. Cheung argues that this category is not the same as content—it is not a matter of counting relevant themes, it is about overall purpose. He writes, "A psalm may have several themes, both wisdom—and nonwisdom-related; but in order to prove itself wisdom, its ruling thrust has to incline towards wisdom" (forthcoming, 32). So it is not identical with content, but, in its evaluation of thematic concerns, it stands close. In my view, content should have priority over form in more traditional assessments.[19] Then the "intellectual tone" resembles the form but is certainly more nuanced—it is about the use of formal and structural devices and yet it is related to communicative purpose (which has an intellectual framework)—and the "didactic speech intention" starts to bring us to context (as does "intellectual tone" in that it takes intellectuals to create such a tone[20]). And then it brings us to whoever first mouthed and then wrote down the wisdom material, although Cheung is more interested in a general teaching intention than in trying to say anything about who these teachers might have been. The intention of didactic speeches also contains elements of form, in that teaching-related formal devices help to establish didacticism. Hence questions of specific context or authorship are left out of these criteria: it is not about composition equaling a specific type of authorship; it is about authors using genres of varying types to communicate, wisdom being just one of those types

---

19. See Dell 2003, where I argued that the content of creation ideas was a key factor in the criteria for determining wisdom psalms.

20. Cf. Whybray's (1974) "intellectual tradition" idea.

of communication. As Cheung writes, "Generic elements are thus not deployed as a kind of 'signature mark' indicating the origin of the psalm. In fact, every writer devises a new genre by creatively incorporating and manipulating the elements of other established genres" (2015, 6).

An Alternative to Wisdom?

It is frustration borne of these definition and classification problems that has led, in some recent work, to questioning the category "wisdom." Weeks (2010) suggests that we reject it as a genre classification in the interests of simply building a piece by piece picture of material with common interests, a mosaic that ultimately demonstrates the broad interconnectedness of the whole Bible.

Coming from a different angle, Kynes (forthcoming) explores the origins of the term that was borne out of nineteenth-century philosophy and well emphasizes the subjective nature of all attempts to classify—often reflective of a scholar's own concerns. He suggests, too, that a broad and more piecemeal approach is preferable to a narrow set of definitions, but he does not want to give up speaking of wisdom altogether given its prominence as a concept in Israelite thought. He calls for a mosaic, that ultimately demonstrates the broad interconnectedness of the whole Bible, rather than a mirror when he writes,

> Perhaps, it is time to break the mirror, scattering its shards throughout the Hebrew Bible and the ancient Near East, so that in gathering them again, interpreters might see the true nature of Israelite 'Wisdom' instead of merely their own reflections. The result will not be a mirror but a mosaic. Though a mosaic may not be as clear, it will likely be more accurate, and, perhaps, more attractive as well. (forthcoming, final page)

His work on intertextuality in relation to Job (Kynes 2012) has shown in particular how finding echoes of, and allusions to, texts within the material often points the way to different associations than a broader term such as wisdom might suggest. If we classify Job as wisdom it tends to lead us away from key psalmic parallels rather than in the direction of them. In this way he confirms the link of Job with Psalms as the closest genre relationship. This point about Job and various genre relationships indicates the direction I am going in this paper. Just because we suggest that the wisdom genre is present in a piece of writing it does not mean it has to be exclusively categorized as such. Wisdom has many different relationships,[21] as in a family.[22] I will explore this idea below.

Questions of Social Context

First, though, I wish to look at the dominance of social context in discussions about the definition of wisdom. The tendency has been—and here Sneed (2011) points us in the right direction—that, as in Jer 18,[23] different categories of context groups—sages, priests, and prophets, for example—have made us see the different genres of wisdom, law, and prophecy as tied to social groups[24] that were often competing with each other and whose literary products ended up being in totally different parts of the canon. Instead, I suggest that we should embrace diversity of genre as a primarily literary aspect rather than a social one, and only then look at its relationship to possible contexts. It is when a book or narrative or psalm is almost entirely made up of wisdom concerns that we can classify it as a part of wisdom (and I hesitate to use the term "wisdom tradition" after Sneed's [2011] clarification), as characterized by a didactic purpose, an ethical concern, and built on personal experience. Then we might start to ask questions about its social context. Furthermore, though, we may need to distinguish between the original world that produced, say, that original proverb, and the literary world that disseminated the proverbs and other wisdom genres. There has been some muddying of the waters between looking to define wisdom but actually being too preoccupied with the original social context of the material that generated it. As Sneed writes, "One cannot necessarily read a setting off from a genre. There is no simplistic one-to-one correspondence between setting and genres. Thus, the relation between settings and genres needs to be viewed as quite flexible" (2011, 55). I would argue, in addition, that there is a difference between

---

21. A phrase coined by Wittgenstein (1958).

22. Michael Fox in his commentary on Prov 1–9 uses the word "family" and indeed the term "family resemblance" to describe wisdom literature when he writes, "Wisdom Literature is a *family* of texts. There are clusters of features that characterize it. The more of them a work has, the more clearly it belongs to the family. In fact, in the case of Wisdom literature, the family resemblances are quite distinctive, especially among the didactic texts." (Fox, 2000, 17, emphasis original). He anticipates here what I want to argue below, but he does not take the idea any further.

23. See discussion of Jer 18:18 in Dell forthcoming a.

24. See Blenkinsopp's book of the same name: *Sage, Priest, Prophet* (1995).

original genre setting and setting as it is revealed by the literary placement of a genre in a final form of literature—which is likely to be much broader. The word genre is still helpful as long as it is defined broadly. The same is true for the categories of form, content, and context; they are helpful as long as they are not too rigid. I would agree with Cheung that the communicated content aspect has to be primary, and thus the very term form criticism is somewhat of a misnomer. However, I think that the terminology of form, content, and context still works. It was looking carefully at small forms that led me to see Job as outside the box of wisdom (Dell, 1991). Common patterns of small forms can be found all over the wisdom literature, the proverbs being in many ways the most readily identifiable.

A Wisdom Core

I wish to uphold the idea that there is a core of wisdom material and that, as I have argued elsewhere (Dell, forthcoming b), Proverbs and Ecclesiastes make up this core. I have already argued that Proverbs is the mainspring of wisdom, but we know that ideas developed even within this book—the first signs of dissatisfaction with the quest for wisdom and understanding begins in Proverbs itself with the sayings of Agur in Prov 30:2–3: "Surely I am too stupid to be human; I do not have human understanding. I have not learned wisdom, nor have I knowledge of the holy ones" (NRSV). What happens when the ethical reward system does not correspond with that key starting point of the wisdom literature: experience? Of course this issue is raised in some depth in the Job dialogue, which gives it an essential wisdom link, one based on content. According to the friends, the righteous and wicked should be rewarded, but according to Job's personal experience this nexus has broken down when the ultimate innocent man suffers many trials. Cheung notices in his work scholarly unease with classifying Job as a mainstream wisdom book and hence with the alignment of Job-like psalms (which are essentially laments) as wisdom psalms (e.g., Ps 73). It needs more than simply a shared content (or even a deliberately subverted content, as also in Job's use of parody) to make up a genre— form and context count. The forms of Job are not generally wisdom ones: the heavenly encounter between God and the Satan, the dialogues, the whirlwind revelation. These may have no biblical parallel, but they are far removed from the piecemeal ethical advice of a series of proverbs. The issue of righteous and wicked behavior may be shared with other wisdom books, so too a sense of God as creator and orderer of the universe, but these are grand themes shared by many books (e.g., Gen 1–11). There are a few proverbs in Job (e.g., 6:5–6; 8:11–12; 12:12–13; 17:5) and a hymn to wisdom in Job 28, but the main wisdom genres are lacking. This has been the problem of breadth in relation to a wisdom definition that has led to its becoming shallow and ultimately meaningless. A line has to be trodden between narrowness and breadth and this is where I believe the concept of family resemblance is a helpful one, which I shall introduce below.

First, though, a mention of Ecclesiastes. It is my contention that this book is much more similar in genre to Proverbs. The book contains whole chapters of proverbs (whether quoted or composed), but they are often accompanied in this book by a qualifying comment that relativizes the material, for example, Eccl 7:1–6 on the house of mourning is relativized by 7:7 "this also is vanity." Indeed the repeated phrase "vanity of vanities, all is vanity" has this relativizing effect throughout the book as a refrain that gives the book its world-weary air. On a formal level there are short instructions and autobiographical narratives as well as example stories such as 9:13–16 and didactic poetry such as Eccl 1:4–9 and 3:2–8. The author often takes over well-known forms only to reuse them in the context of his own reflection—but he stays within the wisdom orbit in that he does not often use forms from other spheres of life. The tone of Ecclesiastes is much more questioning; there is an air of contradiction that is not unknown in Proverbs,[25] but it is just much more developed in this book. Ecclesiastes is less in opposition to Proverbs than a development of the contradictions. Many of the same topics are treated, wealth and work for example, but in Ecclesiastes they are put in the context of death, which relativizes all attempts at finding meaning in making money or in hard work.

A Wisdom Family?

I want to take up Cheung's promotion of family resemblance here, a concept he developed in relation to the wisdom psalms, and apply it to the relationship between Proverbs and Ecclesiastes and beyond. In relation to Cheung's three categories—a ruling wisdom thrust, an intellectual tone, and a didactic intention—when he finds all three in large measure, he considers the psalm under discussion at the center of the wisdom family. Other psalms are on the periphery; they are more distant relatives with

---

25. As argued convincingly by Peter T. H. Hatton (2008).

their "ruling thrust" often in another genre, for example a legal or lament genre. Job is rather like that: there are strong wisdom elements but without the ruling wisdom thrust that Cheung insists is necessary. The dialogue of Job is dominated by laments and uses legal language to mount a case against God.

There needs to be a family resemblance. Thus, if the core of wisdom, the mother and father so to speak, is Proverbs and Ecclesiastes, then other books or literature can be related to them on a scale. Just as I might have a cousin who also has a brother or sister, thus making them more closely related to each other than to me, so a book such as Job might be a cousin of the wisdom core but actually be more closely related to psalmic genres. And so the analogy continues; in this case it is in relation to whole books, but it can be broken down to a sectional level or individual items of interfamilial resemblance—for example, the eyes, gait, or interests of people can be used as the model.[26] This leads to increasing flexibility in genre classification. Returning again to our "wisdom" category, Ben Sira is an interesting case: it is very much in the heartland of the proverb form and the thematic links to both Proverbs and Ecclesiastes are strong. Furthermore, Ben Sira appears to have known the epilogue to Ecclesiastes. Solomon is not mentioned here for authorship, although he is mentioned as one of the famous men in Sir 24.

Genres too have dominant worlds but they are not exclusive, and worlds may well collide in the forging of a new relationship. There is a historical aspect to this family link—we may speak of our ancestors and our successors; in the same way the context of a genre has its ancestry and succession. Genres have a life within the canon where they change and develop (e.g., the old debate about whether apocalyptic as a genre developed out of prophecy or wisdom) as well as a life as it is encountered now by readers. It is ultimately in one's own generation that one encounters any genre in readerly mode. Thus the terminology of today may not be that of tomorrow, but we have to engage with today's debate in order to comprehend what is going on. Relationships across genres are subtle, but defining the ruling thrust of genre—the predominance of its content—is an essential starting point.

---

26. Here Cheung (2015, 19) cites K. S. Whetter (2008, 20), who calls the links between genres "ultimately essential" features akin to "familial bloodlines or DNA," as this applies also in family relationships.

Solomonic Wisdom

Relating back to the evolution of this material brings us back to Solomon. This is not to hark back to social setting but, more subtly, to implied author, which I would argue is a more literary than historical approach. While I imagine that Solomon did not get his reputation from nowhere—and his persona may well have been some kind of inspiration for the didactic world of the sages—I suspect, as do many scholars, that the attribution to him of Proverbs, Ecclesiastes (in a roundabout way), and the Wisdom of Solomon is honorific (Brueggemann 2005). He is however the father of wisdom in that the quest took inspiration from him—and it is interesting that reference to him links the books. He is the symbolic figure who holds this family together. Solomon communicates wisdom across the canon. It is of interest to note that the Solomonic subgrouping of material held sway for a long time when commentators first approached this material in the nineteenth century. Admittedly it was with a belief in authorship by that king. Going further back to precritical times and to the Rabbis, the Baba Bathra relates that Solomon composed Song of Songs in his youth, Proverbs in middle age, and Ecclesiastes when he was in old age. This categorization by ancient (putative) author is a different kind of classification from genre, in some ways historical and yet also, and predominantly, literary. It is, in any case, equally valid. Ultimately, it depends on your criteria and the lens that you are focusing on the material. This grouping by (putative) author would omit not only Job but also Ben Sira, which is clearly a close wisdom relation to Proverbs and Ecclesiastes—a brother or sister maybe. Perhaps any kind of grouping is counterproductive and we should speak of individual works with connecting links (Weeks 2010). On the one hand, any new grouping is a fresh lens on the material and thus helpful in its own way, yet, on the other hand, it seems that any dogmatic insistence on a grouping is an ultimate dead end. Perhaps this is why the frustration with the wisdom category has emerged in recent scholarship: perhaps it has had its day, certainly in the terms in which the debate has been engaged in so far.

An Intertextual Afterthought

This brings me finally, and rather cursorily, to intertextuality. Rather than necessarily seeing like genres as linking material together, the intertextual method as applied to biblical studies also has an alternative ring to it (Dell and Kynes 2012, 2014). With intertextuality one is looking for allusions within the text to works inside the biblical canon (although the parameters of that might well be debated). What intertextuality seems to highlight is unexpected links between books. When I was writing a recent article on Ecclesiastes I was surprised at the extensive links with Gen 1–11 pointed to by scholars (Dell and Kynes 2014). On closer inspection, Gen 1–11 also has been suggested for the wisdom category (Forman 1960), although it is much more clearly narrative, mythological narrative even. However, these kinds of links emerge where one least expects them once an intertextual or inner-biblical approach is taken. The result is more integration across the canon of scripture (in its broadest sense) and less of a piecemeal approach to texts. Perhaps, after all, the literary product that is the Old Testament is ultimately the result of scribal work that seeks to make these links and is a cohesive whole for that reason alone. But this does not nullify the quest for subdivisions and more subtle statements about genres within the whole. The wisdom category is one of these. It has tentacles flowing into many other genres and texts but ultimately it is a useful literary category—and it had real living contexts, however lost to us those may now seem.

Works Consulted

Alster, Bendt. 1997. *Proverbs of Ancient Sumer: The World's Earliest Proverbs Collections*. 2 vols. Bethesda, MD: CDL.

Blenkinsopp, Joseph. 1995. *Sage, Priest, Prophet: Religious and Intellectual Leadership in Ancient Israel*. Louisville: Westminster John Knox.

Bruch, J. F. 1851. *Weisheits-Lehre der Hebräer: Ein Beitrag zur Geschichte der Philosophie*. Strassburg: Treuttel & Würtz.

Brueggeman, Walter. 2005. *Solomon: Israel's Ironic Icon of Human Achievement*. Columbia: University of South Carolina Press.

Cheung, Simon Chi-Chung. 2015. *Wisdom Intoned: A Reappraisal of Classifying Wisdom Psalms*. LHBOTS. London: Bloomsbury.

Crenshaw, James L. 2010. *Old Testament Wisdom: An Introduction*. 3rd ed. Louisville: Westminster John Knox.

Dell, Katharine J. 1991. *The Book of Job as Sceptical Literature*. BZAW 197. Berlin: de Gruyter.

———. 2000. *Get Wisdom, Get Insight: An Introduction to Israel's Wisdom Literature*. London: Darton, Longman & Todd.

———. 2003. "'I Will Solve My Riddle to the Music of the Lyre' (Psalm XLIX 4 [5]): A Cultic Setting for Wisdom Psalms?" *VT* 54:445–58.

———. 2010. "Solomon's Wisdom and the Egyptian Connection." Pages 21–36 in *The Centre and the Periphery: Festschrift for Walter Brueggeman*. Edited by David J. A. Clines, Jill Middlemas, and Else Holt. Sheffield: Sheffield Phoenix.

———. Forthcoming a. "Jeremiah, Creation and Wisdom." In *Perspectives on Israelite Wisdom: Proceedings of the Oxford Old Testament Seminar*. Edited by John Jarick. LHBOTS. London: Bloomsbury.

———. Forthcoming b. "Ecclesiastes as Mainstream Wisdom (without Job)." In *Wisdom Traditions in the Hebrew Bible and Beyond*. Edited by George J. Brooke and Pierre Van Hecke. OtSt. Leiden: Brill.

Dell, Katharine and Will Kynes, eds. 2012. *Reading Job Intertextually*. LHBOTS 574. London: Bloomsbury.

———, eds. 2014. *Reading Ecclesiastes Intertextually*. LHBOTS 587. London: Bloomsbury.

Forman, Charles C. 1960. "Qoheleth's Use of Genesis." *JSS* 5:256–63.

Fox, Michael V. 2000. *Proverbs 1–9*. AB 18a. New York: Doubleday.

Goldingay, John. 1989. *Daniel*. WBC 30. Dallas: Word.

Gunkel, Hermann. 1926. *Die Psalmen: Übersetzt und erklärt*. HKAT. Göttingen: Vandenhoeck & Ruprecht.

Hatton, Peter T. H. 2008. *Contradiction in the Book of Proverbs: The Deep Waters of Counsel*. SOTSMS. Aldershot: Ashgate.

Kynes, Will. 2012. *My Psalm Has Turned into Weeping: Job's Dialogue with the Psalms*. BZAW 437. Berlin: de Gruyter.

———. Forthcoming. "The Nineteenth-Century Beginnings of 'Wisdom Literature' and its Twenty-First-Century End." In *Perspectives on Israelite Wisdom: Proceedings of the Oxford Old Testament Seminar*. Edited by John Jarick. LHBOTS. London: Bloomsbury.

Lambert, W. G. 1960. *Babylonian Wisdom Literature*. Oxford: Clarendon.

Morgan, Donn F. 1981. *Wisdom in the Old Testament Traditions*. Atlanta: John Knox.

Murphy Roland E. 2002. *The Tree of Life: An Exploration of Biblical Wisdom Literature*. 3rd ed. Grand Rapids: Eerdmans.

Rad, Gerhard von. 1966. "The Joseph Narrative and Ancient Wisdom." Pages 292–300 in *The Problem of the Hexateuch and Other Essays*. Translated by E. W. Trueman Dicken. Edinburgh: Oliver & Boyd.

Sneed, Mark. 2011. "Is the 'Wisdom Tradition' a Tradition?" *CBQ* 73:50–71.

Van Leeuwen, Raymond C. 2005. "Proverbs, Book of." Pages 638–41 in *Dictionary for Theological Interpretation of the Bible*. Edited by Kevin

Vanhoozer, Craig Bartholomew, Daniel Treier, and N. T. Wright. Grand Rapids: Baker Academic.
Whybray, R. N. 1968. *The Succession Narrative*. SBT 2/9. London: SCM.
———. 1974. *The Intellectual Tradition in the Old Testament*. BZAW 135. Berlin: de Gruyter.
Whetter, K. S. 2008. *Understanding Genre and Medieval Romance*. Aldershot: Ashgate.
Weeks, Stuart. 2007. *Instruction and Imagery in Proverbs 1–9*. Oxford: Oxford University Press.
———. 2010. *An Introduction to Wisdom Literature*. T&T Clark Approaches to Biblical Studies. London: T&T Clark.
Wittgenstein, Ludwig. 1958. *Philosophical Investigations*. Translated by G. E. M. Anscombe. 2nd ed. Oxford: Blackwell.
Zöckler, O. 1867. *Die Sprüche Salomonis: Theologisch-homiletisch bearbeitet*. Leipzig: Velhagen & Klasing.

Wisdom, Form and Genre

Stuart Weeks

Most of us do not comprehend a phrase by running through all the possible meanings of each component word, any more than we would read through a text by sounding out each letter; even at a very basic level, communication consists of more than the sum of its parts and relies on the recognition of broader shapes and contexts. Above all, though, it depends on an experience of previous communication that is shared by the parties involved, at least in some general sense, and that shapes their interaction. So, for example, the conventional presentation of English verse in lines and stanzas shapes the expectation of readers as soon as they encounter it, just as the way verse is read aloud alerts listeners to its nature. There are different expectations, furthermore, attached to particular poetic forms and meters, and correspondingly there may be different formal conventions in prose: we should not generally, for example, expect to find footnotes in a modern comic novel or to encounter a short story typeset in columns like a newspaper article. It is not just the cover of a book that tells us what we are about to read, and our previous experience of literature may help us to pick up numerous signals about the content before we have read a single word. Once we begin to read, furthermore, the style, subject matter, and choice of vocabulary will all help to consolidate our understanding of what type of text we have before us. But it is important to appreciate both that this remains, in important ways, a process of negotiation and that texts do not simply fall into single, monolithic categories, each directly comparable with the next. Indeed, even the most obvious conventions of prose and verse can yield forms like the prose poem or poetic prose, where the reader is guided more by modes of expression and choice of words than by rhythm or presentation. While it is not difficult to recognize the significance of constraints and conventions that we can describe as generic, it is much harder to talk about genres *tout simple*.

One important reason is that texts quite commonly involve the use of more than one set of generic conventions. The fact that Lionel Shriver's *We Need to Talk about Kevin*, for example, takes the form of fictional letters does not prevent it from being a novel, and there are other novels that use emails, journal entries, police statements, or all sorts of other materials to construct or to further their narrative. When we read such component parts, we expect each to obey the constraints of its own genre, while the work as a whole follows different constraints. This is not a matter of simple compatibility, because the process is not necessarily reversible—a novel might include a police statement, but a police statement could not include a novel—and it is not something that is confined to novels: a play may contain songs, for example, or a poem cite an aphorism or a different sort of poem (as when Wilfred Owen's "Dulce et decorum est" cites Horace). So long as the expectations associated with one type of material can be read in terms of those associated with another, it is possible for genres to subsume each other, and, talking about this phenomenon in novels, Bakhtin (1986, 62) speaks of "primary (simple) genres," which are "altered and assume a special character when they enter into complex ones. They lose their immediate relation to actual reality and to the real utterances of others" and they "enter into actual reality only via the novel as a whole." That distinction may require some qualification—not all genres are easily separable into "simple" or "complex"—but it highlights a common and important way in which genres can be combined. It is also possible for genres to be combined or extended in different ways, effectively forming new genres: Eric D. Hirsch (1967, 106–9) cites the example of Byron's *Don Juan*, which incorporates elements unknown in epic, as an extension of the epic genre; we might view the various sorts of modern crime fiction as extensions of the novel, which add their own conventions and constraints, or recognize the quite different sets of conventions brought together in, say, the science fiction thriller or the historical romance.

We cannot usefully insist that such works must correspond in their totality to any single set of generic conventions, and it is famously difficult to describe the characteristics of specific genres in a way that neither excludes many texts commonly supposed to belong to that genre nor abandons any pretense of precision. Generic classification has to deal, furthermore, with the problem that there are different types of convention and expectation involved in the interaction between text and reader, and it would clearly be unhelpful to insist that all our generic descriptions must relate to some single aspect of texts, be it structural, contextual, or thematic, when the ways in which we naturally link or distinguish texts relate to no such single aspect. If they do not, however, then it is correspondingly impossible to insist that genres are mutually exclusive, let alone that any given text must belong to a single genre. A work may in principle, therefore, belong in one genre according to its form, another according to its content, and yet another according to the context in which it is used. The issue is further complicated by the fact that new genres may be constituted by changes not in the texts themselves, but in the criteria applied to them. Black fiction and Victorian women's novels, for example, are categories that would have been unfamiliar to much earlier generations, and although it would be bold to assert that such categories are any more or less artificial than older ones, their emergence tends to highlight the extent to which generic classification has more to do with the questions and assumptions that we take to our study of texts than with the uncovering of archetypes inherent within them.

Of course, genre is not only a matter of classification, but of composition also, and although it is true that works may be assigned to categories which would have been unknown to their authors, it is surely no less true that authors typically rely heavily on genre, and on their readers' recognition of generic convention. Indeed, for certain types of composition, adherence to, or adaptation of convention is a crucial part of their character: by responding to a fixed set of constraints, for instance, the writers of haikus or sonnets exhibit a compositional skill that is supposed to be admired in and of itself, although, at the other end of the literary spectrum, the same game may be played in the composition of limericks or of certain types of joke. Such strict uses of convention, however, are the exception rather than the rule, and although, of course, poetry may be constrained by conventions of prosody in many traditions, relatively few compositions are governed more generally by some detailed set of rules. Indeed, it is an important insight of modern genre theory that texts are shaped by other texts, not by fixed and immovable abstractions, and that their commonalities are more like family resemblances than the consequence of being modeled on a single archetype. This implies, of course, that we cannot straightforwardly isolate the constituents of a genre by some process of abstraction, and even in the case of sonnets or haikus, such analysis results very swiftly either in a multiplication of subgenres or in the isolation of common features so general as to be almost without consequence: neither of those forms, it transpires, has followed any single set of rules throughout its history, and both have evolved in various ways. In short, the idea of generic convention and communication remains important (and much debated) in the modern study of literature, but most scholars have turned away from an emphasis on genres themselves as anything more than a heuristic tool: there is little appetite these days for the sort of grand generic taxonomies which dominated earlier poetics, or even for the historical study of genres. Indeed, it would probably be true to say that many writers now treat genre as something that is inherent not in texts but in the study of texts.

It would be difficult to say how far the study of the Hebrew Bible has been influenced by such developments, not least because the direct treatment of genre has been, and remains, surprisingly unusual in a discipline that is centered upon a corpus of literature. Since the beginning of the last century, biblical scholars have often instead treated generic issues as an aspect of form-critical study, to the extent, indeed, that many seem either to regard form criticism as a substitute for the study of genre, or at least to accept the use of concepts and vocabulary from form criticism where other scholars would speak of genre. There have been explicit attempts in recent times, furthermore, actually to repackage form criticism as a type of literary analysis, occupying much the same ground as genre studies. I have addressed such attempts in a recent article elsewhere (Weeks 2013), and shall not repeat myself here, but it is important to recognize the confusions that are involved in, and that arise from taking a technique which was designed for recreating sociohistorical situations via their influence on oral traditions, and trying to use it as a way to characterize the connections between literary texts.

In its basic assumptions, form criticism is not wholly unrelated, in fact, either to those modern studies of genre that focus on sociocultural aspects, or to classic Aristotelian perceptions of genre in terms of universals that can be inferred from exemplars: it seeks to abstract a basic underlying form, shaped by the requirements or perceptions of a particular context, from the texts that constitute a *Gattung*. This is like grasping the nature of a Lego® brick by looking at a box full of assorted Lego bricks®: we can comprehend the underlying characteristics of the brick even though the bricks that we actually see may have different shapes, sizes and colors—in fact, it is the degree of variation between the different bricks that enables us to judge what is and what is not essential, and prevents us from assuming that, for instance, "redness" is intrinsic to the nature of a Lego® brick. That does not mean, of course, that its color is somehow a secondary characteristic of any particular brick, but it does mean that we can disregard color, along with size or many other features, when trying to assess the function of "the Lego® brick" or to discern the circumstances that might have influenced its creation and development. In terms of those texts with presumed oral-traditional origins with which form criticism is concerned, this means that we may be looking for different types of connection between the texts, and forms, like genres, are not necessarily to be characterized in terms of the detailed structural similarities often posited in form-critical studies. It is not really surprising that discussions of form have tended to displace studies of genre in biblical studies, because the form-critical form closely resembles the classic, deductive genre that dominated older literary-critical studies (so, similarly, Mitchell 2007, 32). It is difficult, however, to disentangle the form itself from the various other paraphernalia of form criticism, or from the basic form-critical assumption that texts have been built upon forms—and, indeed, to do so would be simply to change the meaning of form. Consequently, biblical scholars tend to import form-critical assumptions into discussions of genre, even when they are not seeking explicitly to undertake form-critical examinations.

This tendency is evident in two well-known, if now rather elderly, British works on Proverbs: Norman Whybray's monograph *Wisdom in Proverbs: The Concept of Wisdom in Proverbs 1–9*, first published in 1965, and William McKane's 1970 commentary, *Proverbs: A New Approach*. Whybray's study does not declare its methodological underpinnings, although he speaks of Prov 1–9 containing "a series of relatively lengthy sections in each of which there is a sustained continuity of thought" and states his intention to examine these "along two well-tried lines of Old Testament literary criticism: the study of the relation of each section to the others, and the examination of the internal structure of each section" (Whybray 1965, 31). What he does in practice is to identify ten discourses, and then to distinguish original from secondary material in each: no overall rationale is outlined, and Whybray frequently treats the secondary character of what he identifies as additions as self-evident, but a retrospective justification is offered by a comparison with Egyptian instructions, which asserts "the credibility of the Book of the Discourses as an example of a known literary form" (Whybray 1965, 71). Although very different in some respects, McKane's commentary is also reluctant to discuss its methodological assumptions, although McKane does begin by rejecting a form-critical belief, widely held at the time, according to which the more sophisticated units typical of instruction literature evolved from the simpler sayings found in sayings collections. This rejection rests on a wide-ranging survey of ancient didactic literature, which enables him to identify and define two distinct types of material, sentence literature and the instruction, with their own separate histories; this in turn leads McKane to group materials in Proverbs according to their membership of each type. In the body of the commentary, indeed, this grouping leads him to treat them out of order—a procedure that accentuates the differences, even if does make the commentary very difficult to use—and also to exclude as secondary any sentence literature that has found its way into instructional material, as is often the case, for example, in Proverbs 3.

Neither of these works, then, declares itself to be form-critical, and McKane, at least, would probably reject that label outright; both of them, moreover, treat Proverbs as literary in nature and origin, rather than as oral-traditional, and each of them rests their case on the belief that Prov 1–9, at least, is modeled on a literary genre that has been borrowed from elsewhere. That belief is very probably correct, and I have argued myself elsewhere that the instruction was probably recognized widely in the ancient Near East as a particular type of composition (Weeks 2007, 4–32). What seems to have made instructions recognizable, however, and so what we might describe as the feature which characterizes the genre, is their self-presentation as advice that is being passed down from one generation to the next: in almost all other respects, extant instructions are highly variable. When Whybray and McKane both try to impose more rigid structural (and in McKane's case, syntactical) definitions, which require them to discount a considerable amount of material, they are arguably still working in a way that is not strictly form-critical, although the influence of form-critical analysis is clearly perceptible. When they then use their definitions to reject the discounted material as secondary, however, they are not just arguing in circles, but also revealing a very particular understanding of the instruction genre not merely as prescriptive, but as in some sense definitional: an ancient writer would not, or even could not have composed an instruction that was the wrong shape or that included materials belonging to a different genre. This procrustean understanding of the instruction turns it from a set of literary conventions into something more essential—a form, shaped by specific needs and context.

For other writers, *Sitz im Leben* becomes the principal import from form criticism, and although it is unusual to read claims that their self-presentation must actually imply a domestic origin for instructions (as, e.g., Camp 1997, 91), a presumed educational setting lies behind a quite common assertion that "father" and "son" must be cyphers in the text for "teacher" and "pupil" (e.g., Murphy 1981, 55). The presentation is in fact, of course, a fictional evocation, which requires us neither to locate instructions in the home, nor to suppose that the language of parenthood must have been taken over in some other real-life context: instructions draw on the reality that parents teach and advise their children, but that does not mean any of the literary instructions in our possession was actually written by a parent for their child, or that ancient parents, for that matter, typically offered advice in the long, poetic forms characteristic of most instructions. The most common presentation of instructions, furthermore, is not as day-to-day teaching, but as a single, special passing on of advice from one generation to the next, usually provoked by retirement or death: at its heart, this is testamentary literature. The form-critical demand for a context is also manifest in treatments of some other texts—as, for instance, when Leo Perdue (Perdue 2008, 158) deals with the mixed generic signals of wisdom psalms by declaring that "Most were likely written to be sung in the liturgical settings of Israelite and Jewish worship (temple and schools)" and goes on (Perdue 2008, 160–64) to speak of the Psalter having been redacted by temple scribes, educated in a wisdom school.

To some extent, perhaps, this is merely a manifestation of the historicism that characterizes biblical studies more generally, and it would be wrong to lay the blame squarely at the door of form criticism, but such attitudes can have the effect of squeezing out more interesting or important ways of understanding what is going on. While the use of genre to evoke context must not be mistaken for a genuine historical connection to that context, that is not the same as saying that the original settings of particular genres must be unimportant, and I have already touched on this in the discussion of primary and secondary genres above. When a novelist, say, incorporates a police report or witness statement into their narrative, that novelist relies on the reader to recognize the implicit forensic context, just as ancient readers would surely have recognized, say, the prophetic use of language from legal disputes. Something similar is going on when instructions evoke the context of parenthood, and, indeed, when other writers borrow conventions from instructions to set the tone or establish the authority of their own compositions. It becomes difficult to appreciate such use of genre, however, if we approach genres through forms, with all their baggage, and if every *Sitz* has to be a *Sitz im Leben*.

The recognition of secondary genres and their implications has, in fact, been one of the most productive areas in the recent study of wisdom literature, although it takes a number of different forms. To take just a few examples, Katharine Dell's assessment of a link between parody and protest in Job (Dell 1991) does not, of course, constitute a straightforward recognition of genre, and her understanding of the book's actual genre as parody raises some significant questions. It does, however, pick up and broaden a long-standing recognition that Job evokes other texts and genres, and puts this recognition to use in interpretation of the book, while some of the more theoretical issues which it raises have been addressed and put on a firmer footing by her student Will Kynes (2011). Job has also been approached from a rather different direction by F. Rachel Magdalene (2007), who sees in its legal language not a mere evocation of the courts, but a progressive presentation of a trial. Elsewhere, Michael Fox has looked to the aretalogies of Isis to throw light on wisdom's self-presentation in Prov 1–9 (Fox 2000, 336–38), and Tremper Longman (1991, 1998) has looked to fictional Akkadian autobiographies to throw light on Qoheleth's account of himself in Ecclesiastes. All these, and many other studies, suggest in effect that the wisdom books make significant use of other genres to communicate aspects of their meaning through their readers' recognition of those genres.

This sort of work is important, and it potentially does much to enhance our understanding of the texts. Inevitably, though, it brings its own problems, some of which arise from our sheer ignorance—of whether, for instance, readers of Proverbs might ever actually have encountered aretalogies, or readers of Job known the intricacies of neo-Assyrian trial procedures. There are some broader questions of method and genre involved, however, perhaps the most important of which concern the very issue of establishing and delimiting genres: this issue is not unique to biblical scholarship, and is fundamental, indeed, to much of the modern debate about genre, but it is not always recognized to be a problem. In this respect, Longman's connection of Ecclesiastes to ancient biographies offers a particularly interesting example, not least because Longman himself is unusual among biblical scholars for his considerable knowledge and awareness of the issues; he devoted much of the first chapter in his book on the autobiographies themselves to an outline of issues in contemporary genre theory, along with a justification of his own ideas about the nature of genre, and about the criteria to be applied for establishing the existence of a genre and the identity of its members (Longman 1991, 3–21). His later commentary on Ecclesiastes also included an exemplary treatment of that work's genre, which takes seriously both the fluidity of genre as a concept, and the need to avoid investigating genre solely as a classification for Ecclesiastes as a whole (Longman 1998, 15–22). Despite all this, it is not really clear what we are to make of the particular resemblances that Longman sees between Akkadian autobiographies and the structure of Ecclesiastes.

To summarize Longman's ideas very briefly, he takes a corpus of fifteen Akkadian texts with certain common features, and describes them as "fictional autobiography," a genre that he further subdivides on the basis of the concluding section in each text. All of the compositions are pseudonymous, and each probably began originally with a first-person self-presentation, which is not always extant, following this with a narrative account of accomplishments; the texts conclude variously, though, with blessings and curses, quasi-apocalyptic material, or didactic admonitions. The last of these subgenres, in which the texts end with admonitions, is compared with Ecclesiastes, which has a first-person introduction (1:12), a first-person narrative (1:13–6:9), and instruction in the rest of the book (although Longman does recognize that there is some advice in the narrative section, citing 4:12 and 5:2 as examples). No extravagant claims are made on the basis of the comparison, but Longman does claim that formal similarities between Ecclesiastes and the Cuthaean Legend, in particular, "demonstrate a generic relationship between the two" (Longman 1991, 122), and the treatment in his commentary correspondingly suggests that he understands Ecclesiastes to be modeled, structurally at least, on the generic conventions of a subgenre among Akkadian fictional autobiographies.

Although I find them compelling, I shall not rehearse here the various objections that have been raised against both Longman's identification of the fictional autobiography genre and his assessment of the structure in Ecclesiastes (they are summarized succinctly in Koh 2006, 106–12).[1] The real question to my mind is what possible significance Longman's observations could have even if their accuracy was beyond reproach. The structure that he defines is so broad, and apparently so capable of variation, that it is difficult to say what exactly would have distinguished members of the genre in the eyes of ancient readers—let alone to exclude coincidental correspondence with it. If readers were able to recognize the genre by its features, moreover, it is not clear that this recognition would serve to convey anything except the fictionality of the account—which they would

---

1. The issues involved in classifying the Akkadian texts are surveyed in Westenholz (1997, 16–24), which describes Longman's genre as created "through a process of arbitrary selection" (19).

presumably have had to grasp already because it is a key distinguishing feature! As for linking Ecclesiastes to the genre, we may reasonably ask how probable it is that either the author or the readers of that book would have been sufficiently aware of an Akkadian genre, which is attested principally in texts that were written several hundred years before the dates normally considered probable for Ecclesiastes, to make that connection. If we are trying to determine the features and reception of inherent genres, consciously employed by writers and not simply imposed on texts by us as a form of classification, then it is surely necessary to demonstrate both that the features of those genres would have distinguished them, and that they could actually have served to shape the original perception of texts.

Despite its strong consciousness of genre as an issue, then, Longman's work does not really seem to engage with the practical problems involved in assigning texts to a genre: the observation of similarities does not suffice to demonstrate conscious and discernable generic affiliations. This is a point that should be emphasized even more strongly, however, with respect to some other, similar claims about Ecclesiastes. A number of scholars have drawn attention in particular to similarities between Qoheleth's account of himself and the language of West Semitic royal inscriptions—which are, of course, more likely in principle to have been familiar to readers of Ecclesiastes than the sort of texts invoked by Longman, although the comparison is sometimes extended to include Assyrian inscriptions as well. The claims made on the basis of these similarities are not all expressed in the same way: Seow, for example, says that Qoheleth is "imitating the style of royal inscriptions" (1995, 283) but goes on to talk of his "imitation of the genre" (284) and about "the adaptation of genres" (285); Koh, on the other hand, is careful to state that there is a "difference in genre" and says less specifically that "Qoheleth may have followed the literary traditions of the ancient royal inscriptions when writing his own work (in order to enhance the literary portrayal of his royal persona)" (2006, 105). These, along with other discussions of particular similarities (e.g., Fox 1989, 174) all imply, however, that, in the first two chapters of the book at least, the writer of Ecclesiastes deliberately evoked the language of royal inscriptions in order to establish or affirm his fictional portrayal of Qoheleth as a king.

Despite the plausibility of such claims, it is important to be aware that the whole notion of a style specific to royal autobiographical inscriptions is problematic. Even the Western Semitic texts commonly cited are from a wide range of dates, places, and contexts, and they were written to serve a variety of purposes: Once we accept the very concept of royal propaganda, indeed, it should not surprise us to find that there existed texts in which kings proclaim their own names and accomplishments, or even that those texts should have expressed themselves in similar ways. We hardly need to presume that they did so in imitation of each other or of some conventional format, and the elements in common between them barely extend beyond self-introduction and the recounting of deeds. That the forms of expression in these texts must be specifically royal, moreover, is difficult to substantiate. Much is made of a supposed formula "I, so-and-so," followed, not always directly, by a reference to the speaker's kingship before an account of deeds, and this certainly resembles Eccl 1:12. It would be difficult to say, however, that this self-introduction is radically different from others in Jewish literature, such as the "I, wisdom" of Prov 8:12, or the "I, Tobit" of Tobit 1:3, neither of which is intended to imply royalty, and the same form is used in numerous self-introductions by God (e.g., Isa 43:15). It is perfectly reasonable to say that "I, so-and-so" is a conventional way for speakers to introduce themselves, and we would expect kings to introduce themselves, therefore, by saying "I, so-and-so, king of such-and-such," or to start their account by saying that they became king. If we had more inscriptions by farmers, however, we might similarly expect them to start "I, so-and-so, farmer in such-and-such a place," and to speak of formulaic *royal* self-introductions is no more meaningful than it would be to speak of formulaic *farmers'* self-introductions: these are just formulaic self-introductions (see Weeks 2012, 30–32). Readers would surely have recognized that Qoheleth was beginning an account of himself in 1:12, but there is no reason to suppose that they would then automatically have associated what followed with any examples of royal propaganda with which they were acquainted, especially when what follows includes so few typically royal accomplishments, and when Qoheleth is careful to state that all his actions were on his own behalf, not those of his country (cf. Weeks 2012, 24–29).

Similar problems beset other such analyses. Leo Perdue, for example, makes an interesting set of comparisons between Ecclesiastes and a variety of other ancient texts, noting particular affinities with Egyptian tomb autobiographies and with royal instructions, which he links to Jewish testamentary literature (Perdue 1994, 194–202). That Ecclesiastes bears a resemblance to tomb autobiographies is beyond doubt, but that resemblance arises partly from the autobiographical character of both, as with royal inscriptions, and partly from a long connection between such autobiographies and instructions in Egypt (Weeks 2007, 5, 11), which means that they often have didactic elements. Perdue does not note, furthermore, that the darker religious ideas which he finds in late autobiographies are by no means specific to such inscriptions, and hence a generic feature, but are rather a characteristic of Egyptian religion and literature more generally from the Ramesside period onward (see Assmann 1979). Royal instructions raise a more interesting issue, because instructions attributed to kings, most notably in Egypt the instructions of Amenemhet and for Merikare, do have a particular character, with a strong interest in government and governance which makes them analogous in some ways to the much later *speculum principum* or *Fürstenspiegel*. Whether they constitute a subgenre that would have been recognized as such in Egypt, let alone Israel, is harder to say, although it is interesting to note that the instruction offered to King Lemuel in Prov 31:1–9 has a similar character.

Like some others before him (most famously Galling 1932, 298, on which see Loretz 1964, 57–65), what Perdue takes from his comparison, however, is not the content, but the idea that Qoheleth is "presented as speaking to his audience either in his old age, shortly before death, or perhaps from the tomb" (Perdue 1994, 202; cf. 2007, 190). This may not be inaccurate, given the way in which Qoheleth's monologue ends, but it has nothing to do with royal instructions in particular, and it is not something that can be determined through some loose association of genre. As I have already noted, it is in the nature of all Egyptian instructions to locate themselves at a point of transition between generations, and so around the time of the speaker's death (which connects them to the tomb autobiographies), but there is virtually nothing in Ecclesiastes that makes it look like an instruction, apart from a belated nod to the genre in the epilogue (12:12 "my son"), and it hardly seems likely that the Qoheleth of 2:18–19, who knows nothing of his successor's qualities, is actually supposed to be instructing him. Perdue uses points of comparison with instructions to assert that Ecclesiastes must in some sense be an instruction, despite its lack of that genre's defining characteristic, or at least that it is somehow enough of an instruction and enough of a tomb autobiography to legitimize reading back the setting of each.

The danger in this sort of analysis lies in its capacity to squeeze out other ways of reading the material. The underlying problems, though, lie not only in the sort of definitional looseness exemplified by Perdue's claims, but, more fundamentally, both in a tendency to suppose that the similarities between texts that we can recognize for the purpose of classification must reflect the existence of a genre known to readers, and in a (rather form-critical) inclination to treat genre and generic convention as a matter of identifying particular text-types, understood in essentially structural terms. It is important to observe, in relation to Qoheleth's presentation, that many ancient readers would have been familiar with fictional or pseudepigraphic memoirs and autobiographies, which are very common amongst ancient compositions. They do not, however, constitute a single type of text, with fixed structures or style, and so although an author might have expected his readers to understand that he was using an accepted literary convention, much as modern novelists would expect their readers to refrain from calling them liars, we cannot really say either that the use of that convention would have required some particular form of expression, or that it would have evoked any additional connotations of context.

This brings me back to the points with which I began this essay. The discourse about genre and convention in biblical studies, influenced so strongly as it is by form criticism, frequently preserves a way of looking at these issues as a matter of whole texts and text-types, and of thinking about genres as exclusive categories to which texts or parts of texts belong. For some purposes, such study is not inappropriate, but it misses the numerous other ways in which genre and convention can link or constrain texts. To take a trivial example, a recent popular guide to modern writing notes that:

> In prose, rhyme is pleasing, amusing, or annoying depending on whether it's deliberate, accidental, or appropriate ... Accidental rhyme seems careless, the product of a writer with a tin ear. In serious or grave material, rhyming word play in general seems inappropriate and at least undignified, if not repellent. (LaRocque 2013, 163)

Competent writers may go to some lengths in order to avoid rhymes in English prose, even at the cost of precision, because they can either mislead readers into a false understanding of the tone intended, or, more probably, lead them to doubt the competence of the writer in expressing that tone. Indeed, writers will tend to avoid poetic cadence more generally in prose, which has its own rhythms, just as poets tend to dispense with the many conjunctions and transitional words that feature heavily in much prose. This is a matter of style, but it is also, more fundamentally, a matter of genre, and it illustrates one of the ways in which the shared expectations of reader and writer not only convey information beyond the literal sense of the words used, but also constrain the choice of those words.

We cannot, perhaps, transfer this particular issue to the study of Hebrew literature, but we can pay much more attention to the presentation of texts. McKane's commentary struggled with the undeniable use of imagery in Prov 5:15–20, where he felt that genre should have imposed a constraint:

> The imperatives in the Instruction are usually associated with a plain, unvarnished mode of communication. Imagery creates more exalted forms of expression; its felicitous use is an important aspect of literary art and it challenges and excites the reader. The Instruction, however, does not aspire to be literature and it sacrifices imaginative outreach to pedestrian clarity. Imagery brings with it problems of interpretation, obscurity and ambiguity, and the concern of the Instruction is above all to be clear and to leave nothing to chance or doubt. (McKane 1970, 317–18)

This is a very strange characterization of instructions, which are generally very literary, poetic works, and it rests largely on McKane's presuppositions about their *Sitz im Leben*, but surely nobody who has read Prov 1–9 in the original would anyway suppose its language to be pedestrian: it is packed with figurative speech and with unusual expressions (note, e.g., the prepositions in 8:2–3), many of which are very difficult and were surely never intended "above all to be clear." To appreciate the texture of that language may not be to slap some simple generic label on the work, but it does offer guidance to its nature and purpose without importing generic assumptions, and says much about the way in which it intends itself to be approached. Instead of viewing, say, Qoheleth's occasional strings of aphorisms simply as inevitable products of genre, we can similarly ask legitimate questions about their function in a work that is not clearly sentence literature, and perhaps investigate similar uses elsewhere. It is not the big generic classifications that offer most insight, but the more subtle ways in which texts are shaped by genre or exploit convention.

Finally, there is no area, perhaps, in which this is more important than the debates around the very character of wisdom literature, and the nature of the relationships between wisdom and other texts. Traditional ways of treating genre create significant obstacles even to talking about wisdom literature, since the three biblical books usually classified that way have little in common formally, and the appearance in other literature of interests or conventions usually associated with one or more of the wisdom books has commonly been described in terms of wisdom influence, implying that such appearances must denote a transfer of wisdom ideas. That is to say, scholarly discussions have tended to bind the formal features of texts to their thought, so that texts with the same ideas or assumptions are expected not to have different forms, while texts with similar forms are presumed to have the same ideas and assumptions. There is no space in this for any classification of wisdom literature that relegates form to a secondary position, or for the idea, conversely, that writers might allude to wisdom texts without importing or at least engaging with wisdom thought more broadly. In many respects, these assumptions are akin to the sort of illegitimate totality transfer about which James Barr complained in the study of biblical vocabulary, and they make it difficult to say, for instance, that the writer of Ps 34 might be borrowing expressions and modes of address from Proverbs for reasons other than to convey a broader set of wisdom ideas (cf. Weeks 2013, and contrast, e.g., Botha 2012). There are various factors that have shaped the terms of these discussions, and the problems are not all down to the treatment of genre, but it is a more sophisticated, and less form-critical approach to genre that offers the best way forward, just as it may do much to enrich the way in which we read the wisdom books themselves. We need to move away from labeling or lumping texts together and toward a better appreciation of the ways in which the biblical writers used convention and allusion to convey tone or nuance.

Works Consulted

Assmann, Jan. 1979. "Weisheit, Loyalismus und Frömmigkeit." Pages 11–72 in *Studien zu altägyptischen Lebenslehren*. Edited by Erik Hornung and Othmar Keel. OBO 28. Fribourg: Universitätsverlag; Göttingen: Vandenhoeck & Ruprecht.

Bakhtin, Mikhail. 1986. "The Problem of Speech Genres." Pages 60–102 in *Speech Genres, and Other Late Essays*. Edited by Caryl Emerson and Michael Holquist. Translated by Vern W. McGee. Austin: University of Texas Press.

Botha, Phil J. 2012. "Psalm 34 and the Ethics of the Editors of the Psalter." Pages 56–75 in *Psalmody and Poetry in Old Testament Ethics*. Edited by Dirk J. Human. LHBOTS 572. New York: T&T Clark.

Camp, Claudia. 1997. "Woman Wisdom and the Strange Woman: Where is Power to be Found?" Pages 85–112 in *Reading Bibles, Writing Bodies: Identity and the Book*. Edited by Timothy K. Beal and D. M. Gunn. Biblical Limits. London: Routledge.

Dell, Katharine Julia. 1991. *The Book of Job as Sceptical Literature*. BZAW 197. Berlin: de Gruyter.
Fox, Michael V. 1989. *Qohelet and His Contradictions*. JSOTSup 71. Sheffield: Almond Press.
———. 2000. *Proverbs 1–9: A New Translation with Introduction and Commentary*. AB 18A. New Haven: Yale University Press.
Galling, Kurt. 1932. "Kohelet-Studien." *ZAW* 50:276–99.
Hirsch, Eric D. 1967. *Validity in Interpretation*. New Haven: Yale University Press.
Koh, Y. V. 2006. *Royal Autobiography in the Book of Qoheleth*. BZAW 369. Berlin: de Gruyter.
Kynes, Will. 2011. "Beat Your Parodies into Swords, and Your Parodied Books into Spears: A New Paradigm for Parody in the Hebrew Bible." *BibInt* 19:276–310.
LaRocque, Paula. 2013. *The Book on Writing: The Ultimate Guide to Writing Well*. Arlington, TX: Grey & Guvnor.
Longman, Tremper. 1991. *Fictional Akkadian Autobiography: A Generic and Comparative Study*. Winona Lake, IN: Eisenbrauns.
———. 1998. *The Book of Ecclesiastes*. NICOT. Grand Rapids: Eerdmans.
Loretz, O. 1964. *Qohelet und der alte Orient: Untersuchungen zu Stil und theologischer Thematik des Buches Qohelet*. Freiburg: Herder.
Magdalene, F. Rachel. 2007. *On the Scales of Righteousness: Neo-Babylonian Trial Law and the Book of Job*. BJS 348. Providence: Brown Judaic Studies.
McKane, William. 1970. *Proverbs: A New Approach*. OTL. London: SCM.
Mitchell, Christine. 2007. "Power, *Eros*, and Biblical Genres." Pages 31–42 in *Bakhtin and Genre Theory in Biblical Studies*. Edited by Roland Boer. SemeiaSt 63. Atlanta: Society of Biblical Literature.
Murphy, Roland E. 1981. *Wisdom Literature: Job, Proverbs, Ruth, Canticles, Ecclesiastes, and Esther*. FOTL 13. Grand Rapids: Eerdmans.
Perdue, Leo G. 1994. *Wisdom and Creation: The Theology of Wisdom Literature*. Nashville: Abingdon.
———. 2007. *Wisdom Literature: A Theological History*. Louisville: Westminster John Knox.
———. 2008. *The Sword and the Stylus: An Introduction to Wisdom in the Age of Empires*. Grand Rapids: Eerdmans.
Seow, C. L. 1995. "Qohelet's Autobiography." Pages 275–87 in *Fortunate the Eyes That See: Essays in Honor of David Noel Freedman in Celebra-*

tion of his Seventieth Birthday. Edited by Astrid B. Beck, Andrew H. Bartelt, Paul R. Raabe, and Chris A. Franke. Grand Rapids: Eerdmans.

Weeks, Stuart. 2007. *Instruction and imagery in Proverbs 1–9*. Oxford: Oxford University Press.

———. 2012. *Ecclesiastes and Scepticism*. LHBOTS 541. New York: T&T Clark.

———. 2013. "The Limits of Form Criticism in the Study of Literature, with Reflections on Psalm 34." Pages 15–25 in *Biblical Interpretation and Method: Essays in Honour of John Barton*. Edited by Katharine J. Dell and Paul M. Joyce. Oxford: Oxford University Press.

Westenholz, Joan Goodnick. 1997. *Legends of the Kings of Akkade: The Texts*. MC 7. Winona Lake, IN: Eisenbrauns.

Whybray, R. N. 1965. *Wisdom in Proverbs: The Concept of Wisdom in Proverbs 1–9*. SBT 45. London: SCM.

Part 2
Case Studies

WHERE CAN WISDOM BE FOUND?
NEW PERSPECTIVES ON THE WISDOM PSALMS

Markus Saur

WISDOM PSALMS AND WISDOM IN THE PSALTER

The book of Psalms in its diversity constitutes a "kleine Biblia" (Luther 1528, 33) and as such depicts a theology of the Hebrew Bible *in nuce*. Thus, it is not surprising to find texts within the Psalter that are shaped by sapiential thought in particular.

However, what is commonly named wisdom within the Hebrew Bible is not a consistent concept. Rather, sapiential thinking characteristically takes place within specific topically defined contexts and, above all, in a characteristic mode of reflective deliberation. Therefore, based upon a necessary blur in the definition of whatever is sapiential—or what is not— it has often been denied categorically that certain texts within the Psalter could be described as wisdom psalms (Crenshaw 2000).

In contrast, features and characteristics of possible wisdom psalms have been collated repeatedly (with varying focuses, though). So, at least the texts in question are identified to the point that a basis for discussion is available.[1]

---

1. R. E. Murphy (1963, 159–61), and J. K. Kuntz (1974, 191–215), collate a catalogue of important stylistic and thematic characteristics of the texts they consider to be wisdom psalms, and Leo G. Perdue (1977, 261–343), in his study "Wisdom and Cult," examines Pss 1; 34; 37; 73; 112; 19B; 127; 32; 119; 49; 19A, under the heading "Didactic Poems and Wisdom Psalms." Cf., in addition, J. Luyten (1979, 59–64), and R. N. Whybray (1995, 160), who emphasizes "that the use of 'wisdom psalms' as a blanket term for all those psalms in the Psalter which express serious thoughts on religious matters ... is a mistaken one. This terminology may be useful if it extends the corpus of wisdom literature by identifying those few psalms and parts of psalms

The debate, already quite controversial in parts, is widened even more by recent research on psalms and the Psalter which added another central aspect. While older research on psalms was mainly concerned with form-critical questions as to the literary genre (*Gattung*) and *Sitz im Leben* of individual psalms, that is, oriented to a large extent towards the questions first raised by Hermann Gunkel (Gunkel 1929; Gunkel and Begrich 1933), a shift in research has occurred in the last decades. Questions of form and genre in regard to individual psalms and the Psalter as a whole have been receding in favor of redaction-critical questions.[2] Both the Psalter as well as individual psalms have quite a long history of literary development, which mirrors a process of theological discussion on certain topics. That discussion is perhaps best described as the procedure of theologically motivated collation of central topoi that were discussed in postexilic ancient Judah. The Psalter presents itself as a 'kleine Biblia' containing a theology of the Hebrew Bible *in nuce* precisely because it came into being over the course of several centuries and because it reflects theologically relevant positionings of that period of time.

The Psalter in its present form is by no means a more or less arbitrary collection of single texts, but rather a book with an introduction (Pss 1–2), five parts (Pss 3–41; 42–72; 73–89; 90–106; 107–145) and an ending (Pss 146–150). The discussion on form and structure of that book has added a great deal to the understanding of psalms and the Psalter as literature, thus helping to focus not only its cultic dimensions but also on those beyond the cult (Wilson 1985, 1992; Zenger and Hossfeld 1993, 2000, 2008; Whybray 1995, 155–57).

The *Verfasserkreise* (authoring circles) behind that work of literature, as has become evident in this context, do not form a homogeneous,

---

which have marked affinities with the acknowledged wisdom books; but a too indiscriminate use of it tends to weaken the distinctiveness of the notion of 'wisdom' in Old Testament studies, and also draws attention away from the question of the character of the Psalter considered as a whole." Crenshaw, based upon a discussion of Kuntz's positions and a reference to the problems that a socio-historical classification of the transmitting circles of wisdom poses, resolves "to question the very category of wisdom psalms" (Crenshaw 2000, 15). Kuntz, on the other hand, rejects this categorical denial (Kuntz 2003). Beyond his 1974 study, he has pointed out the significance of wisdom psalms for the overall profile of the Psalter (Kuntz 2000). Likewise, M. Oeming (2008) and B. Weber (2012) stress the importance of wisdom for a theology of the Psalter.

2. See programmatically E. Zenger (1998) and the commentaries: Hossfeld and Zenger (1993, 2000, and 2008).

sociologically definable group. The topical diversity and the very different accentuations within the Psalter prevent any such enterprise. In fact, the various *Trägerkreise* (transmitting circles) left rather different traces within the composition of the Psalter and within the psalms: standards and educational level of these circles have a crucial influence on the composition and likewise on the theology of the Psalter. Thus, certain areas show a level of productive reflexivity that alludes closely to the texts commonly identified as Old Testament wisdom literature.

The debate on wisdom psalms has been conducted—corresponding to the older research—from a point of view that is oriented primarily toward Gunkel and his form criticism. However, the classical criteria as formulated by Gunkel for the definition of a genre—common cultic context or common *Sitz im Leben*, a common "Schatz von Gedanken und Stimmungen" (Gunkel 1933, 22–23) and a common "Formensprache" (ibid.)—have yielded no results. Thus, there is no denial that with such a method a genre appropriately labeled wisdom psalms cannot be established (Crenshaw 2000). Gunkel himself in his *Einleitung in die Psalmen* (1933) speaks of "wisdom poetry" ("Weisheitsdichtung" [Gunkel 1933, 381–97]) in regard to the texts in question, behind which allegedly stands a distinct mode of poetry ("Dichtungsart" [Gunkel 1933, 382]). Sigmund Mowinckel has adopted that cautious terminology, speaking of "learned psalmography" (Mowinckel 1955, 208–17) instead of "wisdom psalms." Gunkel, and Mowinckel all the more, was convinced that psalms and the Psalter had their proper place in the cult and that a psalm is interpreted appropriately only when understood within its cultic context. However, in the works cited, both Gunkel and Mowinckel betray a certain awareness of the problem of sapiential influences within psalms and the Psalter.[3]

Once we stop regarding the form-critical approach as *the* crucial hermeneutic key towards the interpretation of psalms (but rather as one approach among others), and instead consider especially the outcome of redaction-critical research on psalms and the Psalter, it suddenly becomes much easier to speak of wisdom psalms. Logically, the term then does not mean a form-critically established genre. Rather, it subsumes a certain

---

3. Mowinckel (1955, 213) writes: "As the poets would no longer compose poetry for a definite cultic occasion, the preservation of the modes of composition was no longer supported by their 'place in life', as it used to be, and the different modes and motives were *mixed up*. Therefore we may speak of a *dissolution of the style*" (emphasis original).

group of psalms. A comparable phenomenon would be, for example, the royal psalms or the psalms of Zion, which likewise do not constitute a psalm genre in the form-critical sense, yet are undoubtedly distinguishable as a group of their own within the Psalter.[4] As Kuntz notes, "As is the case with royal psalms, content more than form defines wisdom psalms" (2003, 151).

Indeed, the criteria for a classification of wisdom psalms, thus, become slightly blurred. In fact, however, that indistinctness has quite a productive potential because it allows a more precise view of the texts in their specific individual form. A close reading of Gunkel's *Einleitung* does not hide the fact that particular characteristics of individual psalms often contradict their classification in regard to their alleged genre, and that likewise the assignment of a genre to an individual psalm can only be done *cum grano salis*. It is even possible that form-critical work on psalms at times clouds the awareness as to the particular characteristics of the texts, given that the act of assigning a genre, always more or less formalized, often has a tendency to level out particularities rather than to emphasize them.

The Hebrew Bible contains a wide scope of sapiential thought, which cannot be reduced to just a few clearly definable characteristics. It is, however, evident that within Proverbs, Job, and Qoheleth, the question of how to cope with life and the question of the predictability of the world is discussed heatedly, all the while oriented towards the question whether and in what ways *Tun* and *Ergehen* of the individual are connected. Said sapiential books take different stances regarding the answer to that question. However, all of them have a mode of reflection in common that is grounded in experience and is precipitated in a certain mode of poetry or a distinct "mode of literature."[5]

Due to its broad scope of topics, it seems more adequate to not speak of a tradition in the narrower sense when regarding ancient Israel's wisdom, since a tradition is typically defined by certain marked subjects ("geprägte Sachgehalte" [Steck 1993, 124–47; Becker 2005, 115–28]). While it is true that these subjects are identifiable within Old Testament wisdom literature, they are, on the other hand, quite diverse. Thus, wisdom literature has neither a homogenous profile nor a homogenous *Trägergruppe*. Rather, its

---

4. Regarding royal psalms, see M. Saur 2004; regarding psalms of Zion, see G. Wanke 1966; and C. Körting 2006.

5. See Sneed 2011, 57: "Hebrew wisdom literature should be described as a mode of literature and not strictly a genre."

characteristics lie in the discourse standing behind that literature, which is defined by a plurality of voices and positions. To simply categorize this plurality as wisdom tradition would necessarily be imprecise (Sneed 2011, 54, 62–64, 66–67). Therefore, it seems appropriate to speak of a mode of literature when aiming at the literal level, or, when aiming at the discussions underlying the literary traditions, of a discourse (Saur 2011 and 2012a).

One of the characteristics of wisdom literature—to be found across all areas of sapiential texts—is the genre of proverbs, in other words, a literary form summarizing a certain knowledge, gained through experience, as shortly and concisely as possible, often no more than a bicolon, in order to render it easily accessible for teaching and learning. Such proverbs are found not only in the book of Proverbs, but also in Job, Qoheleth, and psalms like Ps 128. Notably special forms are, for example, the *better-than* proverbs, which compare and rank different matters; likewise the numerical proverbs, which demonstrate a playful handling of knowledge, quite possibly related to riddles. Clearly demonstrated here is the high level to which the *Trägergruppen* of sapiential proverbs were educated, thus fostering the teaching and learning of knowledge. The acrostics, found mainly in the Psalter but also in the Prophets, are of the same kind. These are texts originating in the education sector, with a distinct didactical orientation but also with the aim of expressing something comprehensive, extending from the beginning to the end, from א to ת. It does not come as a surprise, then, that in these texts it is often the Torah that is at the heart and center—the orientation towards the Torah is among the most distinguished educational subject matters in ancient Judah.

Typical for wisdom literature, besides sapiential proverbs, are longer educational and reflective addresses. Such addresses can be found primarily in Job and Qoheleth, but also in the book of Proverbs. In case of the latter, they are located mainly in Prov 1–9 and Prov 30–31. In Prov 10–29 the aim is primarily the mastering of everyday experience through the use of sapiential proverbs. In the reflective texts, on the other hand, a discussion on the efficiency of that everyday wisdom becomes discernible. At the heart of the genre of sapiential proverbs lies the assumption that human *Tun* and *Ergehen* correlate (*Tun-Ergehen-Zusammenhang*) and that one's actions have an immediate effect upon one's life. Meanwhile, in the reflective texts it is precisely the validity of that very assumption that is being questioned. Likewise, the possibilities of human insight are existentially scrutinized. These texts are passed down not only within

Job and Qoheleth—books which in their thinking react upon the conceptual bases of the older compilations of Proverbs—but such texts are also found elsewhere, for example, in Prov 30 or in Pss 49 and 73. The latter two, in turn, seem to have a corresponding relation to Ps 37. Positions that orbit the same fields of topics and problems emerge within these textual constellations, but they cannot be described as a tradition, precisely because there is no homogeneous positioning discernible, neither theologically nor anthropologically. Rather, quite controversial positions are being adopted.

It is not decided yet, whether for sapiential texts there might be other criteria of a more general nature beside the aforementioned, namely, the address as בני or the macarism אשרי. Both do in fact appear in other literary contexts as well, but the didactic undertone of both the address form and the macarism is unmistakable and clearly belongs to the sphere of a successful conduct of life—what the sapiential poets are concerned with.

In view of the evident problems of a definition of wisdom and the characteristics of sapiential texts, it is understandable why there is not any consensus regarding the question of number and demarcation of wisdom psalms. However, it is certainly possible to speak of wisdom psalms or a sapiential impregnation of the psalter, if one is willing to accept a certain level of inquiring reflexivity as one of the characteristics of the sapiential discourse.[6] This reflexivity denotes especially meditation upon the capacity of human insight and the limits of the transparency of the world. On the borders of that definition some blurriness will remain, comparable to the imprecision of a definition of, say, royal psalms or psalms of Zion,

---

6. Exactly this aspect of inquiring reflexivity should be added to Perdue's understanding of wisdom: "Wisdom is man's quest for self-understanding, a self-understanding which derives from his attempts to analyze world order from the perspective of his own experiences and those of his ancestors which are transmitted through tradition, and from his attempts to integrate himself within the cosmological and societal spheres of that world order as he perceives it." (Perdue 1974, 535) It is obvious that these attempts to structure the world on the basis of experience can lead to the experience of the limits of human possibilities. It is exactly at that point, that the sapiential reflections that we find in Job and Qoheleth as well as in texts like Prov 30:1–9 or some wisdom psalms take their beginning. G. von Rad expresses this aspect (regarding the wisdom psalms Pss 37, 49, and 73) thus: "Der Mensch steht ja ... immer in einer Konfliktsituation mit der ihn umgebenden Umwelt. Die Widerfahrnisse, die er zu registrieren hat, sind nie ganz eindeutig, und es ist eine Frage seiner inneren Widerstandskraft, wie er mit dem Unverrechenbaren fertig wird" (von Rad 1970, 266).

concerning which there is likewise no consensus as to their number and exact profile. The following does not seek to take up the extensive debate on the number and demarcation of wisdom psalms. Rather, three exemplary psalms will show how sapiential thought within the Psalter presents itself and in what relations to the conceptual approaches of Proverbs, Job, and Qoheleth, it stands.[7]

Psalm 37 as a Wisdom Psalm

Psalm 37 is an acrostic belonging to the first collection of Davidic psalms within the first book of the Psalter (Pss 3–41). It is constructed quite evenly in its alphabetic structure. Most of the alphabetic stanzas contain two verses or two bicola, respectively. In contrast to the clear formal structure, regarding contents we observe an associative style that is oriented toward the topic of the contrast between the wretched and the righteous, but which does not come to a clear progression of thought (Gunkel 1929, 156). Thus, the tense juxtaposition of formal coherence and associative ambiguity is a key characteristic of the text.

It is the assumed correlation of *Tun* and *Ergehen* that lays the conceptual foundation for this associative exposition of the contrast between the wretched and the righteous. In Ps 37, however, this is not discussed merely on a theoretical level, but rather visualized by the example of the profiled contrast between wretched and righteous. The sapiential literature mode is reflected primarily in the numerous forms of appeal and imperative within the psalm.[8] The first verses already situate the psalm within a certain reading horizon by the vetitive and imperative forms in use: He who seeks to be distinguished from the wretched lets the knowledge about the correlation of *Tun* and *Ergehen* which underlies the text determine his conduct, lest he perish like the wretched, but may rather live like the righteous. Because of

---

7. The texts I will subsequently scrutinize—Pss 37, 49, and 73—all belong to the category of wisdom psalms in the eyes of an *opinio communis* (most recently Kuntz 2000 argued that Ps 73, too, is a wisdom psalm, which he had previously denied [Kuntz 1974]). Limiting myself to these three psalms, however, is in no way meant to deny that, among others, Pss 1, 112, 119, or 128, show sapiential characteristics as well.

8. See Perdue (1977, 280): "The entire poem is an instruction consisting of admonitions", and Weber (2012, 299): "Ps 37 … ist ein dezidierter Weisheitspsalm, der keinerlei Gebetsworte enthält, sondern Belehrung samt Ermahnung und Ermutigung für den Gerechten darbietet."

this orientation, the psalm can be understood as being embossed throughout by a parenetic style with significant parallels in the book of Proverbs, a book that counts the contrast between the wretched and the righteous to be its basic didactic repertoire.

The proximity between Ps 37 and Proverbs is most evident in an almost word-to-word parallel between Ps 37:1 and Prov 24:19. Both verses warn not to get infuriated in view of the wretched and not to envy them. That warning possesses an openly didactical connotation and points to the fact that both texts have their place within the educational sector. The proximity between wisdom on one hand and didactics, instruction, and tuition on the other hand has been elaborated frequently and is found not only in Proverbs but apparently in Psalms as well.

The sapiential stamp upon the psalm stretches beyond 37:1. For example, the *better-than* proverb in 37:16 is a typical sapiential element that is documented abundantly throughout Proverbs and Qoheleth. In a way, this stylistic element establishes hierarchies within reality. Phenomena or matters are being superordinated over each other, in order to render the world understandable and transparent by these patterns of order. Behind the mode of literature, therefore, stands a certain specific view of the world.

The style of Ps 37 is marked by a notably high degree of literary conciseness, as verse 27 exemplarily shows. The three-part structure here disturbs the chain of preceding and following bicola, thereby creating a distinct accent within the psalm. The appeal to refrain from evil and to do good is completed by the appeal to endure. However, this last appeal is essentially a consequence arising from the observance of both preceding commands. The correlation of *Tun* and *Ergehen* is manifest in highest density here: refraining from evil and doing what is good ensures human existence—or so the lesson of the imperatives in verse 27 could be summarized. Precisely because of this mixture of formal density and an orientation toward the *Tun-Ergehen-Zusammenhang*, with regards to content, a sapiential imprint of Ps 37 is undeniable.

The א-stanza in 37:1–2 begins with the admonition not to fret about the wretched because they are about to perish. The ב-stanza in verses 3–4 instructs the reader in five imperatives as to the right conduct. The ג-stanza in verses 5–6 with its judicial accent, created by the use of an imagery of light, corresponds to the overall topic of justice within the psalm. The ד-stanza in verse 7 has the character of a summary: it falls back on verse 1 and emphasizes the importance of remaining still (דמם) before YHWH. The ה-stanza in verses 8–9 elaborates on the topic once more, thus marking the strongly repetitive character of the whole text. In the ו-stanza in verses 10–11, it is announced that the wicked will perish because of their violation of justice, while the humble, the psalm assures, will own the land. The ז-stanza in verses 12–13 marks the contrast between the wicked and the righteous by a special accentuation: God's laughing at the wicked shows who it is that guarantees that both the wicked and the righteous will receive their reward. The ח-stanza in verses 14–15 depicts the correlation of *Tun* and *Ergehen* in the image of the wicked threatening the righteous: the wicked are hit by their own unsheathed sword while the righteous are not harmed. In the ט-stanza in verses 16–17, the doom of the wicked is pictured with regard to their riches. By contrast, the inheritance of the blameless is secured forever according to the י-stanza in verses 18–19. The כ-stanza in verse 20 again focuses on the wicked's downfall. The ל-stanza in verses 21–22 highlights a difference between wicked and righteous regarding loans. The מ-stanza in verses 23–24 emphasizes the ongoing endangerment of the righteous, who nevertheless can rest assured of YHWH's help. Then, in the נ-stanza in verses 25–26, the psalmist explicates, based upon his own experience, that it is impossible for the righteous to fall. It is "im wesentlichen der Standpunkt der Freunde Hiobs, der hier vertreten wird" (Gunkel 1929, 157). Remarkably, the idea of a dimension of the piety of the righteous that extends over several generations and redounds even to his offspring's blessing is brought up here. The ס-stanza in verses 27–28ab sums up the maxim of the conduct of the righteous in the succinct triad "turn from evil—do good—dwell securely forever." The ע-stanza in verses 28c and 29 again underlines the already familiar contrast between the wicked and the righteous. With the פ-stanza in verses 30–31 the communication of the righteous is connected to the concept of wisdom (חכמה) and positioned alongside משפט and תורה. Thus, the coordinates of the conduct of life of the righteous are defined. Here we find ourselves standing at the theological core of the psalm. Accordingly, the צ-stanza in verses 32–33 can be understood as a direct consequence of the preceding: The existence of the righteous is threatened by the wicked. The judicial terminology and the literary conciseness illustrate clearly how intensively the attacks of the wicked threaten the righteous and in what serious danger he is. The short ק-stanza in verse 34 mentions once more the ownership of the land, based upon the orientation toward YHWH and the trust in him. Again narrating from the perspective of the psalmist's experience, the ר-stanza in verses 35–36 emphasizes that the wicked shall indeed perish. However, that hope does not relate to the future exclusively.

Already, it seems, it determines the present. The relevance of the psalm to the present, on the background of its knowledge that the wicked have already perished, corresponds closely to what determines wisdom and its relevance to the present, guided by experience, in general. The ש-stanza in verses 37–38 takes up this idea once more: the future of the wicked is, in fact, already past. In contrast, the salvation of the righteous, as shown in the ת-stanza in verses 39–40, is secured through YHWH. It is he who continuously guarantees that both the wicked and the righteous will in time receive their fair share. The closing phrase in 37:40b resembles the preamble of the Psalter in Ps 2:12: The righteous ones take refuge in and with YHWH.

The axiomatic affirmation of the correlation between *Tun* and *Ergehen*, the dramatic depiction of the contrast between wicked and righteous, the mentioning of wisdom in the mouth of the righteous (verse 30), the *better-than* proverb in verse 16, the many admonitions (as e.g., in verses 1–8), the acrostic structure, the direction in which the text is addressed (i.e., not toward YHWH, like a classical prayer, but rather as an educational address of the psalmist towards his readers or hearers), and the mode of reflection based upon experience (as apparent especially in verses 25–26) all identify Ps 37 as a wisdom psalm.[9] Already Bernhard Duhm noted the psalm had "eigentlich besser in die Sprüche Salomos als in den Davidpsalter hineingepasst" (Duhm 1899, 110). Such a conclusion, however, is only possible if one resolves to hold up a sharp distinction between psalms and wisdom. Psalm 37, on the other hand, bears witness to the fact that a distinction as sharp as that does not make sense and that psalms and wisdom indeed show quite remarkable similarities.

Psalm 37 adds a sapiential perspective to the first Davidic psalter that is grounded in the conviction that the correlation of *Tun* and *Ergehen* is in fact valid (Kuntz 2000, 155). The proximity to Proverbs and to the beliefs of Job's friends is quite impossible to overlook. The question remains, though, of what nature exactly that proximity is. Does Ps 37 represent a stage in the development of sapiential thought that belongs to an old wisdom of, say, preexilic times? If one accepts the notion of linear development within wisdom and thus regards the axiomatic validity of the *Tun-Ergehen-Zusammenhang* as a characteristic of older sapiential thought that

---

9. Cf. Hossfeld and Zenger (1993, 229): "Der Psalm ist eine in Spruchform gebündelte weisheitliche Lebenslehre."

only began to be questioned later on, then one would certainly regard Ps 37 as an older text in comparison. Three aspects, however, seem to contradict this view: First, there is the acrostic structure which shows a level of literary competence that one would rather expect in postexilic texts. Second, the reference to the praying person's subjective experience (as obvious, e.g., in 37:25) adds a level of individuality to the text that seems more likely to indicate a postexilic text. Third and most prominent, however, is the affirmative and stereotypical way with which the validity of the *Tun-Ergehen-Zusammenhang* is being argued.[10] The repetitive affirmation of the wicked's doom and the righteous' well-being as well as the conviction lying behind it raise the question of whether they are not constructed in such intensity so as to react upon voices that—in contrast to Ps 37—emphasize the fragility of this correlation, which was up to then thought to be of existential validity. Perhaps Ps 37 takes part in a discourse that envelops just that very question as to the validity of the correlation of *Tun* and *Ergehen* and in which a number of different positions are being articulated. If so, Ps 37 would implicitly point to the fact that at a certain point the validity of *Tun* and *Ergehen* was no longer as unquestioned as it had formerly been but, on the contrary, was being disputed openly. Psalm 37 reacts to such hostile attempts both in its style and content and thus is not an older text, followed by more recent sapiential texts, but rather is part of the postexilic sapiential discourse. In that regard, Ps 37 indeed has some similarities with Proverbs, though not only with the compilation of proverbs in Prov 10–29 (which is in fact older) but also with the opening chapters in Prov 1–9, which, in rather long educational addresses, try to support and secure the foundations of proverbial wisdom against hostile attacks, the validity of which had recently become fragile.

Within the postexilic sapiential discourse, the question of the validity of *Tun-Ergehen-Zusammenhang* was a central matter of discussion. Both the attackers as well as the defenders of a correlation between *Tun* and *Ergehen* articulate their respective views. Decisive, however, is the simultaneity of such positions. Their differences cannot simply be explained by

---

10. Zenger sees Ps 37 in the context of a later wisdom and, theologically speaking, rather close to the positions that Job's friends take up: "Ohne daß die dabei in der Ijob-Dichtung vollzogene Problematisierung dieser Position erkennbar wäre" (Hossfeld and Zenger 1993, 299). Seybold (1996, 155) thinks the psalm is "wohl spätnachexilisch (hellenistisch?) entstanden"; M. Witte (2014, 51) interprets the text as some kind of "eschatologische Weisheitsdichtung."

reckoning with a development over the course of time. Rather, different positions could be indicative of differences between various *Trägergruppen* in a simultaneous discussion. Psalm 37 takes part in such a discussion, the literary outcome of which are the sapiential texts from postexilic Judah.

Psalm 49 as a Wisdom Psalm

Psalm 49 belongs to the first group of Korahite psalms, which are located within the first and second book of the Psalter (Pss 42–49, and Pss 84–85; 87–88). It closes the first series of Korahite psalms. Its individualistic direction of speech takes up the corresponding perspective from Ps 42–43, where we likewise find a person speaking in the first person singular. In the psalms in the middle of this first series of Korahite psalms, both Zion and kingship are of core theological interest. Central to Pss 42–43, in contrast, is the expression of a deep longing after YHWH and hope in him. This corresponds to the highly reflective style that characterizes Ps 49.

Like Ps 37, Ps 49 is not a prayer in the classical sense but rather an educational reflection. Quite notable is the opening, which consists of 49:2–5 (verse 1 being the heading). Verses 2–3 take a universal perspective which is then impregnated sapientially by verses 4–5: The terms תבונות, חכמות, משל, and חידל all belong to the repertoire of sapiential language. Apparently, this whole opening is constructed in order to put the psalm into a sapiential perspective, that is, letting what follows appear as a sapiential reflection. Therefore, it is indeed adequate to speak of Ps 49 as a wisdom psalm.[11]

Besides the opening, 49:13 and 49:21 function as some kind of chorus, giving the psalm its structure. But there are significant differences between the two of them. While verse 13 states that the human being in all his glory does not endure (בל ילין), verse 21 emphasizes that the human being in his glory does not possess understanding (ולא יבין). While it seems tempting to solve this problem by means of textual criticism, unfortunately this is impossible, since not only do the consonants ל and ב differ, but also the negation is being expressed here with בל and there with לא.[12] In conse-

---

11. See Perdue (1974, 533–36), who places Ps 49 in a sapiential context, based upon the term חידה, and Hossfeld and Zenger (1993, 299): "Der Psalm ist von fast philosophischer Denkbemühung geprägt."

12. Remarkably, at least in the case of בל there is a significantly high rate of usage within Proverbs and the Psalter.

quence, we are forced to accept the differences between verses 12 and 21 as essential for the interpretation of the psalm.

The chorus puts an accent in the middle of the text (49:13). The first main part consists of verses 6–12, within which—corresponding to the book of Qoheleth—human fragility is the central topic. All human beings, the wise and the fool, are doomed. As a consequence, amassing wisdom does not prevent anyone from perishing. While Ps 37 sees a great difference in this regard between the wicked and the righteous—and in fact promises the righteous that he will "prevail in the land"—the author of Ps 49 sees things differently. Although it is possible to distinguish between the wicked and the righteous on the grounds of their conduct, this distinction has no effect on their future: all together are going to die, and all together are like animals. With this insight, Ps 49 proves quite close to Qoheleth, who likewise makes the common fate of death and the proximity between humans and animals his topic again and again.[13]

In the second part (following 49:13) there is a new focus, though not too different. The lexeme כסל in verse 14 is a signpost determining the direction the reading is taking. The psalmist expects, and in fact is quite certain, that God will certainly rescue him from the power of Sheol.[14] The decisive difference from the wicked of Ps 37 is this: though humans share the common fate of death, yet the righteous profit from a continuous relationship with God—a relationship that gives the psalmist some comfort. Even if someone seeks riches and, against all accepted understanding, is successful, the psalmist knows that all this does not last, since everyone has to leave their possessions behind in the end. To the psalmist, however, God's will to maintain the relationship with the one who prays is an unshakeable certainty.[15] It is this fact that is his actual possession—one quite different from riches and glory.

The closing chorus takes up this viewpoint once more at the end of the psalm. Verse 21 at first glance appears to echo the thoughts of verse 13 with its statement on the common human fate of death, but in fact (since it is positioned at the end of the psalm, which intensely attacks foolishness and formulates central new insights into the destiny of the one who

---

13. Regarding the proximity of Ps 49 to Qoheleth, see Hossfeld and Zenger 1993, 300.

14. Regarding Ps 49:16, see Witte 2014, 78–84.

15. See Mowinckel (1955, 215): "Even the experiences of these poets culminate in such a personal religious confidence (xlix 16)."

prays) it has a parenetic color that makes it, similar to several משלים, an implicit admonition: human lack of insight is to be overcome precisely on the ground of the aforementioned reflection, and based upon this reflection it is to be set on a new basis. One of the central recognitions of the psalm is that *Tun* and *Ergehen* in fact do not correspond, insofar as no riches can change the truth that no one will take anything with them in the end. Whoever comes to this insight, though, henceforth remains in a sphere of a lasting relationship with God that claims validity beyond death. To be sure, this is in no way a simple reconstitution of the *Tun-Ergehen-Zusammenhang* on a higher level. Rather, it is a transformation of the *actio-reactio*-ideology into an existentially new orientation of the human being. Psalm 49 thus sketches a piece of inaugurated eschatology in the context of sapiential reflexivity. This form of thinking about limits, however, is to be sharply distinguished from later eschatologies, which, especially in later apocalyptic forms, show almost no insight from wisdom at all.

Psalm 49 is shaped by a specific mode of poetry or mode of literature with a profile that stretches far beyond a simply stylistic level. That is to say, behind the literary mode lies a reflective attitude that is almost impossible to characterize as merely seeking or cautious. Rather, the opening in verses 2–5 is the call of a trumpet, which adds a high level of certainty to the following. True, verse 6 shows the psalmist's insecurity and questions; however it is precisely by that insecurity and by his questions that he has taken a decisive step forward. Psalm 49 thus marks the end of a reflective process. For the one who prays, this process has opened a new understanding of reality.

The positioning of this reflection at the end of the first series of Korahite psalms is quite important. Psalm 49 throws a specific light on the orientation of the first collection of Korahite psalms toward the history of salvation. Neither Zion nor kingship is a lasting property that would have any impact on the future fate of either the people or the individual. Both—Zion and kingship—fall under the overall verdict regarding riches and glory: none of it lasts. It is only the relationship between God and a human being—and established by God—that lasts.

Since traditions rooted in the history of salvation are emphasized so intensively, it is possible that Ps 49 might have been connected to the preceding psalms only after the decline of Zion and kingship. The link established between Pss 42–43 and 49 forms an individualistic (or individualizing) frame for the collection in between. With Ps 49 a wisdom psalm is consciously chosen to close this collection, thus introducing a reflective mode at the end. Perhaps this is to be seen in context with those processes of eschatologizing that characterize the later redactions of the royal psalms and psalms of Zion. At least, it might be worthwhile to investigate the extent to which the eschatological trajectories within those collections can fruitfully be interpreted as a form of inaugurated eschatology (as in Ps 49). It appears undeniable that it was a conscious decision to give a sapiential shape to the first collection of Korahite psalms by having it end with Ps 49—and precisely this circumstance corresponds to the opening of the collection commonly named Psalms of Asaph with Ps 73, another wisdom psalm.

Psalm 73 as a Wisdom Psalm

Psalm 73 not only begins the series of Psalms of Asaph (Pss 73–83), but at the same time opens the third book of the Psalter. The royal psalm Ps 72 closes the second book, and, similar to the structure of the first row of Korahite psalms, the opening Ps 73 distinctly highlights a macrostructural joint of the Psalter. As Ps 49 throws a sapiential light onto the first row of Korahite psalms from the rear, the accent here in Ps 73 works as a sign at the beginning of the collection of following Psalms of Asaph. Whereas Ps 37 can be interpreted as corresponding to Proverbs and Ps 49 seems to have a number of connections to Qoheleth, in Ps 73 it is the constellations of Job that are taken up.[16] The psalmist is concerned with the inexplicable well-being of the wicked, in regard to whose conduct there does not seem to exist a correlation between *Tun* and *Ergehen*.

Three times within this psalm a verse begins with the interjection אך (vv. 1, 13, and 18). This textual marker allows one to divide Ps 73 into three circles of reflection: verses 1–12, 13–17, and 18–28 (Hossfeld and Zenger 2008, 337–38).

In the first part (verses 1–12) the poet engages the problem of the apparently inconsistent *Tun-Ergehen-Zusammenhang*. He perceives the wicked as living in prosperity and peace. Their well-being is obviously undisturbed, not subject to impairment of any kind. Central to the psalmist's lament and irritation is (besides their riches, arrogance, and violence)

---

16. Luyten (1979, 73–80), has analyzed in detail the links between Ps 73 and the book of Job; see also Perdue 1977, 286–87; Weber 2012, 301. Regarding the links between Ps 73 and Qoheleth, see D. Michel 1987, 654–55.

this: according to verse 11 the wicked question whether God is aware of human *Tun* and *Ergehen* at all. Surely, the fundamental question of God's existence is not meant to arise at this point. But since God is thought to guarantee the *Tun-Ergehen-Zusammenhang,* consequently it is he who comes into focus here, at a point where that correlation is becoming fragile. Therefore, the psalmist's question should probably be understood as being this: Does God indeed guarantee that conduct and consequence correlate—or does he not? It seems that, according to verse 1, the psalmist does not question God's presence nor his care for humanity as he perceives it. Nevertheless, the experience of a difference between conduct and consequence is shaking the psalmist.[17] And while Ps 37:1 warns not to envy the wicked, the person praying in Ps 73:3 admits to secretly having been envious of them, since they seem to enjoy a peace he is excluded from.

In the second part, the person praying now draws conclusions from his observations. Since it seems that there is no correlation between *Tun* and *Ergehen*, his strivings up to that point were obviously in vain. The wording of verse 16—חשב, ידע, and עמל—describes a process of problematizing reflection that, in his eyes, throws a new light on things. The מקדשי אל of verse 17 touch a subject that, on the one hand, has cultic connotations but, on the other hand, in the context of sapiential vocabulary points to a form of knowledge that helps the psalmist cope with the problem that *Tun* and *Ergehen* are disconnected: the prospect of the doom of those who caused his irritations in the first place.[18]

In the third part of the psalm (verses 18–28), things suddenly seem to have become reversed. Here, the psalmist takes up the idea of the destruction of the wicked (which is prevalent in Ps 37). Yet, this reversal does not evict a fundamental change of mood in the psalmist. Rather, he sticks to his anger and frustration—especially the statement to have been ignorant and like a beast reminds one of the language and imagery of Ps 49:13, 21 and thus resembles Qoheleth. Crucial to the psalmist, then, is his orientation toward YHWH and his relationship with God, which is emphasized in verses 23–28 at the end of the psalm in the form of a psalm of confidence.

---

17. See Hossfeld and Zenger (2008, 335): "Der Widerspruch zwischen dem weisheitlichen Lebenskonzept … und der gesellschaftlichen Realität … wird für das Ich zu einer strukturellen Lebens- und Glaubenskrise."

18. Regarding that problem, see Michel 1987, 644–47.

As in Ps 49, so in Ps 73 it is the stability of the relationship with God that is the decisive point for overcoming the problems resulting from the disintegration of the *Tun-Ergehen-Zusammenhang*, the disintegration that the psalmist observes and that drives him crazy (Witte 2014, 111). Here— as in Proverbs, Job, and Qoheleth—is by no means a distance from God to be discerned, as has often been imputed to sapiential thought. Wisdom, that is, the human attempt to understand reality around oneself on the basis of one's own experience, is inconceivable without relation to God. Rather, wisdom presents itself as a form of coming to terms with reality that has a person participating in the process of generating insight, yet very much aware of the limitations of such cognitive faculty. Both Ps 73 and Ps 49 express quite openly that decisive moments of cognition cannot be generated humanly, but ultimately have to be based upon an event of revelation. Cognition is connected to intense reflection, one that leads the human being to the מקדשי אל. The nature of these מקדשי אל encounters remains somewhat unclear, yet they lead the poet to the crucially new idea of reflecting on the doom of the wicked. Therefore, it seems adequate to connect these מקדשי אל encounters to some kind of revelatory event, whatever its nature, that becomes cognition only through human reflection: "Irgendwo muß die inhaltlich radikal neue Erkenntnis doch einen über das Übliche hinausgehenden Ursprung haben" (Michel 1987, 647).[19]

Thus, wisdom psalms form a trajectory within the Psalter, which develops its profile out of the quasi-theonomous human reflection. Remarkably, in Ps 73 this profile is being transmitted in a place where otherwise mainly historical aspects are being stressed. W. Brueggemann and P. D. Miller pointed out the connection between Ps 73 and the preceding Ps 72. They suspect that Ps 73 "provides an alternative 'script' for monarchy" (Brueggemann and Miller 1996, 51).[20] Yet, royal motifs are much

---

19. Hossfeld and Zenger (2008, 344–47) interpret the difficult passage similarily, likewise Weber (2012, 301), who emphasizes the cultic background but then notes regarding verse 16: "Die Formulierung ist knapp und entfaltet nicht näher, was dem Sprechenden bei diesem 'Kommen' an Begegnung, Wahrnehmung und Einsicht zuteil wurde. Dass eine tiefe Gotteserfahrung stattgefunden hat, deuten Aussagen in V. 23(f.).28 an."

20. Brueggemann and Miller, in the context of defining the genre of Ps 73, definitely open up further perspectives: "The genre of Psalm 73 is problematic and not obvious to identify. It has the marks of a sapiential psalm, and it is the easiest to read it in this way, as most scholars have done. But our question of interpretation is precisely to consider the interface of *royal* and sapiential (torah) motifs" (Brueggemann and

less prominent in Ps 73 than one would expect, considering their location beside one another—after all, the border between the second and third book of the Psalter, as well as the border between the collections of Psalms of David and Psalms of Asaph, separate them. Nevertheless, the placement of Ps 73 is by no means coincidental—though less in regard to the preceding royal psalm than to the following Psalms of Asaph. That collection (the Psalms of Asaph) transmits texts that focus on history and possibly contain traditions and motives that may well be traced all the way back to the Northern Kingdom of Israel (Seybold 1996, 8–9). Psalm 73, a wisdom psalm, is to be read as a deliberately designed overture to that collection of psalms.[21]

Thus, a process of sapientualizing the Psalter becomes evident. The same process can be seen in the placement of Ps 37 within the first collection of Davidic psalms, the positioning of Ps 49 at the end of the first collection of Korahite psalms, and in other instances, for example, the placement of Ps 1 and Ps 119. All of these texts introduce a reflective mode at macro-structurally central points of the psalter. It is only because of this that the Psalter becomes a book for meditation in the first place.

Upon reading the Psalter, it appears that Ps 73 breaks up the sequence of kingship—history formulated by Ps 72 and Ps 74. Based on the previously expounded problems of the correlation between *Tun* and *Ergehen*, the real power of the dimension behind kingship and history is being explored. In reality, it is the question of God who can be understood as the "alles bestimmende Wirklichkeit" (Bultmann 1954, 26) that is raised here. Where the Psalms of Asaph are determined by a perspective that is fundamentally collective, Ps 73 here individualizes that very perspective and, in the style of a psalm of confidence (*Vertrauenspsalm*), transfers it to the praying individual. This praying person is not only the psalmist of Ps 73 but, moreover, the reader and recipient of both the preceding and following psalms. The horizon within which Ps 73 is to be interpreted thus encompasses both the antecedent royal traditions as well as the subsequent historical traditions. Likewise, vice versa, Ps 73 influences the

---

Miller 1996, 53–54, emphasis original). Precisely this question about the interface of motifs in this psalm needs to be asked not only in regard to the preceding royal psalm, Ps 72, but also regarding the following Psalms of Asaph, which begin with Ps 73.

21. See Hossfeld and Zenger 2008, 353–54. Possibly, verses 1, 10, 15, 27, and 28 reflect the literary process of integrating Ps 73 into the collection of the Psalms of Asaph.

interpretation of the following psalms by expounding the problems of the *Tun-Ergehen-Zusammenhang*, since, of course, the fragility of that correlation has consequences not only for the praying individual, but also for the people and the interpretation of their own history—a history, then, that might not only be reconstructed within the horizon of the *Tun-Ergehen-Zusammenhang*, but, all disruptions notwithstanding, also as a history of God's lasting presence with his people—just as Ps 73 emphasizes the lasting relationship between the person praying and YHWH.[22]

Wisdom in the Psalter?

Where and in what ways is wisdom to be found in the Psalter? Recent research on Psalms has been arguing about whether or not wisdom psalms exist at all, and—in case they actually exist—what their characteristics might be. Bearing in mind what has just been said about Pss 37, 49, and 73, this question is quite easily answered: Comparable to the way royal psalms reflect kingship, its demise, and the rise of messianism, and equally comparable to the way psalms of Zion document a development within the Psalter that begins with preexilic Zion theology and leads right up to its postexilic reorientation, so also wisdom psalms take up central topics of the sapiential discourse that went on in ancient Judah and Israel. The crucial point, however, is not the existence of a specified and definite position, but rather the discursive momentum that mirrors a specific way to deal with reality. It is in that way that Old Testament wisdom literature is connected on a formal level, so to speak. It is only by the analysis of the individual psalms in question that one can begin to bring this connection to light. Normally, the hunt for genres (*Gattungen*) in the form-critical sense tends to cloud the view of those texts, the substance of which cannot be captured by form-critical means alone. It has become apparent in the preceding analysis of Pss 37, 49, and 73, however, that contextualizing the profile of individual psalms (with regards to their content) in a wider perspective than usual may actually help in establishing their classification as

---

22. It is certainly not a coincidence that a collection of psalms with a profile focusing on history is being framed by a psalm that builds upon topics known from the book of Job, since the literary profile of Job, in turn, seems indeed to allude to the Patriarchal history (Schmid 2010, 42, 65) and thus constructs an interface between sapiential and historical traditions. Some quite remarkable convergences on a literary and theological level can be observed here.

wisdom psalms. It is possible to assign each of them a relationship to one of the classic sapiential books of Proverbs, Qoheleth, and Job (with all due caution), though naturally without having to assume literary dependency.[23] Rather, it seems that those very problems debated within classical wisdom literature—that is, the tense relation between the wicked and the righteous, the validity and the problems of the *Tun-Ergehen-Zusammenhang*, the contestation of the fate of death, the significance of God's presence for a successful human life and, last but not least, the question of the transparency of the world and the problem of human cognitive faculty—constitute a complex of topics, which proves powerful both within the transmitting circles (*Trägerkreise*) of wisdom literature and, perhaps even more importantly, shapes debates beyond those texts, as, for example, the wisdom psalms show.

That sapiential topics were being broadly discussed is apparent in the considerable influence that sapiential patterns of thought and language had upon Old Testament literature. Such patterns are discernible not only in Proverbs, Qoheleth, and Job, but also in the primeval history in Gen 1–11 (Schmid 2002; Schüle 2006), in the Prophets (Hermisson 2003; Saur 2012b, 2014a), and precisely in Psalms, too (Saur 2014b). Psalms 37, 49, and 73 are only examples of the overall picture that is the sapiential impregnation of the Psalter.[24] Yet, while wisdom psalms such as Pss 1 or 119 unmis-

---

23. See R. N. Whybray (1995, 158): "It would be justifiable to call a psalm a 'wisdom psalm' only if its resemblance to some part of the Old Testament wisdom books—Proverbs, Job or Ecclesiastes—were so close as to be undeniable." Even with a classification of wisdom psalms as careful as that, Crenshaw remains critical: "True, a few psalms treat the same topics that invigorate the author of the book of Job (Pss 37, 49 and 73) and reflect on life's brevity like Ecclesiastes (Ps. 39), but these subjects probably exercised the minds of all thoughtful people. I do not see any profit in attributing such psalms to the sages when we know so little about the authors and their social contexts" (Crenshaw 2000, 15). The question remains, though, whether the obvious proximity of some psalms to the classic sapiential scriptures does not extend beyond general ideas, after all. The Psalter in its present form as a prayer book and book of meditation is given that very shape primarily by a significant degree of critical reflexivity. And is it not the classification of some psalms as sapiential that enables us to label the milieu from which the Psalter receives that form? Indeed, this is the heuristic capacity of the term wisdom psalms; cf. Oeming (2008, 161–62), and Sneed (2011, 67).

24. Weber in his 2012 article shows "dass die Weisheit als Denk- und Traditionsströmung wesentlichen Anteil an der Buchwerdung des Psalters hat. Ihre "Fingerabdrücke" sind namentlich in der oder den finalen Redaktionsstufe(n) des Psalmenbuchs greifbar" (Weber 2012, 289). Similarly, A. R. Ceresko (1990, 217): "Finally, the

takably point in the direction of a later "Torah-ization" of wisdom,[25] as witnessed especially in Sir 24, here Pss 37, 49, and 73 represent a sapiential perspective that is not formed by the Torah. At the same time, the close relationship between the different writing circles of the Psalter becomes evident. It bears witness to a circumstance with significance for the whole of ancient Israel and Judah: transmitting circles of literature are far better educated, more literate and widely socialized than simplistic classifications let us assume. The transmitting circles of the Psalter are witness to that wide range, and not least because the Psalter is rightfully to be understood as a *kleine Biblia* and *theologia in nuce*. The anchoring of sapiential trajectories within the Psalter thus attests that wisdom is not an isolated foreign body in ancient Israel's history of literature and theology. Rather, it has to be interpreted as an integral part of the world of the Hebrew Bible.

Works Consulted

Becker, Uwe. 2005. *Exegese des Alten Testaments: Ein Methoden- und Arbeitsbuch*. UTB 2664. Tübingen: Mohr Siebeck.

Brueggemann, Walter, and Patrick D. Miller. 1996. "Psalm 73 as a Canonical Marker." *JSOT* 72:45–56.

Bultmann, Rudolf. 1954. "Welchen Sinn hat es, von Gott zu reden?" Pages 26–37 in vol. 1 of *Glauben und Verstehen: Gesammelte Aufsätze* by Rudolf Bultmann. 2nd ed. 4 vols. Tübingen: Mohr Siebeck.

Ceresko, Anthony R. 1990. "The Sage in the Psalms." Pages 217–30 in *The Sage in Israel and the Ancient Near East*. Edited by John G. Gammie and Leo G. Perdue. Winona Lake, IN: Eisenbrauns.

Crenshaw, James L. 2000. "Wisdom Psalms?" *CurBS* 8:9–17.

Duhm, Bernard. 1899. *Die Psalmen erklärt*. Freiburg im Breisgau: Mohr.

Gunkel, Hermann. 1926. *Die Psalmen: Übersetzt und erklärt*. HKAT, Göttingen: Vandenhoeck & Ruprecht.

Gunkel, Hermann, and Joachim Begrich. 1933. *Einleitung in die Psalmen: Die Gattungen der religiösen Lyrik Israels*. HKAT. Göttingen: Vandenhoeck & Ruprecht.

Hermisson, Hans-Jürgen. 2003. "Prophetie und Weisheit." Pages 111–28 in *Weisheit in Israel: Beiträge des Symposiums "Das Alte Testament und*

Psalter itself is clearly the product of the torah/wisdom teachers, and the final form of this collection of songs bears the stamp of their influence and intent."

25. Regarding Ps 1, see Weber 2012, 291–96.

die Kultur der Moderne" anlässlich des 100. Geburtstags Gerhard von Rads (1901–1971), Heidelberg, 18.–21. Oktober 2001. Edited by D. J. A. Clines, Hermann Lichtenberger, Hans-Peter Müller, and Elke Blumenthal. ATM 12. Münster: LIT.

Hossfeld, Frank-Lothar, and Erich Zenger. 1993. *Die Psalmen I: Psalm 1–50*. NEchtB 29. Würzburg: Echter.

———. 2000. *Psalmen 51–100.* HThKAT. Freiburg im Breisgau: Herder.

———. 2008. *Psalmen 101–150.* HThKAT. Freiburg im Breisgau: Herder.

Körting, Corinna. 2006. *Zion in den Psalmen.* FAT 48. Tübingen: Mohr Siebeck.

Kuntz, J. Kenneth. 1974. "The Canonical Wisdom Psalms of Ancient Israel—Their Rhetorical, Thematic, and Formal Dimensions." Pages 186–222 in *Rhetorical Criticism: Essays in Honor of James Muilenburg.* Edited by Jared J. Jackson and Martin Kessler. Pittsburgh: Pickwick.

———. 2000. "Wisdom Psalms and the Shaping of the Hebrew Psalter." Pages 144–60 in *For a Later Generation: The Transformation of Tradition in Israel, Early Judaism, and Early Christianity.* Edited by Randal A. Argall, Beverly Bow, Rodney Alan Werline, and George W. E. Nickelsburg. Harrisburg, PA: Trinity Press International.

———. 2003. "Reclaiming Biblical Wisdom Psalms: A Response to Crenshaw." *CurBR* 1:145–54.

Luther, Martin. 1963. "Vorrede zum Psalter (1528)." Pages 32–37 in *Luther Deutsch. Vol. 5: Die Schriftauslegung.* Edited by Kurt Aland. 2nd ed. Stuttgart: Ehrenfried Klotz.

Luyten, Jos. 1979. "Psalm 73 and Wisdom." Pages 59–81 in *La Sagesse de l'Ancien Testament.* Edited by Maurice Gilbert. BETL 51. Gembloux: Duculot.

Michel, Diethelm. 1987. "Ich aber bin immer bei dir. Von der Unsterblichkeit der Gottesbeziehung." Pages 637–58 in *Im Angesicht des Todes. Ein interdisziplinäres Kompendium I.* Edited by Hansjakob Becker, Bernhardt Einig, and Peter-Otto Ullrich. Pietas Liturgica 3. St. Ottilien: EOS.

Mowinckel, Sigmund. 1955. "Psalms and Wisdom." Pages 205–24 in *Wisdom in Israel and in the Ancient Near East: Presented to Professor Harold Henry Rowley by the Society for Old Testament Study, in Association with the Editorial Board of Vetus Testamentum, in Celebration of His Sixty-Fifth Birthday, 24 March 1955.* Edited by Martin Noth and D. Winton Thomas. VTSup 3. Leiden: Brill.

Murphy, Roland E. 1963. "A Consideration of the Classification 'Wisdom Psalms.'" Pages 156–67 in *Congress Volume: Bonn 1962*. Edited by G. W. Anderson. VTSup 9. Leiden: Brill.
Oeming, Manfred. 2008. "Wisdom as a Hermeneutical Key to the Book of Psalms." Pages 154–62 in *Scribes, Sages, and Seers: The Sage in the Eastern Mediterranean World*. Edited by Leo G. Perdue. FRLANT 219. Göttingen: Vandenhoeck & Ruprecht.
Perdue, Leo G. 1974. "The Riddles of Psalm 49." *JBL* 93:533–42.
———. 1977. *Wisdom and Cult: A Critical Analysis of the Views of Cult in the Wisdom Literatures of Israel and the Ancient Near East*. SBLDS 30. Missoula, MT: Scholars Press.
Rad, Gerhard von. 1970. *Weisheit in Israel*. Neukirchen-Vluyn: Neukirchener Verlag.
Saur, Markus. 2004. *Die Königspsalmen: Studien zur Entstehung und Theologie*. BZAW 340. Berlin: de Gruyter.
———. 2011. "Sapientia discursiva: Die alttestamentliche Weisheitsliteratur als theologischer Diskurs." *ZAW* 123:236–49.
———. 2012a. *Einführung in die alttestamentliche Weisheitsliteratur*. Darmstadt: Wissenschaftliche Buchgesellschaft.
———. 2012b. "'Siehe, du bist weiser als Daniel…' (Ez 28,3): Überlegungen zum Verhältnis von Prophetie, Weisheit und Apokalyptik am Beispiel des Ezechielbuches." *TZ* 68:97–116.
———. 2014a. "Prophetie, Weisheit und Gebet: Überlegungen zu den Worten Agurs in Prov 30,1–9." *ZAW* 126:570–83.
———. 2014b. "Die Weisheitspsalmen Ps 49 und Ps 73 und ihre Bedeutung für die theologische Architektur des Psalters." Pages 121–49 in *Die kleine Biblia: Beiträge zur Theologie der Psalmen und des Psalters*. Edited by Markus Saur. Biblisch-Theologische Studien 148. Neukirchen-Vluyn: Neukirchener Verlag.
Schmid, Konrad. 2002. "Die Unteilbarkeit der Weisheit: Überlegungen zur sogenannten Paradieserzählung Gen 2f. und ihrer theologischen Tendenz." *ZAW* 114:21–39.
———. 2010. *Hiob als biblisches und antikes Buch: Historische und intellektuelle Kontexte seiner Theologie*. SBS 219. Stuttgart: Katholisches Bibelwerk.
Schüle, Andreas. 2006. *Der Prolog der hebräischen Bibel: Der literar- und theologiegeschichtliche Diskurs der Urgeschichte (Gen 1–11)*. AThANT 86. Zürich: TVZ.
Seybold, Klaus. 1996. *Die Psalmen*. HAT 1/15. Tübingen: Mohr Siebeck.

Sneed, Mark. 2011. "Is the 'Wisdom Tradition' a Tradition?" *CBQ* 73:50–71.
Steck, Odil Hannes. 1993. *Exegese des Alten Testaments: Leitfaden der Methodik. Ein Arbeitsbuch für Proseminare, Seminare und Vorlesungen*. 13th ed. Neukirchen-Vluyn: Neukirchener Verlag.
Wanke, Gunther. 1966. *Die Zionstheologie der Korachiten in ihrem traditionsgeschichtlichen Zusammenhang*. BZAW 97. Berlin: Töpelmann.
Weber, Beat. 2012. "'Like a Bridge Over Troubled Water...': Weisheitstheologische Wegmarkierungen im Psalter." Pages 289–306 in *Ex oriente Lux: Studien zur Theologie des Alten Testaments; Festschrift für Rüdiger Lux zum 65. Geburtstag*. Edited by Angelika Berlejung and Raik Heckl. ABG 39. Leipzig: Evangelische Verlagsanstalt.
Whybray, Roger N. 1995. "The Wisdom Psalms." Pages 152–60 in *Wisdom in Ancient Israel: Essays in Honour of J. A. Emerton*. Edited by John Day, R. P. Gordon, and H. G. M. Williamson. Cambridge: Cambridge University Press.
Wilson, Gerald H. 1985. *The Editing of the Hebrew Psalter*. SBLDS 76. Chico, CA: Scholars Press.
———. 1992. "The Shape of the Book of Psalms." *Int* 46:129–42.
Witte, Markus. 2014. *Von Ewigkeit zu Ewigkeit: Weisheit und Geschichte in den Psalmen*. BThSt 146. Neukirchen-Vluyn: Neukirchener Verlag.
Zenger, Erich. 1998. "Der Psalter als Buch: Beobachtungen zu seiner Entstehung, Komposition und Funktion." Pages 1–57 in *Der Psalter in Judentum und Christentum*. Edited by Erich Zenger and Norbert Lohfink. Herders Biblische Studien 18. Freiburg im Breisgau: Herder.

GATTUNG AND *SITZ IM LEBEN*: METHODOLOGICAL VAGUENESS IN DEFINING WISDOM PSALMS

Tova Forti

INTRODUCTION

Since the 1940s, a significant trend has emerged in biblical scholarship toward investigating the influence wisdom literature has exerted upon the whole scriptural corpus (including the prophetic and historical books), replacing the traditional focus on the books customarily regarded as constituting the sapiential literature—Proverbs, Job, and Ecclesiastes.[1] One of the areas this development has affected is the identification of the wisdom psalm. This paper examines how methodological imprecision regarding the criteria for defining this type of psalm has caused widespread confusion and negatively impacted this field of study. It suggests that four elements can help determine those psalms that belong to the creative workshop of the circles of the wise: (1) thematic and ideational features; (2) linguistic and stylistic aspects; (3) an aggregation of wisdom vocabulary; and (4) figurative features. Following a theoretical discussion, an analysis of Psalms 39 and 104 is presented in order to demonstrate how "individual laments" and "hymns of creation" also exhibit wisdom characteristics.

Hermann Gunkel's investigation of the literary types (*Gattungsforschung*) found in the book of Psalms offered biblical scholars a methodological introduction to the form-critical analysis of the psalms and their cult-functional setting (Gunkel and Begrich 1998). The translation of his *An Introduction to Psalms: The Genres of the Religious Lyric of Israel* in

---

1. For different definitions of wisdom for assessing the background and interpretation of biblical literature in general, see Sheppard 1980, 1–12; McKane 1965; Crenshaw 1969, 129–42. Whybray (1968, 481 n. 1) lists a series of studies dedicated to the "wisdom influence upon nonhagiographic literature."

1998 and of Sigmund Mowinckel's *The Psalms in Israel's Worship* in 1962 enabled English-speaking scholars to apply classical form-critical analysis to the Psalms.

In order to establish the *Gattung* into which a class of psalms should be placed, Gunkel argued that, inter alia, they all had to possess a similar *Sitz im Leben*. As Martin Buss argued early on, however, setting is a problematic concept in this context, "refer[ring] either to historical circumstances or to the condition expressly described by the text" (1978, 158–59). Many psalms do not fit into Gunkel's stringent aesthetic scheme; he classified them as "mixed," presenting various literary criteria for identifying "wisdom poetry in the psalms": direct father/son address, admonition and instruction, artistic alphabetic form, and preoccupation with such issues as theodicy, personal experience, individual complaints, and the futility of possessions (Gunkel and Begrich 1998, 293–305). These criteria for the reconstruction of form-critical history became passé, however, when study of Babylonian and Ugaritic poetry revealed that the Mesopotamian psalms of lamentation and the "mixed" biblical psalms exhibit a common range of thematic expressions, including descriptive elements of physical suffering, a sense of divine abandonment, and various hymnic elements addressed to the deity in order to gain his favor.[2]

The stylistic and thematic complexity of many of the psalms also created the need for subcategories—such as the individual and public prayers within the song of prayer class, the former itself being subdivided into the prayer of the afflicted individual and the confessional prayer of the accused. Despite these ever-increasing nuances, however, it remained difficult to definitively ascertain the setting of a number of psalms. Thus while the original setting of the thanksgiving songs or Yahweh's enthronement psalms can be relatively easily identified on the basis of their cultic, ritual, or festival background, that of the wisdom psalms remained difficult, containing no references to either temple rituals/royal court ceremonies or historical allusions.

The fluidity in the number of wisdom psalms adduced by scholars reveals the confusion and lack of consensus in defining the genre. Although

---

2. For a critique of Gunkel's and Begrich's form-critical research, see Kraus 1993, 39–41. For the thematic parallels between Akkadian literature and the individual lament prayers in Psalms, see Widengren 1937; Falkenstein and von Soden 1953; Castellino 1940. See also Avishur 1994; Hilber 2005; Bouzard 1997; Tomes 2005; Lenzi 2010, 303–15.

Mowinckel himself originally only regarded Pss 1, 112, and 127 as wisdom psalms, he subsequently added Pss 19B, 34, 37, 49, 78, 105, 106, and 111 to what he called "learned psalmography."[3] Otto Eissfeldt made similar changes to his inventory, expanding it from Pss 1, 37, 49, 73, 78, 91, and 128 to include 90, 105, 106, 133, and 139 (1965, 124–27). Roland Murphy exhibits the reverse tendency, reducing the number of wisdom psalms in his classification system from twelve to seven.[4] J. Luyten describes the "chaos" of this situation, R. N. Whybray similarly commenting: "To write about 'the wisdom psalms' is … somewhat akin to making bricks without straw, for there is no scholarly agreement at all about the number or the identity of such psalms, or even about the existence of such a category."[5] James Crenshaw concludes, "We have isolated sufficient evidence to suggest that a few psalms share some vocabulary and interests with Israel's sages. Still, we are not justified in taking the further step toward declaring these psalms 'wisdom' and assuming that the sages had a lively interest in the cult prior to Ben Sira."[6] Whybray observes, "It would be justifiable to call a psalm a 'wisdom psalm' only if its resemblance to some part of the Old Testament wisdom books—Proverbs, Job or Ecclesiastes—were so close as to be undeniable" (1995, 158; cf. Oeming 2008, 154–62). Murphy sums up the problem in the succinct statement: "The very idea is as broad as the wisdom literature" (1963, 159). The only generally-accepted criterion being the ideational link to wisdom thought, the question of how speculative reflection forms part of the prayer *Gattung* and the identity of the tradents behind the wisdom psalm remains unresolved.[7]

---

3. Mowinckel 1955, 205–24; idem 1962, 2:104–25. According to Mowinckel, "learned psalmography" was cultivated amongst the circle of erudite/wise scribes who engaged in the writing of noncultic, moralizing, didactic sayings, proverbs, and exhortation.

4. Murphy 1963, 157–67. On the basis of rhetorical features, vocabulary, thematic elements, and forms, Kuntz (1974, 186–222) adds Pss 127 and 133 to Murphy's list.

5. Luyten 1979, 59–81; Whybray 1995, 152. Castellino, for example, designates nineteen psalms as wisdom psalms (1955, 729–835). Engnell, on the other hand, believes that no psalm was originally composed as a didactic poem (1969, 99).

6. Crenshaw 2010, 187–94. For the continuing discussion between Kuntz and Crenshaw, see Kuntz 2003, 145–54; idem 2012, 342–44.

7. Mowinckel discusses the difficulty in distinguishing between the "learned"/"wise" men (חכמים), or possibly "scribes," responsible for the "poetry of wisdom" and other social groups, such as the priests, prophets, and Levites, maintaining that "The psalm poets as a rule belonged to the temple singers [presumably

Which Psalms Merit the Label Wisdom?

In his monumental study *Wisdom in Israel*, Gerhard von Rad endeavored to determine the identity of the individual(s) responsible for the intellectual activity that crystallized practical and empirical knowledge into proverbial rules, wisdom sayings, and poetry, examining the interrelationship between this literary activity and other ideological streams in the Hebrew Bible—such as historiography and prophecy (1972, 4–14). This issue is even more acute in relation to the discussion of psalmody as liturgical literature, the identification of the *Sitz im Leben* of psalms characterized by the ideas and language of wisdom literature and their link with the creative workshop of the circles of the wise men alike being formidable tasks. Arguing that prayer and didactic instructions should not be viewed as antithetical, he suggested that compositions originally composed by poets as cultic psalms were reworked into didactic teachings in the postexilic period—the sapiential features in the psalms thus indicating a literary link with the wisdom milieu rather than reflecting a specific *Sitz im Leben*.

The psalm's status as a liturgical poem recruited to strengthen faith, and religious creed imbuing it with a didactic character, it displays a natural correspondence with wisdom compositions. The context of prayer and communication with God in and of itself is nonetheless too general to justify a specific class of "wisdom psalm." Likewise, from a form-critical perspective, rhetorical questions, numerical sayings, better than sayings, acrostic (alphabetic) arrangements, or the beatitude formula "Happy is/are (אשרי)" are not distinctive to wisdom literature, occurring in other genres—such as prophecy and lamentation.[8] Theologically speaking, while Proverbs recommends that "The fear of the Lord is the beginning of wisdom," not every psalm that contains an expression of piety or makes reference to the notion of retribution can automatically be associated with

---

the final collectors and/or redactors of the psalms].... It is this learned, non-cultic psalmography which is followed up by the post-canonical, late Jewish psalmography" (1955, 207, 216–17).

8. See Whybray 1995, 152–60. The אשרי form introduces cultic blessings, exhortations to trust God, moral ethics, and wisdom observations regarding the nature of reality, occurring virtually exclusively in the Psalms (frequently in Torah psalms) and Proverbs (x 4): see Jacobson 2008, 114.

the wisdom workshop—these themes appearing frequently in the Hebrew Bible and thus not being exclusively sapiential.

The didactic form/content of the psalms exhibits close affinities with the biblical wisdom literature in general.[9] Although the book of Proverbs serves as a guidebook for ethic and social conduct, however, very few of its sayings contain ritual terms or allude to covenantal commandments—such as the Sabbath, the rest mandated for servants, the gifts to be given to the poor, the sabbatical and jubilee years, or the forgiving of debts.[10] Proverbs also evinces little historical sensitivity or context, referring to no historical events or political policies.[11] The absence of intimations regarding formative events in the people's history or traditions concerning God's involvement in their lives in the form of laws, miracles, or theophanies further complicates the contextualization of the biblical wisdom literature within Israelite historiography. The attempt to define the wisdom psalm on the basis of the relation the genre demonstrates to the content of Proverbs therefore cannot be grounded in any specific cultic/ritual or historical context.

Ecclesiastes is primarily a record of personal observation and contemplation—its skepticism being replaced in Job by a theological dispute between Job and his friends. Those psalms that recall the rhetorical, thematic, and formal aspects of these books— such as reflections on

---

9. Perdue (1977) dedicates a chapter "Didactic Poems and the Wisdom Psalms" (261–324), classifying eleven texts into three didactic structures: proverb poems (Pss 1, 19B, 34, 37, 73, 112, 127), 'ashrê poems (32, 119), and riddle poems (49, 19A).

10. While Proverbs warns: "Do not be one of those who give their hand, who stand surety for debts" (22:26) and "Do not remove ancient boundary stones; do not encroach upon the fields of orphans" (23:10), the rationale offered for these directives differs from the covenantal basis given in Deuteronomy: "You shall not move your countryman's landmarks, set up by previous generations, in the property that will be allotted to you in the land that the LORD your God is giving you to possess" (Deut 19:14 NJPS; cf. Prov 22:28). See Kaufmann 1972, 323–27; von Rad 2001, 1:438; Crenshaw 2010, 18–21, 29. For the argument that cult and wisdom are not mutually exclusive, see Perdue 1977, 135–88; Whybray 1995, 152–60; Dell 2004, 445–58. Sneed attributes the priestly and prophetic traditions of Israelite lore to the "literary sages" (2011, 50–71).

11. The attributes to/references to Solomon (1:1; 10:1; 25:1) and "the men of Hezekiah" (25:1) are more appropriately the subject of a literary-redaction discussion than an investigation into the book's historical context and dating: see Whybray 1990, 133–46; Fox 1996, 227–39.

the ephemerality of life formulated in sapiential language and figurative expressions—thus display close affinities with the wisdom genre.[12]

Psalm 39

I shall now analyze two psalms belonging to disparate genres—Ps 39, an individual lament, and Ps 104, a hymn of creation—in order to demonstrate that, despite the diversity in their perspectives, both contain clear sapiential features.

Although H. J. Kraus contends that the reflections in Ps 39 mark it as a didactic poem, he does not identify it as a wisdom psalm in his introductory discussion of didactic poetry (1993, 58–60, 417). Otto Kaiser reconstructs an earlier didactic poem built upon the motif of the brevity of life (39:5–7, 12) (1998, 71–83). Although Crenshaw notes the psalm's affinities with the wisdom tradition, he likewise does not classify it as a wisdom psalm, arguing rather that the similarities between Ps 39 and the reflective wisdom in the books of Job and Qoheleth "suggest either dependence or folk tradition on which the authors of all three works may have drawn" (2010, 188). Will Kynes develops the idea that Ps 39 represents a Job-Psalm or Qoheleth-Psalm, providing a close intertextual study of the connections between it and Job via thematic and lexico-syntactical allusions.[13]

Following Gunkel, the majority of scholars consider Ps 39 to be a lament of the individual in which the petitioner appeals to God (39:13) and describes his afflictions.[14] Although the psalmist opens with a personal confession, he bridles or muzzles his mouth, refraining from lamenting out loud lest he sin with his tongue against God—his suffering being a punishment for his sins that only God can relieve (vv. 9–12). The emotional outburst then shifts to an appeal to God, arguing for a theological solution to human misery and meditating on the transience and vanity of human life and possessions. The focus on suffering and pain (vv. 3, 11) has

---

12. See Murphy 1963; Kuntz 1974, 186–222; Luyten 1979; Ceresko 1990, 217–30; Whybray 1995, 152–60; Brown 2005, 85–102. For philological criteria for the identification of the wisdom thesaurus in the Psalms, see Scott 1971, 192–201; Hurvitz 1988, 41–51; 1991 [Hebrew]).

13. Kynes notes the associations between such passages as Job 6:8–11 and Ps 39:5, 8; Job 7:6–8, 16 and Ps 39:5, 8, 14; Job 10:20–21 and Ps 39:5–6, 14; Job 13:28–14:6 and Ps 39:5–7, 12, 14 (2012, 122–41).

14. Gunkel 1998, 136, 174, 178–79; Briggs and Briggs, for example, define Ps 39 as an elegy (1906, 1:344).

led some scholars to define Psalm 39 as a psalm of sickness and healing—a subcategory of the prayer of the individual (cf. Seybold 1966, 162–63).

The imagery of the moth ותמס כעש חמודו "consuming his precious garment" (39:12) (cf. Isa 50:9) is employed at the point at which the petitioner shifts from refusing to let out his emotions to adducing a series of reasons justifying God's intervention.[15] Following the description of his suffering and entreaty for divine healing—"Take away your plague from me" (v. 11)—the imagery concretely depicts his despair and dissolution. Embedded between the perception of theodicy in the opening strophe ("You chastise a man in punishment for his sin" [12a]) and the declaration of the existential *vanitas* of human beings in the closing strophe ("No man is more than a breath" [12c]), the image becomes a central motif.

The moth picturesquely illustrates the doctrine of divine providence and essence of human existence, its destructive effect highlighting the futile/feeble/fleeting nature of human life and God's omnipotence and eternality. Inserted between the psalmist's recognition that he is being justly punished by God and his reflective declaration that אך כל הבל כל אדם "no man is more than a breath" (39:6), the imagery creates a skeptical, melancholy mood characteristic of speculative wisdom literature.

The figure of the moth occurs frequently in the wisdom literature to symbolize the brevity/vanity of human life.[16] Thus, for example, Job 13:28–14:1 states: "Man wastes away like a rotten thing, like a garment eaten by moths. Man born of woman is short-lived and sated with trouble." As in Job 14:2b, Ps 39 regards human life as a shadow that does not endure. Rather than carrying the customary sense of image or likeness, צלם (v. 7) here appears to signify a fleeting entity (cf. "Man is like a breath; his days are like a passing shadow" [Ps 144:4])—employed ironically here in light of its double meaning.[17] The doctrinal perception of human beings as created in God's "image" (צלם) in the creation story

---

15. Biblical quotations follow the NJPS.

16. See Forti 2008, 160–63. On the rhetorical impact of faunal similes and metaphors within psalmic *Gattungen*, see Kuntz 2008, 46–62.

17. See Ps 102:12; Job 7:2, 8:9, 17:7; Qoh 6:12. Cf. the ideational link between גר "sojourner" and תושב "transient" and the image of the "shadow" in 1 Chr 29:15/Ps 39:7a, 13b and between שכיר "hireling" and צל "shadow" in Job 7:1–2. While *HALOT* (II*צלם, 3:1028) interprets "shadow" in light of the Akkadian *ṣalāmu* "to be dark," the *mêm* of צלם might be an enclitic: see Cohen 1996, 294–95 n. 28.

(Gen 1:26, 27) contrasts starkly with the notion that they are mere "transient shadows" (צל).

הבל "breath" as signifying the brevity—vanity—of life is also closely linked to wisdom literature: "I am sick of it [life]. I shall not live forever; let me be, for my days are a breath" (Job 7:16). In the sense of futility, this term occurs approximately forty times in Qoheleth. In Ps 39, it forms part of a repetitive refrain/*leitmotif* highlighting the limited duration of human life that evokes a reflective atmosphere (vv. 6, 12; cf. also v. 7). The noun תוחלת "hope" (v. 8), a common sapiential term, is also used here as a synonym of תקוה (cf. Prov 10:28), הגיג "thought" (v. 4b) similarly being related to the sapiential terms הגות and הגיון—oral instruction: "My mouth utters wisdom, my speech is full of insight" (Ps 49:4). Outside the Psalms, the noun חלד "life expectancy" also only occurs in Job (11:17). Its parallelism here with חדל (v. 5) constitutes a metathesis, this device serving to accentuate the fact that the duration/span of human life is so short that it ceases virtually the moment it comes into existence, the life expectancy granted a person by God vanishing into nothingness when God summarily terminates it.[18] Finally, the idiomatic expression בטרם אלך ואינני "before I pass away and am gone" (v. 14b) denotes the transience of human life so frequently adduced by Job: "The eye that gazes on me will not see me; your eye will seek me, but I shall be gone" (Job 7:8).[19]

Psalm 39 also employs two stylistic devices characteristic of wisdom literature (see Forti 2008, 157–63). The anaphoric use of the asseverative particle אך (vv. 6c, 7a, 12c) affirms precisely the vanity, transience, and futility of life (cf. Job 13:15, 20; Ps 73:1–2). The usage of the introductory formula אמרתי "I said" (39:2) in sapiential texts marks an inner reflection: "I thought: 'Let age speak; let advanced years declare wise things'" (Job 32:7–8; cf. Ps 53:2; 89:3–5), frequently introducing dialectical discussions in Qoheleth (see 2:1–2; 3:17–18; 7:23; 8:14).[20]

---

18. The compound יוֹשְׁבֵי חָדֶל in Isa 38:11 and the parallelism between חָלָד and שׁוא in Ps 89:48 are also deliberate metatheses between חדל/חלד; see Thomas 1957, 13–14.

19. Cf. Job 3:21; 23:8; 24:24; 27:19. For adverbial idioms signifying the brevity/transience of life and their Akkadian counterparts, see Held 1987, 104–14. Clifford interprets קץ "the end" and מדת ימים "measure of days" as reflecting the psalmist's need to know how long he will suffer rather than how long he will live (2000, 59–66).

20. Von Rad defines this literary genre as *Hoffartsmonolog* (2001, 2:180 n. 10); see also Dahood 1968, 19 n. 2.

Psalm 104

Turning from an individual psalm to a community prayer of praise to the God of creation, Ps 104 is frequently classified as a Torah psalm (Berlin 2005, 71–83). The Torah type is plagued by the same form-critical issues as the wisdom psalm. As Gerald Sheppard notes,

> While other form critical designations carry an implicit assessment of sociological function (e.g., individual lament, thanksgiving song), these two categories seem to reflect only an estimate of the supposed content or subject matter of a psalm. Ps. 1 illustrates why confusion results from the use of this criterion. On the one hand, it is acknowledged that the style and certain expressions in Ps. 1 are idiomatic to [sic] wisdom literature. On the other hand, the Torah seems to be its principal object of concern and it, not the wisdom literature, is commended for study. (1980, 137)

Psalm 104 opens with a summons to bless the Lord, extolling him for his mighty works, and concludes with a petition to destroy the wicked (Levenson 1988). Neither of these themes are closely linked to the lauding of the covenantal commandments so clearly exemplified in the distinctive Torah psalms (1, 19, 119)—whose purpose is to witness to God's power and to the fact that observance of the Torah assures the existence of a well-ordered and cohesive human community.[21] Although the description of creation in Ps 104 recalls the primordial elements depicted in Gen 1, the motifs and flora and fauna adduced in the portrayal of cosmological harmony clearly reflect the wisdom tradition of creation in Job (9:5–10; 38) and Proverbs (3:19–20; 8:22–31), which portrays God as the cosmic Creator who alone knows the ways of wisdom and creation as the subject of human theosophical contemplation (Clifford 1985, 516).

The thematic and ideational elements, linguistic and stylistic factors, and striking use of wisdom vocabulary in Ps 104 have long been recog-

---

21. The argument that the postexilic community identified wisdom with the Torah has led to the proposal that Pss 1 and 119 (book 5) were deliberately placed at pivotal points in the canonical psalmodic collection: see Wilson 1985, 143. According to Mays, "Those who were at work in the final shaping and arrangement of the Psalter were completely committed to torah as the divinely willed way of life" (1987, 11).

nized.[22] Thus, for example, the creation of the sea is adduced as an example of divine wisdom:

> How many are the things You have made, O Lord; You have made them all with wisdom; the earth is full of Your creations. There is the sea, vast and wide, with its creatures beyond number, living things, small and great. There go the ships, and Leviathan that You formed to sport with. All of them look to You to give them their food when it is due. (104:24–27).

Combining climatic and ecological phenomena, the psalm represents creation as a holistic programmatic harmony (vv. 10–14) between the human and the natural, each natural phenomenon finding its "own particular place, function, time, and norms regulating its existence within the complex of cosmic order" (Perdue, 1977, 135). The lack of any reference to the ethnic-national salvation effected by the God of Israel suggests that the author forms part of the wisdom tradition of creation (cf. Prov 3:19–20; 8:22–30; Job 38–39) that promotes the concept of a universal God of creation. Rather than linking ships with the mythological sphere of creation battles (cf. Job 40:25), their juxtaposition with Leviathan—created for God's entertainment—identifies them as worthy objects of wisdom reflection.

The Great Hymn to the Aten includes a similar list:

> All beasts are content with their pasturage; trees and plants are flourishing. The birds which fly from their nests, their wings are (stretched out) in praise to thy ka. All beasts spring upon (their) feet. Whatever flies and alights, they live when thou hast risen (for) them. The ships are sailing north and south as well, for every way is open at thy appearance. The fish in the river dart before thy face; thy rays are in the midst of the great green sea. (Pritchard and Fleming 2011, 326)

The correspondence between the Egyptian and biblical texts demonstrates not only the existence of a universal concept of a beneficent creator but

---

22. Rashi (1040–1105 CE) early on drew attention to the linguistic similarities of שחק "sport with" in 104:26 with Job 40:29 in relation to God's interaction with the animals (Gruber 2004, 618). For Ps 104's affinities with wisdom thought, see Whybray 1974, 154; Jamieson-Drake 1987, 217–35; Gammie 1990, 481–82; Boström 1990, 71–75, 152; Gerstenberger 2001, 226; Terrien 2003, 717; Forti 2011, 359–74.

also a common reservoir of literary traditions in which creation is conceptualized as divine wisdom (*AEL* 2:100).[23]

CONCLUSION

The above discussion illustrates the difficulty in classifying the wisdom psalm, the category not being strictly defined or limited by literary types. The author of this genre recalls sapiential literature via the citation of or allusion to specific texts, employing words, phrases, images, and metaphors borrowed from the wisdom books as a hermeneutical construct for his theological teaching.[24] The date of wisdom psalms is very difficult to establish because wisdom statements are, by definition, didactic/moral rather than historical, with the wisdom tradition spreading throughout the ancient Near East over the course of centuries. Thus while scholars tend to identify wisdom psalms as dating to the lifetime of Ben Sira (ca. 200–150 BCE) or slightly later, some may be preexilic. The wisdom psalms' original composition as poems and their editorial elaboration into independent literary liturgical units must therefore be distinguished, their transformation into prayers most probably being the work of the postexilic scribal-priestly elite in Jerusalem.

WORKS CONSULTED

Assman, Jan. 1992. "Akhanyati's Theology of Light and Time." *PIASH* 7.4:143–76.
Avishur, Y. 1994. *Studies in Hebrew and Ugaritic Psalms*. Jerusalem: Magnes.
Berlin, Adele. 2005. "The Wisdom of Creation in Psalm 104." Pages 71–83 in *Seeking Out the Wisdom of the Ancients: Essays Offered to Honor*

---

23. See Lichtheim 1973–1981, 2:100. Shupak (2001, 409–32) discusses the Egyptian elements in Ps 104: the descriptions of day and night (vv. 20–23), the sea (vv. 25–26), God as the provider of food to humanity (vv. 10–15, 27–28), and God granting life. Dion (1991, 43–71) compares the motif in Ps 104:28: "open Your hand, they are well satisfied" with the symbolic iconography of Aten's hands. The majority of scholars argue for an indirect influence via Canaanite mediation: Craigie 1974, 10–21; Uelinger 1990, 499–526; Assman 1992, 143–76.

24. Given the vague and ambiguous definition of wisdom, Weeks questions the exclusive classification of wisdom psalms via thematic or terminological criteria (2005, 292–307).

Michael V. Fox on the Occasion of His Sixty-Fifth Birthday. Edited by Ronald L. Troxel, Kelvin G. Frieble, and Dennis R. Magary. Winona Lake, IN: Eisenbrauns.

Boström, Lennart. 1990. *The God of the Sages: The Portrayal of God in the Book of Proverbs*. ConBOT 29. Stockholm: Almqvist & Wiksell.

Bouzard, Walter C. 1997. *We have Heard with Our Ears, O God: Sources of the Communal Laments in the Psalms*. SBLDS 159. Atlanta: Scholars Press.

Briggs, Charles A., and Emilie G. Briggs. 1906. *The Book of Psalms*. 2 vols. ICC. Edinburgh: T&T Clark.

Brown, William P. 2005. "'Come, O Children … I Will Teach You the Fear of the Lord' (Psalm 34:12): Comparing Psalms and Proverbs." Pages 85–102 in *Seeking Out the Wisdom of the Ancients: Essayed Offered to Honor Michael V. Fox on the Occasion of His Sixty-Fifth Birthday*. Edited by Ronald L. Troxel, Kelvin G. Frieble, and Dennis R. Magary. Winona Lake, IN: Eisenbrauns.

Buss, Martin J. 1978. "The Idea of *Sitz im Leben*: History and Critique." ZAW 90:157–70.

Castellino, R. G. 1940. *Le Lamentazioni individuali e gli inni in Babilonia e in Israele: Raffrontati riguardo alla forma e al contenuto*. Turin: Societa editrice internazionale.

———. 1955. *Libro dei Salmi*. Turin: Marietti.

Ceresko, A. R. 1990. "The Sage in the Psalms." Pages 217–30 in Gammie and Perdue 1990.

Clifford, R. J. 1985. "The Hebrew Scriptures and the Theology of Creation." TS 46:507–23.

———. 2000. "What Does the Psalmist Ask for in Psalms 39:5 and 90:12?" JBL 119:59–66.

Craigie, Peter C. 1974. "The Comparison of Hebrew Poetry: Psalm 104 in the Light of Egyptian and Ugaritic Poetry." *Semitics* 4:10–21.

Crenshaw, James L. 1969. "Method in Determining Wisdom Influence Upon 'Historical' Literature." JBL 88:129–42.

———. 2010. *Old Testament Wisdom: An Introduction*. 3rd ed. Louisville: Westminster John Knox.

———. 2012. "The Journey from Voluntary to Obligatory Silence (Reflections on Psalm 39 and Qoheleth)." Page 177–91 in *Focusing Biblical Studies: The Crucial Nature of the Persian and Hellenistic Period: Essays in Honor of Douglas A. Knight*. Edited by Jon. L. Berquist and Alice Hunt. LHBOTS 544. New York : T&T Clark.

Cohen, Chaim. 1996. "The Meaning of צלמות 'Darkness': A Study in Philological Method." Pages 287–309 in *Texts, Temples, and Traditions: A Tribute to Menahem Haran*. Edited by Michael V. Fox, et al. Winona Lake, IN: Eisenbrauns.
Dahood, Mitchell. 1968. *Psalms II*. AB 17. New York: Doubleday.
Dell, Katharine J. 2004. "I Will Solve My Riddle to the Music of the Lyre" (Psalm xlix 4[5]): A Cultic Setting for Wisdom Psalms?" *VT* 54:445-58.
Dion, Paul E. 1991. "YHWH as Storm-God and Sun-God: The Double Legacy of Egypt and Canaan as Reflected in Psalm 104." *ZAW* 103: 43–71.
Eissfeldt, Otto. 1965. *The Old Testament: An Introduction*. Trans. by Peter R. Ackroyd. New York: Harper & Row.
Engnell, Ivan. 1969. *A Rigid Scrutiny: Critical Essays on the Old Testament*. Translated by John T. Willis. Nashville: Vanderbilt University Press.
Falkenstein, Adam, and Wolfram von Soden. 1953. *Sumerische und akkadische Hymnen und Gebete*. Zurich: Artemis.
Forti, Tova. 2008. *Animal Imagery in the Book of Proverbs*. VTSup 118. Leiden: Brill.
———. 2011. "Of Ships and Seas, and Fish and Beasts: Viewing the Concept of Universal Providence in the Book of Jonah through the Prism of Psalms." *JSOT* 35:359–74.
Fox, Michael V. 1996. "The Social Location of the Book of Proverbs." Pages 227–39 in *Texts, Temples, and Traditions: A Tribute to Menahem Haran*. Edited by Michael V. Fox et al. Winona Lake, IN: Eisenbrauns.
Gammie, John G. 1990. "From Prudentialism to Apocalypticism: The Houses of the Sages Amid the Varying Forms of Wisdom." Pages 479–97 in Gammie and Perdue 1990.
Gammie, John G., and Leo G. Perdue, eds. 1990. *The Sage in Israel and the Ancient Near East*. Edited by. Winona Lake, IN: Eisenbrauns
Gerstenberger, Erhardt. 2001. *Psalms, Part 2, and Lamentations*. FOTL 15. Grand Rapids: Eerdmans.
Gruber, Mayer I. 2004. *Rashi's Commentary on Psalms*. BRLJ 18. Leiden: Brill.
Gunkel, Hermann, and Joachim Begrich. 1998. *Introduction to Psalms: The Genres of the Religious Lyric of Israel*. Translated by James D. Nogalski. Macon, GA: Mercer University Press.
Held, Moshe. 1987. "Studies in Biblical Lexicography in the Light of Akkadian Parallels." Pages 104–14 in *Studies in Bible Dedicated to the*

Memory of U. Cassuto on the 100th Anniversary of His Birth. Edited by H. Beinart. Jerusalem: Magnes (Hebrew).

Hilber, John W. 2005. *Cultic Prophecy in the Psalms.* BZAW 352. Berlin: de Gruyter.

Hurvitz, Avi. 1988. "Wisdom Vocabulary in the Hebrew Psalter: A Contribution to the Study of 'Wisdom Psalms.'" *VT* 38: 41–51.

———. 1991. *Wisdom Language in Biblical Psalmody.* Jerusalem: Magnes (Hebrew).

Jacobson, Diane. 2008. "Psalm 33 and the Creation Rhetoric of a Torah Psalm." Pages 107–20 in *"My Words Are Lovely": Studies in the Rhetoric of the Psalms.* LHBOTS 467. Edited by Robert L. Foster and David M. Howard. London: T&T Clark.

Jamieson-Drake, David W. 1987. "Literary Structure, Genre and Interpretation in Job 38." Pages 217–35 in *The Listening Heart: Essays in Wisdom and Psalms in Honor of Roland E. Murphy, O Carm.* Edited by Kenneth G. Hoglund, Elizabeth F. Huwiler, Jonathan T. Glass, and Roger W. Lee. JSOTSup 85. Sheffield: JSOT Press.

Kaiser, O. "Psalm 39." 1998. Pages 71–83 in *Gottes und der Menschen Weisheit: Gesammelte Aufsätze.* BZAW 261. Berlin: de Gruyter.

Kaufmann, Yehezkel. 1972. *The Religion of Israel: From Its Beginnings to the Babylonian Exile.* Translated and abridged by Moshe Greenberg. New York: Schocken.

Koehler, Ludwig, Walter Baumgartner, and Johann J. Stamm. 1994–1999. *The Hebrew and Aramaic Lexicon of the Old Testament.* 4 vols. Leiden: Brill.

Kraus, Hans-Joachim. 1993. *Psalms 1–59.* Translated by H. C. Oswald. CC. Minneapolis: Fortress.

Kuntz, J. K. 1974. "The Canonical Wisdom Psalms of Ancient Israel: Their Rhetorical, Thematic, and Formal Dimensions." Pages 186–222 in *Rhetorical Criticism: Essays in Honor of James Muilenburg.* Edited by Jared J. Jackson and Martin Kessler. Pittsburgh: Pickwick.

———. 2008. "Growling Dogs and Thirsty Deer: Uses of Animal Imagery in Psalmic Rhetoric." Pages 46–62 in *"My Words Are Lovely": Studies in the Rhetoric of the Psalms.* LHBOTS 467. Edited by Robert L. Foster and David M. Howard. London: T&T Clark.

———. 2003. "Reclaiming Biblical Wisdom Psalms: A Response to Crenshaw." *CBR* 1:145–54.

———. 2012. "Continuing the Engagement: Psalms Research Since the Early 1990s." *CBR* 10: 321–78.

Kynes, Will. 2012. *My Psalm Has Turned into Weeping: Job's Dialogue with the Psalms*. BZAW 437. Berlin: de Gruyter.

Lenzi, Alan. 2010. "Invoking the God: Interpreting Invocations in Mesopotamian Prayers and Biblical Laments of the Individual." *JBL* 129:303–15.

Levenson, Jon. 1988. *Creation and the Persistence of Evil*. San Francisco: Harper & Row.

Lichtheim, Miriam. 1973–1981. *Ancient Egyptian Literature*. 3 vols. Berkeley: University of California Press.

Luyten, J. 1979. "Psalm 73 and Wisdom." Pages 59–81 in *La Sagesse de L'Ancien Testament*. Edited by Maurice Gilbert. Gembloux: Duculot.

Mays, James L. 1987. "The Place of the Torah-Psalms in the Psalter." *JBL* 106:3–12.

McKane, William. 1965. *Prophets and Wise Men*. SBT 44. Naperville, IL: Allenson.

Mowinckel, Sigmund. 1955. "Psalms and Wisdom." Pages 205–24 in *Wisdom in Israel and in the Ancient Near East*. VTSup 3. Edited by Martin Noth and D. Winton Thomas. Leiden: Brill.

———. 1962. *The Psalms in Israel's Worship*. Translated by D. R. Ap-Thomas. Oxford: Blackwell.

Murphy, Roland. 1963. "A Consideration of the Classification 'Wisdom Psalms.'" Pages 156–67 in *Congress Volume: Bonn, 1962*. VTSup 9. Leiden: Brill.

Oeming, Manfred. 2008. "Wisdom as a Hermeneutical Key to the Book of Psalms." Pages 154–62 in *Scribes, Sages, and Seers: The Sage in the Eastern Mediterranean World*. FRLANT 219. Edited by Leo G. Perdue. Göttingen: Vandenhoeck & Ruprecht.

Perdue, Leo G. 1977. *Wisdom and Cult: A Critical Analysis of the Views of Cult in the Wisdom Literatures of Israel and the Ancient Near East*. SBLDS 30. Missoula, MT: Society of Biblical Literature.

Pritchard, James B., and Daniel Fleming, eds. 2011. *The Ancient Near East: An Anthology of Texts and Pictures*. Princeton: Princeton University Press.

Rad, Gerhard von. 2001. *Old Testament Theology*. Translated by D. M. Stalker. 2 vols. Louisville: Westminster John Knox.

———. 1972. *Wisdom in Israel*. Translated by James D. Martin. Nashville: Abingdon.

Scott, R. B. Y. 1971. *The Way of Wisdom in the Old Testament*. New York: Macmillan.

Seybold, Klaus. 1996. *Die Psalmen*. HAT 1/15. Tübingen: Mohr-Siebeck.
Sheppard, Gerald T. 1980. *Wisdom as a Hermeneutical Construct: A Study in the Sapientializing of the Old Testament*. BZAW 151. New York: de Gruyter.
Shupak, Nili. 2001. "The God from Teman and the Egyptian Sun-God: A Reconsideration of Habakkuk 3:3–7." Pages 409–32 in *Homage to Shmuel: Studies in the World of the Bible*. Edited by Zipora Talshir, Shamir Yonah, and Daniel Sivan. Beer-Sheva: Ben-Gurion University of the Negev Press; Jerusalem: Bialik Institute (Hebrew).
Sneed, Mark. 2011. "Is the 'Wisdom Tradition' a Tradition?" *CBQ* 73:50–71.
Terrien, Samuel. 2003. *The Psalms*. ECC. Grand Rapids: Eerdmans.
Thomas, D. Winton. 1957. "Some Observations on the Hebrew Root חדל." Pages 8–16 in *Volume du Congrès, Strasbourg, 1956*. VTSup 4. Leiden: Brill.
Tomes, Roger. 2005. *"I Have Written to the King, My Lord": Secular Analogies for the Psalms*. HBM 1. Sheffield: Sheffield Phoenix.
Uelinger, Christoph. 1990. "Leviathan und die Schiffe in Ps. 104, 25–26." *Biblica* 71: 499–526.
Weeks, Stuart. 2005. "Wisdom Psalms." Pages 292–307 in *Temple and Worship in Biblical Israel*. LHBOTS 422. Edited by John Day. London: T&T Clark.
Whybray, R. N. 1968. *The Succession Narrative: A Study of II Sam. 9–20 and I Kings 1 and 2*. SBT 9. London: SCM.
———. 1974. *The Intellectual Tradition of the Old Testament*. BZAW 135. Berlin: de Gruyter.
———. 1990. "The Sage in the Israelite Royal Court." Pages 133–40 in Gammie and Perdue 1990.
———. 1995. "The Wisdom Psalms." Pages 152–60 in *Wisdom in Ancient Israel: Essays in Honour of J. A. Emerton*. Edited by John Day, Robert P. Gordon, and H. G. M. Williamson. Cambridge: Cambridge University Press.
Widengren, G. 1937. *The Accadian and Hebrew Psalms of Lamentation as Religious Documents*. Stockholm: Thule.
Wilson, Gerald H. 1985. *The Editing of the Hebrew Psalter*. SBLDS 76. Chico, CA: Scholars Press.

How Wisdom Texts Became Part of the Canon of the Hebrew Bible*

Raik Heckl

In this essay I intend to illuminate how the canon of the Hebrew Bible grew at the end of the Persian period and the beginning of the Hellenistic era. Its beginnings were most likely the book of Deuteronomy and the Pentateuch. One of the following steps in the rise of the canon was the emergence of the Deuteronomistic historical books and the books of the prophets, which later formed the Prophets as the second part of the Hebrew Bible. The books of Job and Proverbs are comparatively of a very different nature. How could it happen that they became part of the foundation texts of Judaism, so formally and theologically different? The discussion of these two examples will help us understand the processes of the emergence of new authoritative religious texts and collections in the postexilic period.

The Framing of the Book of Job

Preliminary Remarks

In the Babylonian Talmud (b. B. Bat. 14b; cf. also 15a) we find the following statement about the authorship of the book of Job:

ומי כתבן משה כתב ספרו ופרשת בלעם ואיוב

> And who did write them (e.g., the books of the Tanak)? Moses wrote his book and the pericope of Balaam and Job.

---

* The subject of the essay was presented for the first time at the 2011 SBL Annual Meeting in San Francisco.

Here the rabbis see Moses not only as the author of the Pentateuch, but also of the book of Job. There was apparently a discussion about this matter in the schools of the rabbis. In a longer passage in the Talmud (b. B. Bat.15a–16b), they deal among other things with the dating of the narrative of Job and compare him with different biblical figures. What reasons could they have had for seeing Moses as the author of Job? In the Pentateuch, the paradigm of Mosaic authorship depends on Moses being the main figure and on the use of Deuteronomic language and content in many passages in the books of Genesis to Numbers (Heckl 2010a, 367). The book of Job is not a Deuteronomistic text. In Deuteronomy, Moses speaks, and in the Deuteronomistic historical books we find many related passages (Heckl 2010a, 367; Ben Zvi 2010, 69). The speeches of Job, however, are not to be compared with these passages. In many points, Job's speeches as well as the speeches of God (Job 38–41) contradict them. And more than this, the secondary framework of Job is highly critical in regard to a radical Deuteronomistic theology as we find it, for instance, in Deut 28.

Job as an Answer to Theological Questions of the Postexilic Period

In Job, we find many connections to other parts of the Hebrew Bible (Witte 2013; Kynes 2013; Frevel 2013; Crenshaw 2013; Schultz 2013, and Schmid 2010). This shows, first of all, that the book did not obtain its current shape before the Persian era. This statement applies equally for the narrative frame as well as for the poetic speeches. In the poetic parts, however, the connections are mostly of an individual nature. We find phrases that are similar to different psalms and to other wisdom books. This means that the discourse of the Job speeches takes up language issues from other texts. If we compare the intertextualities of the poetic parts of Job with those of the framing chapters, we can see the very different nature of the latter.[1] Without doubt, Job uses and refers, for instance, to Ps 8. Michael Fishbane already dealt with this and other similar connections—though following

---

1. Kynes (2012), recently dealt with the connections between Job and Psalms. In particular, the connection between Ps 8:5 and Job 7:17, for instance, is evident. According to Köhlmoos (1999, 362), Ps 8 is the most important intertext of the poetic parts of Job. Frevel (2004, 266–67), generally agrees, but interprets the connection in a different way. In his opinion, the Joban concept is not a critique of Ps 8. He does not see an intentional connection to Job 25:2–6 either. For the discussion of the relationship, compare further Kynes 2012, 69–71.

A. Robert—and saw them as a midrashic use of older literature. He meant "that the earlier biblical texts are exegetically reused, or 'reactualized,' in new contexts" (Fishbane 1985, 286; 2000, 42). In contrast to these individual connections, the framing narrative of Job is connected by scenery, allusions, and quotations first to the book of Deuteronomy, second to the patriarchal stories, and third to the beginning of the books of Samuel. In my monograph on Job (Heckl 2010b), I demonstrated that the concept of the framing narrative as well as the entire framed book is based on the following literary connections.

The reception of Deuteronomy is part of the discourse about the Deuteronomistic theology of history. This discourse constitutes the framing of the book of Job. The ancient reader was to conclude from the quotation of Deut 28:35 in Job 2:7 that there is a connection between the frame narrative and Deuteronomy as well as the Deuteronomistic theology. The patriarchal stories are also an important reference quantity in the narrative framework. It positions Job in the milieu of the patriarchs and assigns to him a great age (Job 42:16) in order to connect Job to them. The connection to the beginning of the book of Samuel is supplied by a group of connected motives, allusions, and structural parallels, as well as by connections with the content.

Two parallels and, at the same time, connected motives lead to the literary relationship with 1 Sam 1–4 (Heckl 2010b, 392; 2013a). First, Eli lectures his children about the impossibility of interceding for one who has sinned against God (1 Sam 2:25a). We find, as a related issue, the intercession of Job for his friends, who provoked the wrath of YHWH (Job 42:7–9; Heckl 2010b, 299). There is, second, the theme of cursing God. This theme appears in the critique of the behaviour of Eli's sons (1 Sam 3), which is the reason for their death (cf. LXX 1Sam 3:13; Heckl 2010b, 244). The same subject occurs in the speech of Job's wife (Job 2:9b) and is connected with the death of Job's children.[2]

The theme of cursing God and the fate of Job's children seem to be derived from the reasoning of the rejection of the Elides in 1 Sam 3:13.[3] We

---

2. See Job 1:5, 13, 19, 22. The theme of the scenes in heaven is the cursing of God. But the theme occurs right before the first scene in which Job fears that his children could have cursed God in their hearts (Job 1:5). Together with their death, the possible cursing of God by Job's children is the background of the prologue.

3. The connection between the prose frame and 1Sam 1–4 explains one particular feature of the narrative: Job fears only that his children sinned against God in their

find in the reconstructed *Vorlage* of the Septuagint to the verse the accusation that Eli's sons cursed God (כי מקללים אלהים בניו).[4] There are connections between the description of their fate and the fate of Job's children.

The other subject, the intercession of Job in Job 42:8–9, depends on the theoretical explanation of Eli in 1 Sam 2:25. The Job of the framing narrative is created as an answer to the rhetorical question of Eli to his sons (Heckl 2010b, 408): "if one sins against YHWH, who will intercede for him?" (Heckl 2010b, 426). The pious sufferer who keeps his relationship with God in spite of his suffering is alone able to perform the intercession that Eli thinks to be impossible. The characterization of Job follows the manner of Eli as well as of Samuel. But Job outrivals not only Eli but also Samuel, if we take the later development of the Samuel story (1 Sam 8) into account. The pious sufferer alone is able to intercede effectively for others to God.[5] There are several other connections, such as the use of the figure of Hanna and her prayer. In the prose framework, the character Job is like a centripetal point to which the references to the different figures in 1 Samuel converge. What is intended is that the readers compare Job with these figures.

Because of this intertextuality, Job already is a paradigmatic character. He is, however, also kept without the mentioning of a patronym, but is praised by God in a way that hardly would have been applied to a stranger in the Hebrew Bible. God's praise of Job that "there is no one on earth like him" corresponds not only to the praise of YHWH in the Psalms, but we also find a similar attribution in the blessings of Moses in Deut 33:29: "Blessed are you, Israel! Who is like you, a people saved by YHWH?"

Furthermore, because the story uses the phrase שוב שבית in Job 42:10 for Job's restoration, a phrase that often is used to express the restoration of Israel after the exile (Heckl 2010, 301), the logical conclusion is that the framed book of Job corresponds not only to the books of Samuel in view of the parallel beginning, but also to the entire corpus of the books of Samuel

---

hearts. When Job's children die, the narrative leaves open the question whether the sin happened.

4. In the Masoretic Text we find a so-called *tiqqun sopherim*. The Masorites left out the א of אלהים in order to lessen the implication of the original phrase that the Septuagint preserves (McCarthy 1981, 77–79).

5. Job as an exemplary interceding figure is therefore connected to Samuel (e.g., 1 Sam 7:5; Jer 15:1). The latter passage is of particular relevance, because it states that there is no effective intercession by Samuel and Moses for others.

and Kings. Thus, the framework and, of course, the entire framed book, is intended to be a counterstory to the Deuteronomistic History of the kingdom of Israel and Judah (1 Sam 1–2 Kgs 25) (Heckl 2010, 477–78). In my opinion, Job, as the pious sufferer who is able to intercede for others represents a pious Israel that keeps its relationship with God in spite of the sufferings of exile and diaspora. This is, of course, a serious critique of the Deuteronomistic theology of blame and punishment, and it is directed against the Deuteronomistic books of Samuel and Kings.

In answering the literary-historical questions about the book of Job, this intertextuality is of utmost importance. All aspects of the contents are connected to it. Therefore, the proposal of the use of an older legend of Job and of the suggestions of far-reaching redactional additions to both the prose frame and the poetic parts are unlikely.[6]

The prose framework of Job, therefore, is part of a discourse about theological literature. The allusions, quotations and, above all, the "imitation" (Genette 1997, 6) of Samuel–Kings[7] presuppose that the intended readers of Job would know the received literature. The function of the framework, therefore, is to present the older poem of Job to an audience who already knew books with prose texts as their authoritative religious texts.

What has happened here? Wisdom content received a prose framework in order to position it within the purview of other prose texts. This serves to introduce a common wisdom theme into new contexts. Thereby, the narrative framework of Job that is able more easily to communicate contents contains the authoritative interpretation of the confined poetic parts. Thus, the Job of the poetic parts could become a paradigm for Israel after the exile and help in the debate about the Deuteronomistic theology—or in other words: Job is the key in the late postexilic reappraisal of the Deuteronomistic theology of history. Job does not stand alone in this aim, but is connected to the priestly-completed Pentateuch (Heckl 2013a, 92–93) and also to the Aramaic temple chronicle in Ezra 6:10.[8]

---

6. Cf., for instance, the concept of Köhlmoos (1999), who sees the origin of Job in a mininarrative from the late preexilic time that was expanded together with the creation of the poetic parts, followed by several redactions.

7. This category of intertextuality indicates conceptual receptions, according to G. Genette (1997); cf. Heckl 2013a, 88–89.

8. The fictional decree of Darius introduces offerings to YHWH for the fate of the Persian king. In the following verses, the curse of YHWH against future kings who contravene the decree of Darius shows sufficiently that the perspective is already

The Prose Framework of Job and the Supposed Changes in the Scribal Curriculum of Ancient Israel

There are two recently published models of how the Israelite/Jewish scribal culture developed. I want to relate my observations upon Job to these theses. These models are D. M. Carr's *Writing on the Tablet of the Heart: Origins of Scripture and Literature* (2005) and K. van der Toorn's *Scribal Culture and the Making of the Hebrew Bible* (2009). Both contributions advocate the theory that in ancient Israel literature arose primarily for the use of a small elite (Carr 2005, 13; van der Toorn 2009, 10). According to Carr, there was only a very slow process of change in the curriculum during the centuries.[9] According to van der Toorn, there was a substantial change in the way literature was used only in late Hellenistic times.[10]

In view of these investigations of Job, I wish to present a different view. Although there was only a small group of literati in the late preexilic, exilic and postexilic periods, the formation of comprehensive literary compositions gives evidence that from the late preexilic time onwards, but above all, in the Persian era, the number of literati and of people who were interested in literature steadily grew. Two known examples illustrate this view. Lachish Letter 3 shows that it was not uncommon that Judean officers were at least able to read and write.[11] The letter also confirms that another possibly literary text—it is called ספר—of a prophet was passed from one person to another for reading. We find something similar in the Bible in Jer 36. The chapter presupposes that a text written by Baruch was read to others several times. Later, after the destruction of the scroll, it states that Baruch wrote a new and extended version of the text.[12]

I assume, therefore, against the view of van der Toorn, that the important changes in the scribal culture and also in the literature occurred not only in Hellenistic times, but earlier. The nature of the literature that arose

---

of the Hellenistic dominion. Cf. the study of the concept of Ezra-Nehemiah in Heckl forthcoming.

9. According to Carr (2005, 45–46), the changes were made by "master scribes."

10. "The Jewish texts produced in the Hellenistic period attest to the presence of a public for books" (van der Toorn 2009, 25).

11. See Renz and Röllig (1995, 412–19); cf., on the text, Schniedewind 2000; Rüterswörden 2001.

12. If it is a literary scene, the text independently presupposes the knowledge of such processes.

from the time of the exile leads to a different theory. In contrast to the literature of the neighbouring cultures, we have primarily prose texts in the books of the exilic and postexilic periods. This almost entirely narrative literature has a clear intentionality. We can assume that this literature no longer served primarily to educate the elite in scribal skills and to introduce them to a firm curriculum of texts, but that now literature served particular interests and could, for instance, follow special religious aims (Heckl 2007, 200–201). With these texts, the authors wanted to inform a broader audience about the presented content, but they also tried to persuade their audience to accept a particular view of religion and history, and thereby urged the readers to identify themselves with the aims of these literary texts (Heckl 2013b, 39–42).

This thread leads back to the secondarily framed book of Job. Obviously, the authors of the prose framework tried to present the older poem to their audience with the aim of providing them with an alternative view of theology of history and eventually, too, with a new view of the known pious sufferer.

The new prose texts were written more or less in everyday speech.[13] Thus they were better able to mediate information and, of course, to communicate intentionality. At the same time, they could address a potentially wider audience. In the case of the framed book of Job, this was an audience that already knew the Pentateuch, and the Deuteronomistic historical books accepted as the authoritative books of the postexilic Judean community.

There is, interestingly, evidence outside the biblical accounts for the use of this technique in reaching a broader, or a new, audience, especially for older literature. The Prophecy of Neferti from the Eighteenth Dynasty[14] and the book of Ahiqar from the Persian period[15] are given a prose framework in order to present older texts to a new audience.

---

13. Eskenazı (1988, 1), uses the differentiation made between prose and poetry (originally made by Hegel) and sees Ezra/Nehemiah as a text created for an age of prose. In her opinion, that mode of literature reports realistically and avoids epic style (185).

14. "Wahrscheinlich bestand ein Interesse daran, das Publikum zu erreichen, das Unterhaltungserzählungen las, und ihm unter dem Vorwand angenehmer Lektüre eine hochpolitische Schrift zu präsentieren" (Blumenthal 1982, 22).

15. The discovery of Aramaic fragments confirmed the thesis that the framing narrative and the proverbs came together secondarily in the book of Ahiqar; cf. Kottsieper 1990–1997, 321. It is also characteristic that the narrative of the Aramaic version uses a later dialect; cf. Niehr 2007, 10–11, 13–14.

The Book of Proverbs

The book of Proverbs also had a long literary history. This is demonstrated by the extrabiblical relationship between Prov 22:17–24:22 and the Instruction of Amenemope. Recently D. M. Carr assumed that a prestage of our book of Proverbs was among the oldest literary texts of ancient Israel (Carr 2011, 403–31). Proverbs 1–9 has to be seen as a relatively late part of the book.[16] In my opinion, the position of the text at the beginning of Proverbs suggests a similar hermeneutical function as that of the framework of Job, even if their literary natures are different.

The Present View of Proverbs 1–9 as a Starting Point

It was known already in the nineteenth century that there is a connection between Prov 1–9 and Deuteronomy.[17] André Robert discussed the intertextuality comprehensively (Robert 1935). Two recent studies also deal with these literary references. G. Reichenbach sees intertextualities between Prov 1–9, Deuteronomy, the priestly creation account, and the prose speeches of Jeremiah. The origin of these connections is, in his opinion, the use of texts during the introduction of pupils to the scribal curriculum. Reichenbach's considerations are based on the thesis of an "oral-written interface" in the ancient Israelite scribal culture (Reichenbach 2011, 297, cites Carr 2005, 305). Literary connections arose because of the oral use and discussion of texts. These discussions lead to the validity of the texts: "Im Lauf der Überlieferung kristallisierten sich bestimmte Teile als gültige Inhalte heraus, die in Form von, ausdrücklich gesagt, *literarischen Traditionen* in Spr 1–9 Eingang gefunden haben" (Reichenbach 2011, 300, emphasis original) .

It seems to me that, conversely, these aspects have to be connected. The wide use of other texts cannot be explained without the presumed acceptance of them. The Pentateuch, Deuteronomy, and Jeremiah, as well, not only claimed authority, but used the authority of persons or literary characters who served as alleged authors (cf. Heckl 2010a; 2013c). An institutional authority can be seen in the background of the Pentateuch

---

16. Gertz 2012, 581–82; Carr (2011, 431), however, suggests that Deuteronomy uses Prov 1–9.

17. Schipper 2012, 6; according to Dell (2006, 105), the religious implications of Prov 1–9 do not belong to a redaction "but form an integral part of the material."

that was very likely the literary program of the priesthood at the second temple. The process that led to the validity of the content of the Pentateuch and Jeremiah happened similarly to the literary history of these books. The reception of passages from one text into another presupposes the knowledge and the authority of the source. At the time when Prov 1–9 was written—at the time of the late Persian Empire at the earliest—the Pentateuch, Deuteronomy, and Jeremiah must have been accepted books of the Jewish community. This early use of these books in Proverbs is similar to the use of scripture in the later Jewish books from the Second Temple period and after. Only the authority of accepted books and the later accepted corpora of the canon of the Hebrew Bible made the use possible.[18]

B. Schipper goes a step further than Reichenbach. He sees a conceptional connection between Prov 1–9 and the Torah. In his opinion, the wisdom literature took part in a discourse on Torah in postexilic times. The redactional history of the book of Proverbs is a witness to this discourse (see Schipper 2012, 282). Schipper shows this with Prov 2, which he sees as the key chapter for understanding Prov 1–9 and its literary connections.[19] According to Schipper, the connections to Deuteronomy are of utmost importance. Prov 2 as well as Prov 1–9 have a Deuteronomic/Deuteronomistic nature. The connections in Prov 2, however, are different from those of the rest of the book. There, we find connections to Deut 6 (see especially Prov 3:1–4; 6:20–23; and 7:1–4), but, in Prov 2, he sees a connection to Deut 28 and to Deut 8:2–6. The latter is part of a very late passage in Deuteronomy that already shows the reception of wisdom content (Schipper 2012, 91). According to Schipper, what happens in Prov 2 is that the demands of Deuteronomy are newly contextualized and thought out: "Im Zusammenhang von Prov 2 erscheint somit das, was Dtn 8 einfordert, als logische Konsequenz aus dem Befolgen der Weisheitslehre. Etwas pointierter formuliert könnte man sagen, dass Prov 2 auf denjenigen reagiert, der sich nach dem Lesen von Dtn 8 fragt, wie er das alles realisieren soll" (Schipper 2012, 92).

Deuteronomy 8, however, already deals with the theology of Deuteronomy from a later perspective. That happens not only in discussing the traditions of the desert wanderings but, without doubt, also in the context of the entire completed Pentateuch, to which Deuteronomy already

---

18. We find this type of scripture use already in the book of Chronicles and in Ezra-Nehemiah.

19. On this he follows H. L. Strack. Cf. Schipper 2012, 1.

belongs.[20] The reference to the written available story from the perspective of Moses has a pragmatic function (Otto 2012, 908–9). The written sources are relevant for the existence of the postexilic addressees. According to E. Otto, the revelation of the Torah was like the manna in the desert, a gracious gift of God that gives life to the people.[21] Accordingly, it is possible that the allusion of Prov 2:6 to Deut 8:3 evokes the entire concept of Deut 8:3 with its connections to the finished Pentateuch. If so, it would be too much to say that Prov 2 sees the demands of Deut 8 as a logical consequence of obedience to the instruction of wisdom (Schipper 2012, 92). Proverbs 2 possibly contains no different view than the view of Torah in Deut 8.

The Speech of Wisdom in Proverbs 8

The relationship between Prov 2 and Deut 8 seems to show a conceptual integration of wisdom literature into the completed Pentateuch. Thus, the question of the connection should be further discussed in Prov 8, where the mention of the creation (8:22–31) seems to presuppose the entire Pentateuch.

The text starts in verses 1–11 with the announcement of the search for wisdom. This happens on the basis of the first-person speech of Wisdom itself, which issues an invitation to itself as a principle. Wisdom boasts of permanence in order to provide a motivation for the invitation. In verses 12–21 the self-characterization dominates. The passage lists the benefits of wisdom, which gives power to kings and to those who dispense justice.[22] Righteousness and glory are connected with wisdom. All of these sentences bear a paraenetic character, which is motivation to accept wisdom. It follows an explanation about the origin and nature of wisdom (Plöger 1984, 87). The passage in Prov 8:22–31, which has been seen as a "Sondertradition" (Plöger 1984, 91) follows after Prov 1 and 8:1–21, where the figure

---

20. "Dtn 8,1–6 ist Teil der nachexilischen Fortschreibung, die das Deuteronomium in den Pentateuch integriert" (Otto 2012, 899).

21. "Die Offenbarung der Tora ist so wie das Manna in der Wüste eine wunderhafte und gnädige Gabe Gottes" (Otto 2012, 912).

22. There is an affinity here to concepts developed on the basis of Jewish monotheism that suggest that YHWH controls history, as he does, for instance, in the presentation of the Cyrus decree and the narrating context in 2 Chr 36:22–23 // Ezra 1:1–4.

who recommends itself in the first-person speeches actually appears. In my opinion, the passage is necessary because it contains the reason for the invitation to seek wisdom and the background of the self-characterization by clarifying wisdom's origin. Without doubt this serves to emphasize the authority of wisdom. It follows a last shorter passage with a paraenesis. Acceptance of wisdom is the choice between life and death.

We find a similar choice between life and death in the framing chapters of Deuteronomy. The decision to keep Torah means life, the opposite, death (Deut 30:15–20). That issue, however, already existed in older parts of the book, as in the chapter on curse and blessing (Deut 28) and implicitly in the paraenesis connected to the single commandments. It seems that it is an original Deuteronomic/Deuteronomistic paradigm.

One could see Wisdom as an alternative to the Torah after the advertising speech. Schipper's considerations in regard to the relationship between Prov 8 and Ps 119 go in this direction. First of all, he points out the large number of references to different terms in the texts. He concludes that similar statements on the Torah in Ps 119 are directed toward Wisdom in Prov 8 (Schipper 2012, 116). Wisdom in Prov 8 and Torah in Ps 119 seem to be two contrasted entities.[23] According to Schipper, the literary history of Ps 119 presupposes the book of Proverbs and reacts to the statements in Prov 2 and 8: "Prov 8 und Prov 2 wären dann von der Perspektive des Verfassers von Ps 119 aus auf einer Ebene anzusiedeln, da beide Texte das geradezu ungeheuerliche Selbstverständnis der Weisheit dokumentieren, das zu leisten, was in der Torakonzeption auf die Zukunft bezogen ist" (Schipper 2012, 119).

Reichenbach especially studied Prov 8:23–31. He came to the conclusion that Prov 8 is based on the reception of Gen 1. He comes to a conclusion comparable to Schipper's when he assumes that Prov 8 contrasts the reference in Gen 1 to the entire Torah and the fulfilment of commandments: "Sind in Gen 1 mit dem Sieben-Tages-Rhythmus die Gebote als die Lebensordnungen der Tora zumindest angedeutet, so findet sich in Spr 8 die durchgehende Präsenz der Weisheitsgestalt im Gang der Schöpfung" (Reichenbach 2011, 227). The implications of this comparison could be that Prov 8 alludes to the priestly creation account and the mythic terminology in order to present Wisdom as a critical alternative to the Torah.

---

23. "Ganz unabhängig von der Frage, ob beide Texte im Sinne einer textuellen Kohärenz zu verbinden sind, erscheinen die Weisheit von Prov 8 und die Tora von Ps 119 als zwei einander gegenübergestellte Begrifflichkeiten" (Schipper 2012, 116).

A glance at the text, however, makes that conclusion unlikely. The passage in Prov 8 starts in verse 23 with the Tetragrammaton as subject and Wisdom speaking as the object. Wisdom declares itself to be the first work of YHWH. The following mention of other works and use of the noun ראשית leaves no doubt that Prov 8 intends a connection to the tradition of origins of the priestly account. The fact that the passage starts with YHWH as the originator, and with the mention of Wisdom as the work of God, shows that it does not present a mythological concept. In Prov 8, Wisdom is not a mythic figure. Wisdom is part of the creation of God. The later tradition history, however, added new mythological aspects. Possibly from that perspective Plöger could say that Prov 8 contains a dangerous argumentation.[24] But what would the Jewish addressees of the late Persian and Hellenistic time conclude? It must have been obvious to them that, according to Prov 8:23, Wisdom is presented within a clearly monotheistic conceptualization. YHWH is solely and exclusively the principle of the world, and Wisdom as a created work of YHWH is part of that concept and not a competing concept.

In that speech, however, Wisdom is also quite near to God as the first work. The demand of obedience in the last paraenesis in Prov 8:32–36, with its prospect for positive or negative effects, could be seen as a disparate issue in the realm of the common monotheistic concept. Theologically quite surprising is the statement in Prov 8:35: כי מצאי מצא חיים ויפק רצון מיהוה "Indeed one who finds me finds life, and he will receive favor from YHWH." The obedience to Wisdom seems to be, after all, an alternative to the fulfilment of Torah. The position of Prov 8 in the context of Prov 1–9, however, contradicts this assumption.

Contextualization

The existence of wisdom themes and formulations with an affinity to the wisdom literature in the Pentateuch contradicts the view of Prov 8 as a critique of Torah. Deuteronomy already uses wisdom language (Weinfeld (1983, 244–60). This must have been known to the ancient recipients of Prov 8, and, also, the received creation account in Genesis has its relationship to wisdom. Therefore, H. Gese speaks of a sapientialization of

---

24. According to Plöger (1984, 91), it is a "nicht ungefährliche[s] Profil" of wisdom.

Torah.²⁵ Besides Gen 1, he mentions Deut 4:5–6.²⁶ This passage calls the commandments and laws (חוקים ומשפטים) the wisdom and knowledge of the Israelites in contrast to the other people (חכמתכם ובינתכם). The incomparability of Israel in this text is based on the nearness of God (4:7) and on the Torah (4:8). Interestingly, it is this well-known and very late passage which also alludes to the priestly creation account (see Deut 4:15–19; Otto 1996, 218–19).

There existed seemingly a synthetic interest within the completion of the Pentateuch that connected wisdom themes to the Torah. This could belong to the background of the reception of Deuteronomy and Torah in Prov 1–9. First, the use of the phrase יראת יהוה for the characterization of wisdom at the beginning and at the end of Prov 1–9 indicates that context. Two key phrases subordinate knowledge and wisdom to the fear of God: In Prov 1:7 "fear of YHWH is the beginning of knowledge" (יראת יהוה ראשית דעת), and in Prov 9:10 "the beginning of wisdom is the fear of YHWH" (תחלת חכמה יראת יהוה).

The phrase is connected to a formulation used by Deuteronomy and the Deuteronomic literature (ירא את יהוה) that describes the nature of the relationship to God on the basis of the commandments of Deuteronomy.²⁷ In Deut 31:12, however, to fear YHWH is already catechetically connected to the communication of the content of Torah. Listening to the reading of Torah and the mediation of its contents leads to the fear of YHWH, which enables the listener to keep the commandments and to attain future salvation (Deut 31:13; Heckl 2011, 242). We find the very same formulation as in Deuteronomy in Prov 24:21. However, it puts together two subjects: the fear of YHWH and of the king. So, in the older passage of Proverbs, the fear of God does not yet have the paradigmatic implications as in Prov 1–9 and Deuteronomy.

---

25. "Denn wenn nicht allein und nicht in erster Linie menschliches Tun von diesem Gesetz betroffen wird, sondern das Sein, wenn das Gesetz Transzendenz abbildet, zeichenhaft hinweist auf das göttliche Sein und so die Wahrheit als göttliche Ordnung vermittelt und verwirklicht, so ergibt sich eine Analogie zur Schöpfungsordnung und der daraus sich ableitenden Ordnung menschlichen Lebens, der die sogenannte Weisheit auf der Spur ist" (Gese 1977, 68–69).

26. Gese (1977, 70), states that according to Deut 4:6: "Ja die Toralehre wurde in Israel für den heidnischen Gesichtspunkt geradezu als Weisheit bezeichnet."

27. This affinity was seen already by Weinfeld 1983, 274.

Relevant for the interpretation of the connections to the Torah in Prov 1–9 is, first, the framing by the theme the fear of God and, second, the fact that we already find in Prov 1:2–3 a connection to Deut 4:5–6. It is necessary to be cautious with alleged connections discovered by a concordance. In our case, the connection is additionally confirmed by the subject of the "fear of God" in Prov 1:7, which precedes the different connections to Deut 6:4–9, especially in Prov 3:1–4, 6:20–23, and 7:1–4. Seen together with this pointer, the mention of צדק and משפט in Prov 1:2–3 cannot be independent of Deuteronomy either.

Deut 4:5–6	Prov 1:2–3
ראה למדתי אתכם חקים ומשפטים כאשר צוני יהוה אלהי לעשות כן בקרב הארץ אשר אתם באים שמה לרשתה	לדעת חכמה ומוסר להבין אמרי בינה
ושמרתם ועשיתם כי הוא חכמתכם ובינתכם לעיני העמים אשר ישמעון את כל־החקים האלה ואמרו רק עם־חכם ונבון הגוי הגדול הזה	לקחת מוסר השכל צדק ומשפט ומישרים:

What does this mean for the interpretation of Prov 8? Following this introduction, Wisdom also precedes the following works of creation in Prov 8:22–36, dependent on Gen 1, but the intended readers would recognize this connection to the Torah. The Torah as a literary document beginning with the creation and as an instruction about how to fear God is itself a witness for wisdom.

Thus, Prov 1–9 connects the older collections of wisdom literature with the content of the authoritative texts of the late postexilic time. Within the context of Prov 1–9, we find ourselves with Prov 8 on the way to the identification of Torah and Wisdom, which we explicitly find in Sir 24:23–34. The ancient reader, arriving from Prov 1, encounters the connections to Deuteronomy in Prov 2 and later. The intention is that the reader should infer the identity of Wisdom and Torah because of the reference to the creation.

The fact, however, that Wisdom speaks and declares by itself in Prov 1 and 8, must be explained. B. Schipper states that, in contrast to Prov 8, the Torah is not figured as a personal character in Ps 119 (Schipper 2012, 117). It needs, however, to be borne in mind that in Prov 8:23 Wisdom introduces itself as an object and emphasizes its difference from YHWH. This shows that the context of the wisdom book most likely influenced the special characteristic of Wisdom in Prov 1 and 8. Another question is what tradition led historically to the far-reaching association of the origin of the wisdom of Torah. The influence of the common classical view in the ancient world that the origins of religious books lie in the deity itself is very likely. YHWH is still mentioned as a scribe of texts and books in the Pentateuch (e.g., Exod 24:12; Deut 5:22). Even if Moses as the mediator of Torah was emphasized in the completed Pentateuch, YHWH remained recognizable as the traditional God of wisdom in ancient Israel (see Heckl 2013, 191–94, 196–99).

Summary

In the third part of the canon, we have the Writings, some traditional books with a long literary and tradition history. Two traditional wisdom books were received by means of a synthetic concept that had its basis in the Pentateuch and possibly in other older prophetic books. The already-accepted Pentateuch was primarily the authoritative basis of this reception. The process of reception, though, did not preserve these texts unchanged. It is thrilling to see that, with Job and the book of Proverbs, the postexilic authors or editors tried to present traditional texts of a possibly great age in the light of the newly-composed literature of the exilic and postexilic time. This process can also be seen in the composition of other books, for instance, the book of the Psalms.

That Prov 1–9 was introduced into the older traditional composition of the book shows, at the same time, that this was necessary. These texts were used in the training of scribal skills. They also formed the backbone of the teaching of ethical principles, but they had not been accepted as foundational literature by those who accepted the Torah. By the use of framing and secondary introduction, traditional books became acceptable to a new audience and classical texts had a new context.

The reception of texts was undertaken from a particular perspective and with an interpretation from the context of the accepted religious literature. In this way, parts of the traditional literature of Israel were given their places beside the already quasi-canonical books. Now they enhanced the range of the literature used not only by new additions to books, but also by presenting other theological positions of a sometimes competitive character.

In the case of Proverbs, it was the life teaching used in training, over the centuries, and in the case of Job, it was the blaming of God that became a neighbor of Deuteronomistic theology. The reception of Job and Proverbs both introduced the emphasis on the individual's relation to God and on a universal view of YHWH as the God of the world beyond the realm of Israel.

The ways used to introduce the book of Job and Proverbs into the already accepted books is in each case different. Job uses the prose style of the Pentateuch and the Deuteronomistic historical books; Proverbs imitates the style of the Deuteronomic paraenesis in order to lead the reader to the inference that the content of the original wisdom book corresponds to the claims of the Torah.

The reception of both books and their integration into new literary and theological contexts also shows that here we are dealing with a relatively free use of older literature in the Persian and Hellenistic era and not with traditions of the provider groups (*Trägergruppen*). Thus, our considerations confirm the criticism of the classical theses about the wisdom tradition: "The Hebrew wisdom tradition, as defined by most scholars of Hebrew wisdom, is not a tradition or movement, and it does not reflect a worldview. It is a mode of literature that is only loosely homogeneous. Its main function, if we can speak of modal settings, was to train young scribes" (Sneed 2011, 71). After the development of intentional literature after the exile, this literature lost its relevance and had to be introduced into the new context of literature.

Works Consulted

Ben Zvi, Ehud. 2010. "On the Term Deuteronomistic in Relation to Joshua–Kings in the Persian Period." Pages 61–71 in *Raising Up a Faithful Exegete: Essays in Honor of Richard D. Nelson*. Edited by Kurt L. Noll and Brooks Schramm. Winona Lake, IN: Eisenbrauns.

Blumenthal, Elke. 1982. "Die Prophezeiung des Neferti." *ZÄS* 109:1–27.

Carr, David M. 2005. *Writing on the Tablet of the Heart: Origins of Scripture and Literature*. Oxford: Oxford University Press.

———. 2011. *The Formation of the Hebrew Bible: A New Reconstruction*. New York: Oxford University Press.

Crenshaw, James L. 2013. "Divine Discipline in Job 5:17–18, Proverbs 3:11–12, Deuteronomy 32:39 and Beyond." Pages 178–89 in Dell and Kynes 2013.

Dell, Katharine J. 2006. *The Book of Proverbs in Social and Theological Context*. Cambridge: Cambridge University Press.

Dell, Katharine, and William L. Kynes, eds. 2013. *Reading Job Intertextually*. LHBOTS 574. New York: Bloomsbury.

Eskenazi, Tamara C. 1988. *In an Age of Prose: A Literary Approach to Ezra-Nehemiah*. SBLMS 36. Atlanta: Scholars Press.

Fishbane, Michael A. 1985. *Biblical Interpretation in Ancient Israel*. Oxford: Clarendon.

———. 2000. "Types of Biblical Intertextuality." Pages 39–44 in Congress Volume: Oslo, 1998. Edited by André Lemaire and Magne Sæbø. VTSup 80. Leiden: Brill.

Frevel, Christian. 2004. "Eine kleine Theologie der Menschenwürde: Ps 8 und seine Rezeption im Buch Ijob." Pages 244–72 in *Das Manna fällt auch heute noch: Beiträge zur Geschichte und Theologie des Alten, Ersten Testaments; Festschrift für Erich Zenger*. Edited by Frank-Lothar Hossfeld and Ludger Schwienhorst-Schönberger. Freiburg im Breisgau: Herder.

———. 2013. "Telling the Secrets of Wisdom: The Use of Psalm 104 in the Book of Job." Pages 157–68 in Dell and Kynes 2013.

Genette, Gérard. 1997. *Palimpsests: Literature in the Second Degree*. Lincoln: University of Nebraska Press.

Gertz, Jan C., Angelika Berlejung, Konrad Schmid, and Markus Witte, eds. 2012. *T&T Clark Handbook of the Old Testament: An Introduction to the Literature, Religion and History of the Old Testament*. London: T&T Clark.

Gese, Hartmut. 1977. "Das Gesetz." Pages 55–84 in *Zur biblischen Theologie: Alttestamentliche Vorträge*. Munich: Kaiser.

Heckl, Raik. 2007. "Die Religionsgeschichte als Schlüssel für die Literargeschichte: Eine neu gefasste Überlieferungskritik vorgestellt am Beispiel von Ex 32." *TZ* 63:193–215.

———. 2010a. "Augenzeugenschaft und Verfasserschaft des Mose als zwei hermeneutische Konzepte der Rezeption und Präsentation literarischer Traditionen beim Abschluss des Pentateuchs." *ZAW* 122:353–73.

———. 2010b. *Hiob: Vom Gottesfürchtigen zum Repräsentanten Israels; Studien zur Buchwerdung des Hiobbuches und zu seinen Quellen*. FAT 70. Tübingen: Mohr Siebeck.

———. 2011 "Die Präsentation tradierter Texte in Dtn 31 zur Revision der dtr Geschichtstheologie." Pages 227–46 in *Deuteronomium: Tora für eine neue Generation*. Edited by Georg Fischer, Dominik Markl, and Simone Paganini. BZABR 17. Wiesbaden: Harrassowitz.

———. 2013a. "The Relationship Between Job 1–2, 42 and 1 Samuel 1–4 as Intertextual Guidance for Reading." Pages 81–93 in Dell and Kynes 2013.

———. 2013b. "Remembering Jacob in the Late Persian/Early Hellenistic Era." Pages 38–80 in *Remembering Biblical Figures in the Late Persian and Early Hellenistic Periods: Social Memory and Imagination*. Edited by Diana V. Edelman and Ehud Ben Zvi. Oxford: Oxford University Press.

———. 2013c. "Mose als Schreiber: Am Ursprung der jüdischen Hermeneutik des Pentateuchs." *ZABR* 19:179–234.

———. Forthcoming. *Neuanfang und Kontinuität in Jerusalem: Studien zu den hermeneutischen Strategien im Esra-Nehemia-Buch*. FAT. Tübingen: Mohr Siebeck, 2015.

Kottsieper, Ingo. 1990–1997. "Weisheitstexte in aramäischer Sprache: Die Geschichte und die Sprüche des weisen Achiqar." *TUAT* 3:320–47.

Kynes, William L. 2012. *My Psalm Has Turned into Weeping: Job's Dialogue with the Psalms*. BZAW 437. Berlin: de Gruyter.

———. 2013. "Job and Isaiah 40–55: Intertextualities in Dialogue." Pages 94–105 in Dell and Kynes 2013.

McCarthy, Carmel. 1981. *The Tiqqune Sopherim: And the Other Theological Corrections in the Masoretic Text of the Old Testament*. OBO 36. Fribourg: Universitätsverlag; Göttingen: Vandenhoeck & Ruprecht.

Meinhold, Arndt. 1991. *Die Sprüche: Kapitel 1–15*. ZBK 16.1. Zurich: TVZ.

Niehr, Herbert. 2007. *Aramäischer Aḥiqar*. JSHRZ NS 2/2. Gütersloh: Gütersloher Verlagshaus.

Otto, Eckart. 1996. "Deuteronomium 4: Die Pentateuchredaktion im Deuteronomiumsrahmen." Pages 196–222 in *Das Deuteronomium und seine Querbeziehungen*. Edited by Timo Veijola. SESJ 62. Göttingen: Vandenhoeck & Ruprecht.

———. 2012. *Deuteronomium 1–11*. HThKAT. Freiburg im Breisgau: Herder.

Plöger, Otto. 1984. *Sprüche Salomos (Proverbia)*. BKAT 17. Neukirchen-Vluyn: Neukirchener Verlag.

Reichenbach, Gregor. 2011. *Gültige Verbindungen: Eine Untersuchung zur kanonischen Bedeutung der innerbiblischen Traditionsbezüge in Sprüche 1 bis 9*. ABG 37. Leipzig: Evangelische Verlagsanstalt.

Renz, Johannes, and Wolfgang Röllig. 1995. *Handbuch der Althebräischen Epigraphik*. Darmstadt: Wissenschaftliche Buchgesellschaft.

Robert, André. 1934. "Les attaches littéraires bibliques de Prov. I–IX." *RB* 43:42–68, 172–204, 374–84.

———. 1935. "Les attaches littéraires bibliques de Prov. I–IX." *RB* 44:344–65, 502–25.

Rüterswörden, Udo. 2001. "Der Prophet in den Lachisch-Ostraka." Pages 179–92 in *Steine, Bilder, Texte: Historische Evidenz ausserbiblischer und biblischer Quellen*. Edited by Christof Hardmeier. ABG 5. Leipzig: Evangelische Verlagsanstalt.

Schipper, Bernd U. 2012. *Hermeneutik der Tora: Studien zur Traditionsgeschichte von Prov 2 und zur Komposition von Prov 1–9*. BZAW 432. Berlin: de Gruyter.

Schmid, Konrad. 2010. *Hiob als biblisches und antikes Buch: Historische und intellektuelle Kontexte seiner Theologie*. SBS 219. Stuttgart: Katholisches Bibelwerk.

Schniedewind, William M. 2000. "Sociolinguistic Reflections on the Letter of a 'Literate' Soldier (Lachish 3)." *ZAH* 13:157–67.

Schultz, Richard L. 2013. "Job and Ecclesiastes: Intertextuality and a Protesting Pair." Pages 190–203 in Dell and Kynes 2013.

Sneed, Mark. 2011. "Is the 'Wisdom Tradition' a Tradition?" *CBQ* 73:50–71.

Toorn, Karel van der. 2009. *Scribal Culture and the Making of the Hebrew Bible*. Cambridge: Harvard University Press.

Weinfeld, Moshe. 1983. *Deuteronomy and the Deuteronomic School*. Oxford: Clarendon.

Witte, Markus. 2013. "Does the Torah Keep Its Promise? Job's Critical Intertextual Dialogue with Deuteronomy." Pages 54–65 in Dell and Kynes 2013.

Riddles and Parables, Traditions and Texts: Ezekielian Perspectives on Israelite Wisdom Traditions

Mark W. Hamilton

In a recent article Mark Sneed challenges the widespread assumption that "Hebrew Wisdom literature represents a worldview, tradition, and movement distinct from those of the priests and prophets and that it provides an alternative to Yahwism, that it is antirevelatory" (Sneed 2011, 53–54). He argues that genres do not equal worldviews and thus that we should exercise caution in moving from texts to the mindsets of those creating and using them. Such an understanding of wisdom texts, in particular, would vitiate an approach equating texts with worldviews, especially one that imagined such a worldview as characterized by such vague qualities as optimism, skepticism, and despair (cf. Crenshaw 1998, 10). Sneed disputes the oft-repeated claim that because Israelite wisdom texts stem from a readily identifiable, highly self-conscious social group called the sages, they must have differed in their viewpoints from other recognizable social groups called priests or prophets and functioned analogously to similar groups in Mesopotamia, Egypt, and other ancient Near Eastern societies. To be sure, if taken to its ultimate conclusion, Sneed's approach risks both tautology ("texts are about texts") and a nihilism that would render a history of ideas parlous at best; but when used carefully, it properly allows us to avoid crying interpolation or redaction whenever a text from an allegedly different worldview has the temerity to appear where it ought not.

More debatable, however, is his further claim that all the biblical texts derive from "scribal scholars" who, whatever their social roles (priests, prophets, sages, courtiers) "were united in their role as scribes and in their common scribal training" and whose "role as scribes should be given more weight than whether they were also simultaneously priests, prophets, or sages" (Sneed 2011, 64). It obviously does not automatically follow that because two individuals share a status or occupational identity or even produce similar texts that they cannot identify themselves, and be identified by others, as belonging to a distinct tradition. So in our own time an economics department may contain professors who espouse neo-Marxist, Friedmanite, or neo-Keynesian views, or a divinity school might include Protestant, Catholic, Muslim, and agnostic faculty, just to take two examples. Traditions need not be isolated from other viewpoints to maintain their own integrity.

On the other hand, Sneed rightly challenges the major points of the dominant construction. Therefore, I propose that we consider the problem that he raises from a different direction, that is, by examining ancient scribal practices and the ways in which ideas (including both literary forms and the proposals they carry) migrate from one intellectual circle to another. This demonstration further requires reexamination of the ways in which complex literary works, such as most biblical texts, combined genres in ways that produced new potentialities for meaning-making. In short, we need to consider how texts refract worldviews, however difficult such an endeavor might prove.

As a minor contribution to such an enterprise, this essay proceeds in two moves. The first reflects briefly on what we might mean by tradition. The second considers a particular complex literary work and its use of recognizable wisdom genres in ways that interpenetrate the rest of the work: the book of Ezekiel. I shall argue that notions of neither an airtight tradition called wisdom nor a mere textual phenomenon (whatever that means) can explain the evidence of Israelite texts and that we must, instead, think of interlocking intellectual circles that created, preserved, reused, and reinterpreted texts as fit representations of their ideas about the world, or at any rate the ideas they thought worthy of interaction and commentary.

On Tradition

To begin, what does such a contested notion as tradition mean? Most definitions assume two things: first, that pastness is somehow involved, usually as a warrant for current decisions (Weber 1978, 1:226–27; 2:954), but always as a matter of self-consciousness. For example, artistic and intellectual traditions, however we wish to define them, reflect deeply on their own pasts, or at any rates their own givenness, and set themselves up as somehow distinct from, though not necessarily antithetical to, other traditions that they or others identify. Groups may invent traditions, not out of whole cloth, to be sure, but through creative appropriations, adaptations, or amalgamations of their imagined past(s) as instantiated in ritual, story, and symbol (Hobsbawm 1983).

The second point is that, as Edward Shils put it forty years ago, "Traditions are beliefs with a particular social structure; they are a consensus through time" (Shils 1971, 126). He goes on to argue that traditions are "beliefs with a sequential social structure … which are believed by a succession of persons who might have interaction with each other in succession or at least in a unilateral (even if not intergenerationally continuous) chain of communication" (ibid.). A tradition, in Shils's accounting, need not foreground its own pastness, but it does offer continuity as a conclusive argument for or against any proposed action or commitment. In addition to the presentness of the past, for Shils, traditions understand the present as "the reinforcement of responsiveness to the past" and the "past as an object of attachment" (or repulsion in some cases). Beliefs held by those within a tradition may arrive from many sources and be held for a range of reasons and with varying intensity, but they assume the sacredness of past discoveries (so, Einstein builds on Newton, or Mendelssohn repristinates Bach).

On such an understanding, to speak of an Israelite "wisdom tradition," as Professor Sneed asks us to stop doing, would be to imply that its participants (social structure) held views that distinguished them from others, that they regarded these views as sanctioned by antiquity and therefore inviolable, and that they drew on their viewpoint to critique others. Nothing in such a definition would imply an incapacity to learn from other viewpoints or the sort of closed-in world that Sneed rightly critiques in the reconstructions of some other scholars. Nor does such a view of tradition compel us to search for a single closed group that held to the tradition or saw itself as the defender of it.

This latter point speaks to a key element in arguments for an Israelite wisdom tradition embodied in a "body of literature that reflects specific interests at variance with Yahwistic texts in general" and that stems from "a distinct class" (Crenshaw 1998, 21; but Steiert 1990; differently, Perdue 1997, 84–90; 2008, 49–80). Without assessing the dubious usefulness of the term "class" for antiquity, one must ask whether this sort of reconstruction fits what we know of scribal practice in the ancient Near East.

Certainly a profession called scribe existed in most, if not all, societies in the region from the third millennium BCE on. And certainly membership in this profession required significant training, which in turn required a level of élan sustainable by group solidarity, as well as societal commitment of economic and social capital to the scribal enterprise. At the same time, however, Mesopotamian scribes at any rate, were responsible for a range of literary texts in multiple genres, and their relationship to these texts ranged in intensity from mere copying to adaptation to free creation (van der Toorn 2007, 110; Veldhuis 2000; cf. Beaulieu 2007, esp. 17–18), just as their motivations varied according to the potential uses of the texts and their own commitments (Pearce 1993). In the cases of persons creating advanced texts in cuneiform such as those pertaining to rituals, bi- or trilingual lexical texts, or omina, the training level must have been very high indeed. Thus the empirical evidence for a group responsible only for wisdom texts is sparse, but it does make sense to speak of scribal traditions in less rigid ways.[1]

On the other hand, several aspects of Israelite and other Northwest Semitic wisdom texts might be explained as features of a self-conscious tradition, as Shils defines it. He argues that traditions have both formal and substantive properties, with the former including a structure that allows modes of transmission and renewal (Shils 1971, 133–35) and the latter including "traditionality of legitimation" (à la Weber), valuation of the past, the enactment of values in ritual, and a strong sense of collective identity, among other features. The wisdom texts of the Hebrew Bible, in particular, seem to reflect such a reality as they (1) deliberately evoked their own circle of ancient authorities (Job, Ethan the Ezrahite, Agur ben Yakeh, Lemuel, or Solomon rather than the patriarchs and matriarchs as in the prophetic tradition or Moses in the priestly traditions);[2] (2) used such evocation to lend authority to new texts in some way, though the authority had to be uncontestable to be effective (hence Job's proffering of various authorities from the "first man" [אִישׁ רִאשׁוֹן; Job 15:7; cf. 8:8; also Ezek 28, which situates the wise king of Tyre in the primordial garden] to YHWH as the sole witness to the beginning of time); (3) self-consciously excluded, marginalized, critiqued, or co-opted other authorities (hence the querying

---

1. On problems connecting the Israelite to the Mesopotamian (and derivative) traditions, see the discussion in Cohen 2013, 7–14; cf. Lambert 1960, 1–2, 10–13.

2. Something similar seems to have occurred in the formation of the Ahiqar tradition. See the discussion in Weigl 2010, 756–64 and infra.

of special revelation in both Job and Qoheleth); and (4) discussed the relationship of past to present in ways that privileged a certain construction of the former.

At some level, then, the texts that modern scholars identify as Israelite wisdom reflect a tradition in a loose sense. That is, the wisdom teachers lent weight to the argument of the text because they cited teachers revered for making commendable arguments, who had especial appeal to their audience, or at least to themselves, that other authorities did not have. The texts in question can plausibly be argued to have interacted with each other (Steiert 1990, 168–86). However, it is difficult to know how to allocate credit for the features of these texts that distinguish them from other genres. For example, it is true that a text like Proverbs cites certain figures and not others (no prophets, for example), but is this fact a reflection of living in a tradition, or simply a function of genre decisions (as in the counterfactual scenario in which prophets did not write משלים)? What about a text like the Psalter, in which the superscriptions allude to a wider range of persons engaged in the music business? Imagining a wisdom tradition as discrete and self-contained, much less antithetical to other traditions would assume a group that is simultaneously both more and less open to other traditions and their authoritative teachers, a situation that we do not know to have existed and that seems self-contradictory (though admittedly groups often do believe formally contradictory things). At this point then, we have reasons for acknowledging that the evidence points in more than one direction and that overprecision is to be avoided.

This inconclusiveness has been a factor in biblical scholarship for some time, in part because of the difficulty of defining the content and boundaries of wisdom. Hence the long discussion that ensued from Fichtner's (1949) proposal to find Isaiah among the sages, the rise and fall of a pan-wisdom approach to many biblical texts (see Crenshaw 1969), and the reconsideration of possible connections between prophecy and wisdom, with varying results (MacIntosh 1995; Soggin 1995; Williamson 1995). Clearly we face a problem of both evidence and conception. The way out of the morass involves rethinking the problem of how ideas migrate from one setting to another. To consider this larger question, it will be important to understand how Ezekiel, the test case at hand, has appropriated wisdom elements in a complex work. It will then be possible to think through what the evidence suggests about the larger question of how ideas migrated among circles in ancient Israel.

The Case of the Book of Ezekiel

Let me turn, then, to a suitably complex work that embeds multiple genres: Ezekiel. Scholars have argued for connections between the book and a range of ancient Near Eastern genres, ritual practices, and texts from city laments (Odell 2000; Petter 2011) to the *mīs pî* ritual (Strine 2014) to (more convincingly) the Erra Epic, the Babylonian story of a pestilence deity run amok during his brief assumption of Marduk's role as cosmocrator (Bodi 1991), among others.[3] Some of these proposals seem more probative than others, but the basic sense of Ezekiel's cosmopolitan horizons remains. The creators of Ezekiel knew the oral traditions, not only of Israel but of its neighbors,[4] though the work's freedom in recasting those motifs

---

3. The points of contact include vocabulary and such motifs as the seven executioners, the crowd, the absence of the deity from his shrine (though that theme is more widely attested and not specific to Erra), the navel of the earth, and the song of the sword (Ezek 21), among other items.

4. A most interesting case of this appears in the book's oracles to the king of Tyre, who appears as a model of חכמה, indeed as the "first man" (איש ראשון). The prophet contrasts two narratives and two narrators. The first, the king of Tyre, portrays himself as a divine figure of great wisdom, wiser than the greatest Canaanite sage. It seems reasonable to think that, given what we know about ancient Near Eastern royal self-praise, Ezekiel apparently had access to Tyrian royal propaganda, though Tyrian texts are rare and not helpful on this point (see the broader issue of Phoenician influence discussed in Bogaert 1991; Lipiński, 2004). (Perhaps he participated in the exchange of texts that ancient Near Eastern intellectuals sometimes practiced [for the overall practice, see Gadotti and Kleinerman 2011].) At a minimum, Ezekiel attributes to Tyre a political discourse that legitimates commerce as a sign of divine presence. However, the language of political deconstruction is the language of a decomposing narrative. Ezekiel's YHWH exposes the king of Tyre as a foolish braggart, a false hero who meets a deservedly horrific end.

As Vladimir Propp noted in his classic little book *Morphology of the Folktale* (1994, 62) the narrative function of the exposed false hero often links to one in which the true hero is revealed. Here, the poem implies a true hero, YHWH, who does not merely declare a fate but makes it happen. It would follow that the poem assumes that the instrument of Tyre's fall, the slayers of his folly-filled wisdom, were commissioned by YHWH to undertake the grim duty. Many prophetic texts make such an assumption explicit, but this one only assumes it. The latency of the narrative works because it contrasts with the first narrative and narrator a second, more trustworthy one, YHWH. For YHWH's narrative, the wisdom of Tyre proves empty, its regal sage a fool. Yet the character of the narrator remains undeveloped, the drama of his quest or mission unexpressed.

mark it as something other than mere bricolage, but a skilled production. More germane to the discussion at hand, the book not only cites ancient sages such as Job, Noah, and Danilu in the much-discussed text in Ezek 14 but also employs on some occasions wisdom genres in constructing its overall message.

As Renz has argued in a most insightful study of the book's rhetoric, the book of Ezekiel organized the material stemming from the circles of its prophetic namesake to articulate a viewpoint that would promote the survival of Israel in exile. As he puts it, "Both the full integration into the Babylonian culture and the attachment to unreconstructed traditions of the past would have provided an inadequate basis for the survival of this community as a distinct entity. In a context where the survival of the community was in question, the book provided an argument well suited to the situation" (Renz 1999, 234). In other words, the radical requirements of the long sixth century BCE (i.e., the 630s through the 520s) prompted the creator(s) of the book of Ezekiel to innovate while drawing on a range of traditional ideas and literary practices. Shils again: "The results of original creation or discovery ... become a point of redirection of the line of tradition, retaining some elements of the tradition, diminishing the prominence of others and introducing novelty as well" (Shils 1971, 144).

Even if one does not accept the arguments of Odell (2000, 2005) that the mixture of genres in Ezekiel moves the book (though not its namesake) out of the realm of prophecy and into something more like wisdom literature, any analysis of the work must nevertheless account for its incorporation of literary complexes that engage nonprophetic materials (see Pohlmann 2006, 166). As Nay (1999) has shown, much of Ezekiel must be understood as a dialogical text creating meaning by the display of multiple voices.

To come to the case at hand, then, the book occasionally employs the jargon of wisdom on several occasions, using terms such as מָשָׁל (12:22–23; 17:2; 18:2; 21:5; 24:3), חִידָה (17:2), חכם (27:8–9; 28:3), and חכמה (28:4–5,

---

Most crucially for the issue under consideration here, the text of Ezek 28 explicitly subverts the Tyrian monarch's claims to have חכמה. However, this fact does not imply that having wisdom or being a sage would be problematic as such any more than the critique of violent, negligent priests in Ezek 22:26 renders the priesthood nugatory. The problem is that the Tyrian king was a bad sage, deluded, arrogant, and destructive. The prophetic oracle does not critique a wisdom mindset, therefore, but an abuse of power.

7, 12, 17) in technical ways[5] to refer to oral productions that pithily express some important idea, controversial or not, as in Ezek 12:22–23:

> Human being, what is this *mashal* of yours concerning the land of Israel, "the days stretch out and every vision perishes"? Therefore, say to them, "thus says the lord YHWH, stop using this *mashal* [LXX: παραβολή] and do not mashalize it again in Israel." Instead, say to them, "the days draw near for the utterance of every vision."[6]

> בן אדם מה המשל הזה לכם על אדמת ישראל לאמר יארכו הימים ואבד כל חזון: לכן אמר אליהם כה אמר אדני יהוה השבתי את המשל הזה ולא ימשלו אתו עוד בישראל כי אם דבר אליהם קרבו הימים ודבר כל חזון.

That is, the passage envisions a prophetic correction of a popular proverb (it is לכם), not because wisdom material comes from different circles than prophecy or is critical of prophecy, but because the *mashal* erroneously assumes the end of prophetic communication. Hence Ezek 12:24's insistence that "any lying vision" (כל חזון שוא) and "deceptive divinatory practices" (מקסם חלק; LXX: μαντευόμενος) will cease. Their truthfulness, not the media of delivery nor the social location of the deliverer, is in question. Yet this relatively familiar and uncomplicated text reveals the capacity of the Ezekiel tradition to respond in a complex way to a literary genre not strictly at home in prophecy, but familiar to many persons (not just sages), and to absorb (so to speak) that genre and its underlying ideas into the prophetic ambit.

---

5. It is instructive to consider the use of this vocabulary in other prophetic books. The noun משל appears in Isa 14:4; Jer 24:9; Mic 2:4; and Hab 2:6; the verbal form occurs in Isa 14:10 (relating to the public reputation of monarchs); 28:14 (as a proverb-speaker); and 46:5. The word חכם occurs in Isa 3:3; 5:21; 10:11; 19:11–12; 29:14; 31:2; 40:20; 44:25; Jer 4:22; 8:8; 9:11, 16; 10:7, 9; 18:18; 50:35; 51:57; Hos 13:13; 14:10 (as part of the redactor's overarching comment on the book's purpose and the proper strategy for reading it); and Obad 8. Meanwhile, the abstract noun חכמה appears in Isa 10:13; 11:2; 47:10; 29:14; 33:6; Jer 8:9; 9:22; 10:12; 51:15; 49:7 (twice). Finally, חידה occurs elsewhere in the prophets in Hab 2:6 (indeed eight of its fourteen appearances in the Hebrew Bible occur in one chapter, Judg 14). A thorough study of the use of this vocabulary lies beyond the scope of the present paper, but it would probably show that texts use these words in both technical and nontechnical ways. Sometimes wisdom is the property of a small elite, sometimes a characteristic of many human interactions. It may be public or private, focused on grand politics or domestic life, and so on.

6. Unless otherwise specified, all translations are mine.

On Birds, Trees, and Lions: Ezekiel 17–19

A more complex, and therefore more interesting, case of Ezekiel's use of parabolic material appears in a set of texts that seem deliberately interwoven, Ezek 17 and 19.[7] Three times, the text includes prolonged discussions of a set of agrarian images known elsewhere in the Bible and well beyond.

The foundational piece from which the others spring appears in Ezek 17:1–10, which reads

> And YHWH's word came to me:
> Human being, riddle a riddle [חוד חידה] and tell a parable [ומשל משל]
>   to the house of Israel and say to them, thus says the lord YHWH:
> "The giant griffin with giant wings outspread,
> Its pinions full and colorful, came to Lebanon
> And took off the cedar's top.
> It broke off its branches' crown,
> Brought it to Canaan's land
> And put it in the traders' town.
> And it took the land's seed and put in a sowable field,
> A slip[8] near abundant water, putting it next a willow.
> It sprouted, and it became a vine,
> Spreading high and low.
> Its limbs hung, its roots underslung it,
> And it was a vine, putting out shoots and
> Sending forth branches.
> Yes, the one griffin is great, giant-winged and full-feathered.
> Yes, the vine's roots turned outward[9] from itself,
> And its branches sent out (tendrils) to get sustenance from the beddings
>   of its plantings.
> In the good field, on the many waters it was planted
> To make twigs, to bear fruit, to be a luxuriant vine."

---

7. But see the structural conversations in Renz (1999, 72–92). The interrelationships of the texts seem to corroborate a remark by Zimmerli (1979, 25) that "not only behind the book in its present form, but also behind the composition of its individual parts, there stands a definite plan." Whether one attributes this plan to Ezekiel himself is a different question.

8. Following Greenberg's (1983a, 311) connection of קח to Akkadian *qū* ("slip") rather than as a verb form.

9. Note the pun כנף/כפן in this text. The wordplay forms a sort of equation between the spreading wings of the bird and the spreading branches of the vine. But see Zimmerli 1979, 354–55.

Say, thus says the lord YHWH, "Will it succeed?
Will not its roots be torn out and its fruit soured?
And all the tendrils of its branches be dried out?
Will it not wither and will not a great arm or a mighty people rip it out by the roots?
Will the planted really flourish?
Will it not be כגעת?[10]
An east wind will dry what will be dried.
On the beddings of its plantings will it dry out."

The high level of repetition of stock phrases and disenjambment point to an oral register for the text, especially when one considers the contrast between it and the prophet's explanation of the riddle/parable in 17:11–21. The connections among a giant beast and life and death, especially considering the poem's final image of the dessicating east wind, point to a plausible background for the idea of the text in ancient Near Eastern stories, possibly via the Gilgamesh stories, which did circulate in the Levant (Steymans 2010).[11]

If we had only the parable itself, the meaning of it would be, well, a riddle. Is the removal of a treetop and its transplantation good or bad? Surely the morphing of a cedar or juniper crown into a vine places the story in the realm of fantasy (dare we say, magic?). And while Ezekiel elsewhere speaks negatively of רכלים ("merchants"; see Ezek 17:4; 27:3, 12–13, 15, 17, 20, 22–24; cf. 1 Kgs 10:15; Nah 3:16; Song 3:6; Neh 3:31; also רכולה in Ezek 26:12; 28:5, 16, 18), he mostly has in mind Tyrians or Phoenicians more generally (see the historical background in Lipiński, 2004), apparently not the reference in this text. Most significantly, a possible interpretation of the *mashal* alone would be that the villain was YHWH, who plots to kill the vine, surely an act that any ancient Israelite would regard as a great material loss.

Yet the interpretation in the text of Ezekiel itself goes in a very different direction. The prophet operates with a hermeneutic of substitution,

---

10. Another pun, perhaps? Greenberg (1983a, 313) takes this form to relate to נגע, without discussion. Another option would be to derive it from גוע ("to languish"; hence "like something languishing"), and still another to posit an intentional pun.

11. On the connection to Ninurta's hunt of the Anzu bird and of that theme to Neo-Assyrian's monarchy reappropriation of the Gilgamesh Epic, see Ataç 2010; Watanabe 1998.

bordering on allegory (see, in an exaggerated way, Fohrer 1955, 94), in which an item in the story stands for an item in history. Thus he writes

> The king of Babylon came to Jerusalem and took its king and its nobles and brought them to him toward Babylon. And he took from the seed of the kingdom and made a covenant with him and imposed on him a curse and deported the leaders of the land so it would be a lowly kingdom unable to rise, to keep his covenant so it would endure. But he rebelled by sending his messengers to Egypt to [ask them to] give him horses and many troops. Will he succeed? Will the one doing these things escape? Will the one breaking covenant survive? (17:12–15)[12]

In short, Ezekiel creates a set of matched pairs:

The griffin	king of Babylon
The city of merchants	Babylon
The treetop	Jerusalem's king and nobles
Spreading out vines	going to Egypt (?)

Such a strategy of replacement has precedents in Ezekiel's world, for example in commentaries on mystical texts from Nineveh and a Hurrian-Hittite bilingual from Bogazköy/Hattusa. KBo 32.14 (= COS 1.82, trans. Gary Beckman)[13] is a multitablet work that includes a series of parables and their interpretations, separated by a refrain that Gary Beckman translates as "Leave that story. I will tell you another story. Listen to the message. I will speak wisdom to you." Accordingly, a parable of a mountain expelling a deer stands for a man who fled his town, or a deer grazing stands for an envious district governor, or a beautiful copper cup for a son neglecting filial piety. The connections between parable and events in the world of politics are not obvious (hence the labeling of their interrelationships as wisdom) but are highly interesting.

Similarly, a text that one of its editors speaks of as cultic commentary (SAA 3.37 = K 3476) comments on a ritual, equating both the kindled

---

12. Ezekiel 17's point is to cast the covenant-breaking Judahite king as the villain of the piece, as also in 2 Kgs 17 and possibly Hos 10:4.

13. The editors (Otten and Rüster 1990, iv) describe the text this way: "Vollständig erhaltene zweikolumnige Tafel; Rs. Nach Z. 22 aus Raumgründen einkolumnig angelegt mit Wechsel von hurritischem und hethitischem Text. Ohne Kolophon, aber die Weisheitssprüche verbinden den Text mit Nr. 12: also vielleicht Tafel 3?"

fire and the bowing king with Marduk, the dignitaries beating clappers (*kiskilāti*) with the gods, the fire in the brazier with Tiamat's companion Qingu, and so on. That is, in such texts, a mantic reading strategy of a ritual, in which a = b, prevails (Livingstone 1989, 92–95). Ezekiel, similarly, offers a mantic interpretation at home in the world of scholarly divination and prophecy, a world with which he was very familiar.

Nor is this all. In 17:22–24, the Ezekiel text offers a second interpretation of the *mashal*:

> Thus says the lord YHWH, "And I will take the lofty top of the cedar and place it.[14] From its crown I will pluck a lofty branch and plant it on a high, looming mountain. I shall plant it on the high mountain, Israel. And it will raise branches and bear fruit and be a noble cedar. And every bird,[15] every fowl will dwell in the shade of its branches. And all the trees of the field will know that I am YHWH when I fell the tall tree and grow the short tree, dry out the luxuriant tree and invigorate the withered tree. I, YHWH, have spoken and will act!"

The second interpretation is at considerable variance from the first, indeed its reversal. The emplotment of Israel's history in the form of the story of the bird and the cedar tree, because it can take advantage of the disjuncture between the patent and latent meanings of each story now made parallel, allows for a new, indeed antithetical meaning. While the juxtaposition of hope and doom in the prophets is not only not unusual, but in fact part of their redactors' stock in trade, the reversal here does not seem primarily to be explicable as a later development, but something that arises from the choice to speak of Israel's history by means of fable.

Here again, substitution of one element for another happens. But in this case the griffin becomes YHWH, and the cedar remains a cedar rather than morphing into a vine. The original parable's final move, in which the plant dies, gives way to a new situation emphasizing the deity's gracious decision about the plant's fate. Far from being a stand-in for Babylonian power, YHWH appears here as the sovereign of history whose word may change to suit changing needs, and an oracle of doom may become an admittedly ambiguous oracle of hope. What has been an oracle of doom becomes one of hope.

---

14. LXX omits the final verb.
15. Greek θηρίον, "animal," avoids the redundancy of MT.

A final turn in the life of the plant imagery comes in Ezek 19's parable of a pride of lions. After Ezek 18's famous attempt at revising a then-famous proverb, "the ancestors have eaten sour grapes, and the children's teeth are set on edge," and thus again at reframing the proper uses of oral tradition, 19:1–14 casts the historical events following the death of Josiah as a parable about the "princes of Israel" (נשׂיאי ישׂראל). Framing the parable as a "lament" (קינה; 19:1, 14), apparently a sort of abbreviated city lament (Carvalho 2009), Ezekiel describes two fierce young lions who turn out to be Jehoahaz and either Jehoiachin or Zedekiah, his successors. The key move for our purposes comes in 19:10–14, in which the prophet shifts from leonine to botanical imagery, picking up much of the vocabulary of Ezek 17:

> Your mother is like a vine in your blood,[16] planted on waters,
> Fruitful and multibranched is she on the many waters.
> And she has thick limbs, fit for rulers' staffs,
> And her height soars among the boughs,
> Seen afar for its many branches.
> But it was rooted up in anger, hurled to the ground,
> And the east wind dried it, stripped its fruit away.
> And its mighty boughs dried up. A fire devoured it.
> So now it is planted in a wasteland, in a dry and parched land.
> And fire comes from its boughs, consumes its limbs and fruit.
> So there is no thick limb to it, no staff for ruling.
> It is a lament and will be a lament.[17]

The shift from zoomorphic to botanical imagery is unsurprising in the world of an oral text. The bereft mother whose children have been sport for foreign kings is herself desolate. One expects the mother's desolation at the loss of her children, especially in the absence of a hero. The story is a lament precisely because no hero appears, no villain is plainly identified

---

16. On the problem of בדמך, see Greenberg, 1983a, 353; Fohrer 1955, 19 ("wie ein Weinstock im Weinberg" emending the text to בכרם, apparently modeled very loosely on LXX).

17. MT: קינה היא ותהי לקינה. LXX understands the previous phrase, ending with שבט למשל, as part of the following phrase: φυλή εἰς παραβολὴν θρήνου ἐστὶ καὶ ἔσται εἰς θρῆνον ("it is a staff for a parable of lament, and will be a lament"), which seems almost unintelligible, but reflects an understanding of the Hebrew משל as a noun (cf. the use of παραβολή in LXX Ezek 12:22–23; 16:44; 17:2; 18:2–3; 19:14; 20:49; and 24:3).

(though the Babylonians come close to that role), and no resolution of the pride's lack obtains. Also, it should not be surprising that the mother's grief would change her into another sort of being. Think of Ovid's later (and literary) tale of Baucis and Philemon (in which they transform into oak and linden trees as a reward for their hospitality [*Metam.* 8.611–724]) or, perhaps, the salinification of Lot's wife (Gen 19:26).

However, the metamorphosis of mother Judah into a grapevine returns to the congeries of images in Ezek 17, with a detailed use of the earlier story's vocabulary:

גפן (17:6–8; 19:10)
קומה (17:6; 19:11)
שתולה (17:8, 10; 19:10, cf. 13)
מים רבים (17:5, 8; 19:10)
דליות (17:7; 19:11)
רוח הקדים (17:10; 19:12)
פרי (17:8–9; 19:12, 14)
יבש (17:9–10; 19:12)

The close relationship between the two texts might be explained in several ways: (1) chapter 17 is primary, with 19 being a gloss on it; (2) chapter 19 is earlier, with 17 being an expansion or reworking; or (3) the two originated simultaneously as the prophet employed multiple oral forms to comment on the politics of his time. It is difficult to choose an option with certainty, though the placement of the viticultural imagery within the parable of the lion's pride might argue for its secondary status vis-à-vis Ezek 17. However that may be, in the written form of the book of Ezekiel, 19:10–14 offers an interpretation of 17:1–10, namely, a return to the doom-saying view of 17:12–15 (again arguing that 17:22–24 comes from a later setting in the development of the text, perhaps in late exilic or early postexilic period).[18]

What does this analysis of these clearly interrelated texts, which the book of Ezekiel describes as parabolic (משׁל, παραβολή) show? At least three things, I think. First, the prophetic book uses both a genre and a technique of interpreting the genre that appears in other environments. The technique of multiple interpretations of a single text appears in several literary environments in the ancient Near East, including divinatory texts

---

18. But on the relationships of these texts, see Greenberg 1983b.

RIDDLES AND PARABLES, TRADITIONS AND TEXTS 255

(Winitzer 2006), a priestly literary genre closely associated with wisdom (see Joseph's mastery of oneiromancy and dream interpretation in Gen 41–46 and Daniel's similar skills in Dan 2–7). The notion that an esoteric text can bear more multiple exoteric meanings appears in several literary and intellectual environments.

Second, Ezekiel explicitly presents this set of texts in chs. 17–19 as the interpretation of a "parable" or "riddle," that is, as reversing the relationship between the surface and deep meanings of the original vision, inviting the audience to understand its immediate past (the Babylonian absorption of the Judahite state) as a drama of cosmic significance, emphasizing Ezekiel's emplotment of Israel's history as *Unheilsgeschichte* (Peterson 2013). While marking a representation of history as an exoteric משל has a nice parallel in Ps 78:2 (אפתחה במשל פי), in describing it as the more esoteric category חידה and juxtaposing the two labels, Ezekiel has gone a different way, marking history itself as a species of wisdom accessible to the deity and those properly taught by the deity. In that sense, the text seems to fit Fishbane's description of mantic exegesis of oracular texts (Fishbane 1985, esp. 458–99). He argues that in such texts, particularly in the early sixth century BCE and before, "the prophet-receiver of the vision or imagery is directly informed of its meaning by the addressing divine voice" (Fishbane 1985, 506). Text and commentary inextricably intertwine to suggest both a cluster of ideas (content) and a process of interpretation that renders the text pregnant with interpretive possibilities.

At a formal level, to be sure, the Ezekiel texts do not easily correspond to Fishbane's oracle types, which he argues are "initially both non-symbolic and non-esoteric. Indeed, the very evocative and communicative force of these oracles depends on their comprehensibility, on the exoteric plain sense of the language employed" (Fishbane 1985, 507). Yet the Ezekiel texts do not fit his other textual category for mantological exegesis, dreams. They lie somewhere in between.

Third, the fact that the Ezekiel text is hard to place within the expected range of prophetic texts deserves comment. Fishbane himself offers a clue when he understands Ezek 19 as a reuse of Gen 49, a transformation of a blessing into an oracle (Fishbane 1985, 502). In other words, the capacity of genres for manipulation allows the prophet to create something new, something that Ezekiel understands as the interpretation of the חידה/משל of Ezek 17. This is why Zimmerli (1979, 360; cf. Hals 1989, 115–17) understands Ezek 17:1–10 as "the prophetic adoption" of "Wisdom animal and plant fables" (though not quite an allegory, contra Fohrer 1955, 94–97).

But what does "prophetic adoption" mean? This question states concisely the crux of the problem at hand. The answer is that, by presenting the story of the eagle and the tree as parabolic material, and YHWH as both the teller of the tale and its virtuosic interpreter, Ezek 17–19 has posited YHWH as the ultimate sage and has rendered prophecy and wisdom as two sides of the same coin, that is, as two media of divine communication with humankind. The notion of the divine sage is, of course, widespread in the ancient Near East and certainly underlies texts such as both the wisdom poem in Job 28 and the climactic divine speeches in Job 38–41, even if the former speech does not so much deconstruct wisdom by the means of wisdom as celebrate the infinite depth of wisdom, and therefore the necessity of the divine revelation of the latter, however enigmatic it proves to be. In short, both the fusion of traditions presupposed by Ben Sira, say, and the grounding of wisdom traditions in the divine realm are foreshadowed by Ezekiel.

Conclusions

So far, then, in testing Sneed's questioning of the existence of a discrete wisdom tradition, that is, a self-conscious group aware of its own past and committed to working out its view by means of certain literary genres and not others, the task has been to sharpen his critique in several ways. First, reference to a scribal social location alone cannot vitiate the regnant theory, since scribes could share social location and some social behaviors while still distancing themselves from each other intellectually (even if historical knowledge of their inner disputes may lack sufficient data to perceive all the details of these differences). Second, however, Israelite texts from one intellectual milieu could use literary genres and the ideas they carried from a range of other milieux. In the Hebrew Bible, Ezekiel offers perhaps the most extraordinary case of such literary virtuosity, with its almost baroque exuberance in using prophetic, priestly, and (as I have argued) wisdom materials.

Third, the combination of these two sets of data prompts the question of whether either social milieu or scribal/literary convention provides an adequate category for explaining the material we have. It seems too easy to depict wisdom literature as simply a mode of scribalism concerned with practical wisdom for everyone or Israel's way of avoiding parochialism and seeking truth that is "applicable to all peoples, not just the Israelites" (Sneed 2011, 71), just as it seems difficult to match texts neatly to a closed intellectual circle in a distinctive social setting. On the one hand, texts do not exist isolated from ideas and the social contexts that create and sustain them. Not only does a figure like Ezekiel clearly have a view of the world that assumes the survival and, to some degree, legitimacy of the "other" outside Israel, and thus shares with wisdom a cosmopolitan outlook compatible with a robust notion of divine revelation through prophecy. In short, something seems amiss in our categories, as though we have not quite shaken off the older ways of construing things.

Yet, if we are to move in new directions, where should we begin? Surely Sneed has helped us by pointing to the incongruence of certain wooden constructions of wisdom literature that equate literary genre with social uses. However, is there a way to reframe our notions of wisdom traditions? If, as Shils argues, "traditions are beliefs with a particular social structure," then what social structures gave birth to, and nurtured, the various sorts of texts present in the Bible? What were the features of the intellectual circles in which the creators of wisdom and prophetic texts, to take just two examples, operated? How did those circles overlap, and how did they relate to other Israelites, both intellectual elites and the much larger group of persons who were not? And how did the ideas created in one setting move to another?

The answer to these questions remains quite obscure at this point, though perhaps a few things are clear, such as: (1) the texts that we call wisdom and prophetic were collected and transmitted together at least as early as the Hellenistic period, and arguably earlier, a fact that implies a perceived congruence between them prior to their joint transmission and collection; (2) the ideas informing them, however, overlapped and cross-fertilized much earlier, owing to the close physical proximity of their creators (Jerusalem and other Israelite cities were small places, the number of Hebrew speakers relatively small, and the distances required to share texts limited) and their shared educational experiences (assuming the existence of only a few schools in the ancient Israelite kingdoms, probably associated with the temples and priesthoods of those polities); and (3) both wisdom texts and Ezekiel operate on the assumption that the movement from surface meaning to real meaning requires the disciplined pursuit of understanding taught by a sage, in the latter's case, the sage being the deity whose pupil, the prophet, transmits the deep knowledge to others. Put differently, the distinction between a wisdom text and a prophetic text lies less at the level of the ideas in them than at the level for constructing and interpreting them, but even this difference is one on a continuum, not a radical distinction in kind. The task ahead is to build on Sneed's helpful intervention and reconsider how ideas moved about in ancient Israel and thus made the texts constituting the Bible possible.

WORKS CONSULTED

Ataç, Mehmet-Ali. 2010. "Representations and Resonances of Gilgamesh in Neo-Assyrian Art." Pages 261–86 in *Gilgamesch: Ikonographie eines Helden/Gilgamesh: Epic and Iconography*. Edited by Hans U. Steymans. OBO 245. Fribourg: Academic Press; Göttingen: Vandenhoeck & Ruprecht.
Beaulieu, Paul-Alain. 2007. "The Social and Intellectual Setting of Babylonian Wisdom Literature." Pages 3–19 in *Wisdom Literature in Mesopotamia and Israel*. Edited by Richard J. Clifford. SymS 36. Atlanta: Society of Biblical Literature.
Bodi, Daniel. 1991. *The Book of Ezekiel and the Poem of Erra*. OBO 104. Fribourg: Universitätsverlag; Göttingen: Vandenhoeck & Ruprecht.
Bogaert, Pierre-Maurice. 1991. "Le Chérub de Tyr (Ez 28,14–16) et l'hippocampe de ses monnaies." Pages 29–38 in *Prophetie und geschichtliche Wirklichkeit im alten Israel: Festschrift für Siegfried Herrmann zum 65. Geburtstag*. Edited by Rüdiger Liwak and Siegfried Wagner. Stuttgart: Kohlhammer.
Carvalho, Corrine. 2009. "Putting the Mother Back in the Center: Metaphor and Multivalence in Ezekiel 19." Pages 208–21 in *Thus Says the Lord: Essays on the Former and Latter Prophets in Honor of Robert R. Wilson*. Edited by John J. Ahn and Stephen L. Cook. LHBOTS 502. New York: T&T Clark.
Cohen, Yoram. 2013. *Wisdom from the Late Bronze Age*. WAW 34. Atlanta: Society of Biblical Literature.
Crenshaw, James L. 1969. "Method in Determining Wisdom Influence upon 'Historical' Literature." *JBL* 88:129–42.
———. 1998. *Old Testament Wisdom: An Introduction*. Rev. ed. Louisville: Westminster John Knox.
Day, John, Robert P. Gordon, and H. G. M. Williamson, eds. 1995. *Wisdom in Ancient Israel: Essays in Honour of J. A. Emerton*. Cambridge: Cambridge University Press
Fichtner, Johannes. 1949. "Jesaja unter den Weisen." *TLZ* 74:75–80.
Fishbane, Michael. 1985. *Biblical Interpretation in Ancient Israel*. Oxford: Clarendon.

Fohrer, Georg. 1955. *Ezechiel*. HAT 13. Tübingen: Mohr Siebeck.
Fokkelman, Jan. 2010. "Job 28 and the Climax in Chapters 29–31: Crisis and Identity." Pages 301–22 in *Literary Construction of Identity in the Ancient World*. Edited by Hanna Liss and Manfred Oeming. Winona Lake, IN: Eisenbrauns.
Forti, Tova. 2008. "A New Criterion for Identifying 'Wisdom Psalms.'" Pages 365–79 in vol. 1 of *Birkat Shalom: Studies in the Bible, Ancient Near Eastern Literature, and Postbiblical Judaism Presented to Shalom M. Paul on the Occasion of His Seventieth Birthday*. Edited by Chaim Cohen, Victor Avigdor Hurowitz, Avi Hurvitz, Yochanan Muffs, Baruch J. Schwartz, and Jeffrey H. Tigay. Winona Lake, IN: Eisenbrauns.
Gadotti, Alhena, and Alexandra Kleinerman. 2011. "'Here Is What I Have. Send Me What I Am Missing': Exchange of Syllabi in Ancient Mesopotamia." *ZA* 101:72–77.
Greenberg, Moshe. 1983a. *Ezekiel 1–20*. AB 22. New York: Doubleday.
———. 1983b. "Ezekiel 17: A Holistic Interpretation." *JAOS* 103:149–54.
Hals, Ronald M. 1989. *Ezekiel*. FOTL 19. Grand Rapids: Eerdmans.
Haran, Menahem. 2005. "Observations on Ezekiel as a Book Prophet." Pages 3–19 in *Seeking Out the Wisdom of the Ancients*. Edited by Ronald L. Troxel, Kelvin G. Friebel, and Dennis R. Magary. Winona Lake, IN: Eisenbrauns.
Hobsbawm, Eric. 1983. "Mass-Producing Traditions: Europe, 1870–1914." Pages 263–307 in *The Invention of Tradition*. Edited by Eric Hobsbawm and Terence Ranger. Cambridge: Cambridge University Press.
Lambert, W. G. 1960. *Babylonian Wisdom Literature*. Oxford: Clarendon.
Lipiński, Edward. 2004. *Itineraria Phoenicia*. OLA 127; Studia Phoenicia 18. Leuven: Peeters.
Livingstone, Alasdair. 1989. *Court Poetry and Literary Miscellanea*. SAA 3. Helsinki: Helsinki University Press.
Lust, Johan. 2004. *Messianism and the Septuagint*. BETL 178. Leuven: Peeters.
Macintosh, A. A. 1995. "Hosea and the Wisdom Tradition: Dependence and Independence." Pages 124–32 in Day, Gordon, and Williamson 1995.
Moyn, Samuel. 2013. "On the Nonglobalization of Ideas." Pages 187–204 in *Global Intellectual History*. Edited by Samuel Moyn and Andrew Sartori. New York: Columbia University Press.

Nay, Reto. 1999. *Jahwe im Dialog: Kommunkationsanalytische Untersuchung von Ez 14,1–11 unter Berücksichtigung des dialogischen Rahmens in Ez 8–11 und Ez 20*. AnBib 141. Rome: Pontifical Biblical Institute.
Odell, Margaret S. 2000. "Genre and Persona in Ezekiel 24:15–24." Pages 195–220 in *The Book of Ezekiel: Theological and Anthropological Perspectives*. Edited by Margaret S. Odell and John T. Strong. SymS 9. Atlanta: Society of Biblical Literature.
———. 2005. *Ezekiel*. SHBC. Macon, GA: Smyth & Helwys.
Otten, Heinrich and Christel Rüster, eds. 1990. *Die Hurritisch-Hethitische Bilingue und weitere Texte aus der Oberstadt*. KBo 32. Berlin: Mann.
Pearce, Laurie E. 1993. "Statements of Purpose: Why the Scribes Wrote." Pages 185–93 in *The Tablet and the Scroll: Near Eastern Studies in Honor of William W. Hallo*. Edited by Mark E. Cohen, Daniel C. Snell, and David B. Weinberg. Bethesda, MD: CDL.
Perdue, Leo G. 1997. "Wisdom Theology and Social History in Proverbs 1–9." Pages 78–101 in *Wisdom, You are My Sister: Studies in Honor of Roland E. Murphy on the Occasion of His Eightieth Birthday*. Edited by Michael L. Barré. CBQMS 29. Washington, DC: Catholic Biblical Association.
———. 2008. *The Sword and the Stylus: An Introduction to Wisdom in the Age of Empires*. Grand Rapids: Eerdmans.
Peterson, Brian. 2013. "Ezekiel's Perspective of Israel's History: Selective Revisionism." Pages 295–314 in *Prophets, Prophecy, and Ancient Israelite Historiography*. Edited by Mark J. Boda and Lissa M. Wray Beal. Winona Lake, IN: Eisenbrauns.
Petter, Donna Lee. 2011. *The Book of Ezekiel and Mesopotamian City Laments*. OBO 246. Fribourg: Academic Press; Göttingen: Vandenhoeck & Ruprecht.
Phinney, D. Nathan. 2009. "Portraying Prophetic Experience and Tradition in Ezekiel." Pages 234–43 in *Thus Says the Lord: Essays on the Former and Latter Prophets in Honor of Robert R. Wilson*. Edited by John J. Ahn and Stephen L. Cook. LHBOTS 502. New York: T&T Clark.
Pohlmann, Karl-Friedrich. 2006. "Forschung am Ezechielbuch 1969–2004." *TRu* 71:60–90, 164–91, 265–309.
Propp, Vladimir. 1994. *Morphology of the Folktale*. Translated by Laurence Scott. Revised by Louis Wagner. Austin: University of Texas Press.
Renz, Thomas. 1999. *The Rhetorical Function of the Book of Ezekiel*. VTSup 76. Leiden: Brill.
Shils, Edward. 1971. "Tradition." *CSSH* 13:122–59.

Sneed, Mark. 2011. "Is the 'Wisdom Tradition' a Tradition?" *CBQ* 73:50–71.
Soggin, J. A. 1995. "Amos and Wisdom." Pages 119–23 in Day, Gordon, and Williamson 1995.
Steiert, Franz-Josef. 1990. *Die Weisheit Israels: Ein Fremdkörper im Alten Testament? Eine Untersuchung zum Buch der Sprüche auf dem Hintergrund der ägyptischen Weisheitslehren*. Freiburger Theologische Studien 43. Freiburg im Breisgau: Herder.
Steymans, Hans Ulrich. 2010. "Gilgameš im Westen." Pages 287–345 in *Gilgamesch: Ikonographie eines Helden/Gilgamesh: Epic and Iconography*. Edited by Hans U. Steymans. OBO 245. Fribourg: Academic Press; Göttingen: Vandenhoeck & Ruprecht.
Strine, Casey A. 2014. "Ezekiel's Image Problem: The Mesopotamian Cult Statue Induction Ritual and the Imago Dei Anthropology in the Book of Ezekiel." *CBQ* 76:252–72.
Toorn, Karel van der. 2007. *Scribal Culture and the Making of the Hebrew Bible*. Cambridge: Harvard University Press.
Veldhuis, Niek. 2000. "Sumerian Proverbs in Their Curricular Context." *JAOS* 120:383–99.
Vogelzang, M. E. 1995. "Learning and Power During the Sargonid Period." Pages 17–28 in *Centres of Learning: Learning and Location in Pre-Modern Europe and the Near East*. Edited by Jan Willem Drijvers and Alasdair A. MacDonald. BSIH 61. Leiden: Brill.
Watanabe, Chikako E. 1998. "Symbolism of the Royal Lion Hunt in Assyria." Pages 439–50 in *Papers Presented at the 43rd Rencontre Assyriologique Internationale: Intellectual Life of the Ancient Near East*. Edited by Jiří Prosecký. Prague: Oriental Institute.
Weber, Max. 1978. *Economy and Society*. Edited by Guenther Roth and Claus Wittich. Translated by Ephraim Fischoff et al. 2 vols. Berkeley: University of California Press.
Weigl, Michael. 2010. *Die aramäischen Achikar-Sprüche aus Elephantine und die alttestamentliche Weisheitsliteratur*. BZAW 399. Berlin: de Gruyter.
Williamson, H. G. M. 1995. "Isaiah and the Wise." Pages 133–41 in Day, Gordon, and Williamson 1995.
Winitzer, Abraham. 2011. "Writing and Mesopotamian Divination: The Case of Alternative Interpretation." *JCS* 63:77–94.

Zimmerli, Walther. 1979. *Ezekiel 1: A Commentary on the Book of the Prophet Ezekiel, Chapters 1–24*. Translated by Ronald E. Clements. Hermeneia. Philadelphia: Fortress.

Part 3
Ancient Near Eastern Comparison

THE CONTRIBUTION OF EGYPTIAN WISDOM TO THE STUDY OF BIBLICAL WISDOM LITERATURE

Nili Shupak

Although the wisdom genre was prevalent in many Ancient Eastern cultures, including Sumer, Babylon, Canaan, and even Emar (Syria), Egyptian wisdom has proved to be the most important for the study of biblical wisdom literature. As 1 Kgs 5:10 informs us, it was widely known and esteemed during the biblical period, Solomon's wisdom "surpassing the wisdom of all the people of the east (בני קדם), and all the wisdom of Egypt." The publication of this corpus thus constituted a watershed in the modern study of biblical wisdom literature.[1] This discussion demonstrates how comparison of the biblical and Egyptian wisdom corpora has helped to elucidate issues debated within the field of biblical studies: the dating of the biblical wisdom literature, the stages of its development, who wrote it and for whom, its *Sitz im Leben*, and—most recently—whether it constitutes a genre distinct from law and prophecy.[2]

The first part reviews Egyptian wisdom literature, highlighting the features that are significant for study of the biblical wisdom corpus. The second part discusses how it aids our understanding of issues relating to biblical wisdom literature.

---

1. Biblical quotations follow the RSV with minor modifications.
2. Although I shall touch on this issue indirectly, the reader is directed towards Sneed's article (ch. 2 in this volume) for a more extensive review of this subject.

Egyptian Wisdom Literature

Its Genres and Characteristics

Wisdom literature flourished in Egypt from the middle of the third millennium to the first centuries BCE.[3] Popular among members of the educated classes, the compositions were copied and handed down from generation to generation over the centuries. A considerable number having been preserved in a number of copies, most of these can be fully reconstructed, with thirty known works being extant to date. Like contemporaneous Ancient Near Eastern sapiential corpora, Egyptian wisdom consists of two subgenres—didactic and speculative.[4] The former is practical in nature, being designed to provide answers to quotidian questions and problems, such as how to succeed in business, fulfill professional obligations, and how to behave towards various types of people. The latter is critical, protesting against administrative and moral injustice and political, religious, and social failings. On occasion, following the admonitions, the reign of a future ideal king is depicted.

Both types understand the world in general, and human life in particular, to be ruled by the laws of *mꜣʿt*—justice and righteousness. Employing a vocabulary that reflects sapiential ideas and themes, they also share the goal of passing down knowledge derived from life experience and philosophy. This task being usually restricted to men of authority and standing, wisdom literature is always attributed to (real or fictional) authors, unlike other genres, which are mostly anonymous.[5]

The following discussion focuses on didactic wisdom, examining three sets of didactic texts ascribed to three types of authors: vizier's instructions to his son—the Instruction Addressed to Kagemni and the Instruction of Ptahhotep (end of the Old Kingdom and beginning of the

---

3. Egyptian possesses no term for "wisdom" as an abstract concept, this term being borrowed from biblical studies. The closest parallel is *rḫ* "to know."

4. The scholarly literature also refers to speculative wisdom as complaint or prophetic literature. For arguments against this approach and a discussion of the works belonging to this literary genre, see Shupak 1989–1990, 5–40.

5. The exceptions to this rule are the Instruction of a Man to His Son and the Loyalist Instruction. Although these have been regarded as the work of anonymous authors, Verhoeven (2009, 87–98) has recently suggested that the latter was composed by a vizier named Kairsu. See also Assmann 1983, 69, and n. 37 below.

Middle Kingdom); a king's instructions to his son—the Instruction of Djedefhor, the Instruction Addressed to Merikare, and the Instruction of Amenemhet (end of the Old Kingdom and the Eleventh and Twelfth Dynasties of the Middle Kingdom); and a scribe's instructions to his son—the Instruction of Any and the Instruction of Amenemope (Nineteenth and Twenty-First Dynasties, New Kingdom and beginning of the Third Intermediate period).[6] Within this complex two instructions are exceptional—the Instruction of a Man to His Son and the Loyalist Instruction (beginning of the Twelfth Dynasty, Middle Kingdom period). While these contain advice for sons destined to become high officials, they are primarily encomia to the king encouraging his subjects to serve him steadfastly and loyally.[7]

This genre is known in Egyptian as *sbꜣyt*, a term parallel to the Hebrew מוּסָר, deriving from the verb *sbꜣ*. The determinative depicting a man holding a staff, it designates both teaching and corporal punishment, thereby indicating the process whereby knowledge was transmitted from teacher to pupil in the ancient world—that is, by beating words into the student.[8] Used of any document designed to teach and instruct, *sbꜣyt* indicates not only the content of the work but also a literary genre, identified by its framework, structure, style, and language.

The most common form it takes is a father's instruction of his son—as in Proverbs and Ecclesiastes. Herein, the speaker-father frequently belongs to an upper or middle social class—a king, vizier, or scribe. Generally said to be advanced in years, he seeks to guide his son "in the way of life/god," drawing on his life experience to direct his son/heir into the proper path.

Works of this type customarily bear a title that refers to "teaching," "instruction" (*sbꜣyt*), or "teaching for life," the name of the author and his title(s), and the name of the addressee.[9] The prologue sets out the circum-

---

6. For the translation of the Egyptian texts, see Lichtheim (1973–1980) with occasional modifications by the author. The verse numbering of Any follows Quack (1994). The dates given here are general, the precise point at which these works were composed still being subject to debate.

7. With the exception of some samples from the Instruction of Ankhsheshonqy and the Instruction of Pap. Insinger, dated to the Ptolemaic period, which help to clarify issues in the older texts, this discussion does not address the Demotic Instructions.

8. Like *sbꜣyt*, מוּסָר denotes both instruction and corporal punishment; see Prov 1:8; 13:24; 15:5; 23:13. See Shupak 1993, 33–34.

9. Real-life father-son relationships are quite plausibly to be understood in this context, sons regularly inheriting their father's profession. Thus, for example, Ptah-

stances surrounding the handing down of the instruction—the father's senescence (Ptahhotep) or imprisonment (the Instruction of Ankhsheshonqy)—and its goal. The body of the composition contains advice, teaching, admonitions, and proverbs associated with the profession the son is destined to inherit from his father. It also adduces general ethical values and recommends ways of behavior in diverse life circumstances. The epilogue reinvokes the circumstances calling for the voicing of the instructions or its writing, and at times, also reiterating their target.[10]

This literary model remained constant over an extensive time period, the uniform structure, sophisticated stylistic features, and textual divisions suggesting that it began life as a written genre. While the framework occasionally employs narrative, the body of the text is poetic rather than prose in form, typically making use of rhythm, parallelism, wordplays, repetition of similar words or sounds, keywords, and refrains.[11] These literary artifices are supplemented by metaphors and similes taken from daily life.[12] Different types of proverbs can be discerned—those comparing two things

---

hotep refers to the son as his father's "staff of old age"—a designation indicating an assistant or apprentice. At the same time, the relationship also clearly serves as a literary device—as in the Loyalist Instruction.

10. In some works, not all these parts are extant or the order in which they appear differs. In some, the epilogue possesses a divergent nature—as the argument between the father and son in the Instruction of Any—or is absent altogether.

11. For examples of stylistic means, see, e.g., the Instruction of Amenemope: For parallelisms (members, verses, chapters), see Amenemope 1, 7–8; 5, 10–11; 24, 9–10 (synonymous); 3, 11–12; 5, 20–6, 12; 10, 10–11 (antithetic); 4, 4–5; 4, 12–13; 5, 12–13; 6, 14–15 (synthetic). For repetitions of expressions, verses, and proverbs, see "secure in the hand of the god" (14, 1; 24, 20), "abomination to god" (x 4 times in chapters 10, 13, 17); "If you come before him in the morning" (20, 16; 26, 4); "If you make your life with these (words), your children will see [their good results]" (5, 18–19; 17, 15–16). For identical openings of consecutive verses, see the "better ... than ... ($3h$ ... r) repetitions in chapter 6. For the use of keywords, see field ($3ht$ [x 3]; sht [x 2]), furrow (x 2), and to be safe (x 2) in chapter 6 and hidden (x 3), men (x 2), tongue (x 3), belly (x 2), good (x 3) in chapter 8. For wordplays, see "the boat of the silent – in the wind" (a play on the homonyms $m3^cw$ "wind" and $m3^c$ "true" [a typical appellation for the silent man, who is called "the true silent man"] in chapter 7:10, 11); the "heated man" who "tears down, he builds up with his tongue" (chapter 9:12, 3), resembles the creator god who "tears down and builds up every day (chapter 25:24, 15). For dual meanings, see $wd3$ signifying "storehouse/to be safe" at the end of chapter 1:4, 6, etc.

12. The crocodile thus serves as a symbol of unexpected danger and covetousness and an object of honor and fear; see Merikare 98; Ptahhotep 168; Amenemope 13, 4; 22, 9–10. Sailing in a boat similarly constitutes a metaphor for life in this world and a

via the term "like" or "as" (*mi*), comparisons without any conjunctions, and "better ... than ..." (*ꜣḫ ... r*) proverb.[13] The author frequently adduces proverbs in support of his statements.[14]

The instructions are generally formulated in the second person as a positive or negative command: Thus do/do not do. On occasion, they are conditional and refer to specific life situations: If you find yourself in x situation, act in such and such a manner.[15] Infrequently, the body of the instruction is formulated in the first-person singular, the author's experience forming the basis from which he draws a moral (cf. the royal instructions in Merikare and Amenemhet). In the majority of cases, the first verse of each section is distinguished by red rubric (heading) (see Ptahhotep, Merikare, Amenemhet, and the Loyalist Instruction). The Instruction of Amenemope is unique in being systematically divided into chapters headed by a number in red. In some works, the end of the verse is also denoted by red dot.[16]

Egyptian wisdom literature also employs distinctive language and terminology.[17] Various terms designate teaching—*sbꜣyt* (instruction), *mtr(t)* "reproof," *sḫr* "counsel. Education and study are signified by *sbꜣ* "to teach," *mtr* "to reprove," *sḏm* "to hear, listen," *rdi ḥꜣty* "to give one's heart to," *wḥʿ* "to explain, resolve."[18] The results of acquiring/failing to acquire knowledge are designated in wisdom terms: *rḫ* "(practical and acquired) knowledge,"

---

means to gain the next; see Ptahhotep 93; Amenemhet E15 ; Amenemope 4, 12–5, 6; 10, 10–11; 20, 5–6.

13. For proverbs likening two things, see Ptahhotep 358; Merikare 94; Amenemope, 5, 14–15; 6, 1–2, 7–8; 26, 6–7. For proverbs of equivalence, see Merikare 31; Amenemope 7, 16–17; 17, 7; 26, 6. For "better than" proverbs, see Merikare 129; Amenemope 9, 5–8; 16, 11–14.

14. Cf. Ptahhotep 116, 343; Merikare 128–129; Amenemope 19, 11–13; 20, 5–6; 26, 6–7. See in particular the ends of the chapters in Amenemope 5: 18–19; 17, 15–16; 23, 8–11. See Gunn 1926, 282–84.

15. The conditional occurs primarily in the older instructions—Kagemni, Ptahhotep, Merikare.

16. The divisions and verse endings marked in red ink were apparently teaching aids indicative of the material to be studied. The custom of denoting the verse endings fell into decline towards the end of the first millennium, each verse subsequently being written separately with a space in between (see Amenemope): see Brunner 1988, 76–78.

17. For a detailed discussion for each term, see Shupak 1993.

18. *Sḏm*—whose meanings range from listening/obeying to understanding and assimilating the sage's words—functions as a keyword in the opening section and con-

si₃ "charismatic wisdom," *s₃₃* "acquired knowledge/charismatic wisdom/ professional expertise;" the instructor is referred to as *rḫ/rḫ iḫt*—that is, the "one who knows/wise man," *s₃₃* "sage," or *ḥmww* "craftsman, skilled"; the one who fails to avail himself of the instruction is a fool—*iwty- ḥ₃ty* one who "lacks understanding, sense," *ḥm* "simpleton," *wḫ₃* "fool," *gwš* "crooked." Human types and traits are frequently adduced: the *grw/grw m₃ʿ* "(truly) man silent man," the *qb* "cool-tempered, level-headed man," the *ḥrw* "calm" person, the *šmm/ḥmm* "heated man," the *ʿwn-ib* "covetous person," the *ḥnty* "greedy person," *grg* "to lie" (primarily in speech), the *(s)ʿḏ₃* "to lie, to behave falsely," and so on. Terms for sapiental sayings and proverbs: *ḫn* "saying," *ṯs* a "well-constructed saying, maxim," *mdt nfrt* "good speech," and so on. Parts of the body are identified as serving as instruments for acquiring wisdom: *ns* "tongue" (speech), *ib/ḥ₃ty* "heart" (thoughts and intellect), *ḫt* "belly" (thought, drive and emotion).

As this brief survey indicates, wisdom thus constituted a delimited literary genre in Egypt characterized by distinctive linguistic, stylistic, literary features and devices.

The Ideology of Egyptian Wisdom Literature

The Image of Man

Like wisdom literature in general, Egyptian wisdom literature is traditionally anthropocentric. While it does not engage in lengthy descriptions of human traits, it addresses human action and modes of behavior whence human nature may be deduced. At its basis lies the belief that the world is organized in accordance with a cosmic order established at creation—*m₃ʿt*, that is, justice, truth. The objective of human behavior is harmony with this principle: "Great is justice, lasting is its effect, unchallenged since the time of Osiris. One punishes the transgressor of its laws" (Ptahhotep 88–90).[19] Conduct that violates this order must be corrected—deeds and acts that infringe the social ethic (falsehood, covetousness, gluttony, wrath, lack of restraint, gossip, etc.) or the religious framework (disdain of the

---

stitutes a leitmotif throughout. Cf. the play on this root in the epilogue of *Ptahhotep* (507–63) in particular.

19. No term parallel to *m₃ʿt* existing in any modern language, it is translated, according to the context, as truth, justice, righteousness, or order.

temple and its attendants, impropriety during religious rituals, etc.).[20] The teacher-sage's task being to set young men on the path of life that leads to *mꜣꜥt*, he instructs them in how to establish, maintain, and exemplify this by inculcating integrity, truth, modesty, self-restraint, self-control, silence, generosity, mercy, and so on.[21] Human beings, characteristics, and values are frequently categorized according to antithetical pairings in order to sharpen the opposing concepts—the wise versus the fool, the silent versus the heated man, the silent versus the greedy man, the good woman versus the evil woman, and so on.[22]

The Attitude toward Cult and Religion

Didactics, education, and the inculcation of proper socioethical behavior lying at its center, Egyptian wisdom rarely adduces rites or rituals. While it presumes the existence of the cultus, few instructions relate to the offering of sacrifices, the celebration of holy days, or the performance of ceremonies.[23] Among the extant Egyptian didactic wisdom works from the Old and Middle Kingdoms, only one contain detailed references to worship of the divinity—Merikare (63–67) addressing the erection of monuments, the priest's daily obligations in the temple, and the offering sacrifices and meal-offerings. While the king commands his son "Supply the offerings, revere the god" (112), this instruction relates to a monarch-elect, one of whose principal duties was service as high priest in the temple. Alongside the common request—issued in a pragmatic tone—that the addressee "Work for god with offerings that make the altar flourish, he will work for you also, with carvings (of inscriptions)" (129–130; cf. 64, 66), Merikare

---

20. Cf. falsehood (Ptahhotep, epilogue 533; Amenemope 13, 5), covetousness (Ptahhotep proverb 19), spreading gossip (Ptahhotep proverb 8), etc.

21. The sage endorses *mꜣꜥt* and follows its path (Ptahhotep, epilogue, sections 1, 5, 7). The wise king possesses the essence of *mꜣꜥt* (Merikare 34) and speaks a "message of *mꜣꜥt*" (Amenemhet C1). The king orders the performance of *mꜣꜥt* (Merikare 46, 128) and officials are admonished to speak it in court (Man for His Son 9, 10; Amenemope 20, 14).

22. See Shupak 1993, 258–67; 2009, 245–50. While the good/evil woman do not appear in antithetical parallelism, the contrast can be adduced from a comparison of the sections dealing with these two figures, in the instructions of Ptahhotep and Any in particular: see Shupak 2011, 310–23.

23. Kagemni and Ptahhotep do not relate to any cultic demands; Djedefhor only refers to the ritual for the dead.

also contains the unique statement: "The character (or 'loaf,' Eg. *byt*) of the upright is preferred to the ox of the evildoer" (129)—that is, ethical behavior is preferable to the offering of sacrifices accompanied by wrongdoings.[24] Biblical scholars being familiar with such dicta in the prophetic literature, in the ensuing I shall return to the issue of whether this idea can in fact be adduced from this passage.[25]

When the ideal of personal piety began to emerge following the Amarna period, increased emphasis was placed upon religious and cultic aspects of human behavior. Thus, for example, Any cautions his addressees that they must act properly within the temple and as the god's statue is brought outside the temple and the believers turn to it to receive an oracle (16, 4–9; 17, 1–4; 20, 12–17). Meal offerings and sacrifices to the gods are also to be devotedly observed: "Incense is given them as daily food in order to strengthen the master of the revelations" (20, 17). While Amenemope—composed in roughly the same period—contains no direct demands for ritual practice, its author prohibits any falsification of the god's oracle when recorded (chapter 20), also cautioning against exploiting the temple and interfering in the appointment of those who serve in it (chapter 5). The temple also serves as the background against which the "silent man" and "hot-tempered man" are contrasted (chapter 4). Elsewhere, allusion is made to the daily prayer to the sun god, Aten, and the monument of the deceased erected in the temple that enables him to participate in the daily sacrifice to the god (10, 12–15; 11, 2–3).

These later instructions also reflect a special attitude that relates to the god's image as well as to his worship. Early Egyptian wisdom texts exhibit the belief that *mꜣꜥt*—which corresponds to the gods' will—is determined by acts and consequences. The person who conducts himself in accordance with it is thus rewarded, while he who violates it is punished: "One knows not what may happen, what god does when he punishes" (Kagemni 2, 2); "He who hears is beloved of god; he whom god hates does not hear" (Ptahhotep 545–546). The deterministic approach alluded to in the last verse is also reflected throughout Ptahhotep.[26] Statements such as "He who opposed you, they [the gods] hate him; misfortune was declared on him in the womb" (ibid., 216–217) and the "perfect" son is "god's gift"

---

24. With *byt* signifying both "character" and "loaf of bread," a wordplay appears to exist here.

25. See p. 288 below.

26. Contra Miosi 1982, 78–83.

(ibid., 633) indicate the fact that a man's fate is considered to be determined by the god before he is born. This perception contravenes the cause and effect/act and consequences principle, and becomes more dominant in New Kingdom wisdom compositions.

Any juxtaposes the earlier idea of god as punisher—expressed in the request that the fate of the enemy be placed in his hands (B 15, 12–16; 20, 10–12; 21, 14–16)—with the new spirit of personal piety: "Man is in the image of God" (23, 8–9).[27] At the same time, the gulf between human beings and the gods—already evinced in such statements as "People's schemes do not prevail; god's command prevails" (Ptahhotep, 115–116)— grows ever wider: "Does (such a thing) not happen to men? Their plan is one thing, but that of the Master of Life differs from it" (Any 21, 9–10).[28] The contrast between divine omnipotence and human feebleness is even more forcefully illustrated in Amenemope: "Man is clay and straw; god is his builder" (chapter 25). God is the supreme punisher (chapters 2, 3, 6), "sealing (the verdict) with his finger" (chapter 18). His ways are unknown to mortals: "You do not know the plans of god, and should not be weeping for tomorrow" (chapter 21:22, 5–6 = chapter 22:23, 8–9).

Lying and cheating—traditionally the individual's responsibility (Cf. Ptahhotep 133; Any 15, 9; 18, 4–9)—are now explained as constituting an "abomination to god."[29] God decides the fate of man as he wishes, without taking the latter's plans into consideration: "The words men say are one thing, the deeds of god are another" (chapter 18:19, 14–17). The link between responsibility and personal success is thus severed. While a person who followed *mꜣʿt* could formerly have expected to prosper, now his success lies in the hands of a god who grants it arbitrarily: "*Mꜣʿt* is a great gift of god; he gives it to whom he loves (or wishes)" (chapter 20:21,

---

27. The Instruction of Any makes no reference to *mꜣʿt*. For the significance of this fact, see Quack 1994, 71–72.

28. See Volten 1937, 118, who adds the word "master"—a logical insertion in light of the fact that the passage refers to the fickleness of fate and man's inability to control his destiny, similar to the words of the sage in Amenenope 19, 16–17. For a contrary view, see Quack 1994, 72.

29. Occurring four times in Amenenope, this expression alludes to false, hypocritical speech (chapter 10 [x 2]), the recording of false testimony (chapter 13), and deceitful weights and measures (chapter 17). In Any, it is applied to attacking one's opponent (15, 13) and shouting in the temple (17, 11–12), replacing the expression "abomination of the *ka*" (referred to thrice in Ptahhotep) and similarly referring to unseemly social behavior (124–125; 159–160; 188–190).

5-6).[30] Within this framework, man's only recourse is to submit himself—like the ideal "silent one"—into god's hands: "Settle into the arms of god" (22, 7-8; 23, 10-11);[31] "You shall pray to the Aten ... he will give you what you need for this life and you will be safe from fear" (end of chapter 7).

The Social Background of Egyptian Wisdom Literature

The wisdom instructions known from the Old and Middle Kingdoms are customarily the work of prominent upper-class figures. Thus, for example, the Instructions of Kagmeni and Ptahhotep are attributed to viziers, those of Djedefhor, Merikare, and Amenemhet to kings. Their intended audience thus being heirs to the throne and/or high-ranking officials, their subject matter relates to such issues as the viziers' judicial role (Ptahhotep, proverbs 13, 17,[32] 28-29), the fostering of loyal servants (Ptahhotep, proverb 14), the way in which the affluent should be treated, compassion towards lower-ranking persons, generosity to one's family and the needy (ibid., 74-77, 264-267, 339, 481-494; et al.), avoidance of boasting in wealth (ibid., proverbs 9, 30), recognition that "A little something stands for much" (Kagemni 1, 3-6), and so on.

They also frequently reflect a practical, utilitarian attitude. Ptahhotep recognizes the possibility of changes in status owing to vicissitudes of fate—perhaps tomorrow you will need the help of those dependent upon you today: "Sustain your friends with what you have ... one knows not what will be" (Ptahhotep 339-349, 175-177, 428-432). The welfare of senior officials is recognized as dependent both upon those subject to his authority and those who are in charge of him. Ptahhotep addresses these issues at length, recommending submissiveness and respect to those over one (60-67, 119-144, 145-150, 175-180, 388-398, 441-447, etc.).

The Loyalist Instruction and the Instruction of a Man for His Son similarly address high-ranking officials in the king's court and administrators, whom the lower classes exist to serve: being a "useful flock for their masters," "One lives by the work of their hands" (Loyalist Instruction, chapters

---

30. For a divergent interpretation, see Lichtheim 1992, 99–100.
31. Cf. also the conclusion of chapters 5 and 25.
32. Contra Vernus (1999), this text—inscribed on the tomb of the vizier Rekhmire (see Shupak 1992, 14)—clearly evinces that the instruction is directed towards high rather than lower middle-class officials.

9 and 14). A significant disparity exists between this view and the identification with the wretched and ill-fated found in later sapiential texts.

The shift to the new emphasis is evident in the New Kingdom and Third Intermediate period instructions of Any and Amenemope.[33] A minor official, a scribe in the queen's mortuary temple, one of Any's principal themes is the proper attitude to be exhibited toward those in high positions: submission, respect, a willingness to be helpful that borders on bribery, and refraining from "using one's elbows" to get ahead (21, 11–13). A talented man can become a scribe even without the necessary pedigree: "The head of the treasury has no son; the master of the seal has no heir. The scribe is highly respected for his hand; his office has no children" (20, 5–6).[34]

Amenemope, who served in the agricultural administration, was also a mid-level official. Reflecting the personal piety of his time—expressed most notably in the cultivation of compassion towards the unfortunate—he speaks in the "language of the poor," taking the side of the weak: "Beware of robbing the wretch and acting violently against the cripple" (chapter 2); "Do not covet the property of the poor, nor hunger after his bread" (chapter 11); "Do not assess a man who has nothing.... If you find a large debt against a poor man, make it into three parts; release two, let one remain" (16, 5–7; cf. 20, 21–21, 4; 26, 13–14). He also directs his attention to widows and the handicapped—dwarves, the blind and the lame.

The Egyptian wisdom instructions from the end of the Old through to the New Kingdom and Third Intermediate periods thus represent the worldview and life experience of various officials—from the scribes in government offices dependent on the elite to those underneath them. As Ecclesiastes notes, each official exists within a chain of command: "For the high official is watched by a higher, and there are yet higher ones over them" (5:7).

The Development of Egyptian Wisdom Literature

Over the course of the three thousand years in which it flourished, neither the literary framework (fatherly instruction to son) nor purpose (directing the son-pupil into the right paths of life) of Egyptian wisdom

---

33. For the disparity between Middle and New Kingdom wisdom literature, the former being associated with the social elite of the royal court and the latter with the "sub-elite scribes," see Ragazolli 2010, 157–70.

34. Cf. Merikare 62.

literature underwent any fundamental transformation. Earlier material being adapted and expanded, the content changed in line with historical circumstances, the issues faced by specific generations, and the (real or fictitious) identity of the authors and their social standing.

With the establishment of a central government during the Old Kingdom period (2682–2145 BCE), the need arose to educate a whole class of officials. The Instruction Addressed to Kagemni and the Instruction of Djedefhor were composed to help meet this demand. The spirit of this period was informed by the principles of *mꜣꜥt* and act and consequence, the sages' advice relating primarily to interpersonal relations in acknowledgement of the fact that the individual formed part of society. The image of the ideal man as modest, meticulous, silent, and calm that continued to lie at the center of the sapiential worldview emerged at a very early stage (cf. Kagemni). In the only text to have survived in full from this period (the end of the Old Kingdom/beginning of the Middle Kingdom)—the Instruction of Ptahhotep—reference is thus made for the first time to the personal/family circle—sons, wives, and women in general. The lengthy epilogue in praise of heeding fatherly advice, set within a didactic framework, recalls the debate between a father and son in the Instruction of Any dated centuries later.

Following the First Intermediate period (2145–2025/2020 BCE), during which the central government collapsed and a wave of anarchy swept across the country, the stabilization of the government during the Middle Kingdom (2019–1794/1793 BCE) led to increased efforts to reinforce the monarchy's status and position. The four instructions written in this period thus unsurprisingly focus on the king. In Merikare and Amenemhet, the king—or the author writing in his name—draws on his life experience and historical circumstances in order to advise his son/heir on foreign and internal affairs. Both texts present the pharaoh in unusual fashion—as a mortal capable of error and acknowledging misfortune rather than the omnipotent son of god.

The Loyalist Instruction and the Instruction of a Man for His Son—from the same period—on the other hand, espouse the traditional figure of the ideal king, accentuating his proximity to the gods. The principles that had existed in the Old Kingdom prior to the crisis witnessed during the Intermediate period now being questioned, these texts champion loyalty to the king, representing the welfare of all Egyptians as being dependent completely on his mercy. This fact is reflected in the various rewards he grants to his loyal supporters—from education, security, and economic success in this world, to preparations for the next. Juxtaposed alongside these are instructions regarding the traits high officials should seek to cultivate—silence, restraint, modesty, generosity, friendship, and similar traits. These resemble the ideal human characteristics fostered during the Old Kingdom. The pursuit of mꜣʿt they seek to instill in their addressees is intended to enable them to "pass through life in serenity" (Loyalist Instruction, Introduction).

This horizon is expanded in works dating from the Middle Kingdom period, the reward and punishment meted out now extending beyond this world into the next. Merikare, for example, thus notes that the consequences of a man's deeds follow him after death, when they are weighed and judged. The Instruction of Amenemhet and the Loyalist Instruction both contain extensive advice concerning the preparations a man should make for his death.

The sapiential instructions from the New Kingdom period (1550–1070/1069 BCE) continue to indicate how a man can succeed and maintain good relations with his intimate social circle—family, neighbors, friends, and superiors, and so on. At the same time as addressing traditional themes such as the need to build a house and marry, the eschewing of adultery with strange women, quarrels and lies, the use of restraint and forbearance, good table manners, and so on, they also, however, reflect the piety characteristic of the age following the religious revolution of the Amarna period (1388–1334 BCE).[35] This stressed the direct contact between a man and god, especially faith in a personal protector god. Thus, for example, Any is marked by a religious tone not found in any previous works, the son addressed being admonished to behave properly on diverse ceremonial and cultic occasions. Similarly, the principle that whoever clings to mꜣʿt will be rewarded is gradually replaced in Amenemope by the belief that men are completely dependent upon god who, holding mꜣʿt in his hands, determines men's fate as he wishes, irrespective of their desires, or actions (19, 14–17). Granting mꜣʿt arbitrarily to whomever he "loves" (21, 5–6), a human being has no choice but to place himself in god's hands, in the manner of the "true silent man" who "positions himself on the side"— behaves modestly and trusts in god (Amenemope chapter 4).

The new spirit is also reflected in a revised ethical perception. While the social framework had formerly taken center stage, the religious ethic

---

35. For the close affinities between Amenemope and Ptahhotep, see Shupak 2012.

now comes to occupy a sizable portion of Egyptian wisdom literature. The *gr* "silent man"—the social ideal (Kagemni, Ptahhotep)—gives way to *gr mꜣꜥ* "the true silent man" or ideal religious adherent. Life becoming increasingly complex, "Man adapts himself to the will of god, even if he does not understand it" (Brunner 1988, 57).

The New Kingdom sapiential texts also begin to challenge the traditional monolithic view and acknowledge the possibility of differences of opinion. The argument between father and son in Any, for example, reflects two divergent concepts of education, the father espousing the traditional concept that everyone can acquire knowledge, the son maintaining that "Each man is led by his nature" (22, 14–15), not everyone is suited for learning.

The content of the instructions thus varies, some reflecting historical events (Merikare, Amenemhet), others religious developments (Any, Amenemope). While the advice given in the earlier documents addresses the elite, high officialdom (Kagemni, Ptahhotep, Loyalist Instruction, Man for His Son) or heirs to the royal throne (Merikare, Amenemhet), the later texts relate to low- or middle-ranking officials (Any, Amenemope). All nonetheless seek the same goal—schooling towards the living of the perfect life as conceptualized in terms of health, wealth, dignity, and reputation.

The Authors of the Egyptian Wisdom Literature and Its *Sitz im Leben*

One of the key questions debated by scholars is whether the authors to whom the Egyptian wisdom texts are attributed were real or fictitious.[36] There is no reason to doubt the identity of the authors of the instructions of the scribes Any and Amenemope; the scribes were the circle creating Egyptian literature in general and the wisdom instructions in particular. This is not the situation with the alleged authors of other works—Kagemni, Ptahhotep, Djedefhor, Merikare, and Amenemhet— who were well-known figures in ancient Egypt. While Kagemni and Ptahhotep were historical personages, they lived long after the period attributed to them in the instructions delivered in their name. The Instruction of Amenemhet is ascribed, according to the Egyptian sources themselves, to the

---

36. Cf. Grumach 1972, 20–21; Parkinson 2002, 237–39. According to the latter, the framework of handing down a legacy or a will from father to son constitutes a literary device rather than a real circumstance.

scribe Kheti.[37] One may, therefore, assume that the reference is to fictitious authors. Either way, during the New Kingdom these texts were regarded as the authentic writings of the authors to whom they are attributed. The famous Ramesside Pap. Chester Beatty IV contains a eulogy referring to the written works of these men as their "heirs":

> (2,5) As for the learned scribes [sšw rḫ-iḫt]
> from the time after the gods,
> who foretold [sr] what was to come,
> their names remain forever …
> (2,7) They did not make for themselves pyramids of copper,
> or stelae of iron,
> They left no children as heirs …
> to pronounce their names;
> They made heirs for themselves of books,
> and instructions [sbꜣywt] they had composed …
> (2,9) The instructions [sbꜣywt] are their pyramids,
> the reed pen their child,
> and the back of the stone their wife …
> (2,11) Portals and graves [lit. mansions] were made for them
> (but) they have crumbled.
> Their ka-servants [i.e., mortuary service] are [gone]
> Their tombstones are covered with dust,
> Their graves are forgotten;
> (but) their names are (still) pronounced because of their books [lit. papyrus rolls]
> (2,13) which they made when they existed …
> (3,3) Man perishes, his corpse is dust,
> all his relatives come to the ground;
> (but) it is the book that makes him remembered
> in the mouth of the reciter.
> More effective is a book [lit. a papyrus roll] than a well built house,
> Than a tomb in the west [i.e., the necropolis];
> Better than a sturdy castle,
> Than a stela in the temple.
> (verso 2,5–3,10; 6,11–6,14)

---

37. Pap. Chester Beatty IV states that Kheti was one of the eight great writers of ancient Egypt, explicitly observing that "He wrote a papyrus scroll with the instruction of King Shetepibre (Amenemhet I)." Amongst the eight are Djedefhor, Ptahhotep, and Kairsu (author of the Loyalist Instruction).

Uniquely, this gives us a glimpse into the way ancient Egyptians regarded their cultural heroes. The authors of the instructions (sbꜣywt) are described as "learned scribes" (sšw rḫ-iḫt) who express their thoughts in well-phrased maxims known as ṯs "knot(s)."[38] Strikingly, they are said to possess the art of foreseeing the future (sr)—an apparent reference to their ability to understand mꜣʿt, the set rules controlling cosmic and human history, which imbues them with the capability to give useful advice, referring to both the present and the future [39] The authors of the Egyptian wisdom literature are called "learned scribes" in the Pap. Chester Beatty IV. This fits with the identification of the authors of Any and Amenemope as scribes. Thoth, the god of the latter, also being the god of wisdom, the ancient Egyptians made no distinction between the scribal institution and the circle responsible for the composition of wisdom texts. The composers of the Egyptian instructions, therefore were the scribes whose literary activity included the writing of various literary genres, among them sapiential literature. The special nature of wisdom literature stems from its literary genre rather than from the group of people responsible for creating it.

The scribe-author is frequently portrayed as a venerable aged man tasked with transmitting the wisdom of the ancients to his sons/heirs/pupils:[40]

> It goes well with him when he has heard.
> When he grows old and attains honor,
> He will tell likewise to his children,
> Renewing the teaching [sbꜣyt] of his father ...
> He will tell the children,
> So that they will tell their children. (Ptahhotep, 588–594)

This may be compared with the following:

> Justice [mꜣʿt] comes to him [the sage] distilled,
> Like the sayings of the ancestors.

---

38. For the Egyptian term ṯs and its Hebrew equivalent, see p. 287 below.

39. See Fox 1980, 127–29; Brunner 1966, 29–35.

40. Kagemni's father is referred to in the epilogue as knowing the "ways and character of men." Ptahhotep, who asks the king to appoint his son after him, opens his statements with a detailed depiction of his senescence. Any's and Amenemope's sons being identified as scribes, their fathers can be assumed not to have been young when they came to write their texts. Merikare's father recalls memories of times past, with Amenemhet being described as speaking from the next world.

Copy your fathers, those who anteceded you ...
See, their words endure in the writing.
Open that you may read and imitate the learned one. (Merikare, 35–36)

The scribe constitutes a link in the handing down of traditional wisdom, which reaches him "distilled"—that is, in an abridged form, his authority deriving from this process and his life experience. Such figures were not only lauded and esteemed but were sometimes venerated as saints, their graves in Memphis forming cult and pilgrimage sites.[41]

The authors, copiers, and teachers of sapiential instructions were all active within the Egyptian educational framework, which varied according to time and place. In all periods there operated a private instruction from father to son or from professional patron to apprentice, alongside a more official learning that was situated in the king's court and in the temple in the capital city, and probably in other large cities as well, and later, within a system of guilds of scribes.

The rise of the New Kingdom witnessed the development of a new educational institution known as the House of Life. Located in proximity to the temple, this formed a kind of school of higher education for those seeking to specialize in various sciences—medicine, magic, omenology, embalming, astronomy, foreign languages, international relations, and so on.[42] The most detailed extant evidence regarding the mode of study comes from the artisans village of Deir el-Medina during the Ramesside period. Significantly, this contains no designated school structure, students apparently meeting outside or in a private residence in the provinces.[43]

---

41. Remnants of the cult of Djedefhor, Kagemni, and Ptahhotep from the Old and New Kingdom periods have been discovered at Giza: see Shupak 2001, 543–44, and n. 30 above.

42. Significantly, this institution is referred to in the Book of the Temple (see below) as an independent institution connected to the royal house but without any link to the temple area. This location may reflect the fact that the curriculum included sciences studies by students intended for various positions and not necessarily for priesthood (Quack 2002, 171). Thus far only one House of Life—dated to the Eighteenth Dynasty—has been discovered, at Tel El-Amarna. It is plausible to assume that one also existed at Elephantine during the ninth–sixth centuries BCE and at Edfu during the Greek period: see Burkard 1980, 79–115.

43. This despite the vigorous educational activity conducted therein—attested by the numerous ostraca bearing school exercises; see McDowell 1996; Hagen 2007, 38–51; Warnemünde 2011, 21–22. The approximately 150 ostraca discovered in the

In the capital, the king's sons and those of his officials studied together in the royal court and temple. From the Middle Kingdom onwards, an educational institution known as the *Kap*, located in the king's court, provided an education for Egyptian princes, children of relatively low origins, and the sons of the rulers of conquered countries brought to Egypt specifically for this purpose. Merikare, for example, refers to a man of virtue with whom the prince "chanted the writings"—that is, studied with him in the palace (line 51).

Our knowledge about studies in the temple has recently been enriched by Joachim F. Quack's endeavor to reconstruct the Book of the Temple. Dated to the Middle Kingdom or beginning of the New Kingdom and preserved in hundreds of fragments from the Roman period (Quack 2002: 159–71), this contains "instructions for a senior teacher (Oberleher)" who is in charge of the education of the priests' sons/heirs. The learning materials include guidelines for performing songs of praise, behavior befitting the temple, rules for conducting rituals, and instructions concerning the needs of the palace and different regions across Egypt. While the study corpus designed for the priests does not contain any wisdom instructions, Quack is convinced that these formed part of the reading material housed in the temple's library. He thus assumes that they are hiding within the general instructions regarding proper behavior.

Most significant in the present context is a corpus of school-related writings from the Ramesside period published by Sir Alan Gardiner (1937).[44] This corpus sheds light on the atmosphere of the ancient Egyptian school, the identity of the teachers and students, the study methods employed, and the material learned. Classical wisdom works formed the backbone of the curriculum, their copying and memorization serving as one of the primary rubrics for learning how to read and write. This fact

---

temple of Ramses II at Ramesseum containing material from sapiential texts, letters, and beginners' textbook known as *Kemit* (i.e., the complete), together with exercises for writing hieroglyphics and drawings of figures, suggest the existence of a school there during this period. A letter from the end of the Twentieth Dynasty similarly indicates that such an institution may also have existed in the temple of Mot at Karnak; see Brunner 1957; Schlott 1989; Wente 1995, 2011–21; Warnemünde 2011, 16–22.

44. This corpus, published under the title *Late Egyptian Miscellanies*, was translated by Caminos (1954) into English. It includes exchanges of letters between teachers and students, encomia to the king and to the scribe's profession, prayers to the gods, epistolary formulae, wisdom instructions, etc.

is attested by the dozens—on occasion even hundreds—of poor-quality copies done using cheap writing materials (wooden and stone tablets and ostraca) that served the students and apprentice scribes in the circles of the Egyptian school.[45] These copies frequently contain selections from the works the students studied, sometimes also bearing the teacher's corrections marked in red ink.

The plethora of sapiential quotations found in other literary genres—royal inscriptions, autobiographies, funerary literature, and cultic texts—indicate that this genre formed an integral part of the regular education of the professional scribes. It thus constituted part of the upper class's oral repertoire.[46] The great esteem in which these writings were held is manifest by the lengthy period of time over which they continued to be handed down, copies being made hundreds or even thousands of years after the composition of the original texts.[47]

---

45. Over two hundred ostraca of Amenemhet, dozens of Djedefhor, over seventy of the Loyalist Instruction, approximately a hundred and fifty of the Instruction of a Man for His Son, seven copies of Ptahhotep, and eight copies of Amenemope have been discovered.

46. Intellectuals were accustomed to appealing to sapiential instructions in proof of their argument or as a way of showing off their erudition. Thus, for example, in the Nineteenth-Dynasty Pap. Anastasi I, the scribe Hori accuses his colleague, Amenemope, of quoting the words of Djedefhor without understanding them: "You have come (to me) loaded with great secrets; you told me a wisdom saying (*ts*) of Djedefhor. (But) you do not know whether it is good (positive) or bad (negative), what chapter comes before or after it" (11, 1–2). An instructive example also occurs in the Eighteenth Dynasty Installation of a Vizier, wherein the king adduces Ptahhotep (264–269; 418) in order to reinforce the code of juridical behavior; see Brunner 1988, 38; Guglielmi 1984, 354–55; Shupak 1992, 14–16; The custom of quoting from such works continued through the eighth century BCE into the Hellenistic-Roman period, with Djedefhor still being quoted in the second century CE; for additional examples, see Guglielmi 1984, 347–64; Brunner 1979, 105–71. The fact that they also occur in other genres and constituted part of private libraries evinces that they were also frequently used outside formal educational circles; see Osing 1997, 139–42; Hagen 2012, 243–45.

47. Although the majority of these copies have reached us from Ramesside school circles (Shupak 2001), the copying of classical works continued until a much later date. Thus, for example, copies of Djedefhor, Amenemhet, Any, and Amenemope have survived from the Twenty-Fifth/Twenty-Sixth Dynasties: see Jasnow 1999, 194–95; Hagen 2012, 244–46.

The Contribution of Egyptian Wisdom Literature to the Understanding of Biblical Wisdom Literature

Among ancient wisdom literatures the Egyptian corpus is most relevant to the study of biblical literature. Within the latter, the Instruction of Amenemope—addressed to his youngest son and dated to the eleventh–tenth centuries BCE—is the most significant. The publication of this document some ninety years ago (1923) constituted a turning point in the study of biblical wisdom literature and its comparison with biblical sapiential texts has remained firmly on the research agenda ever since.[48] While Proverbs also exhibits substantive and literary affinities with other Egyptian wisdom instructions, Amenemope is unique in providing direct literal parallelisms. These occur in particular in the first part of the third collection in Proverbs known as The Words of the Wise (Prov 22:17–23:11).

Having discussed the direct parallels between the Words of the Wise and the Instruction of Amenemope extensively elsewhere (see Shupak 2005, 203–20), in the following I shall focus on the contact between Egyptian wisdom instructions and biblical wisdom literature in general.

The Contact between Egyptian and Biblical Wisdom

The two bodies resemble one another in structure, literary form, style, vocabulary, and principal topics.[49] As observed above, Egyptian didactic wisdom instructions typically open with a prologue that sets out the work's title, purpose, and author's and addressees' identity. The first collection in Proverbs evinces a similar prologue (1:1–6). On occasion, the reason for the instruction's composition and/or transmission are noted either at the beginning or conclusion. Thus, for example, Ptahhotep opens with a poem depicting how the Egyptian sage was prompted to write his work due to

---

48. The only complete papyrus to have survived—dated to the mid-seventh century BCE—is that in the British Museum (10474). Seven fragmentary copies have also been discovered, the majority of which are ascribed to the Saitic and Persian periods (sixth–fifth centuries BCE), but two belong to the Twenty-First/Twenty-Second Dynasties (eleventh–eighth centuries BCE).

49. The following discussion refers to Proverbs as a whole rather than the nine collections comprising it. A detailed comparison of the latter type would require a separate study, which lies beyond the scope of the present discussion.

his realization of his advanced age (lines 1–23). This text displays affinities with the description of old age at the end of Ecclesiastes (12:1–7).

Like the—fictitious or real—royal authors of such Egyptian wisdom works as Djedefhor, Merikare, and Amenemhet, Proverbs and Ecclesiastes are also attributed to a monarch: King Solomon.[50] Similarly, like Any and Amenemope, the third (22:17–24:22) and fourth (24:23–34) collections in Proverbs are ascribed to sages/scribes. Ecclesiastes also belongs to this class: "Besides being wise, Koheleth also taught the people knowledge, weighing and studying and arranging proverbs with great care" (12:9). The father-son framework typical of Egyptian sapiential instruction manuals likewise frequently occurs in the first and third collections of Proverbs, as well as in the epilogue to Ecclesiastes.

Egyptian wisdom literature being primarily poetic in form, it abounds in the types of parallelisms prevalent within the biblical wisdom corpus.[51] Interweaving similes and metaphors, Proverbs also makes use of similar literary devices culled from daily life in order to convey its message (cf. Prov 1:17–19; 6:6–8; 30:24–31). Like his Egyptian counterpart, the Hebrew sage reasons by quoting popular proverbs, typically introducing these by כי.[52] Both literary corpora also repeat words and/or use similar sounds. They thus share anaphoric structures—consecutive verses beginning with an identical particle or word: ל (Prov 1:2–4, 6), אל (3:27–31), ב (8:24–25, 27–29), איש (16:27–29), דור (30:11–14), תחת (ibid., 21–23), and so on; alliteration: בעס, כסה (12:16), רש, רשע, רע (28:3–5); homonyms: יום צרה and צר (Prov 24:10), סירים and סיר (Eccl 7:6); and double entendres: מחתת, a fracture/destruction and fear (Prov 10:15); אף and אפים, nose/anger (Prov 30:33).

Both wisdom literatures also make use of short proverbs—pithy conclusions or morals, instructions—admonitions and preaching by father to son/teacher to pupil, and didactic stories—narratives originating in per-

---

50. Although the eighth collection in Proverbs (31:1–9) is also ascribed to an ancient king (Lemuel) it concerns an instruction he received from his mother. Likewise, while the fifth collection (Prov 25–29) is not attributed directly to Hezekiah, it attests to the presence of wisdom-related activity in his court: "These also are proverbs of Solomon, which the men of King Hezekiah of Judah copied" (Prov 25:1).

51. See Prov 1:8–9, 15; 2:1; 3:1, 21; 23:15, 19, 22, 25–26; 24:13; Eccl 12:12. For examples of the stylistic phenomena characteristic of the Egyptian wisdom instructions detailed below, see n. 11 above.

52. See Prov 1:17, 32; 2:21–22; 6:23; 8:11; 6:10–11//24:33–35; Eccl 7:6; 9:4.

sonal experience, related in the first person, and intended to teach a lesson.⁵³ As in the Egyptian counterparts the proverbs in Proverbs can be divided into various types: those that liken two things via the use of "like" or "as" (Hebrew כ) (e.g., Prov 10:26; 25:13; 26:11); those that compare two things by juxtaposing them without any conjunction (e.g., Prov 11:22; 25:14, 25, 28; 26:17); and "better than" proverbs (Hebrew ... מ ... טוב) (e.g., Prov 17:1; 22:1; 28:6).⁵⁴

The use of antithetical words or concepts common in Egyptian wisdom is also prevalent in biblical wisdom.⁵⁵ On occasion identical pairs are adduced: the wise man (נבון) versus the fool (אויל/לץ) (e.g., Prov 9:8; 10:1, 8; 13:1; 15:20), wisdom (חכמות) versus foolishness (כסילות) (Prov 9), the wicked (רשע) versus the righteous (ישר/צדיק) (e.g., Prov 3:33; 10:16, 20, 24, 30; 11:11; 12:6).⁵⁶ The motif of the bad versus the good woman—only adduced as a direct antithesis in Prov 5—is interwoven throughout the first collection (Prov 2:16–19; 5; 6:24–35; 7:5–27), also concluding the book as a whole (31:3 versus 31:10–31).

Egyptian wisdom literature and biblical literature also share a common wisdom vocabulary—terms relating to education, study, instruction, contrasting traits, words of wisdom and the body organs linked to their acquisition, and so on.⁵⁷ The affinities derive primarily from the fact that the two corpora deal with similar topics rather than reflect any borrowing or influence. The authors' call for their audiences to "listen" (שמע // *sḏm*) to their instruction, for example, is typical of all ancient wisdom writings.⁵⁸ Both the Egyptian *sbȝyt* and its Hebrew parallel מוסר have a double meaning—to rebuke (with words) and to beat

---

53. For short proverbs, see, e.g., Prov 10:5; 13:7; Ptahhotep: "Good speech is more hidden than greenstone" (proverb 1); Merikare: "Good nature is a man's heaven" (31). For father-son instruction, see Proverbs, first (chs. 1–9) and third (chs. 22:17–24:22) collections; Eccl 12:12. For didactic stories, see Prov 4:1–4; 7:6–27; 24:30–34; Merikare 68–75; 119–125; Amenemhet C3–F7.

54. For rhetorical questions, see Prov 6:27–28, 17:16; Amenemhet A8–F9; the Instruction of a Man for His Son 3, 1–3. For proverb types in Egyptian wisdom, see pp. 268–69 above.

55. See p. 271 and n. 22 above.

56. For an extensive discussion of these pairs, see Shupak 1993, 238–39, 261–67.

57. For a detailed discussion of this topic, see Shupak 1993.

58. See Ptahhotep 49, 507–563; Amenemhet D1; Amenemope 3, 9; Prov 1:8; 2:2; 4:1, 10, 20; 5:1, 13; 8:32–34; 12:15, etc. See Shupak 1993, 51–57. Terms deriving from שמע // *sḏm* carry diverse senses: hearken, pay attention, obey, understand.

(with a rod)—indicating the principal ancient teaching method of beating knowledge into the student. The semantic field "fool" comprises two categories: the negative (Heb. נבל, ליץ, אויל, and Late Eg. *lḫ* and *swg*) and the positive (Heb. כסיל, פתי, חסר לב, and Egyptian *ḥm, iwty ḥꜣty*, and *wḫꜣ*). The expression "abomination to god"—or "abomination of the *ka* (man's personality)"—that occurs in Ptahhotep and Amenemope parallels the "abomination to the Lord" (תועבת ה') in Proverbs, both phrases relating to interpersonal relations and deceitful behavior.[59]

Other biblical terms exclusive to biblical sapiential literature are also elucidated by Egyptian literature, apparently being borrowed from the latter. Thus, for example, the Hebrew תחבלות (cf. Prov 11:14; 20:18; 24:6; Job 37:12)—derived from חֶבֶל "rope"—parallels the Egyptian *ṯs*, (lit. a knot) which signifies a pithy, well-formed wisdom saying that must be "unknotted" (Shupak 1993, 313–17).[60] The divine designation תֹּכֵן לִבּוֹת "who weighs the hearts," which occurs twice in the biblical texts—both in Proverbs (21:2; 24:12; cf. תכן רוחות "weighs the spirits" [16:2])—reflects the Egyptian belief in the judgment of the dead, in the course of which the deceased's heart is weighed on a scale against the goddess *Mꜣʿt* (justice) or her symbol, and Thoth, as the god of wisdom, records the verdict (Shupak 2014b: 2–5). The expressions חדרי-בטן "innards of the belly" as denoting the seat of human reason and thought (cf. Prov 18:8//26:22; 20:27, 30) and איש חמה "heated man" (together with its synonyms)—also exclusive to Proverbs—are similarly clearly borrowed from Egyptian motifs.[61]

Biblical wisdom literature dealing—like its venerable counterpart—with questions and issues posed by human life, the two corpora also address with similar topics, concepts, and ideas: the need to heed and obey

---

59. The phrase occurs twelve times in Proverbs, e.g., 3:32; 6:16–19; 11:1, 20; 12:22. See Shupak 2012, 149–51; 2014a.

60. Untying the knots—i.e., understanding the words of wisdom—is the task of the sage who is called *wḥʿ* "one who understands/explains" (lit. unties knots); see Ptahhotep, 611; Amenemope 3, 10; 28, 14–15 (Shupak 1993, 63–65).

61. Occurring four times in the second collection of Proverbs (18:8//26:22; 20:27, 30), the phrase חדרי-בטן "innards of the belly" appears to be an adaption of the Egyptian expression "casket of the belly" (Amenemope 3, 13). The "heated man" (איש חמה/חמות, Prov 15:18; 22:24–25; בעל חמה, 29:22; and גְּדָל חמה, 19:19) and the synonymous phrases (בעל אף, Prov 22:24–25; איש אף, 29:22)—which only appear in Proverbs—correspond to the Egyptian term *šmm/ḫmm* "hot-tempered" (elsewhere also characterized as "hot-mouthed," "hot-hearted," and "hot-bellied"), which designates a negative type of person in Egyptian literature.

words of instruction, encomia to eloquence and to the wise son who hearkens to his father's words, censure of the foolish son, recognition of human ignorance of what fate holds in store, restraint in various circumstances, giving to the needy and protecting the poor and weak, abjuration of taking bribes and perverting justice, and so on.

In both wisdom traditions there are almost no direct ritual instructions.[62] The statement "The character of the upright is preferred to the ox of the evildoer" (Merikare 129) is striking in this regard. Portraying the idea that ethics are more important than ritual that we find around a thousand years later in biblical prophecy (Isa 1:11–17; Hos 6:6; Amos 5:21–25; Mic 6:6–8), it suggests that this notion can be traced as far back as the second millennium BCE. The presence of a similar thought in Proverbs— "The sacrifice of the wicked is an abomination to the Lord, but the prayer of the upright is his delight" (Prov 15:8); "To do righteousness and justice is more acceptable to the Lord than sacrifice" (21:3; cf. 27:1)—may thus reflect the influence of Egyptian wisdom as much as biblical prophetic thought.[63]

Both wisdom literatures also share a belief in the dogmatic doctrine of retribution (Prov 10:27–30; 28:13, 17–19, 22; 29:1, 3, etc.). Only late wisdom texts—Amenemope and Job—raise doubts regarding this idea. The notion of family retribution also appears in Amenemope and Proverbs and Job.[64] Underlying their schemes is also the utilitarian stress on

---

62. See p. 271 above. Merikare and other late instructions form an exception to this rule.

63. According to Kaufmann (1964, 643–45), the Egyptian concept found in Merikare differs from the biblical demand in its assumption that the sacrifices serve as food to sustain the gods, its utilitarian approach that stresses the reward given to the person who brings the sacrifice ("The god is aware of him who acts for him" [Merikare 130]), and address of individual rather than national ritual. Yet, as Kaufmann himself acknowledges, Proverbs also refers to individual sacrifice. In my view, despite Kaufmann's attempt to underscore the difference between the biblical and the Egyptian concept, the author of Merikare explicitly contends that uprightness is more important than sacrifices. This text still being in vogue during the New Kingdom period, it may have influenced the sayings in Proverbs, thence finding its way into biblical prophecy.

64. See Prov 3:33; 11:21; 13:22; 14:26; etc.; Job 5:3–4; 31:7–10. The hypothesis that the enigmatic nature of Lady Wisdom (חָכְמוֹת) in Prov 1, 8, 9 reflects the Egyptian goddess Mзʿt is of interest here. While Kayatz (1966) notes the affinities between these two figures, Egyptian wisdom texts relate to mзʿt as an abstract noun (justice) rather than as a goddess. Similarly, in contrast to Lady Wisdom—God's primordial creature

the beneficial/harmful rather than the ethical tenet of good/bad.[65] They also appear to have developed along similar lines. A substantial number of scholars identify two or three stages, or strata—in the evolution of the wisdom tradition: day-to-day "secular" wisdom derived from the experience of the speaker/instructor/father/sage succeeded by a "religious" wisdom in which fear of God takes the place of the wisdom of the human father or teacher. At this stage the sage's teaching is identified with God's law, and God assumes the role of the teacher.[66] Adducing this process in order to determine the ancient and later material in Proverbs, these scholars presuppose that the second and fifth collections (10–22:16 and 25–29) are older than the first (1–9), sixth (30:1–14), eighth (31:1–9), and ninth (31:10–31). Egyptian sapiential literature also evinces evidence of a two-stage process—an early "secular" wisdom subsequently replaced from the Amarna period onward by a "religious" wisdom.[67]

The shift is witnessed in the instructions written during the New Kingdom and the Third Intermediate periods—Any and Amenemope—which focus more heavily on cult and ceremony, human fate as lying in god's hands irrespective of the individual's behavior/deeds, human ignorance of the future vs. divine omnipotence, and the direct link between man and god, the latter ruling over all.[68] It is also manifest in the semantic field of the "silent man." Originally presented as the ideal of interpersonal relations, this figure is replaced by the ideal religious adherent—the "true silent man." His antithesis—the "heated man"—who instigates quarrels and harms those who befriend him, is similarly identified as a person who

---

and representative rather than an independent-supreme entity—Mꜣʿt symbolizes the harmonic order ruling the cosmos, to which both kings and gods are subordinate.

65. See Prov 3:13–18; 4:10, 14–19; 11:25–26; Rofé 2006, 381–84.

66. See Skladny 1962; McKane 1970; Whybray 1965, 1974; Fox 2011. The later stratum is generally attributed to the editors of Proverbs, who placed maxims of faith next to ancient "secular" sayings (Rofé 2006, 405–8). According to other scholars (see Weeks 1994; Dell 2006), however, the religious sayings constituted part of the early material.

67. See pp. 277–78 above. As Assmann (1979, 11–72) has demonstrated, the personal piety of the Amarna period, which left its mark on the wisdom instructions of the time, developed gradually out of the preceding wisdom literature.

68. This phenomenon may be compared with the late stratum of biblical wisdom. As McKane (1970, 10–22) observes, words that carry a positive connotation in the ancient stratum take on a negative tone in the later one. Thus, for example, מועצות "counsels" becomes "intrigues." See also תחבלות, חכם, etc.

merely pretends to be a religious man (Amenemope, chapter 4). Demotic instructions identify the "wise man" with the "man of god" (Pap. Insinger) with the "fool" being denounced as "wicked" (ibid.). Similarly, the "abomination to the *ka*" (human personality) (cf. Ptahhotep) is replaced by the "abomination to god" (Amenemope*). Recognition of this developmental scheme within the Egyptian wisdom tradition can contribute to our understanding of the chronological layers within the biblical wisdom corpus.*

The Divergences between Egyptian and Biblical Wisdom

While the two corpora display close affinities, their disparities cannot be overlooked. These stem primarily from their different religious frameworks—polytheism vs. monotheism. The Egyptian compositions contain allusions to numerous myths—the Destruction of Mankind and God's Battle against the Sea (Merikare 130–138), for example—and references to various pagan concepts and customs: the ceremony for spitting on the serpent Apophis who threatens to swallow the sun (Amenemope 10, 20), the description of the god Khnum as forming creatures on his potter's wheel (ibid., 12, 15–17), or belief in the next world and the judgment of the dead therein (Merikare 53–57, 127–130; Amenemope 17, 22–18, 1), and so on. They also refer to the Egyptian gods, from the head of pantheon—the sun god Re—to more minor gods: Thoth, god of wisdom and the scribes, Hapy, the god of the Nile's inundation, and Aten, the sun-disc god.

Further differences originate from the disparate geographical background and fauna. In the Egyptian wisdom literature, the Nile serves as a framework for the depiction of human life. Thus, for example, sailing symbolizes the ship of life, the channels of the river representing the courses followed by human life. The Egyptian sages discerned affinities between the human and natural world, esteeming the crocodile for its silence and denouncing it for its covetousness, for example, or likening the enemies to crocodiles and lions, the scribe's finger to the beak of the ibis, and the rapidity with which wealth can disappear like a goose taking off in flight.

The target audience of the two corpora also differs. The Egyptian authors having been trained in official frameworks designed to provide an education for those destined for administrative positions within state institutions, their compositions are addressed to senior and middle-ranking officials. The sources of Hebrew didactic wisdom literature were far more numerous and varied. Proverbs is composed of two types of sapiential sayings—(1) popular proverbs passed down orally relating to daily life in the village, family or tribal setting, or city and (2) instructions and advice, which represent the world of values and spheres of interest of members of the upper class and originated in the circle of scribes and high officialdom, in the school, and the royal court.[69] The former appear to have been collected, edited, and written down by scribes belonging to the latter circle, who added the second group of texts—that is, their specific material. In its extant form, Proverbs thus resembles the Egyptian instruction manual, whose main purpose was to educate the cadres of officialdom for administering government institutions, interwoven into which are wisdom sayings originally directed at all class levels, from the farmer, shepherd, orphan, and widow to the judge, adviser, emissary, and monarch.

The Instruction of Amenemope and Proverbs

As observed above, the discovery of the Instruction of Amenemope constituted a watershed in the study of biblical wisdom literature in general and Proverbs in particular. The two texts both reflect the literary structure, content, and ideas found in other Egyptian wisdom instructions—a utilitarian approach, the belief in retribution, and lack of direct interest in the cultus, and so on.[70] At the same time, Amenemope also exhibits a new approach. Emphasizing the direct relationship between a man and his god, it propounds that the world order (*mꜣʿt*) is solely dependent on god and

---

69. Skladny (1962) differentiates between four collections of sayings in Proverbs, addressing diverse circles: young people (10–15), officials in service to the king (17–22:16), the common man/farmer (25–27), and the ruling class—"mirror of the ruler" (28–29). See also Hermisson 1968, 123–25; McKane 1970, 9.

70. Some samples for these common features: the prologue in Prov 1:1–7, which employs, as the introduction of Amenemope, a series of infinitives to express the purpose of the work ("to know ... to understand ... to acquire ... to give"); the "better ... than ..." proverb that frequently occurs in Amenemope (primarily at the end of chapters) and Proverbs (12:9; 15:16–17; 16:8, 19; 17:1); the quotation of a proverb at the end of a chapter (see Prov 1:17–18, 32; 2:21–22; Amenemope, chapters 2, 3, 6), similar topics: a small estate from god's hand—or attaining it with love, with a happy heart, or in uprightness—is better than great wealth (Prov 15:16 // Amenemope 9, 5–8; 16, 11–14; Prov 16:8 // Amenemope 9, 5–6), mercy towards one's enemy or rival while allowing the god to determine his retribution (Prov 20:22; 25:21–22; Amenemope, 5, 3–6; 22, 3–8), an individual's ignorance of his fate, which lies wholly in god's hand (Prov 27:1; Amenemope, 19:13; 22, 5–6; 23, 8–9). See Fox 2008.

takes the side of the poor and the weak. It thus evinces a closer correspondence with biblical ethics.

Alongside this general affinity, Prov 22:17–24:22—that is, the third collection known as the Words of the Wise—displays evidence of direct contact with Amenenope. Particularly striking is the impression of the Egyptian work in the first part of the collection, chapters 22:17–23:11. The key word in the Hebrew text, שלשום (*ketiv*; *qere* שָׁלִישִׁים [22:20]), traditionally having constituted a lingual-textual enigma, is elucidated by the fact that the Egyptian instruction is divided into thirty chapters. Also other ideas and images, foreign to the Hebrew background, become clear when considering Egyptian wisdom. This chapter is too short for proper illustration of this contact, which I have dealt with extensively elsewhere (e.g., Shupak 1996: 21–24; 150–55; 2005: 203–20). The foreign concepts and images in Prov 22:17–23:11 are not unique to Amenemope, being common to the Egyptian wisdom tradition preceding and following it alike.[71] Undoubtedly, however, there is unparalleled contact between Prov 22–23 and the Egyptian work, evinced in the concentration and succession of the parallel items. This almost certainly indicates that the Hebrew author of these chapters had a copy of the Egyptian composition before him.[72] Yet, this is not a case of mechanical copying

---

71. Some of these common concepts and images are: the belly as the seat of human intelligence, thoughts, and feelings (Prov 22:18–19 // Amenemope 3, 11–13; cf. Amenemope 3, 8–15; 22, 11–16; 23, 4), cf. Ptahhotep 235–248, 264–269, 412–414; Merikare 143–144; Loyalist Instruction 2, 5–6; Man for His Son 7, 2; 19, 8; Any 20, 9–11; the negative man is the "heated/ hot tempered" (or its synonyms [Prov 22:24–25 // Amenemope 11, 13–17) rather than a fool or evil (cf. Amenemope 4, 17; 5, 9–19; 6, 1–6), cf. Ptahhotep 350–352, 373–378; table manners (Prov 23:1–3, 6–8 // Amenemope 23, 13–18; 14, 3–5, 17–18), especially common in Egyptian wisdom literature; cf. Kagemni 1, 3–11; Ptahhotep 119–144; Any 21, 31; 23, 13–20; Insinger 5, 12–6, 24. Many Egyptian traces are also concealed in the second part of the Words of the Sages, Prov 23:12–24:22. See Shupak 2005, 214–16.

72. According to the prevailing scholarly opinion, Proverbs was influenced by the Instruction of Amenemope, mainly 22:17–23:11. While the majority of scholars have rejected Grumach's (1972) thesis regarding a common Egyptian source (*Alte Lehre*) for Prov 22:17–24:22 on the grounds that the reconstruction of such a source must remain speculative (see Römheld 1989, 13–114; Fox 2008, 25–26), differences of opinion still exist regarding whether direct or indirect contact was responsible for the affinities. In my view (Shupak 2005), the former can be evinced (see also Römheld 1989; Emerton 2001; Overland 1996, 275–291). Bryce (1972) goes so far as to distinguish three stages during which the Egyptian material was interwoven into Proverbs:

or borrowing: not all the material brought in the Egyptian instruction occurs in the Hebrew composition and vice versa. Moreover, the Egyptian material was reworked and adapted to its new Israelite environment. Thus, for example, the expression "casket of the belly" (Amenemope 3, 13)—associated with the Egyptian scribal craft—was reduced to "belly" (Prov 22:18); the duck common on the Nile landscape (Amenemope 10, 4–5) replaced by the eagle (Prov 23:5), and religious customs and elements typical of Hebrew culture with no analogy in ancient Egyptian culture added (cf. גואל "redeemer" [Prov 23:10–11], עולם גבול "an ancient landmark" [22:28; 23:10–11], and the name of God [22:18–19, 22–23]). The author or editor of Prov 22:17–23:11 can thus be seen to have borrowed carefully and selectively from Amenemope, adapting the Egyptian instructions to monotheistic faith and Israelite setting.

Chapter 4 of Amenemope also exhibits close affinities with Ps 1 and Jer 17:5–8. All three of these passages contrast two types of people—the "heated" versus the "true silent man" (Amenemope), the "righteous" versus the "wicked" (Ps 1), and the "man who trusts God" versus the "man who trusts in man" (Jeremiah). In each, the good fate of the positive type and the bitter end of the negative one is demonstrated via appeal to

---

adaptation, assimilation, and integration. Some scholars hold that the author—or editor—of Proverbs possessed a Hebrew or Aramaic translation of Amenemope that reached Jerusalem during the Saitic period or as early as the Twenty-Fifth Dynasty (Schipper 2001, 307–18; 2005, 53–72, 232–48; Laisney 2007, 246; Fox 2008). If this were the case, however, we might expect far more Aramaisms in the parallel portion of Proverbs. The scribal circle in Jerusalem appears to have known Egyptian; Egyptian wisdom works almost certainly formed part of their study corpus. This hypothesis has recently been reinforced by Calabro's (2012) demonstration of the existence of a tradition of Hieratic writing in Judah prior to the Persian period whose roots most likely go back to the pre-New Kingdom period, and by Hess (1989, 249–65), who argues that a scribal tradition existed in Jerusalem during the Amarna period (fourteenth century BCE) that continued up to the Israelite period and included Egyptian language usages and expressions. Recently, Fox (2014) proposed an original explanation for the affinity between the Egyptian work and Prov 22:17–23:11 by reconstructing the technique used for adapting the Egyptian material: utilizing an Aramaic translation of the Egyptian work written on a scroll, the author of these chapters of Proverbs selected parts by rolling it forwards and backwards, refashioning these in line with his aims and agenda and adding his own new material. This theory assumes that the Hieratic columns in the original scroll paralleled the Aramaic scroll, but a scroll written in alphabetic Aramaic script is much shorter than a scroll written in Hieratic script, containing hundreds of signs.

a floral metaphor: a tree planted beside streams of water (Ps 1 and Jeremiah) / planted in a garden (?) (Amenemope) vs. the chaff blown away by the wind (Ps 1), a bush in the desert (Jeremiah), and a wild tree that grows in the forest (?) (Amenemope). Although the link between the three passages is clear, the meaning of the floral terms in Amenemope remains obscure. Such similes also being common in ancient literature (cf. Hos 13:3; Isa 29:5; Job 29:19; Ps 52:10; 92:13–14), it is difficult to determine whether the Egyptian source influenced the Hebrew or whether all three passages drew upon a common Ancient Near Eastern tradition.[73]

Also of note is the fact that Amenemope forms a link in a long chain of Egyptian wisdom literature, thereby reflecting an age-old tradition that may be traced back to the middle of the third millennium BCE. It thus demonstrates close affinities with the preceding wisdom instructions—in particular Ptahhotep (early second millennium BCE) and Any (middle of the second millennium). A comparison of Ptahhotep, Prov 22:17–23:11 and Amenemope reveals that eight of the fourteen parallels between Prov 22–23 and Amenemope also occur in Ptahhotep.[74] The collection Words of the Wise nonetheless exhibits a more specific contact with Amenemope than with Ptahhotep, the latter demonstrating no evidence of the direct contact and literal parallels existing between Prov 22–23 and Amenemope. This fact further corroborates the conjecture that the author of Proverbs was directly acquainted with Amenemope.[75]

---

73. For various suggestions concerning the habitat of the trees, see, e.g., Drioton 1962; Posener 1973; Israeli 1990; Laisney 2007, 74–75. For a detailed comparison between chapter 4 in the Egyptian work and Ps 1 and Jer 17, see Shupak 1993, 175–77; Creach 1999, 34–46; Garsiel 2012, 9–23.

74. See Shupak 2012, 132–62.

75. Recent research has highlighted the similarities between the Egyptian royal instructions (Merikare and Amenemhet) and Prov 28–29, together with the affinity of both and the Egyptian Loyalist Instructions, with the sayings related to monarchs in the other chapters of Proverbs (see Blumenthal 2003; Tavares 2007). Despite the centuries-long chronological gap between these texts, this suggests that the sayings in Proverbs most likely refer to a real royal institution. This being the case, they are to be dated to the Israelite monarchical period (contra Weeks 1994, 46–56).

The Conclusions to Be Drawn from the Comparison

The Antiquity of the Material in Proverbs

The supposition of direct contact between Amenemope—composed during the eleventh–tenth centuries BCE and based on a preceding Egyptian wisdom tradition going back almost a millennium—suggests that wisdom literature may well have flourished within Israel as early as the first millennium BCE. In light of this fact and the evidence provided by 1 Kgs 1–9 regarding the close contacts between Israel and Egypt during Solomon's reign, it is reasonable to conjecture that the ancient stratum of Proverbs—whether originally oral or written—developed within King Solomon's court (970–930 BCE).[76] While this reinforces the traditional attribution of Proverbs to Solomon, archeological evidence is uncorroborative. No direct signs of Egyptian presence in Israel can be adduced in the wake of the collapse of Egyptian rule in Asia in the twelfth century BCE, the majority of Egyptian objects discovered being Phoenician imports. The contact between Israel and Egypt during Solomon's reign thus appears to have been much more indirect than direct.[77] Egyptian influence consequently seems to have penetrated on a more widespread scale only in later periods. As this most likely occurred when close cultural and political contact developed between Israel and Egypt, the most fitting time

---

76. See Solomon's marriage to Pharaoh's daughter, the parallel administrative arrangements and official titles in the two countries, the building of the chariot towns, the sending of missions southward via the Red Sea to bring luxury items in imitation of the pharaonic custom, and the plan and decorations of the Temple in Jerusalem (see Williams 1975; Strange 2004).

77. Egyptian scribes, poets, and musicians were active in the Phoenician port cities, wherein Egyptian works were translated into Canaanite and brought to Jerusalem. Direct contact with Egypt also possibly existed during this period via Egyptian scribes present in the king's court in Jerusalem (see David's scribe, Shisha, whose sons were scribes in the court of his son, Solomon [1 Kgs 4:3]; see n. 80 below) or local scribes who acquired their education in Egypt. Egyptian influence continued even after Egyptian rule in the region, as evidenced by the hundreds of amulets—primarily from the Iron Age (1000–700 BCE)—discovered in various places in Israel that reflect distinctively Egyptian beliefs and traditions (Herrmann 1994) and hieratic inscriptions that evince a hieratic writing tradition in Judah prior to the Persian period (Calabro 2012). Fox's opinion (2008, 35) that no Egyptian influence in the area existed between the eleventh century BCE and end of the eighth, scribes versing themselves in Akkadian rather than Egyptian, thus appears untenable.

appears to be Hezekiah's reign in Judah (726–697/6 BCE.), which paralleled the Twenty-Fifth/Twenty-Sixth Dynasties in Egypt. Hezekiah maintained close connections with the pharaohs of the Twenty-Fifth Dynasty;[78] in the time of the Twenty-Sixth Dynasty, the Saitic period, following the rise of Assyria, which threatened Egyptian hegemony, Egypt began to become more open to contacts with neighboring countries. Support for this hypothesis can be found also in the picture of vigorous wisdom activity in this period depicted in the Bible as well as from Egyptian testimonies. Proverbs 25:1 thus witnesses the renewal and flourishing of wisdom activity in Hezekiah's court, and copies of Egyptian wisdom instructions preserved from the Twenty-Fifth/Twenty-Sixth Dynasties inform us of a similar situation in Egypt.[79]

Egyptian wisdom influence may have continued over a broader period. Jewish communities that maintained contact with their brethren in Jerusalem existed in Egypt through the beginning of the mid-seventh century until the destruction of the Temple in 587 BCE. The most famous was that in Elephantine (see Jer 43:7; 44:1). This may form the background for the contact with later Egyptian wisdom literature—in the form of the Demotic instructions—composed during the last centuries before the Common Era.

The *Sitz im Leben* of the Biblical Wisdom Literature

Comparative research also helps to explain the *Sitz im Leben* of the biblical wisdom tradition. Most of the Egyptian wisdom works—including Amenemope—served as study material in scribal school and other educational frameworks. One may assume, even if there is no direct evidence, that during the First Temple period such institutions dedicated to educating high-ranking officials existed in the royal court. These simultaneously served as the basis for the development of biblical wisdom literature and

---

78. In the time of Hezekiah there were close political connections with Egypt: a pro-Egyptian party was active in Judah (see Isa 30:1–5; 31:1–3), and Tirhaka, of the Twenty-fifth Dynasty, came to the aid of Hezekiah in his war against Sennacherib (2 Kings 19:9; Isa 37:9).

79. As attested by the copies of Amenemope dating to the Saitic and Persian periods, and copies of Djedefhor, Amenemhet, and Any, which belong to the Twenty-Fifth/Twenty-Sixth Dynasties (see nn. 47 and 48 above).

the assimilation of Egyptian and other foreign cultural elements.[80] At least parts of the biblical wisdom books and selections from famous Egyptian wisdom works—in the original or translation—were likely to have been studied herein.[81] In this context, the fact that Proverbs evinces literal parallels to Amenemope as well as concepts, motifs, and expressions known from other Egyptian works composed centuries earlier should come as little surprise. The book of Proverbs is thus a book of education and guidance that reflects the values and worldviews of Ancient Near Eastern scribes and high officials, particularly those in Egypt.[82]

WORKS CONSULTED

Assmann, Jan. 1979. "Weisheit, Loyalismus und Frömmigkeit." Pages 11–72 in *Studien zu altägyptischen Lebenslehren*. Edited by Erik Hornung and Othmar Keel. OBO 28. Fribourg: Universitätsverlag; Gottingen: Vandenhoeck & Ruprecht.

———. 1983. "Schrift, Tod und Identität: Das Grab als Vorschule der Literatur im alten Ägypten." Pages 64–93 in *Schrift und Gedächtnis*. Edited

---

80. It is quite reasonable to assume that the first school in Israel was established under the influence of the Egyptian model. Expressions prevalent in Egyptian school writings from the Ramesside period occur in biblical wisdom works: מוסר as an epithet for instruction, שבט beating as a study incentive, אזן as an organ of study, עצל —the lazy student, חסר לב—the foolish student, קר רוח—the ideal man, etc. This vocabulary recalls the ambience and teaching methods of Egyptian schools (Shupak 1987: 98–119). The world of the Hebrew scribe is also akin to that of Egyptian writing and education. David's scribe was known as שיא/ שושא/ שישא (1 Kgs 4:3; 1 Chr 18:16; 2 Sam 20:25; 2 Sam 8:17 [שריה])—a transliteration of the Egyptian term *sš šʿ t* ("scribe of letters"). קסת and דיו (Ezek 9:2–3, 11; Jer 36:18), both of which belong to the scribe's craft, similarly derive from the Egyptian *gsti* (the scribe's slate) and *ryt* (ink). The existence of a school does not negate the possibility of education in other frameworks, such as the family, apprenticeship, or scribal guilds (see 1 Chr 2:55). A school may have also existed within the Temple precincts to train the priest serving in the cultus.

81. Supporting the idea that school forms the *Sitz im Leben* of Proverbs, are the following scholars: Mettinger 1971, 140–57; Olivier 1975; Lemaire 1981; Rofé 2006, 390–91; Perdue 2008, 103–7; Demsky 2012, 22–23, 169–211; Hurovitz 2012, 25. Other scholars disagree: Whybray 1974, 33–43; Haran 1988; Weeks 1994, 153–56; Davies 1995.

82. The terminology relating to the learning process prevalent in Proverbs also supports this view (Shupak 2003).

by Aleida Assmann, Jan Assmann, and Christof Hardmeier. Munich: Fink.

Blumenthal, Elke. 2003. "Die Rolle des Königs in der ägyptischen und biblischen Weisheit." Pages 1–36 in *Weisheit in Israel : Beiträge des Symposiums "Das Alte Testament und die Kultur der Moderne" anlässlich des 100. Geburtstags Gerhard von Rads (1901–1971), Heidelberg, 18.–21. Oktober 2001*. Edited by D. J. A. Clines, Hermann Lichtenberger, Hans-Peter Müller, and Elke Blumenthal. ATM 12. Munich: LIT.

Brunner, Hellmut. 1957. *Altägyptische Erziehung*. Wiesbaden: Harrassowitz.

———. 1966. "Die 'Weisen', ihre 'Lehren' und 'Prophezeiungen' in altägyptischer Sicht." *ZÄS* 93:29–35.

———. 1979. "Zitate aus Lebenslehren." Pages 105–71 in *Studien zu altägyptischen Lebenslehren*. Edited by Erik Hornung and Othmar Keel. OBO 28. Fribourg: Universitätsverlag; Göttingen: Vandenhoeck & Ruprecht.

———. 1988. *Altägyptische Weisheit: Lehren für das Leben*. Zurich: Artemis.

Bryce, Glendon E. 1972. *A Legacy of Wisdom: The Egyptian Contribution to the Wisdom of Israel*. Lewisburg, PA: Bucknell University Press.

Burkard, Gunther. 1980. "Bibliotheken im Alten Ägypten." *Bibliothek: Forschung und Praxis* 4:79–115.

Calabro, David. 2012. "The Hieratic Scribal Tradition in Preexilic Judah." Pages 77–85 in *Evolving Egypt: Innovation, Appropriation, and Reinterpretation in Ancient Egypt*. BARIS 2397. Edited by Keery Mühlestein and John Gee. Oxford: Archaeopress.

Caminos, Ricardo A. 1954. *Late Egyptian Miscellanies*. BEStud 1. London: Oxford University Press.

Creach, Jerome F. D. 1999. "Like a Tree Planted by the Temple Stream: The Portrait of the Righteous in Psalm 1:3." *CBQ* 61:34–46.

Davies, G. I. 1995. "Were There Schools in Ancient Israel?" Pages 199–211 in *Wisdom in Ancient Israel: Essays in Honour of J. A. Emerton*. Edited by John Day, Robert P. Gordon, and H. G. M. Williamson. Cambridge: Cambridge University Press.

Dell, Katharine J. 2006. *The Book of Proverbs in Social and Theological Context*. Cambridge: Cambridge University Press.

Demsky, Aaron. 2012. *Literacy in Ancient Israel*. Jerusalem: Bialik Institute (Hebrew).

Drioton, E. 1962. "L'apologue des deux arbres." Pages 76–80 in *Drewnii mir: Festschrift for V. V. Struve*. Edited by N.W. Pigulewskaja. Moscow: Izdatelstvo Vostocnoj Literatury.

Emerton, J. A. 2001. "The Teaching of Amenemope and Proverbs XXII 17–XXIV 22: Further Reflections on a Long Standing Problem." *VT* 51:431–65.

Fecht, G. 1965. *Literarische Zeugnisse zur "Persönlichen Frömmigkeit" in Ägypten: Analyse der Beispiele aus den ramessidischen Schulpapyri*. Heidelberg: Winter.

Fox, Michael V. 1980. "Two Decades of Research in Egyptian Wisdom Literature." *ZÄS* 107:120–35.

———. 2008. "The Formation of Proverbs 22:17–23:11." *WO* 38:22–37.

———. 2011. "Terms for Wisdom in the Book of Proverbs." Pages 13–24 in *Wisdom, Her Pillars Are Seven: Studies in Biblical, Post-biblical and Ancient Near Eastern Wisdom Literature*. Edited by Shamir Yona and Victor A. Hurowitz. Beersheva 20. Beersheba: Ben-Gurion University Press (Hebrew).

———. 2014. "From Amenemope to Proverbs." *ZAW* 126:76–91.

Gardiner, Alan H. 1935. *Hieratic Papyri in the British Museum: Third Series; Chester Beatty Gift*. 2 vols. London: British Museum.

———. 1937. *Late Egyptian Miscellanies*. BAe 7. Brussel: Fondation égyptologique Reine Élisabeth.

Garsiel, Moshe. 2012. "Intertextual Dialectics on the Issue of Reward and Punishment: The Case of Psalm 1, Jeremiah 12 and 17." Pages 9–27 in *The Wisdom Literature in the Old Testament and Ancient Near East*. Beit Mikra 57. Edited by Nili Shupak and Yair Hoffman. Jerusalem: Bialik Institute (Hebrew).

Grumach, Irene. 1972. *Untersuchungen zur Lebenslehre des Amenope*. MÄS 23. Munich: Deutscher Kuntsverlag.

Guglielmi, Waltraud. 1984. "Adaption und Funktion von Zitaten." *SAK* 11:347–64.

Gunn, Battiscombe. 1926. "Some Middle Egyptian Proverbs." *JEA* 12:282–84.

Hagen, Fredrik. 2007. "Ostraca, Literature and Teaching at Deir el Medina." Pages 38–51 in *Current Research in Egyptology 2005: Proceedings of the Sixth Annual Symposium*. Edited by Rachel Mairs and Alice Stevenson. Oxford: Oxbow.

———. 2009. "Echoes of 'Ptahhotep' in the Greco-Roman Period?" *ZÄS* 136:130–35.

———. 2012. *An Ancient Egyptian Literary Text in Context: The Instruction of Ptahhotep.* OLA 218. Leuven: Peeters.
Haran, Menahem. 1988. "On the Diffusion of Literacy and Schools in Ancient Israel." Pages 81–95 in *Congress Volume: Jerusalem, 1986.* Edited by J. A. Emerton. VTSup 40. Leiden: Brill.
Hermisson, Hans-Jürgen. 1968. *Studien zur israelitischen Spruchweisheit.* Neukirchen-Vluyn: Neukirchener Verlag.
Herrmann, Christian. 1994. *Ägyptische Amulette aus Palestina/Israel: Mit einem Ausblick auf ihre Rezeption durch das Alte Testament.* OBO 138. Fribourg: Universitätsverlag; Göttingen : Vandenhoeck & Ruprecht.
Hess, Richard S. 1989. "Hebrew Psalms and Amarna Correspondence from Jerusalem: Some Comparisons and Implications." *ZAW* 42:249–65.
Hurowitz, V. A. 2012. *Proverbs: Introduction and Commentary.* 2 vols. Mikra Leysrael. Tel Aviv: Am Oved; Jerusalem: Magnes (Hebrew).
Israeli, Shlomit. 1990. "Chapter Four of the Wisdom Book of Amenemope." Pages 464–84 in *Studies in Egyptology Presented to Miriam Lichtheim.* 2 vols. Edited by Sarah I. Groll. Jerusalem: Magnes.
Jasnow, R. 1999. "Remarks on Continuity in Egyptian Literary Tradition." Pages 193–210 in *Gold of Praise: Studies on Ancient Egypt in Honour of Edward F. Wente.* SAOC 58. Edited by Emily Teeter and John A. Larson. Chicago: Oriental Institute of the University of Chicago
Kaufmann, Yehezkiel. 1964. *The Religion of Israel.* 4 vols. Jerusalem: Bialik Institute (Hebrew).
Kayatz, Christa. 1966. *Studien zu Proverbien 1–9: Eine form und motivgeschichtliche Untersuchung unter Einbeziehung ägyptischen Vergleichsmaterials.* WMANT 22. Neukirchen-Vluyn: Neukirchener Verlag.
Laisney, V. 2007. *L'Enseignement d'Aménémopé.* StPohl 19. Rome: Pontificio Instituto Biblico.
Lemaire, André. 1981. *Les écoles et la formation de la Bible dans l'ancien Israël.* OBO 39. Freiburg: Universitätsverlag; Göttingen: Vandenhoeck & Ruprecht.
Lichtheim, Miriam. 1973–1980. *Ancient Egyptian Literature.* 3 vols. Berkeley: University of California Press.
———. 1992. *Maat in Egyptian Autobiographies and Related Studies.* OBO 120. Fribourg: Universitätsverlag; Göttingen: Vandenhoeck & Ruprecht.
Marlo, Hilary. 2007. "The Lament over the River Nile: Isaiah XIX 5–10 in Its Wider Context." *VT* 57:229–42.

McDowell, A. 1996. "Student Exercises from Deir el-Medina: The Dates." Pages 601–8 in vol. 2 of *Studies in Honour of William Kelly Simpson*. Edited by Peter Der Manuelian. Boston: Museum of Fine Arts.

McKane, William. 1970. *Proverbs*. OTL. London: SCM.

Mettinger, Tryggve N. D. 1971. *Solomonic State Officials: A Study of the Civil Government Officials of the Israelite Monarchy*. ConBOT 5. Lund: Gleerup.

Miosi, F. T. 1982. "God, Fate and Free Will in Egyptian Wisdom." Pages 69–111 in *Studies in Philology in Honour of Roland James Williams: A Festschrift*. SSEA 3. Edited by Gerald E. Kadish and Geoffrey E. Freedman. Toronto: Benben.

Olivier, J. P. J. 1975. "Schools and Wisdom Literature." *JNSL* 4:49–60.

Osing, Jürgen. 1997. "School and Literature in the Ramesside Period." Pages 131–42 in *L'Impero Ramesside: Convegno Internazionale in onore di Sergio Donadoni*. Edited by Alessandro Roccati. Rome: Università degli studi di Roma "La Sapienza."

Overland, Paul. 1996. "Structure in the Wisdom of Amenemope and Proverbs." Pages 275–91 in *"Go to the Land I Will Show You": Studies in Honor of Dwight W. Young*. Edited by Joseph E. Coleson and Victor H. Matthews. Winona Lake, IN: Eisenbrauns.

Parkinson, R. B. 2002. *Poetry and Culture in Middle Kingdom Egypt: A Dark Side to Perfection*. London: Continuum.

Perdue, Leo G. 2008. *The Sword and the Stylus: An Introduction to Wisdom in the Age of Empires*. Grand Rapids: Eerdmans.

Posener, G. 1973. "Le chapitre 4 d'Aménémope." *ZÄS* 99:129–35.

Quack, Joachim. 1994. *Die Lehren des Ani: Ein neuägyptischer Weisheitstext in seinem kulturellen Umfeld*. OBO 141. Fribourg: Universitätsverlag; Göttingen: Vandenhoeck & Ruprecht.

———. 2002. "Die Dienstanweisung des Oberlehrers aus dem Buch vom Tempel." Pages 159–71 in *Ägyptologische Tempeltagung: Würzburg, 23–26 September, 1999*. Edited by Horst Beinlich et al. ÄAT 33. Wiesbaden: Harrassowitz.

Ragozilli, Chloé. 2010. "Weak Hands and Soft Mouths: Elements of a Scribal Identity in the New Kingdom." *ZÄS* 137:157–70.

Rofé, A. 2006. *Introduction to the Literature of the Hebrew Bible*. Jerusalem: Carmel (Hebrew).

Römheld, K. F. Diethard. 1989. *Wege der Weisheit: Die Lehren Amenemopes und Proverbien 22,17–24,22*. BZAW 184. Berlin: de Gruyter.

Schipper, Bernd U. 2001. "Kultur und Kontext-zum Kulturtransfer zwischen Ägypten und Israel/ Juda in der 25. und 26. Dyn." *SAK* 29:307–18.

———. 2005. "Die Lehre des Amenemope und Prov. 22,17–24,22." *ZAW* 117: 53–72; 232–48.

Schlott, Adelheid. 1989. *Schrift und Schreiber im Alten Ägypten*. Munich: Beck.

Shupak, Nili. 1987. "The 'Sitz im Leben' of the Book of Proverbs in the Light of a Comparison of Biblical and Egyptian Wisdom Literature." *RB* 94:98–119.

———. 1989–1990. "Egyptian 'Prophecy' and Biblical Prophecy: Did the Phenomenon of Prophecy Exist in Ancient Egypt?" *JEOL* 31:5–40.

———. 1992. "A New Source for the Study of the Judiciary and Law of Ancient Egypt: 'The Tale of the Eloquent Peasant.'" *JNES* 51:1–18.

———. 1993. *Where Can Wisdom Be Found? The Sage's Language in the Bible and in Ancient Egyptian Literature*. OBO 130. Fribourg: Universitätsverlag; Göttingen: Vandenhoeck & Ruprecht.

———. 1996. *The Book of Proverbs: World of the Bible*. Tel Aviv: Davidson-Itai (Hebrew).

———. 2001. "'Canon' and 'Canonization' in Ancient Egypt." *BO* 58:535–47.

———. 2003 "The Terminology of Biblical Wisdom Literature as a Tool for the Reconstruction of Learning Methods in Ancient Israel." *VT* 53:416–26.

———. 2005. "The Instruction of Amenemope and Proverbs 22:17–24:22 from the Perspective of Contemporary Research." Pages 203–20 in *Seeking Out the Wisdom of the Ancients: Essays Offered in Honor of Michael V. Fox*. Edited by Ronald L. Troxel, Kelvin G. Friebel, and Dennis R. Magary. Winona Lake, IN: Eisenbrauns.

———. 2009. "Positive and Negative Human Types in Egyptian Wisdom Literature." Pages 245–60 in *Homeland and Exile: Biblical and Ancient Near Eastern Studies in Honour of Bustenay Oded*. Edited by Gershon Galil, Markham J. Geller, and Alan R. Millard. VTSup 130. Leiden: Brill.

———. 2011. "Female Imagery in Proverbs 1–9 in the Light of Egyptian Sources." *VT* 61:310–23.

———. 2012. "'To Teach the Ignorant about Knowledge': The Instruction of Ptahhotep and Biblical Wisdom Literature." Pages 132–62 in *The Wisdom Literature in the Old Testament and Ancient Near East*. Edited by Nili Shupak and Yair Hoffman. Beit Mikra 57. Jerusalem: Bialik Institute (Hebrew).

———. 2014a. "The Abomination of Egypt: New Light on an Old Problem." Pages 1–12 in *Jubilee Volume in Honor of V. A. Hurowitz*. Edited by S. Paul and M. Gruber. Beersheba: Ben-Gurion University Press (Hebrew).

———. 2014b. "Weighing in the Scales: How an Egyptian Concept Made Its Way into Biblical and Post-biblical Literature." Pages 225–33 in *Festchrift for Prof. Zipora Talshir*. Edited by K. Verman. Beersheba: Ben-Gurion University Press.

Skladny, Udo. 1962. *Die ältesten Spruchsammlungen in Israel*. Göttingen: Vandenhoeck & Ruprecht.

Strange, J. 2004. "Some Notes on Biblical and Egyptian Theology." Pages 345–58 in *Egypt, Israel, and the Ancient Mediterranean World: Studies in Honor of Donald B. Redford*. Edited by Gary N. Knoppers and Antoine Hirsch. PAe 20. Leiden: Brill.

Tavares, Ricardo. 2007. *Eine königliche Weisheitslehre? Exegetische Analyse von Sprüche 28–29 und Vergleich mit den ägyptischen Lehren Merikaras und Amenemhats*. OBO 234. Fribourg: Academic Press; Göttingen: Vandenhoeck & Ruprecht.

Verhoeven, Ursala. 2009. "Von der 'Loyalistischen Lehre' zur 'Lehre des Kairsu': Eine neue Textquelle aus Assiut und deren Auswirkungen." ZÄS 136: 87–98.

Vernus, Pascal. 1999. "Le discours politique de l'Enseignement de Ptahhotep." Pages 139–52 in *Literatur und Politik im pharaonischen und ptolemäischen Ägypten: Vorträge der Tagung zum Gedenken an Georges Posener 5.–10. September 1996 in Leipzig*. Bibliothèque d'Étude 127. Edited by Jan Assmann and Elke Blumenthal. Cairo: Institut français d'archéologie orientale.

———. 2010. *Sagesses de l'Égypte pharaonique*. 2nd ed. Arles: Actes Sudes.

Volten, Aksel. 1937. *Studien zum Weisheitsbuch des Anii*. Copenhagen: Levin & Munksgaard.

Warnemünde, G. 2011. "'Es geht nichts über die Bücher': Schule und Ausbildung im Alten Ägypten." *Kemet* 20.4:16–22.

Weeks, Stuart. 1994. *Early Israelite Wisdom*. Oxford: Clarendon.

Wente, Edward F. 1995. "The Scribes of Ancient Egypt." *CANE* 4:2211–21.

Whybray, R. N. 1965. *Wisdom in Proverbs: The Concept of Wisdom in Proverbs 1–9*. SBT 45. London: SCM.

———. 1974. *The Intellectual Tradition in the Old Testament*. BZAW 135. Berlin: de Gruyter.

Williams, R. J. 1975. "'A People Come Out of Egypt': An Egyptologist Looks at the Old Testament." Pages 231–52 in *Congress Volume: Edinburgh, 1974*. VTSup 28. Leiden: Brill.

Contributors

Katharine J. Dell, University of Cambridge

Tova Forti, Ben Gurion University

Michael V. Fox, University of Wisconsin at Madison

Mark W. Hamilton, Abilene Christian University

Raik Heckl, University of Leipzig

Will Kynes, Whitworth University

Douglas Miller, Tabor College

Markus Saur, University of Kiel

Annette Schellenberg, University of Vienna

Nili Shupak, University of Haifa

Mark R. Sneed, Lubbock Christian University

Stuart Weeks, University of Durham

Index of Ancient Works

Biblical Literature

Genesis

1	134, 213, 231, 234
1–3	101, 106
1–11	14, 155, 158, 200
1:26	212
1:27	212
9:8–17	122
12:1	134
12:1–3	101
17	122
19:26	254
37	15
37–50	14, 104
39–50	15
41–46	255
49	255

Exodus

7:11	89
12:27	77
20:5	134
21:2–11	131
22:20–21	131
22:20–26	131
22:25	132
23:6	132
24:12	235
28:3	89

Leviticus

25	131
26	119
26:3	119
26:9	119
26:14–15	119
26:44	119

Numbers

12:6–8	119
27:1–11	104

Deuteronomy

4:5–6	233–34
4:5–8	139
4:6	45, 89, 119
4:7	233
4:8	233
4:15–19	233
5:22	235
6	43, 229
6:4–9	234
7:6–8	134
8	229, 230
8:1–6	230
8:2–6	229
8:3	230
12–26	29
15:1–18	131
16:11–12	131
18:15	119
18:18	119
19:14	209
24:6	131
24:10–15	131
24:17–22	131
28	222, 229, 231
28:23–24	123
28:30	123

Deuteronomy (cont.)

28:35	223
28:43	123
30:11–14	126, 139
30:15–20	123, 231
31:12	233
31:13	233
33:29	224
34:10	119

Judges

14	248

1 Samuel

1–4	223
2:25	223, 224
3	223
3:13	223–24
7:5	224
8	224
25	56
25:3	56
25:33	56

2 Samuel

8:17	297
9–20	15
11–20	14
16:23	46
20:25	297
25:30	90

1 Kings

1–2	14, 15
1–9	295
4:3	117, 295, 297
5:10	265
7:14	89
10	55, 145
10:15	250

2 Kings

17	251
19:9	296
25:19	117

1 Chronicles

2:55	297
18:16	297
29:15	211

2 Chronicles

36:22–23	230, 250

Ezra

1:1–4	230
6:10	225
7:11	117

Nehemiah

3:31	250

Esther

4:14	104

Job

1–2	57
1:1	98, 99, 135
1:5	137, 138, 223
1:8–9	99
1:13	223
1:19	223
1:22	223
2:7	223
2:9	223
2:11	135
3	57
3:11–19	102
3:19	132
3:21	212
4	57
4:12–21	43, 108
4:13–21	56
5	57
5:3–4	288
6:5–6	155
6:8–11	210
7:1–2	211
7:2	211
7:6–8	210
7:7–8	148

INDEX OF ANCIENT WORKS

7:8	212	28:28	99
7:9	102	29–31	133
7:13–14	56	29:19	294
7:16	210, 212	31:7–10	288
7:17	222	31:16–17	131
8:8	244	31:19	132
8:9	211	31:19–21	131
8:11–12	155	32:2	135
9:5–7	125	32:7–8	212
9:5–10	213	32:8	127, 128
9:8	125	32:18	128
9:23–24	125	33:14–18	108
10:20–21	210	33:15–16	56
11:7–9	127	36:2–4	108
11:17	212	37:12	287
12:12–13	155	38	213
12:14–19	125	38–39	214
12:17–21	132	38–41	56, 105–6, 125, 128, 222, 256
13:15	212	38–42	108
13:20	212	38:1–42:6	57, 102
13:28–14:1	211	38:4–5	127
13:28–14:6	210	40:25	214
14:2	211	40:29	214
14:13	134	42:7–9	223
15	57	42:7–16	133
15:7	244	42:7–17	57
15:7–8	127	42:8	138
15:18	90	42:8–9	224
16:9	134	42:10	224
17:5	155	42:10–17	126
17:7	211	42:16	223
19:4–11	134		
19:13–19	131	Psalms	
19:25–27	102	1	58, 98–99, 102, 181, 187, 198, 200–201, 207, 209, 213, 293–94
23:8	212		
23:10	102	1–2	182
24:24	212	2:12	190
25:2–6	222	3–41	182, 187
25:29	132	8	106, 222
26:7–10	125	8:4	148
26:11	125	8:5	222
26:12–13	125	19	99, 102, 150, 213
27:19	212	19A	181, 209
28	127, 155, 256	19B	181, 207, 209
28:25–27	124	32	150, 181, 209

Psalms (cont.)

34	175, 181, 207, 209
37	150, 181, 186, 187–92, 195–96, 198–99, 200–201, 207, 209
37:1	188, 196
37:1–2	188
37:1–8	190
37:3–4	188
37:5–6	188
37:7	188
37:8–9	188
37:10–11	189
37:12–13	189
37:14–15	189
37:16	188, 190
37:16–17	189
37:18–19	189
37:20	189
37:21–22	189
37:23–24	189
37:25	191
37:25–26	189, 190
37:27	189
37:27–28	189
37:28	189
37:29	189
37:30	190
37:30–31	189
37:32–33	189
37:34	189
37:35–36	189
37:37–38	190
37:39–40	190
37:40	190
39	4, 150, 200, 210–12
39:2	212
39:3	210
39:4	212
39:5	210, 212
39:5–6	210
39:5–7	210
39:6	211–12
39:7	211–12
39:8	210, 212
39:9–12	210
39:11	210–11
39:12	210–12
39:13	210, 211
39:14	210, 212
42–43	192, 194
42–49	192
42–72	182
49	150, 181, 186–87, 192–95, 197–201, 207, 209
49:1	192
49:2–3	192
49:2–5	192, 194
49:4	212
49:4–5	192
49:6–12	193
49:12	193
49:13	192–93, 196
49:14	193
49:16	193
49:21	192–93, 196
52:10	294
53:2	212
68:20–35	101
72	123, 195, 197–98
72:5	123
72:7	123
72:17	123
73	154, 181, 186–87, 195–99, 200–201, 207, 209
73–83	195
73–89	182
73:1	195–96, 198
73:1–2	212
73:1–12	195, 212
73:3	196
73:10	198
73:11	196
73:13	195
73:13–17	195
73:15	198
73:16	196
73:17	196
73:18	195
73:18–28	195–96
73:23–28	196

73:27	198	1–9	43, 45–46, 74, 89, 124, 128, 147, 153, 165–66, 168, 174, 185, 191, 228, 229, 230, 232–35, 286, 289
73:28	198		
74	198		
76:12	101		
78	61, 207	1:1	73, 79, 209
78:2	255	1:1–6	284
82:8	101	1:1–7	291
84–85	192	1:2	80
87–88	192	1:2–3	234
89:3–5	212	1:2–4	285
89:48	212	1:2–6	98
90	207	1:2–7	89
90–106	182	1:4	59
91	207	1:5	50, 59
92:13–14	294	1:6	80, 90, 285
97:1–6	101	1:7	99, 233–34
102:12	211	1:8	127, 267, 286
104	4, 106, 210, 213–15	1:8–9	285
104:10–14	214	1:15	285
104:10–15	215	1:17	285
104:20–23	215	1:17–18	291
104:24–27	214	1:17–19	285
104:25–26	215	1:20–33	128, 147
104:26	214	1:32	285, 291
104:27–28	215	2	229, 230–31, 234
104:28	215	2:1	127, 285
104:31–35	101	2:1–8	105
105	207	2:2	286
106	207	2:5	127
107–145	182	2:6	127, 230
108	101	2:16–19	286
111	207	2:20–21	102
112	181, 187, 207, 209	2:21–22	285, 291
119	78, 102, 181, 187, 198, 200, 209, 213, 231, 234	2:22	102
		3	166
127	181, 207, 209	3:1	285
128	150, 185, 187, 207	3:1–4	229, 234
133	207	3:3–4	131
139	207	3:13–18	147, 289
144	101	3:19	46
144:4	211	3:19–20	124, 213–14
146–150	182	3:21	285
		3:27–31	285
Proverbs		3:32	287
1	234–35, 288	3:33	286, 288

Proverbs (cont.)		8:30	46
3:35	102	8:32–34	286
4:1	286	8:32–36	232
4:1–4	286	8:35	232
4:10	286, 289	9	286, 288
4:14–19	289	9:1–6	128
4:18	102	9:8	286
4:20	286	9:10	99, 233
5	286	10–15	291
5:1	286	10–20	89
5:11	102	10–22:16	289
5:13	286	10–29	124, 185, 191
5:15–20	174	10:1	73, 209, 286
6:1–3	132	10:4	132
6:6–8	285	10:5	286
6:10–11	285	10:7–9	102
6:12–15	102	10:8	50, 286
6:16–19	287	10:15	285
6:20–23	229, 234	10:16	286
6:20–35	43	10:16–17	102
6:23	285	10:20	286
6:24–35	286	10:24	286
6:27–28	286	10:25	102
7	25	10:26	286
7:1–4	229, 234	10:27–30	288
7:5–27	286	10:28	212
7:6–27	286	10:30	102, 286
8	3, 41, 46, 102, 106, 128, 147, 230–32, 234–35, 288	11:1	287
		11:3	124
8:1–11	230	11:11	286
8:1–21	230	11:14	58, 287
8:2–3	174	11:15	124
8:11	285	11:20	287
8:12	171	11:21	288
8:12–21	230	11:22	286
8:13	98	11:25–26	289
8:15–16	91	11:26	124
8:21	98	12:5	59
8:22–30	214	12:6	286
8:22–31	124, 213, 230	12:9	291
8:22–36	234	12:15	286
8:23	232, 234	12:16	185
8:23–31	231	12:18	102
8:24–25	285	12:22	287
8:27–29	285	13:1	286

13:7	286	20:30	287
13:14–17	102	21:2	287
13:18	132	21:3	137, 288
13:20	124	21:17	132
13:21	102, 124	21:31	136
13:22	288	22–23	292, 294
13:24	267	22:1	286
14:12	102	22:6	59
14:26	288	22:8	124
14:31	124	22:16	55
14:34	58	22:17	19, 73, 90
14:35	91, 124	22:17–23:11	284, 291–94
15:1	59	22:17–24:22	13, 45, 228, 285–86, 292
15:3	134	22:18	293
15:5	267	22:18–19	292–93
15:8	137, 288	22:20	292
15:16	291	22:22–23	132, 293
15:16–17	291	22:24–25	287, 292
15:18	287	22:26	209
15:20	286	22:28	293
15:24	102	23:1–3	292
15:29	134	23:5	293
16:2	287	23:6–8	292
16:4	124	23:10	209
16:7	124	23:10–11	293
16:8	291	23:12–24:22	292
16:18	102	23:13	267
16:19	291	23:15	285
16:20	102	23:17–18	102
16:25	102	23:19	285
16:27–29	285	23:22	285
17–22:16	291	23:25–26	285
17:1	286, 291	24:3	59
17:16	286	24:6	287
17:17	131	24:10	285
18:8	287	24:12	124, 287
18:12	102	24:13	285
19:10	132	24:14	102
19:19	287	24:19	188
19:20	102	24:20	102
20:18	287	24:21	233
20:21	102	24:23	19, 73, 90
20:22	291	24:23–34	285
20:24	127	24:24	58
20:27	287	24:30–34	286

INDEX OF ANCIENT WORKS

Proverbs (cont.)

24:33–35	285		
25–27	291		
25–29	285, 289		
25:1	73, 90, 209, 285, 296		
25:6–7	132		
25:13	286		
25:14	286		
25:21–22	291		
25:25	286		
25:28	286		
26:11	286		
26:17	286		
26:22	287		
27:1	288, 291		
28–29	291, 294		
28:3–5	285		
28:6	286		
28:13	288		
28:17–19	288		
28:22	288		
28:27	131		
29:1	288		
29:3	288		
29:19	132		
29:21	132		
29:22	287		
30	58, 186		
30–31	185		
30:1	135		
30:1–9	45, 73, 186		
30:1–14	289		
30:2–3	154		
30:3–4	127		
30:11–14	285		
30:21–23	132		
30:24–31	285		
30:33	285		
31	55		
31:1	73–74, 135		
31:3	286		
31:1–9	73, 132, 172, 285, 289		
31:10–31	286, 289		

Ecclesiastes

1–2	60
1:3–11	122, 126
1:4	126
1:4–9	155
1:9–10	126
1:12	169, 171
1:12–2:11	105
1:12–2:26	81
1:13	103, 105
1:13–6:9	169
1:14–15	103
2:1	103
2:1–2	212
2:1–23	103
2:2	103
2:3	80
2:7	132
2:18–19	172
2:24	103
2:24–26	93, 103
2:26	127
3:1–8	126
3:2–8	155
3:10–11	105
3:10–15	93
3:11	127
3:12–13	103
3:14–15	105, 126
3:16	133
3:16–17	103
3:17	93
3:17–18	105, 212
3:22	125
4:1	103, 133
4:1–3	103, 105
4:1–8	93
4:2–3	103
4:4–8	103
4:5	132
4:7–12	131
4:9–12	103
4:9–16	91
4:12	169
4:13–16	93, 103

4:17	137	Song of Songs	
5:1	108, 137	3:6	250
5:1–7	93, 103, 105		
5:2	99, 169	Isaiah	
5:7	99	1:11–17	288
5:7 (Hebrew)	133, 275	1:23	131
6:1–2	105	1:25–27	131
6:11–12	127	3:3	248
6:12	211	5:8	131
7:1–6	155	5:21	248
7:6	285	10:1–2	131
7:7	155	10:11	248
7:11–12	103	10:13	248
7:13–14	105	11:2	248
7:14	127	11:4–5	131
7:15–18	103	14:4	248
7:23	212	14:10	248
7:29	93	19:11–12	248
8:1–9	91	19:12	90
8:2–4	132	24:1–6	122
8:10	131	28:14	248
8:12–13	93, 103	29:5	294
8:14	212	29:14	90, 248
8:16–17	93, 127	30:1–5	296
8:17	105	31:1–3	296
9:1	105	31:2	248
9:1–3	134	33:6	248
9:2	137	37:9	296
9:4	285	38:11	212
9:13–16	155	40–55	106
9:13–18	103	40:4	122
10:7	132	40:20	248
10:14	127	43:15	171
11:5	105	44:25	248
11:5–6	127	45:17	136
11:9	103, 105	46:5	248
12:1–7	106, 285	47:10	248
12:7	105	50:9	211
12:8	81	54:6–8	134
12:9	80, 285	54:9–10	122
12:9–11	98, 103	58:7	132
12:11	90	61:1–3	131
12:12	80, 172, 285–86	65:17	122
		66:22	122

INDEX OF ANCIENT WORKS

Jeremiah
- 4:22 — 248
- 4:23–26 — 122
- 8:8 — 57, 90, 248
- 8:8–9 — 118–19
- 8:9 — 248
- 9:11 — 248
- 9:16 — 248
- 9:17 — 89
- 9:22 — 248
- 9:23–24 — 90
- 10:7 — 248
- 10:9 — 248
- 10:12 — 248
- 15:1 — 224
- 17 — 294
- 17:5–8 — 293
- 18 — 153
- 18:18 — 2, 90, 248
- 20:14–18 — 57
- 22:11–17 — 131
- 23:5 — 131
- 24:9 — 248
- 31:33 — 101
- 31:33–34 — 126
- 31:35–37 — 122
- 33:20 — 122
- 33:25–26 — 122
- 36 — 226
- 36:18 — 297
- 36:32 — 117
- 43:7 — 296
- 44:1 — 296
- 49:7 — 248
- 50:35 — 248
- 51:15 — 248
- 51:57 — 248

Ezekiel
- 9:2–3 — 297
- 9:11 — 297
- 12:22–23 — 247–48
- 12:24 — 248
- 14 — 247
- 17 — 249–52, 253–55
- 17–19 — 249–56
- 17:1–10 — 249–50, 254
- 17:2 — 247
- 17:4 — 250
- 17:5 — 254
- 17:6 — 254
- 17:6–8 — 254
- 17:7 — 254
- 17:8 — 254
- 17:8–9 — 254
- 17:9–10 — 254
- 17:10 — 254
- 17:11–21 — 250
- 17:12–15 — 251, 254
- 17:22–24 — 252, 254
- 18 — 253
- 18:2 — 247
- 18:7 — 132
- 19 — 249, 253–56
- 19:1 — 253
- 19:1–14 — 253
- 19:10 — 254
- 19:10–14 — 253–54
- 19:11 — 254
- 19:12 — 254
- 19:13 — 254
- 19:14 — 253–54
- 21 — 246
- 21:5 — 247
- 22:6–12 — 131
- 22:26 — 247
- 24:3 — 247
- 26:12 — 250
- 27:3 — 250
- 27:8 — 89
- 27:8–9 — 247
- 27:12–13 — 250
- 27:15 — 250
- 27:17 — 250
- 27:20 — 250
- 27:22–24 — 250
- 28 — 244, 247
- 28:3 — 247
- 28:4–5 — 247
- 28:5 — 250

28:7	248	3:1–3	131
28:12	248	6:6–8	288
28:16	250		
28:17	248	Nahum	
28:18	250	3:16	250
34:11–16	118		
34:20–22	131	Habakkuk	
36:26	136	2:6	248
36:26–28	101		
37:13–14	101	Zephaniah	
38:19–20	122	1:14–18	101
40–48	126		
		Haggai	
Daniel		2:6	122
2–7	255	2:21–22	122
7–12	101, 126		
9	31	Zechariah	
		1–6	126
Hosea		1:1–6	31
6:6	288	14:6–8	122
10:4	251		
13:3	294	Malachi	
13:13	248	3:5	131
14:10	248		

LXX

Joel			
2:10	122	1 Samuel	
2:28–29	101	3:13	223–24
Amos		Ezekiel	
5:11–12	131	12:22–23	253
5:12	132	16:44	253
5:18–20	101	17:2	253
5:21–25	288	18:2–3	253
6:1–6	131	19:14	253
8:4–5	131	20:49	253
8:8–9	122	24:3	253
9:8	118		

Deuterocanonical Works

Obadiah			
8	248	1 Enoch	
		1:7	123
Micah			
2:1–2	131	4 Ezra	
2:4	248	5:1–13	123

INDEX OF ANCIENT WORKS

Sirach (Ben Sira)		19:20	129
1:1	124	22:27–23:6	81
1:1–10	81	24	22, 55, 129, 156, 201
1:4	124	24:1–9	124
1:9	124	24:1–29	81
1:10	127	24:8–12	136
1:26	127	24:23	129
2:8	134	24:23–24	234
3:1	74	24:25–29	129
3:8	74	24:33	129
3:12	74	29:4–6	132
3:17	74	31:12–32:13	132
3:18	74	33:7–15	125
3:21–24	127	33:25–32	132
3:30–4:10	131	34:5–7	127
4:20	74	34:21–24	137
6:5–17	131	34:30–31	137
6:18	127	35:1–5	137
6:32–37	127	35:6–13	137
6:34–37	129	35:15	137
7:9	137	36:1–22	81
7:30	137	38:11	137
8:18	135	38:24	118
10:1–5	132	38:34	136
10:6–7	131	38:34–39:3	57
10:22	135	38:34–39:8	129
11:34	135	39:1–8	136
15:1	127, 129	39:6	127–28
15:7–8	127	39:12–35	81
16:11–12	134	39:24	129
16:15–16	129	41:14	74
16:16	134	42:15–43:33	81, 125
16:18–19	125	43:33	127
16:23	125	44:1–15	129, 136
17:1	136	44:1–50:24	81
17:6–7	127	44:5	129
17:11	129	45:6–22	137
17:11–12	136	45:23–26	137
17:11–14	129	46:1	129
17:15	134	48:3	129
17:17	136	48:7	129
17:19–20	134	48:22	129
18:1–7	81	48:24–25	129
18:11–14	134	49:8	129
18:33	132	50:1–21	137

50:22–24	81	19:6	125
50:27	80	19:18	125
51:12	81		
51:23	74, 107, 117	DEAD SEA SCROLLS	
51:25	74		
		1Q	
Tobit		26	25
1:3	171	27	25
Wisdom		4Q	
1–5	123	184	25
1:1	129, 132, 135	185	25
1:4	127	298	25
1:8	134	299–301	25
1:9	134	415 2 ii	58–59
2:10–12	131	415–418	25
2:21–22	127	420–421	25
2:21–24	128	423	25
2:22	128	424	25
3:9	134	525	25
6:1–2	129		
6:9	129	RABBINIC LITERATURE	
6:12–16	127		
6:21	129	b. Baba Bathra	
7	55	14b	221
7:1–6	128	15a	221
7:7	127–28	15a–16b	222
7:14	128		
7:15	128	EGYPTIAN LITERATURE	
7:15–21	127		
7:17–20	125	Admonitions of Ipuwer	53
7:21–8:1	124	Complaints of Khakheperre-sonb 47, 53	
8:1	124	Dispute Between a Man and his Ba 53	
8:4	124	Great Hymn to the Aten	214
8:21	127	In Praise of Ancient Scribes (Immortality	
9:9	124	of Writers)	72–73
10	56	Installation of a Vizier	283
10–19	136	Instructions in Negative Form	79
11:21–12:2	136	Instruction of Amenemhet	70, 80,
11:23	134	81, 172, 267, 269, 271, 274, 276, 277,	
12:11–18	136	278–79, 283, 285–86, 294, 297	
12:27	129	Instruction of Amenemope	13, 47, 71,
13	133	78, 79, 81, 132, 267–69, 271–75, 277,	
13:8–9	129	278, 280, 283–95, 297	
18:11	132		

Instruction of Amennakhte 71–72, 73, 79
Instruction of Ankhsheshonqy 47, 72, 267–68
Instruction of Any 71, 79–80, 267–68, 271–73, 275, 277–78, 280, 283, 285, 289, 292, 297
Instruction of Chety (Duachety) 70–73
Instruction of Hori 72
Instruction to Kagemeni 72, 266, 269, 271–72, 274, 276, 278, 280–81, 292
Instruction of a Man for His Son 70, 266–67, 271, 274, 276, 278, 283, 286, 292
Instruction of Prince Hardjedef (Djedefhor) 72, 267, 271, 274, 276, 278–79, 281, 283, 285, 297
Instruction to Merikare 72, 80, 81, 172, 267, 268–69, 271–72, 274–78, 280–82, 285–86, 288, 290, 292, 294
Instruction of Pap. Insinger 267, 290, 292
Instruction of Ptahhotep 48, 53, 55, 72, 73, 266–67, 267–69, 270–74, 276, 277–81, 283, 284–85, 286–87, 290, 292
Loyalist Instruction 70, 267–69, 274–79, 283, 292
Pap. Anastasi I 283
Pap. Chester Beatty IV 279, 280
Prophecies of Neferti (Neferit) 53, 73, 227
Tale of the Eloquent Peasant 53

Syrian and Mesopotamian Literature

Ahiqar (Achikar) 72–73, 79, 81, 227, 244
Babylonian Counsels of Wisdom 76
Cuthean Legend 169
Erra Epic 246
Etana 28
Gilgamesh Epic 27, 76, 250
Hymn to Ninurta 28
Instruction of Shurupak 46, 48, 73, 76

Ludlul Bēl Nemeqi 76, 82
Šamaš Hymn 28
The Series of the Fox 28
The Series of the Poplar 28
Shupe'awilum 73
Sidu 28

Greek Literature

Ovid, *Metamorphoses* 8.611–724 254

Ostraca

Lachish Letter 3 226

Index of Modern Authors

Alster, Bendt 84, 146, 158
Alter, Robert 58–59, 63
Apostel, Leo 120
Assmann, Jan 124, 139, 172, 175, 215, 266, 289, 297–98
Ataç, Mehmet-Ali 250, 258
Avishur, Y. 206, 215
Bakhtin, Mikhail 162, 175
Barr, James 104, 110
Baumgartner, Walter 12, 13, 33, 211, 218
Beaulieu, Paul-Alain 27, 33, 244, 258
Becker, Uwe 184, 201
Begrich, Joachim 182, 201, 205–6, 217
Ben Zvi, Ehud 93–94, 113, 118, 139, 222, 236
Berlin, Adele 213, 215–16
Bickel, Susanne 73, 84
Blenkinsopp, Joseph 99, 110, 153, 158
Blumenthal, Elke 227, 236, 294, 298
Bodi, Daniel 246, 258
Bogaert, Pierre-Maurice 246, 258
Boström, Lennart 214, 216
Botha, Phil J. 175
Boucher, Madeleine 97, 100, 110
Bouzard, Walter C., Jr. 206, 216
Briggs, Charles A. 210, 216
Briggs, Emilie G. 210, 216
Bright, John 57, 63
Brown, William P. 57, 59, 63, 98, 110, 210, 216
Bruch, Johann F. 13, 148, 158
Brueggemann, Walter 90, 104, 110, 157, 197–98, 201
Brunner, Helmut 69, 79, 81, 84, 269, 278, 280, 282–83, 298

Bryce, Glendon E. 292, 298
Buccellati, Giorgio 52, 63
Bultmann, Rudolf 198, 201
Burkard, Gunther 281, 298
Buss, Martin J. 41–42, 63, 90, 110, 206, 216
Calabro, David 293, 295, 298
Caminos, Ricardo A. 282, 298
Camp, Claudia 166, 175
Carr, David M. 19, 22, 24, 33, 54, 63, 82, 84, 117–18, 135, 139, 226, 228, 236
Carvalho, Corrine 253, 258
Castellino, R. G. 206–7, 216
Ceresko, Anthony R. 200–201, 210, 216
Černý, Jaroslav 84
Cheung, Simon C. C. 3, 150–52, 154, 155–56, 158
Clifford, Richard J. 18, 19, 24, 33, 46, 48, 63, 212–13, 216
Cocceius, Johannes 96, 110
Coggins, Richard 28–29, 33
Cohen, Chaim 211, 217
Cohen, Yoram 47, 63, 244, 258
Collins, Jeff 40, 63
Collins, John J. 17, 22, 25–26, 34, 58, 64, 88–89, 99, 102, 106, 108, 110, 116, 121, 125–26, 128, 137, 139–40
Copi, Irving M. 54, 64
Corbett, Edward P. J. 97, 111
Craigie, Peter C. 215–16
Creach, Jerome F. D. 294, 298
Crenshaw, James L. 2, 7, 12, 13, 14, 15, 16–18, 20, 23–24, 28–29, 34, 42–43, 58, 64, 77, 84–85, 87, 88–89, 92–93,

-321-

Crenshaw, James L. (cont.) 95–97, 109, 111, 115, 140, 147, 148, 181–83, 200–201, 205, 207, 209–10, 216, 222, 236, 241, 243, 245, 258
Culler, Jonathan D.   31–32, 34, 94, 111
Dahood, Mitchell   212, 217
Davidson, Robert   91, 92, 111
Davies, G. I.   297–98
Dell, Katharine J.   3, 13, 16, 22–24, 31, 33–34, 48–49, 60, 62, 64, 97, 111, 116, 140, 146–48, 150, 151, 153–54, 157–58, 158–59, 168, 176, 209, 217, 228, 236–37, 289, 298
Demsky, Aaron   297–98
Derrida, Jacques   60, 64
Dion, Paul F.   215, 217
Dodd, C. H.   101, 111
Dowd, Garin   40, 64
Drioton, E.   294, 299
Driver, S. R.   12, 34, 91, 111
Duhm, Bernhard   2, 7, 190, 201
Duncan, Mike   54, 64
Dutcher-Walls, Patricia   61, 64
Eagleton, Terry   54, 64
Edzard, Dietz Otto   32, 64
Eichrodt, Walther   96
Eissfeldt, Otto   207, 217
Emerton, J. A.   292, 299
Engnell, Ivan   207, 217
Erman, A.   13, 34–35
Eskenazi, Tamara C.   227, 237
Falkenstein, Adam   206, 217
Faulkner, Raymond   80, 85
Fecht, G.   299
Fichtner, Johannes   15, 35, 85, 245, 258
Fischer-Elfert, H. W.   69, 70
Fishbane, Michael A.   61, 64, 222–23, 237, 255, 258
Fleming, Daniel   219
Fohrer, Georg   250–51, 253, 255, 259
Fokkelman, Jan   259
Forman, C. C.   158–59
Forti, Tova   3, 4, 50–51, 64, 211, 214, 217, 259
Foster, Benjamin R.   85

Fowler, Alastair   32, 35, 40, 57, 59–60, 64, 94–95, 111
Fox, Michael V.   3, 5, 12, 26, 35, 43–46, 61, 64–65, 69, 70, 72, 74, 76, 80, 81, 83, 85, 89, 105, 111, 147, 153, 159, 168, 170, 176, 209, 217, 280, 289, 291, 292–93, 295, 299
Frevel, Christian   222, 237
Frow, John   40, 47, 59–60, 65
Gabler, Johann   96
Gadamer, Hans-Georg   11, 35
Gadotti, Alhena   246
Galling, Kurt   172, 176
Gammie, John G.   90, 111, 214, 217
Gardiner, Alan H.   85, 282, 299
Garsiel, Moshe   294, 299
Genette, Gérard   225, 237
Gerstenberger, Erhardt   214, 217
Gertz, Jan C.   228, 237
Gese, Hartmut   13, 35, 139, 140, 232–33, 237
Gadotti, Alhena   246, 259
Goff, Matthew J.   11–12, 17, 25–26, 30, 35, 57–58, 59, 65, 128, 140
Goldingay, John   18, 58, 65, 110–11, 150, 159
Gottwald, Norman K.   87, 111
Grabbe, Lester L.   115, 140
Gray, John   27, 35
Greenberg, Moshe   249–50, 253–54, 259
Greenstein, Edward L.   57, 65
Groome, Thomas H.   101, 112
Gruber, Mayer I.   214, 217
Grumach, Irene   278, 292, 299
Guglielmi, Waltraud   283, 299
Gunkel, Hermann   2, 7, 18, 60, 77, 85, 90, 146, 148–49, 159, 182–83, 187, 189, 201, 205–6, 210, 217
Gunn, Battiscombe   269, 299
Hagen, Fredrik   281, 283, 299–300
Hallo, William W.   60, 65
Hals, Ronald M.   255, 259
Hamilton, Mark W.   3, 6
Haran, Menachem   259, 297, 300
Hatton, Peter T. H.   155, 159

INDEX OF MODERN AUTHORS

Heckl, Raik   3–4, 222, 223–25, 226–27, 228, 233, 235, 237–38
Hegel, Georg W. F.   227
Held, Moshe   212, 217–18
Hermisson, Hans-Jürgen   200, 201–2, 291, 300
Herrmann, Christian   295, 300
Hess, Richard S.   293, 300
Hilber, John W.   206, 218
Hirsch, E. D.   162, 176
Hobsbawm, Eric   243, 259
Høgenhaven, Jesper   24, 35
Hossfeld, Frank Lothar   182, 190, 192, 193, 195–97, 198, 202
Hurowitz, Victor A.   85, 297, 300
Hurvitz, Avi   210, 218
Israeli, Shlomit   294, 300
Jacobson, Diane   208, 218
Jamieson-Drake, David W.   214, 218
Jasnow, R.   283, 300
Jeremias, Joachim   101, 112
Kaiser, Otto   93, 112, 210, 218
Kampen, John   57–58, 65, 108, 112
Kaufmann, Yehezkiel   209, 218, 288, 300
Kayatz, Christa   288, 300
Kidner, Derek   18, 49, 65
Kitchen, Kenneth A.   53, 65
Kleinerman, Alexandra   246, 259
Koehler, Ludwig   211, 218
Koh, Y. V.   169, 170, 176
Köhlmoos, Melanie   222, 225
Körting, Corinna   184, 202
Kottsieper, Ingo   227, 238
Kovacs, Brian   46
Kraus, Hans Joachim   206, 210, 218
Krüger, Thomas   119, 120, 126, 140–41
Kuntz, Kenneth J.   42, 65, 181–82, 184, 187, 190, 202, 207, 210, 218
Kynes, Will L.   2, 3, 6, 11, 13, 31, 32, 34–35, 69, 75, 79, 83, 85, 152, 157–59, 168, 176, 210, 219, 222, 237–38
Laisney, Vincent P. M.   85, 293–94, 300
Lambert, W. G.   27, 28, 35, 52, 65, 76, 82, 85, 148, 159, 244, 259
Landes, George M.   100, 112
Lange, Armin   126, 141
LaRocque, Paula   173, 176
Lemaire, André   297, 300
Lenzi, Alan   206, 219
Levenson, Jon   213, 219
Lichtheim, Miriam   27, 35, 52–53, 58, 65–66, 85, 214–15, 219, 267, 274, 300
Lipiński, Edward   246, 250, 259
Livingstone, Alasdair   252, 259
Lohfink, Norbert F.   28, 29–30, 31, 35
Longman, Tremper, III   168–69, 176
Loretz, O.   172, 176
Lust, Johan   259
Luther, Martin   181, 202
Luyten, Jos   181, 195, 202, 207, 210, 219
Macintosh, A. A.   245, 259
Magdalene, F. Rachel   168, 176
Marlo, H.   300
Mathieu, Bernard   73, 84
Mays, James L.   213, 219
McCarthy, Carmel   224, 238
McDowell, A.   281, 301
McKane, William   24, 35, 105, 112, 165–66, 174, 176, 205, 219, 289, 291, 301
McKenzie, John L.   19, 36
McKenzie, Steven L.   30–31, 36
McLaughlin, John L.   2, 7
Meinhold, Arndt   238
Meinhold, Johannes (Hans)   12, 36, 88
Mettinger, Tryggve N. D.   297, 301
Michel, Diethelm   105, 195–97, 202
Miller, Douglas B.   3, 5, 105, 112
Miller, Patrick D.   197–98, 201
Miosi, F. T.   272, 301
Mitchell, Christine   40–41, 66, 165, 176
Morgan, Donn F.   14, 16, 36, 148, 159
Mowinckel, Sigmund   150, 183, 193, 202, 206–8, 219
Moyn, Samuel   259
Murphy, Roland E.   14, 20, 23, 36, 90, 91, 93, 95–96, 99, 104, 105, 112, 116, 141, 148, 159, 166–67, 176, 181, 203, 207, 210, 219
Nay, Reto   247, 260

324 INDEX OF MODERN AUTHORS

Newsom, Carol A. 25, 32, 36, 40–41, 66, 94–95, 102, 112
Nicklesburg, George W. E. 32, 36
Niditch, Susan 41, 66
Niehr, Herbert 227, 238
Nihan, Christophe 119, 141
Odell, Margaret S. 246–247, 260
Oehler, Gustav Friedrich 96, 112
Oeming, Manfred 182, 200, 203, 207, 219
Olbrechts-Tyteca, Lucie 98, 112
Olivier, J. P. S. 297, 301
Osing, J. 283
Otten, Heinrich 251, 260
Otto, Eckart 229–30, 233, 238
Overland, Paul 292, 301
Parkinson, R. B. 278, 301
Pearce, Laurie E. 244, 260
Penchansky, David 2, 8, 105, 112
Perdue, Leo G. 74, 86, 118, 141, 167, 171–72, 176, 181, 186–87, 192, 195, 203, 209, 214, 219, 243, 260, 297, 301
Perelman, Chaim 98, 112
Peterson, Brian 255, 260
Petter, Donna Lee 246, 260
Phinney, D. Nathan 260
Plöger, Otto 117–18, 230, 232, 238
Pohlmann, Karl-Friedrich 247, 260
Porten, Bezalel 86
Posener, Georges 294, 301
Preuß, Hans Dietrich 141
Preuss, Horst Dietrich 13, 36, 139
Pritchard, James B. 219
Propp, Vladimir 246, 260
Quack, Joachim F. 80, 86, 267, 273, 281–82, 301
Rad, von, Gerhard 11, 12, 13, 14, 15, 20, 22, 30, 36, 88–89, 93, 96–97, 100, 109, 112–13, 147, 150, 159, 186, 203, 208–9, 212, 219
Ragozilli, Chloé 275, 301
Rankin, Oliver 91
Reichenbach, Gregor 228, 231, 238
Renz, Johannes 226, 238
Renz, Thomas 247, 249, 260

Robert, André 222–23, 228, 239
Rofé, A. 289, 297, 301
Röllig, Wolfgang 52, 66, 226, 238
Römheld, K. F. Diethard 292, 301
Rowley, H. H. 91, 113
Rüster, Christel 251
Rütersworden, Udo 226, 239
Saur, Markus 3, 4, 24, 36, 49–50, 66, 184–85, 200, 203
Schearing, Linda S. 28, 36
Schechter, Solomon 86
Schellenberg, Annette 3, 4, 118, 126, 131, 141
Schipper, Bernd U. 43, 45, 66, 81, 86, 119, 141, 228, 229, 230, 231, 234, 239, 293, 302
Schlott, Adelheid 282, 302
Schmid, Hans Heinrich 122, 141
Schmid, Konrad 117, 119, 141–42, 199, 200, 203, 222, 239
Schniedewind, William M. 118, 142, 226, 239
Schüle, Andreas 200, 203
Schultz, Hermann 2, 8
Schultz, Richard L. 222, 239
Schwienhorst-Schönberger, Ludger 12, 20, 36, 49–50, 66
Scott, R. B. Y. 13, 15, 20, 28, 37, 92, 95, 98, 104–5, 113, 210, 219
Seow, C. L. 60, 66, 170, 176–77
Seybold, Klaus 191, 198, 203, 210–11, 220
Sheard, Cynthia Miecznikowski 98, 113
Sheppard, Gerald T. 15–16, 22, 24, 37, 205, 213, 220
Shils, Edward 243–44, 247, 261
Shupak, Nili 3, 7, 51, 53, 66, 79, 80, 86, 215, 220, 266–67, 269, 271, 274, 281, 283–84, 286–87, 292, 294, 297, 302–3
Skaldny, Udo 289, 291, 303
Smart, Ninian 41, 66
Smend, Rudolf 13, 37, 88, 91, 93, 113
Sneed, Mark R. 3, 6–7, 12, 18–21, 22–23, 24, 30, 37, 40, 41, 66, 69, 74–75, 77, 81, 86, 115–17, 118–19, 139, 142,

145–46, 149–50, 153, 159, 184–85, 200, 204, 209, 220, 236, 239, 241–42, 243, 256, 261, 265
Soden, Wolfram von 206, 217
Soggin, J. A. 245, 261
Sparks, Kenton L. 18–19, 37, 40, 43, 61, 66, 77, 86, 90, 94, 113
Stamm, Johann J. 211, 218
Steck, Odil Hannes 115, 120, 142, 184, 204
Steiert, Franz-Josef 243, 245, 261
Steymans, Hans Ulrich 250, 261
Strack, H. L. 229
Strange, J. 295, 303
Strauß, Hans 59, 66
Strine, Casey A. 246, 261
Swales, John M. 26, 37
Sweeney, Marvin A. 93–94, 113
Talmon, Shemaryahu 15, 37
Tanzer, Sarah J. 26, 37
Tavares, Ricardo 294, 303
Taylor, C. 86
Terrien, Samuel 214, 220
Thomas, D. Winton 212, 220
Tomes, Roger 206, 220
Toorn, Karel van der 19, 27, 28, 37, 49, 67, 117–18, 130, 142, 226, 239, 244, 261
Uelinger, Christoph 215, 220
VanderKam, James C. 118, 142
Van Leeuwen, Raymond C. 22, 37, 47–48, 67, 90, 113, 147, 159–60
Veken, Jan van der 120
Veldhuis, Niek 244, 261
Verhoeven, Ursala 266, 303
Vernus, Pascal 274, 303
Vidal, Clément 120, 142
Vogelzang, M. E. 261
Volten, Aksel 273, 303
Wanke, Gunther 184, 204
Warnemünde, G. 281–82, 303
Watanabe, Chikako E. 250, 261
Weber, Beat 182, 187, 195, 197, 200, 201, 204
Weber, Max 242, 244, 261

Weeks, Stuart 3, 5, 11–12, 14–15, 17, 22–23, 28–29, 30, 31, 32, 37–38, 49, 67, 115–19, 121–22, 130, 133, 138, 142–43, 147–49, 152, 157, 160, 164, 166, 171–72, 175, 177, 215, 220, 289, 294, 297, 303
Weigl, Michael 244, 261
Weinfeld, Moshe 19, 37, 232–33, 239
Wente, Edward. F. 282, 303
Westenholz, Joan Goodnick 169, 177
Westermann, Claus 31, 38
Wette, W. M. L. de 31, 38
Whetter, K.S. 156, 160
Whybray, R. N. 12, 15, 16, 23, 38, 52, 58, 67, 70–71, 86, 90–91, 107, 113, 115, 118, 143, 146–47, 150–51, 165–66, 177, 181–82, 200, 204–5, 207–8, 209–10, 214, 220, 289, 297, 303–4
Widengren, G. 206, 220
Williams, Ronald J. 27, 38, 295, 304
Williamson, H. G. M. 245, 261
Wills, Lawrence M. 100, 113
Wilson, Gerald H. 22, 38, 182, 204, 213, 220
Wilson, Robert P. 28–29, 30, 38
Winitzer, Abraham 254–55, 261
Witte, Markus 17, 24, 38, 191, 193, 197, 204, 222, 239
Wittgenstein, Ludwig 3, 94, 153, 160
Wolff, Hans Walter 15, 38, 89, 92, 113
Wright, Benjamin G., III 17, 21–22, 25–26, 38
Wright, G. Ernest 13, 38
Yardeni, Ada 86
Zahn, Molly 78, 86
Zenger, Erich 182, 190, 191–93, 195–98, 202, 204
Zimmerli, Walther 92, 113, 249, 255, 262
Zimmerman, H. J. 78, 86
Zöckler, O. 148, 160

www.ingramcontent.com/pod-product-compliance
Lightning Source LLC
Chambersburg PA
CBHW021846300426
44115CB00005B/37